Law Enforcement and Public Health

Isabelle Bartkowiak-Théron • James Clover
Denise Martin • Richard F. Southby • Nick Crofts
Editors

Law Enforcement and Public Health

Partners for Community Safety and Wellbeing

Springer

Editors
Isabelle Bartkowiak-Théron
Tasmanian Inst. Law Enforcement Studies
University of Tasmania
Hobart, TAS, Australia

James Clover
Faculty of Health and Community Studies
MacEwan University
Edmonton, AB, Canada

Denise Martin
School of Business, Law and Social
Science
Abertay University
Dundee, UK

Richard F. Southby
Milken Institute School of Public Health
The George Washington University
Washington, DC, USA

Nick Crofts
Centre for Law Enforcement and Public
Health School of Population and Global
Health
University of Melbourne Global Law
Enforcement and Public Health
Association
Melbourne, VIC, Australia

ISBN 978-3-030-83915-4   ISBN 978-3-030-83913-0   (eBook)
https://doi.org/10.1007/978-3-030-83913-0

This Springer imprint is published by the registered company Springer Nature Switzerland AG
The registered company address is: Gewerbestrasse 11, 6330 Cham, Switzerland

We would like to dedicate this book to all the first responders and emergency personnel who have worked hard to see the world go through (almost!) the COVID-19 pandemic. Your efforts have been remarkable, and we are grateful for the work you do, protecting and caring for our families. To all individuals and families suffering from wars, poverty or illness, our thoughts go to you, and our efforts in our work are constantly directed at trying to make a positive difference to you, locally, and internationally.

Isabelle, James, Denise, Richard, and Nick

To Amélie and Nicolas: because you make EVERYTHING better and brighter, every day. And to Ouschka: because you deserve one too.

Isabelle

To Barb, Gabrielle, and Jack: For continuing to listen to all my crazy ideas, yet still encouraging me to keep exploring. And to my fellow editors and contributors for allowing me to be part of this special project.

James

For Aaron the best boy.

Denise

*To Janet, my wife, for her love,
encouragement, and intellectual support.*

Richard

*To my best friend and mainstay, Kerri, and my
wonderful daughters;
and my inspiring friends, Bill Stronach, Auke
van Dijk, and David Patterson.*

Nick

Foreword

From Incrementalism to Radical Restructuring: A Preface

Law enforcement and public health (LEPH) have much in common. They share to a considerable degree the same operating spaces as they address specific ills like drug overdose, violence, road safety, and mental illness as well as the deeper social determinants of health and security like poverty and inequality. Both claim preventive roles in relation to social harms but devote considerable resources to responding to harms that have already occurred. Law enforcement is organized to be reactionary, responding to individual symptoms of social problems, and society enlists them to do so. It has been difficult to align individual and population approaches in the advancement of security, just as it has been difficult to achieve this alignment in the advancement of health.

Recognizing these spaces of common ground, the Global Law Enforcement and Public Health Association (GLEPHA) has initiated this collection of papers on the many and diverse facets of the LEPH intersection. We should remember the LEPH idea has a longer history, dating back to the first LEPH global conference in 2012 in Melbourne, Australia. The founders of the conference, Nick Crofts and Bill Stronach, from the Center for Law Enforcement and Public Health, shared the vision of bringing people together from both fields to recognize their commonalities and examine how they could harmonize their missions and practices. This was no easy feat and continues to be a challenge. Historically, public health academics and practitioners have been dubious, knowing that policing can be and has been harmful to health. Public health researchers argue that police are a social determinant of health. In any given interaction, policing agents—through their privileged tools of coercion and law—can undermine people's mental and physical health. In a more distal sense, police play a role in sorting people into different life outcomes through the discretion granted them to funnel people into the criminal legal system, known to have tragic consequences for health.

Despite some scepticism around the LEPH idea, this rich collection of chapters is evidence that there is an appetite to cross boundaries and tackle shared problems.

Since its inception, the LEPH conference series spawned a network of practitioners and scholars working in a shared space of intellectual dialogue and peer-to-peer exchange of practical ideas. This book is a testament to the fact that GLEPHA has made gains in requiring actors from across LEPH to come together, recognize the limits of their practices, and reflect on the insularity of their institutional cultures. The LEPH idea has come alive by inviting participants to render themselves vulnerable, challenge their own framings, and develop common language to delineate this shared space. Pursuing this goal has been and will continue to be challenging for GLEPHA because all institutions contain residues of past ways of seeing.

In its detail, this book reveals the ways in which the LEPH idea has evolved and taken shape over the past decade, both in terms of substantive/operational areas of inquiry and in the nature of the collaborations that have produced these chapters. The authors of this collection are practitioners and researchers, working collaboratively to advance our understanding of institutional partnerships, the keys to successful inter-operability, and the factors (e.g., institutional, cultural, legal, financial) that limit the full potential and sustainability of joined-up initiatives. This collection also shows in action the ways in which academics are interrogating their disciplinary limits in efforts to advance LEPH theory and methods. Perhaps most importantly, this book also signals the need for researchers and practitioners to challenge their standpoints—shaped by their geographies, occupations, and positions of privilege— to propel the evolution of LEPH towards a focus on the needs, concerns, and experiences of our most vulnerable populations, particularly in the Global South.

Centring the Global South and centring all marginalized populations in the advancement of theory, methods, evidence, and practice has been important to the LEPH agenda since its inception. Yet, this commitment has been and continues to be extraordinarily difficult to fulfil. The bulk of LEPH scholarship and the bulk of participation at LEPH conferences have been dominated by the knowledge and experiences of people from upper-middle and high-income countries. Because of this, certain kinds of institutions and institutional arrangements for advancing public safety and health are taken for granted. Moving forward, the LEPH idea may best evolve and grow by creating spaces for a plurality of voices to challenge dominant assumptions and frameworks about how we govern in furtherance of common goods. Bringing a diversity of thinking and experiences to writing, networking, and institutional innovation will help GLEPHA enhance its commitment to equality in all forms.

Prevailing over marginalization and inequality is at the heart of the current agenda for advancing the LEPH idea. In one part of the world, the United States, there is a reckoning over police brutality, but state institutional violence is a recognized lived experience in many parts of the world. Prevailing over inequality calls for broad and sustained attention to the structural conditions that make community safety and well-being possible. Inequality, including but not limited to structural racism, continues to be woven into the fabric of laws, policies, and institutions that shape public safety, health, and wellbeing. The harmful effects of laws that sort people into different life trajectories can be exacerbated by the harms of weak public health infrastructures and institutional dysfunction. The COVID-19 pandemic has shed harsh light on social health inequities arising from broken health systems in many parts of the world.

Recognizing the many visible and invisible vectors of inequality, we believe that GLEPHA, and the LEPH idea, face their greatest challenge to date. Implicitly, the LEPH idea was based on an incremental view of change. How could we alter the mentalities, institutions, and practices of policing to generate less harm to the public's health? How could law enforcement and public health institutions collaborate operationally or strategically to act on shared social problems? How could the best thinking and tools of public health be brought to bear on the practice of policing to instil considerations of health into the doing of police work? What do public health researchers and practitioners need to know to understand the demand conditions on police and the lived realities officers face as they seek to provide temporary remedies to people in distress and communities plagued by crime?

Perhaps it is no longer sufficient to stimulate new thinking about how police and public health can better align. We have long understood that prevention beats response, and that prevention entails addressing the deep structural drivers of crime and illness as social determinants of health. Investment in housing, education, public amenities coupled with policies that significantly reduce glaring racial and economic inequality through new tax and fiscal policies is essential, not just to short- or medium-term improvement but to the viability of democratic societies. GLEPHA is a global organization that can foster dialogue about the signs, symptoms, and roots of inequality within and across LEPH. How might the people and institutions driving the LEPH idea forward build in design elements—to conferences, publications, practices—that foster creative thinking about the legal and institutional arrangements that could give concrete effect to the LEPH idea in different parts of the world. What the solution will look like will depend on where you live and how governance is imagined.

The answer to the question of whether this incremental approach is the best way forward to advance LEPH is necessarily dependent on context. Some may argue that a mission of incremental, sensible improvements in long-entrenched institutional and professional arrangements will not add sufficient value in a world where more is demanded. In the United States, some people are calling for the abolition of police, based on the argument that the police institution is built to violently sort people and populations into unequal trajectories. What an institutional 'replacement' would look like is now a part of the American conversation. Yet, there is no guarantee that what might be built in its place would be good for public health unless the structural determinants of health are fruitfully addressed through the deep issue that connects other social systems, institutions, and laws.

Likewise, in the face of COVID-19, we are seeing the limits of public health agencies in responding to epidemics driven by dramatic underlying inequities. Health agencies are still set up and funded on a model of 'disease control and prevention' rather than promoting the broad social wellbeing that makes communities strong. People working in public health are struggling with the practical questions of turning the analyses of social epidemiology into institutions and practices fostering social equity. 'Defund public health' would be a terrible slogan, not least because the defunding has already happened and is part of the problem; but reimaging public health and its institutional design is more urgent than ever.

GLEPHA could continue to nourish and grow conversations about the future of incrementalism. But perhaps there is a place for it to create viable opportunities for scholars, researchers, and people with lived experience to illuminate new possibilities. We live in a moment where notions of abolition and reinvention are in the current thought space of everyday people. That said, the idea of reinventing governance and building new institutions is not a new idea, especially in low- and middle-income economies where state authority and capacity is illegitimate, weak, or both. LEPH was always meant to be a global idea. Perhaps there is space to reflect on what new institutions—working to harmonize law enforcement and public health—could look like, who should own them, who should direct them, and what tools and authority could be granted to them to advance security, health, and wellbeing at the population level. Into the future, GLEPHA should foster not simply a space for dialogue, but a strong listening stance in order to learn what might be possible or what might be out of our reach because we did not see what was in our periphery.

Department of Criminal Justice, Temple   Jennifer Wood
University, Philadelphia, PA, USA

Beasley School of Law, Temple   Scott Burris
University, Philadelphia, PA, USA

University of Cape Town, Rondebosch,   Clifford Shearing
Cape Town, South Africa
Griffith University, Brisbane, QLD,
Australia

Contents

About the Contributors

Nicole L. Asquith, PhD is Professor of Policing and Emergency Management at the University of Tasmania and the Director of the Tasmanian Institute of Law Enforcement Studies in Australia.

Murray Billett is a human rights activist, specializing in conflict resolution, police administration, and related education with a focus on the fabulous GLBTQ2 diverse communities.

Scott Burris, JD is Professor of Law and Public Health at Temple University in Philadelphia, Pennsylvania, USA, and Director of the Center for Law and the Public's Health. His work focuses on the effects of laws and law enforcement practices on population health.

Cal Corley, MBA served with the Royal Canadian Mounted Police for over 35 years. He has since operated as a strategic advisor in private practice, including overseas supporting policing reform.

Emily Craven is the Director of the Sex Worker Education and Advocacy Taskforce (SWEAT), Cape Town, South Africa.

Franck David has been a National Development Worker at People First (Scotland) since March 2020, which is a role he enjoys very much. Before taking up this post he was the Executive Assistant to the CEO and the Board of a public body in Edinburgh. Franck's professional activities have essentially been in the public sector. He was a clerk at the Scottish Parliament for 10 years.

Emily Diamond, PhD is a professor and researcher at the Wright Institute in Berkeley, California, USA. Her work focuses on health inequality, occupational health, and public health.

Auke van Dijk, MA is senior strategist with the Netherlands National Police. His academic background is in International Relations Theory and International Political Economy. He has been involved in Law Enforcement and Public Health since 2012 and is a member of the board of the related Global Association.

Nadine Dougall, PhD is an Associate Professor in Statistics, Data Science and Mental Health, School of Health & Social Care, Edinburgh Napier University, Scotland. She is Co-Director of the Scottish Centre for Law Enforcement and Public Health and leads a programme of work on the intersection between policing and health, with specific interests in mental health distress and suicide.

Grant Edwards, MA retired from the Australian Federal Police after a 34-year career. Grant is a passionate advocate in the field of mental health, and his personal lived experience was shown on the ABC's Australian Story in 2017.

Penny Egan-Vine, AM, BMed, BSurgery is a former Trauma and Grief Counsellor in Albury, NSW, Australia. She is also the Chairperson of the Murray Valley Sanctuary Refugee Group, whose vision is to assist refugees in order that they can achieve independence and integration. She is a member of the Order of Australia.

Donna Maree Evans holds a Bachelor of Laws and Master of Social Change and Development with Distinction and is enrolled in a PhD programme with RMIT University, Australia. Her career includes 25+ years of experience in private and community legal practice; court administration; criminal justice programme and project management; community legal education; research and advocacy.

William Graham, PhD is a Senior Lecturer in Criminology at Abertay University, Dundee, Scotland. He is a former senior police officer in Glasgow, in the Strathclyde Police force and now part of Police Scotland, and he retired in 2010 after 30 years of service. His research interests include policing, violence reduction, criminal justice policy transfer, and organized crime.

Wayne Helfrich is educated in pharmacology and has 20 years of experience in disease management. He is a committed life-long human and health rights activist for queer and other marginalized population groups. Wayne moved from academia to private practice to NGO sector and now finds himself in full-time politics and policy design.

Inga Heyman, PhD is a Lecturer in Mental Health Nursing and Lead for Interprofessional Learning at Edinburgh Napier University, Scotland. Her research, teaching, and clinical practice interests lie in the policing, health care, and public protection interface. Prior to joining higher education, Inga worked in clinical practice for 30 years across a range of law enforcement and public health (LEPH) areas within Australian and Scottish health and police services.

Melissa Jardine, PhD is an international policing consultant with extensive experience working with or in relation to policing agencies in South and Southeast Asia, Africa, and Central Asia. Her interests include police culture, education and reforms, transnational crimes, and gender-responsive policing.

Daniel J. Jones, MA is an Inspector with the Edmonton Police Service and a PhD candidate at the University of Huddersfield, UK. Daniel is hoping to see changes in the policing construct that are trauma informed and in line with a public health model of policing.

Roberta Julian, PhD is a Professor of Sociology and Foundation Director of the Tasmanian Institute of Law Enforcement Studies (TILES) at the University of Tasmania, Australia. Her research is applied, collaborative, and multidisciplinary with a focus on issues of social and criminal justice in three major areas: immigrant and refugee settlement, policing, and forensic studies.

Dan Jurman worked over 20 years serving vulnerable populations through non-profit work in New Jersey, Florida, and Pennsylvania. Dan began serving as the first Executive Director of the new Pennsylvania Office of Advocacy and Reform in the PA Governor's Office where his focus is working to reform government services to create positive outcomes for people whose circumstances have made them vulnerable.

Katy Kamkar, PhD, CPsych is a Clinical Psychologist at the Centre for Addictions and Mental Health (CAMH). She is an Assistant Professor at the University of Toronto, Canada, and the Chair of the Canadian Psychological Association (CPA), Traumatic Stress Sector.

Zoe Kizimchuk Cert IV Community Services has worked in the alcohol and other drug sector for the past 10 years, specializing in drug education and health literacy. A collector of skills, Zoe moves eagerly between a broad selection of activities, including (but never limited to!) non-empirical research, resource creation, game design, illustration, and data systems.

Liz Komar, JD is the Director of Strategic Initiatives at Fair and Just Prosecution and a former Assistant District Attorney.

Miriam Aroni Krinsky, JD is the founder and executive director of Fair and Just Prosecution—a national network of elected prosecutors in the United States working towards common-sense, compassionate criminal justice reforms—and a former federal prosecutor.

Dale McFee served with the Prince Albert Police Service and became President of the Canadian Association of Chiefs of Police before retiring to become the Deputy

Minister of Corrections and Policing for the Saskatchewan government. Dale returned to policing as the Chief of Police for the Edmonton Police Service.

Elida Meadows, BA (Hons) Communications, MA has worked in policy and research in the mental health, drug and alcohol, and multicultural sectors for the past 15 years. A researcher, consultant, and historian, Elida's interests include the movement of people through diaspora, displacement, migration, pilgrimage, and travel and the marginalization of people in Western society. Her publication and research interests have explored intersections of place, time, liminality, and identity, and she has presented talks and conference papers on various topics including identity, travel literature, migration history, and heritage.

John Middleton, PhD was a Director of Public Health in an English Health administration for 27 years before moving on to national and international public health professional roles. He is currently President of the Association of Schools of Public Health in the European Region (ASPHER). He has retained a strong interest in policing, law enforcement crime, violence, and public health throughout these different roles.

Juani O'Reilly, GradCert, PH is a police veteran with the Australian Federal Police. Juani has been regularly involved in academic research, through her work at the Australian National University and Flinders University. In particular, the 'Policing the Neighbourhood: Australian Peace-keeping, Capacity Building and Development in Timor-Leste, Solomon Islands and Papua New Guinea' project aimed to provide a solid foundation for future AFP involvement in the region. It also looked at the governance of illicit synthetic drugs which identified various ways in which law enforcement have engaged with external institutions in furtherance of reducing the supply of illicit synthetic drugs.

Konstantinos Papazoglou, PhD, CPsych is a licensed psychologist (clinical and forensic). His research work focuses on law enforcement stress, trauma, wellness, performance, and resilience. He is the founder and director of the ProWellness Inc., a division of his psychology professional corporation, in Toronto, Ontario, Canada. In addition, he is also the principal founder of the POWER Project: A non-profit public benefit corporation in San Diego, California, USA. He completed his postdoctoral appointment with Yale School of Medicine. He served as a police officer for 15 years with the Hellenic national police and he resigned as a police captain. He authored numerous scholarly articles, edited books, and presented in many major conferences.

Michael Peters is a Programme Manager with Community and Housing Initiatives at the YMCA of Northern Alberta. He holds a diploma in Child and Youth Care Counselling and has over 20 years of experience in the field. Michael lives with his wife and their two young boys in Edmonton, Alberta, Canada.

Brandon del Pozo, PhD is a public health, policing, and addiction researcher. He served 19 years as a police officer in the New York City Police Department and for four as the chief of police of Burlington, Vermont, USA.

Karl A. Roberts, PhD is Professor of Policing and Criminal Justice at the Western Sydney University, Australia, and is a consultant with the World Health Organization on health security and law enforcement. His research explores the interface between policing processes and public health, and his interests include policing during pandemics, violence and suicide prevention, and police well-being.

Clifford Shearing, PhD holds professorships in the Law Faculty at the University of Cape Town in South Africa, Griffith Institute of Criminology at Griffith University in Australia, and the School of Criminology at the University of Montreal, Canada.

Norm Taylor, MEd has practiced as an independent executive advisor and educator for over 40 years, with a concentration in policing for the past 25 years. In 2002 he co-founded and continues to serve as Programme Director for the CACP Executive Global Studies, leading over 200 police leaders into research studies in 50 countries to date. Since 2016 he has also served as the Editor-in-Chief of the peer-reviewed *Journal of Community Safety and Well-being*. He holds an Honorary Commission in the Ontario Provincial Police of Canada.

Stuart Thomas, PhD is Professor of Forensic Mental Health at RMIT University in Melbourne, Australia. His background is in psychology and law and his research interests include outcome measurement, law enforcement and public health, missing persons, and stigma.

Matthew Torigian, MPA had a 29-year career with the Waterloo Regional Police, including 7 years as Chief of Police before taking on the role of Deputy Minister of Community Safety for the province of Ontario, Canada. He now serves as a Distinguished Fellow at the Munk School for Global Affairs and Public Policy at the University of Toronto, Canada.

Shelley Turner, PhD is an adjunct Senior Lecturer in Social Work at Monash University, Australia. Her research focuses on young people's lived experiences of the criminal justice system and knowledge co-production. She has extensive policy and practice experience in youth justice and was clinical manager of Australia's first Youth Drug and Alcohol Court (YDAC) programme.

Shirleyann Varney, BA (Hons) Economics has been involved in the community services sector in Australia and UK over the past 13 years. She is committed to the ongoing development of educational initiatives that empower individuals, families, and the wider community to understand and reduce the harms from alcohol, tobacco, and other drug use. Shirleyann is the current CEO of the Drug Education Network.

Chris White has brought his own mental health experiences into his work for over 20 years, supporting lived experience participation and engagement across the mental health sector. He is a strong believer in the power of stories and how they can bring greater awareness and understanding of mental health issues.

Jennifer Wood, PhD is a Professor in the Department of Criminology at Temple University in Philadelphia, Pennsylvania, USA. Her research focuses on the many intersections between policing and public health, including changes in how officers intervene with people experiencing health vulnerabilities such as mental illness.

Lesslie Young, RGN, SCM is the Chief Executive Officer of Epilepsy Scotland, the national charity representing those living in Scotland with epilepsy. Her interest in the misinterpretation of ictal and post-ictal behaviour leading to the possible inadvertent entry to the criminal justice system has led to changes in approach, the development of policies and procedures in Police Scotland and the Crown Office and Procurator Fiscal Service in Scotland.

About the Editors

Isabelle Bartkowiak-Théron, PhD is an Associate Professor in Policing and Emergency Management at the University of Tasmania, Australia. She specializes in socio-legal studies, with a particular interest in police interaction with vulnerable people. She is the lead senior researcher on the vulnerability, police education, and law enforcement and public health research streams at the Tasmanian Institute of Law Enforcement Studies. In her teaching capacity, she coordinated the Tasmania Police Recruit Course for the University for ten years, within which she still teaches on police interactions with vulnerable people and the related legislation. An award winning educator, she is the recipient of the University of Tamania 2020 Teaching Excellence Medal. Isabelle sits on the Board of Directors of the Global Law Enforcement and Public Health Association, heads up the Education Special Interest Group, and sits on the First Responders Mental Health Special Interest Group, as well as the Prosecutors Group. She has been the deputy chair of the Tasmanian Human Research Ethics Committee since 2018. She occasionally consults on the UNODC on vulnerability matters and international curricula. Isabelle sits on various international journal editorial committees and on international and Australian charitable, professional, and research governance boards, the Australian Institute of Police Management Ethical Review and Research Governance Advisory Committee, and the Australia New Zealand Society of Criminology. She sat on the Australian Crime Prevention Council as the executive member for Tasmania and on the Tasmanian Sentencing Advisory Council until 2021. She has two amazingly wonderful children and is often seen with knitting needles in hand.

James Clover, MPA has been responsible for a variety of roles in policing including undercover operations, gangs, high-risk offender assessment and management, training, hate crime investigations, and combating human trafficking and sexual exploitation. He has represented Canadian police education and training in his previous roles as a National Advisory to Police Training and the Chair for the implementation of the National Police Training Inventory. He has conducted research and provided consultation to several countries, including Tampa Florida (2014) and Melbourne Australia (2012). In 2018, James was awarded the 2018

International Policing Award from the Canadian Association of Chiefs of Police. James was named a Police Fellow with the Global Law Enforcement and Public Health Association in 2020. Since 2015, he has instructed within the Department of Public Safety & Justice Studies, Faculty of Health and Community Studies at MacEwan University in Edmonton, Alberta, Canada. It is not uncommon to see James working at his desk with one or two pugs sitting on his lap.

Denise Martin, PhD is a Professor of Criminology at the University of Abertay in the city of Dundee, Scotland. She has had a long career as a researcher in the field of Criminal Justice and her work has involved working with vulnerable groups and practitioners across a range of issues. Her interests are primarily around partnership working and examining ways to effectively support communities resolve issues around crime and anti-social behaviour. She also has a strong interest in learning and education in the field of criminal Justice, specifically leadership and organizational change. She has worked on projects focusing on alternatives to custody for young offenders (with the Children's Society), understanding the experience of school aged children's crime victimization, and evaluating coaching for women offenders. Professor Martin has also been awarded funding from a variety of organizations, including the Scottish Prison Service for a project of prison officer professionalization, the Home Office to examine emergency service collaboration, and Police Scotland to evaluate a National Crime Unit established to Investigate Child Abuse cases and an evaluation of the Prevention First initiative, to introduce a preventative approach to tackling local community issues like anti-social behaviour and violence. She has published a number of articles and edited two books, one on *Crime, Anti-Social Behaviour and Schools* (Hayden and Martin 2011, Palgrave Macmillan) and one on Police Research (*Introduction to Policing Research: Taking Lessons from Practice*, Brunger, Tong, and Martin (2015)). She has been the Associate Director for the Education and Leadership Network for the Scottish Institute of Research since November 2016. She is a member of the Law Enforcement and Public Health Special Interest Group for Education.

Richard F. Southby, PhD is Executive Dean and Distinguished Professor of Global Health Emeritus, Milken Institute School of Public Health, The George Washington University, Washington, DC, USA. Prior to joining the George Washington University in 1979, he was Senior Lecturer in Social and Preventive Medicine at Monash University and Director of Health Services Research and Teaching, School of Public Health and Tropical Medicine at the University of Sydney, Australia. In 1975 he was seconded to be Full-Time Commissioner on the Australian Hospitals and Health Services Commission in Canberra. He is currently an Honorary Professor in the Faculties of Medicine at the University of Melbourne, Monash University, and the University of Sydney. Since 1984 he has been Director of the Interagency Institute for Federal Health Leaders, which is the major continuing professional development programme for senior health professionals from the US Army, US Navy, US Air Force, US Public Health Service, and the Department of Veterans Affairs. Since 1989 he has been a member of the Metropolitan Police

Department Reserve Corps, Washington, DC, rising to the rank of Commander and serving as Commanding Officer. He is Senior Educational Adviser to the Metropolitan Police Department.

Nick Crofts, AM MBBS, MPH, FAFPHM is an epidemiologist and public health practitioner who has been working in the fields of HIV/AIDS, illicit drugs, harm reduction, and law enforcement for over 30 years. His major epidemiological work has been on the control of HIV and hepatitis C among injecting drug users in Australia (for which he received an NHMRC Senior Research Fellowship) and globally, including almost every country in Asia, for which he received the International Rolleston Award from the International Harm Reduction Association in 1998, and was made a Member of the Order of Australia in 2018. He was at the Burnet Institute for Medical Research and Public Health for 19 years, where he was instrumental in building its Public and International Health arms, and was Deputy Director for 5 years. He was Director of Turning Point Alcohol and Drug Centre for 3 years, and then at the Nossal Institute for Global Health for 3 years. He was Visiting Senior Research Fellow at the UN Interregional Crime and Justice Research Institute in Turin in 2012 and is currently a Senior Expert at the International Development Law Organization in The Hague, resident in Amsterdam. He has been a member of Australia's National Council on AIDS three times and has performed multiple consultancies for WHO, UNAIDS, UNODC, AusAID, and other bilateral and multilateral agencies. As a designer and technical director of AusAID's flagship HIV/AIDS programme in Asia, ARHP 2002–2007, he was instrumental in building capacity among SE Asian police forces in relation to HIV and has worked in many settings forging relationships between police and public health. Through the Centre for Law Enforcement and Public Health, of which he is founding Director, he founded the Law Enforcement and HIV Network (LEAHN) in 2009, convenes the International Working Group on Policing Marginalised Communities, and is Director of the annual Law Enforcement and Public Health Conferences (LEPH2019, Edinburgh, October 2019) from which the Global Law Enforcement and Public Health Association has grown. He is married to his best friend, Kerri, and has four remarkable young women as daughters.

Abbreviations

ACE	Adverse Childhood Experience
AOD	Alcohol and Other Drugs
CIT	Crisis Intervention Teams
CLEPH	Centre for Law Enforcement and Public Health
CVE	Countering Violent Extremism
DEN	Drug Education Network
GLEPHA	Global Law Enforcement and Public Health Association
HIV	Human Immunodeficiency Virus
LEAN	Law Enforcement Against Narcotics
LEPH	Law Enforcement and Public Health
LGBTIQ	Lesbian, Gay, Bisexual, Transgendered, Intersex and Queer
LGBTQ2	Lesbian, Gay, Bisexual, Trans, Intersex, Queer, and Two Spirited
LMIC	Low- and Middle-Income Countries
NGO	Non-Governmental Organization
OPS	Overdose Prevention Sites
PEPFAR	President's Emergency Plan for AIDS Relief
SAPS	South African Police Service
SDOH	Social Determinants of Health
SOLD	Supporting Offenders with Learning Disabilities
SWEAT	Social Workers Education and Advocacy Task Force
SWEEP	Sex Worker Empowerment and Enabling Environment Prog.
UN	United Nations
WHO	World Health Organization
YMCA	Young Men's Christian Association

Part I
Historical and Conceptual Issues

Chapter 1
Conceptual and Practice Tensions in LEPH: Public Health Approaches to Policing and Police and Public Health Collaborations

Isabelle Bartkowiak-Théron, James Clover, Denise Martin, Richard F. Southby, and Nick Crofts

Introduction

The intersections of law enforcement (especially police, but also other professions involved in criminal justice, such as public prosecutors) and public health are manifold, covering the widest range of social issues. Partnerships between police and health agencies have a long history in practice, with an evolving history of collaborations, and are increasingly seen as critically important. This cross-sectoral approach to complex social issues has been inadequately recognised and understood.

One aim of this collection is to consolidate literature on the topic of law enforcement and public health (LEPH); it is also to provide a critical analysis of how effective police and public health partnerships have been to date. Questions of effectiveness (and cost-effectiveness) are at the forefront of public policies, not only because of measures of austerity, but also because of relatively recent analyses that

I. Bartkowiak-Théron (✉)
Tasmanian Inst. Law Enforcement Studies, University of Tasmania, Hobart, TAS, Australia
e-mail: isabelle.bartkowiaktheron@utas.edu.au

J. Clover
Faculty of Health and Community Studies, MacEwan University, Edmonton, AB, Canada

D. Martin
School of Business, Law and Social Science, Abertay University, Dundee, UK

R. F. Southby
Milken Institute School of Public Health, The George Washington University, Washington, DC, USA

N. Crofts
Centre for Law Enforcement and Public Health School of Population and Global Health, University of Melbourne Global Law Enforcement and Public Health Association, Melbourne, VIC, Australia

© The Author(s), under exclusive license to Springer Nature Switzerland AG 2022
I. Bartkowiak-Théron et al. (eds.), *Law Enforcement and Public Health*,
https://doi.org/10.1007/978-3-030-83913-0_1

have revealed redundancies or gaps in problem-solving. More recently still, there has been scrutiny around the remits of policing and of public health, and reinvigoration of the question as to whether such problem-solving should better sit in early primary health prevention, rather than in the hands of police at (crisis) intervention stage (Bittner, 1967; Toumbourou et al., 2007; Millie & Herrington, 2014; Punch & James, 2017).

Although the justice and law enforcement industries are partners in the delivery or in facilitating access to public health services and outcomes, the essential role of brokerage played by police has only recently started to be formally acknowledged by other stakeholders (Asquith & Bartkowiak-Théron, 2017; Wood et al., 2015; Wood & Watson, 2017). In light of such a late acknowledgement, it should not come as any surprise that with issues characterised as being the responsibility of either the health system or the criminal justice system, outcome measures have been similarly demarcated (van Dijk et al., 2015) and that reliable measures of service referrals, collaboration or integration have been hard to find. There is now much evidence that such polarisation, in core business and evaluation, is detrimental to any process and that law enforcement and public health agencies often work with the same clientele, sometimes simultaneously, often at different times and according to a different timeline. They also sometimes work at cross-purposes.

This collection gathers some of the leading thinkers and practitioners in the articulation of LEPH partnerships, in a consolidation of the scholarly work done to recognise and enhance joined-up solutions to complex social problems (van Dijk et al., 2019). Together, we analyse the principles critical in the building of efficient, sustainable and productive cross-disciplinary partnerships between health and police. In painting the landscape with a broad-brush, we provide a canvas for our contributors to build an argument for the necessity of law enforcement and public health collaborations (LEPH). We define key terms and break down the major themes that underpin this collection.

A Rationale for LEPH

The need to build efficient partnerships to address complex issues—very often characterised as 'wicked issues' (Fleming & Wood, 2006)—is not a new idea (Bittner, 1967; Punch & Naylor, 1973; Punch, 1979; Butterfoss et al., 1993). However, systemic siloed practices, policies, agencies, underpinning assumptions, workforces and budgets have created disparate cultures in the law enforcement and public health sectors (Burris et al., 2010; Shepherd & Sumner, 2017). This disjunction has often led to the failure to address complex social issues adequately, resulting in an aggravation of crime, antisocial behaviours, ill-health and ultimately death. This has particularly been documented in the fields of substance use, sexual assault or mental health (themes that are explored in further depth in Chaps. 8, 9 and 12 of this collection).

The sharing and complementarity of information and responsibilities, especially in the fields of policing, criminal justice, and public health, present challenges as far as ways of working and the daily job routine is concerned (Shepherd & Sumner, 2017). It also creates difficulties in the design of policies and in the allocation of budgets across multiple government areas, co-opted evaluation measures, mixed methods analysis, goal sharing and shared visions (Burris et al., 2010; Bartkowiak-Théron & Asquith, 2016). The study of partnerships, in practice, theory and policy, constantly reveals issues with their creation, sustainability, resourcing, overarching goals and actual machinery.

As a result of such a conflicting terrain, it is unsurprising that public health has underestimated the role of law enforcement in helping to achieve its goals. Unremarkably, law enforcement has done the same in failing to recognise the importance of its function as a partner in fulfilling the overall public health mission. However, these historically specialised fields are increasingly beginning to understand the inextricable links between public safety and public health. In part, such realisation of how enmeshed both fields are has resulted from deliberations about health practitioners as procurers of public safety, as much as about the role of police as public health interventionists and facilitators (Wood & Watson, 2017; Asquith & Bartkowiak-Théron, 2017). Part of this is a shift in thinking about law enforcement officers as guardians, as opposed to warriors (Wood & Watson, 2017), and of health practitioners as facilitators of public safety. At the centre of such deliberations and re-conceptualisations of roles and remits, leaders and managers, especially at local government level, are essential to bring a new organisational 'flavour' and sensitivity to business as usual, shaping debates and shifting policies and practices towards more integrated practices (Sharma & Hossain, 2019).

In some way, the movement of LEPH is guided by community imperatives for joined-up, more visibly effective solutions. As we explore the various contributions in this collection, we are made very aware of conflict in how police and the public health operate—both in the shared and separate spaces. The health and wellbeing of communities is an all-of-system responsibility, and continuing to operate in silos to meet that responsibility will not further the efforts to achieve satisfactory outcomes for all involved.

In shaping this introductory chapter, we want to emphasise an urgent need to develop knowledge and broaden theoretical positioning, and to advocate for practices that have less to do with collaboration and more to do with a fundamental integration of services. We aim to do so by dedicating a whole collection to the analysis of not solely the conceptual, ethereal idea of partnerships, but in showcasing examples where partnerships, collaboration or integration have worked, or failed, and in drawing on the very large literature in public health on this topic, and the, perhaps more limited but increasing literature in criminology and policing.

Key Themes

Five key themes underpin this collection. We see these themes as essential in setting the tone of the book, and all contributing authors have used these as guides in considering the ways in which to focus an argument around LEPH. While not all themes are addressed in all chapters, most chapters address one or more of these.

1. The first key theme revolves around the underpinning principles of public safety that inform approaches to LEPH and how these dominate or conflict across sectors. In considering LEPH, one must systematically consider what issues or components of a crisis are prioritised in a field of practice or in a scholarly argument that focuses on dealing with vulnerable populations (Karpati et al., 2002). One of the main issues here is that such prioritisations are not always easy to reconcile or holistically address, which raises the question as to why such reconciliation seems unsurmountable in the first place. Some examples or case studies in this collection do demonstrate, however, that some collaboration principles can effectively reconcile and showcase the mechanics of such integration in practice.

2. Collaboration and partnerships as an organising principle of LEPH and the ways in which they work effectively are the second main theme of this collection. The benefits of collaborative approaches and the challenges in working in effective, collaborative manners are scrutinised and often characterised as non-negotiable practice that should be more of a norm than an exception. Authors explore and provide evidence of the various ways in which collaboration has been successful (what were the internal/external drivers that impacted on these: structures, culture, resources or relationships) and also highlight what went well/not so well in other situations.

3. It is only logical, then, to focus on governance frameworks as a subsequent theme, and how these support or hinder the progress of LEPH collaborations and integration. In examining how LEPH collaborations can unfold to their full potential, it is necessary to analyse the broader structural elements that work collectively to enhance or inhibit policy, strategy and legislation development to support the LEPH agenda (Julian et al., 2017).

4. Resources through times of austerity or challenging circumstance that are likely to impact us globally over the next few years is our fourth theme. Budget cuts have plagued the health system across many countries for a number of years in the Global North, with the Global South suffering from constant lack of critical resources overall. In examining how LEPH collaborations work in both cases, we can learn deeply from situations where collaborations, built from the ground up, have been the necessary accommodations to shrinking budgets that are out of synch with government and public demands to do more. Such resourcing issues continue to impact upon the LEPH agenda, with agencies often reverting to looking inwards when times become too tough, financially. But, we argue, one way to resolve these financial and other resource limitations is thinking how best

to use both monetary and other opportunities and assets, such as physical, environmental and people resources in better and more effective ways.

5. The building of evidence across the broad field of LEPH is crucial in recognising both success and failure. However, collaborative partnerships are often difficult to measure, due to diverging core businesses, performance indicators and (hard or soft) measures of impact (van Dijk et al., 2015). The point remains that evidence should inform the field about how to approach or create a momentum in LEPH to support its longer term and continued growth as a field of critical importance. Here we argue that programme evaluation should form a key aspect of the LEPH space. More critically, we mean evidence not through applying a narrow or prioritised methodological approach, but in a way that builds knowledge of what is effective, where, when and who, taking into consideration that adaptions need to take place depending on the contexts in which LEPH innovations occur.

Structure of the Book

This book is built in three parts which progressively examine the conceptualisation and operationalisation of the LEPH field.

Part I combines contributors' considerations of historical and conceptual issues relating to LEPH.

In Chap. 2, John Middleton provides a reflexive account of how he observed the development of the collaboration of law enforcement and public health throughout his career, and how it has always been a reality of public health administrators. What essentially existed as 'communities of interest' slowly progressed into partnerships of necessity which then became statutory to address complex issues of emergency. The sheer array of issues presented in this chapter is an illustration of the broad range of topics that are, or should be, addressed in partnership, due to their complexity. It also highlights the sobering dawn of LEPH problems which present new and unparalleled challenges, from cyber-crime to climate change.

James Clover provides a careful, and much needed (re-)consideration of the definition, role and remit of police in Chap. 3. By asking the question of what police do, and what we want them to do, Clover examines the morphing of a role that was initially perceived and codified as solely revolving around incidents of crime, into the reality of responding to the nature of incidents, that are less about criminality and more deeply rooted into pre-existing situations of deprivation.

In Chap. 4, Bartkowiak-Théron and Asquith reprise the issue of vulnerability as a core concept in the LEPH field, but examine the recent worldwide events that have precipitated a renewed attention and an un-deniability of the universal nature of vulnerability. Increased attention and media coverage of the #Defundthepolice and Black Lives Matter movements, as well as the heart-breaking death of George Floyd, present sobering and important calls to action.

It is only natural to place, early on in this collection, the communication/dissemination of what works and how to do it in LEPH partnerships through education and training of practitioners. There are many models for accomplishing the education and dissemination of goals that preoccupy not only many of our contributing authors but also many practitioners who have shaped LEPH debates. Some of these models include work-integrated learning, coaching and mentoring, online delivery of theory and practice modules, etc. It is justified to question what models underpin curriculum development and educational strategies that are emerging in this field. In Chap. 5, Richard F. Southby and Brandon Del Pozo dissect the need for strong education practices to facilitate the operationalisation of LEPH partnerships. Societal expectations of law enforcement are evolving globally, and these have implications for the education and training of police and their expanded roles in society. The 'militarisation' of law enforcement is evident in many countries and has resulted in undesirable practices and negative reactions from communities. The professionalisation of policing demands more collaboration and partnerships in education, training, professional development, expansion of applied research and evidence-based policing.

Each part of this book finishes with a chapter, introduced by one of the editors, which features the voice of professionals on specific issues explored in the previous chapters or introduces new issues of interest that are relevant to the part's main topic. It was important for us, as editors who constantly engage in both the practical and scholarly fields, to include voices from both practitioners and academics in this collection. Particularly, we insisted on the importance of providing some visibility to the many issues that are of prevalence in LEPH, especially those that are of crucial importance to practitioners. We have therefore provided practitioners with a platform to describe the intersect of police and health and how that intersection impacts their respective field of work. We called these ground-up contributions to the collection 'Community voices', and we have placed them in the parts of the collection that they illustrated best.

To conclude Part I, Jurman and Turner highlight the importance of communication and procedural justice to effectively engage with vulnerable groups. Chapter 6 starts with an analysis of the impact of adverse childhood experiences, by Dan Jurman. Adverse childhood experiences are traumatic events that happen before the age of 18 years. Their prominence came to the fore in the 1990s after a study by the Centers for Disease Control and Prevention linked their occurrence with significant negative outcomes in adult life, from substance and dependency issues to crime or further victimisation. The second one, from Shelley Turner's social work perspective, provides some insight into the brokerage role police officers play in the broad public health continuum, insisting on the importance of adaptable communication techniques and skills.

Part II explores in further depths the kinds of partnerships that are needed for LEPH to function. In many communities and organisations cross-disciplinary partnerships are celebrated precisely because they are still relatively unusual (if not, at least not documented as such), but that does not necessarily mean they are effective at solving wicked problems. Authors provide a critical stance and dedicate close attention to scientifically sound evidence on what works at every level in partnerships, and what brings the demise of joint ventures. In Chap. 7, Taylor, Corley,

McFee and Torigian provide a critical account of various reflective practitioner perspectives on transformational leadership. They accompany their analysis with case studies that go a long way to inform what collaborative leadership must look like to sustain these partnerships.

In Chap. 8, Thomas, Heyman, White and Dougall consider the widely documented issue of law enforcement and mental health, but argue that current partnerships are failing to meet the needs of a significant proportion of the population who have mental health-related needs but do not meet the threshold for admission to public mental health services. For that 'missing middle', as they dub it, other community-based care and support are also insufficient. Their contribution also looks to pockets of innovation internationally that have sought to address this significant unmet need.

Through examining specific case studies focusing on the prevention of crime, violence and anti-social behaviour, Martin and Graham explore some of the benefits of partnerships for resolving LEPH issues in Chap. 9. They address some of the challenges around sustaining partnerships in the longer term, including for example, limited resources, shifting priorities and political pressures. They argue such challenges can serve to re-enforce siloed practices and what the authors call 'retreatism into organisational cultures and norms'. They also address the importance of ensuring strategic planning and evaluation, ensuring the effectiveness of these programmes is captured.

In Chap. 10, Brandon Del Pozo argues that there is merit in attempting to overcome institutional and cultural obstacles to facilitate LEPH integration. The development of joined practices is in dire need for an evidence-base, which, he argues, can only be obtained in the consolidation of practice and study in the shape of an applied research centre for policing and public health at a major university. The rationale for such a centre would be the cultivation of 'a lasting and widespread relationship between [both] fields, in their theoretical grounding and in practice'. He further emphasises the current, detrimental situation of misunderstanding (sometimes hostility) between both fields.

Chapter 11 concludes this part of the book, with Craven, Evans, Helfrich, Komar, Krinsky and Peters exploring the terms and conditions that become established in the relationships that have to be maintained with communities. Their analysis of shared and mutual problem-solving spaces highlights the challenges that exist when different siloed agencies and groups strive to work together. Michael Peters picks up on Shelley Turner's focus on youth and discusses the importance and effectiveness of early intervention networks, and the positive effects these can have when they are sustained throughout time. Donna Evans then harnesses the expertise of two colleagues, Emily Craven and Wayne Helfrich, to provide an analysis of the collaboration that occurs in South Africa between police and sex workers, and the essential support that is provided by non-governmental organisations (NGOs) to communities at risk. Both South African vignettes provide an account of the deep-seated barriers that still remain, and of the various stigma that can provide progress or impede transparent collaborations. Krinsky and Komar, as a final contribution to Part II, provide a remarkable piece that advocates for a shift in prosecutorial practice. With the inauguration of Overdose Prevention Sites (OPS) in Philadelphia, Pennsylvania, OPSs and prosecutors became unlikely partners in one of the most forward thinking and proactive harm minimisation initiatives in the USA.

The primary purpose of law enforcement and public health partnerships is to address complicated issues that go beyond disciplinary boundaries, for which sole stakeholder action provides sub-optimal solutions. Such issues are explored in Part III of this collection, which focuses on issues of importance in LEPH.

As such, Chap. 12 looks at the alcohol and other drugs sector, through the lens of an Australian perspective on illegal drug regulation and prevention. Meadows et al. focus on the topic of harm minimisation (using two specific case studies) and on the lack of articulation of law enforcement and health policies, with an outlook to the future that seems to go in the right direction. However frustrating the lack of operational guidelines can be for stakeholders involved in the management of drugs in the community, international and local policies seem to slowly coalesce.

In Chap. 13, Egan-Vine, Bartkowiak-Théron and Julian outline the specific case of refugee resettlement, via two case studies in which collaboration and lack of knowledge on issues of displacement and migration failed community members. The case studies, emotional in nature, highlight the complexity of the situation of refugees relocating to unknown countries and the necessity for the LEPH fields to not only collaborate together, but also with local agencies to contribute to community safety and wellbeing, particularly in regional and rural areas of the country of resettlement.

Kamkar et al., in Chap. 14, provide an analysis of the gaps and stigma revolving round first responder mental health. While the topic of mental health is altogether well documented in policing and public health, with much said about topics such as Crisis Intervention Teams, Crisis Assessment Teams and similar, the concomitant toll experienced by first responders (police, firefighters, paramedics, etc.) is only a nascent field which is yet growing rapidly in political attention and scrutiny.

Melissa Jardine and Auke Van Dijk explore the oft silent voice of the 'Global South' and of low- and middle-income countries (LMICs). Chapter 15 highlights the significant potential to examine LEPH partnerships in LMICs: they present different understandings as to who the police are and what they should do, compared to what is described in dominant Global North scholarship. The fact that such a chasm in operational and conceptual frameworks is increasingly documented in policing literature shows that there is much to learn from the Global South LEPH practices.

Finally, in Chap. 16, Karl Roberts provides some important analysis of the COVID-19 situation, and the new perspectives brought to the field by the emergency created by the pandemic, at the very moment we are putting this book together. Roberts outlines the difficulties public agencies, particularly police, face when they have to engage, suddenly and quickly, with agencies they usually do not work with. Difficulties include, but are not limited to, lack of mutual understanding of processes, policies and practices and lack of trust. Other, more logistical problems lie in the protecting of officers from infection, safe handling of samples and effective management of stress, anxiety and possible bereavement amongst police staff. All of this in a context of likely high staff attrition.

Part III community voices, as Chap. 17, reprise and go beyond some of the themes explored in the preceding chapters. Dan Jones provides an account of the importance of being attuned to vulnerabilities in the field, as a police officer, but then goes on with a candid analysis of the impact of such sensitivity on police officers themselves, as collateral trauma. The following two contributions focus on work with social minorities. While Murray Billett focuses on the case of the LGBTQ2 communities, Frank David discusses an initiative that specifically focuses on working with offenders with learning disabilities. Both contributions discuss the deeply entrenched stigma and barriers experienced by individuals, and how community attitudes and joined up services go a long way to support people living in situations of social disadvantage to live better lives, or turn their lives around altogether. Emily Diamond then shines a spotlight on autism, an issue that we fail to address holistically in police education, and which has until very recently been glaringly missing from operational policies. In a similar vein, Lesslie Young provides us with an essential introduction to the topic of epilepsy in the LEPH context, especially how misconstrued symptoms and subsequent misguided police intervention can have dramatic consequences on the life of an individual.

Conclusion

One of the major strengths of this book is its focus on issues relating to forming and sustaining partnerships that aim to address persistent issues of deprivation and ill-health, and their possible consequences on offending or victimisation. This collection aims to move beyond just describing problems and recommending collaborative approaches to solving them, to examining what these collaborative approaches look like. We are mindful, however, to acknowledge that as the first consolidated collection on the LEPH topic, the range of issues discussed is far from being exhaustive, especially since LEPH is a growing field. Rather than putting together a catalogue-like list of issues that would have come at the cost of deep discussion of some issues, we are very aware that this book is only the first step towards documenting many more issues of importance in LEPH, and we welcome the future opportunities to do so. Our next contributions will unravel an intricate web where it is pointed out that for example, alcohol, tobacco and drug use are pervasive issues that impact many others: there is an argument to be made that alcohol and substance use are right at the intersection of law enforcement and public health. Many scholars and practitioners discuss multiple morbidities in intricate details. Regardless of any future work on the matter, we engage in a hefty debate around how a public health approach to any topic relevant to law enforcement (whether on substance use, and any other). The list of topics that we would have liked to include is long and range from county lines to sexual abuse, the full alcohol and other drugs (AOD) sector (including vaping), human trafficking or natural disasters. We have no doubt that future work will include those.

Obviously, as we close our work on this collection and handout this manuscript to the publishers, it is impossible to ignore events and lessons that befell the year 2020. The pandemic is still upon many countries as we write these words, although some, like Australia, New Zealand and Mongolia, seem to be faring much better than others. As such we are grateful for the many contributors to this collection who have made room in their calendars to write a chapter for us, discuss angles of analysis and manage, at the same time, the pain and trauma that was, and still is, COVID-19. In the same context, we would like to acknowledge some other issues that we wanted to include in this book, but that, despite our invitations to authors to write on the topic, were too raw in the social and scholarly psyche, still, to write about in strong, analytical words. As such, we pay our respects to the Black Lives Matter movement, and to all the individuals, families and neighbourhoods that have suffered at the hands of totalitarian discourses on violence, or were met with deafening silence. This, too, sits at the centre of the LEPH intersection, and we will make every effort to acknowledge and promote practices that are free of stigma, trauma-aware and inclusive.

We have set out our intentions and key themes for this collection and hope these provide the starting point for what we believe is a critically important collaborative space. We have drawn together a range of voices, perspectives and experiences from practitioners, researchers and stakeholders. These voices have mutually covered some of the key challenges that those working at the intersections of Law Enforcement and Public Health face. More importantly, they weave a narrative of recognition and dedication to the importance of strengthening the connections between Law Enforcement and Public Health to ensure a holistic approach that aims to reduce the often hazardous and disruptive forces that structural inequalities can bring. This is not an easy endeavour. What we learn is that many obstacles are presented, not least that sometimes conflicting priorities of safety and security. As is described in some places in this book, these priorities can appear to be at odds and insurmountable (Bartkowiak-Théron & Asquith, 2016). What we learn though and what we hope that readers and students using this publication learn are that there are ways to overcome challenges through working collaboratively and appreciating the perspectives of others. These glimmers of hope are important particularly as current tensions remain both between Law Enforcement and Public Health and in society more broadly. We hope this collection offers an opportunity for people to learn, reflect and consider how we can continue to improve and sustain the growing intersections between Law Enforcement and Public Health to improve people's lives.

References

Asquith, N. L., & Bartkowiak-Théron, I. (2017). Police as public health interventionists. In N. L. Asquith, I. Bartkowiak-Théron, & K. Roberts (Eds.), *Policing encounters with vulnerability* (pp. 145–170). Palgrave.

Bartkowiak-Théron, I., & Asquith, N. L. (2016). Conceptual divides and practice synergies in law enforcement and public health: Some lessons from policing vulnerability in Australia. *Policing and Society, 27*(3), 276–288.

Bittner, E. (1967). Police discretion in emergency apprehension of mentally ill persons. *Social Problems, 14*(3), 278–279.

Burris, S., Wagenaar, A. C., Swanson, J., Ibrahim, J. K., Wood, J., & Mello, M. M. (2010). Making the case for laws that improve health: A framework for public health law research. *Milbank Quarterly, 88*(2), 169–210.

Butterfoss, F., Goodman, R., & Wandersman, A. (1993). Community coalitions for prevention and health promotion. *Health Education and Research: Theory and Practice, 8*(3), 315–330.

Fleming, J., & Wood, J. (2006). *Fighting crime together: The challenges of policing and security networks*. University of New South Press.

Julian, R., Bartkowiak-Théron, I., Hallam, J., & Hughes, C. (2017). Exploring law enforcement and public health as a collective impact initiative: Lessons learned from Tasmania as a case study. *Journal of Criminological Research, Policy and Practice, 3*(2), 79–92.

Karpati, A., Galea, S., Awerbuch, T., & Levins, R. (2002). Variability and vulnerability at the ecological level: Implications for understanding the social determinants of health. *American Journal of Public Health, 92*, 1768–1772.

Millie, A., & Herrington, V. (2014). The Great Debate: How wide or narrow should the police's remit be? *Public Safety Leadership Research Focus, 2*(4), 1–10.

Punch, M., & James, S. (2017). Researching law enforcement and public health. *Policing and Society, 27*(3), 251–260.

Punch, M., & Naylor, T. (1973). The police: A social service. *New Society, 24*(554), 358–361.

Punch, M. (1979). The secret social service. In S. Holdaway (Ed.), *The British police* (pp. 102–117). Edward Arnold.

Sharma, R., & Hossain, M. M. (2019). Strengthening public health partnerships in India: Envisioning the role of law enforcement during public health emergencies. *Indian Journal of Community Medicine: Official Publication of Indian Association of Preventive and Social Medicine, 44*(3), 188–192. https://doi.org/10.4103/ijcm.IJCM_110_19

Shepherd, J. P., & Sumner, S. A. (2017). Policing and public health—Strategies for collaboration. *Journal American Medical Association, 317*(15), 1525–1526.

Toumbourou, J. W., Hemphill, S. A., Tresidder, J., Humphreys, C., Edwards, J., & Murray, D. (2007). Mental health promotion and socio-economic disadvantage: Lessons from substance abuse, violence and crime prevention and child health. *Health Promotion Journal of Australia: Official Journal of Australian Association of Health Promotion Professionals, 18*, 184–190.

van Dijk, A., Hoogewoning, F., & Punch, M. (2015). *What matters in policing? Change values and leadership in turbulent times*. Policy Press.

van Dijk, A., Herrington, V., Crofts, N., Breunig, R., Burris, S., Sullivan, H., Middleton, J., Sherman, S., & Thomson, N. (2019). Law enforcement and public health: Recognition and enhancement of joined-up solutions. *The Lancet, 393*(10168), 287–294.

Wood, J. D., & Watson, A. C. (2017). Improving police interventions during mental health-related encounters: Past, present and future. *Policing and Society, 27*(3), 289–299.

Wood, J. D., Taylor, C. J., Groff, E. R., & Ratcliffe, J. H. (2015). Aligning policing and public health promotion: Insights from the world of foot patrol. *Police Practice and Research, 16*(3), 211–223.

Chapter 2
The Historical Public Health and Social Work Role of the Police

John Middleton

Introduction

In some political administrations and cultures, the idea of public health and the police working together seems to be an alien one. For me, it has been an essential part of my career in public health. This chapter will describe some of the joint working between the police and public health policymakers and services over 30 years in two local authorities the West Midlands of England, Sandwell and Coventry. I will describe how some joint working seems to me to be essential—'partnerships of necessity'. Examples include emergency preparedness and response, safeguarding children and vulnerable adults, response to acute mental health problems, alcohol and problems of addiction, offender management and rehabilitation and preventing racial violence. All these have had, in the UK, some statutory framework in which the responsibilities of different agencies are defined and their actions working together are described.

Some areas of joint working may be considered as 'communities of interest', where initiatives have been taken by police and public health coming together to look at a problem, not because they have to, but because they recognise a need: such as accident prevention and domestic violence. In the early days of the Sandwell community safety partnership, this too was a community of interest—a non-statutory joining of interests in recognition of the need to work together to reduce crime and

This contribution is based on the EUPHA/ ASPHER sponsored lecture at the 2019 conference of the Law Enforcement and Public Health in Edinburgh Scotland (October 22, 2019): *Public health problems are multidisciplinary so why do we train for them separately?* https://www.slideshare.net/johnmiddleton7965/public-health-problems-are-multidisciplinary-why-do-we-train-for-them-separately.

J. Middleton (✉)
Association of Schools of Public Health in the European Region, Brussels, Belgium
e-mail: john.middleton@aspher.org

improve health. There has been, in addition, considerable innovation in what might be described as the epidemiology of violence and crime and evidence-based intervention. In these I will describe some of my involvement with the Campbell Collaboration and getting research into practice on problems that reduced crime and improved health, and how this knowledge informed the actions of the Sandwell Community Safety Partnership through the years 2000s.

Some of the partnerships of necessity that became statutory during my time as a director of public health were, at first, communities of interest. They went through their exploratory 'forming' and 'storming' phases and became established 'norming' and 'performing' organisations taking care of routine business (Tuckman, 1965). Community safety partnerships continue to be the overarching bodies representing local authorities, the police, health services and public health, fire services, community and minority representatives and charged with planning to prevent crime and violence at local administrative level. They have shown their value despite being tested through different national political ideologies over time. Drug and alcohol partnerships have not survived as consistently. The development of partnerships between police and public health requires enthusiasm, expertise, mutual respect and commitment by senior officers and officers working at the frontline. Joint training is essential. Co-location is beneficial where joint decision-making in real time is necessary as in children's safeguarding and mental health responses.

Progress in partnerships has been undermined by austerity policies that have cut resources. They are undermined more significantly by disruptive reorganisations of services, the moving around of senior service managers and changes of administrative boundaries. There have also been contentious and highly divisive policy initiatives from national governments over the years, including the Anti-Social Behaviour Orders (ASBO) and the PREVENT anti-terrorism strategy, which have tested local partnerships. Partnerships can also be undermined by political indifference. In the age of pandemic and populism, it is more vital than ever that public health and police forces continue to work together and develop effective partnerships, for the safety and health of the communities they serve.

Early Work with the Police and Public Health

Coventry Health Promotion Team

In my first public health training post, from 1983 to 1986, I was attached to Coventry Health Authority. The District Medical Officer, Dr. George Pollock, was about to set up the Coventry Health Promotion group of senior people from health, local authority and blue light services. Priorities for the group included cardiovascular disease, smoking and accident prevention. Police and fire services were interested in cardiovascular and cancer prevention as an occupational health concern; as major employers in the city, they wanted to be good employers, and it was an imperative to have fitter personnel. In the accident prevention work, police leadership with council road safety led us to propose Coventry become a no drink-driving city by the year 2000. This included the launch of a Coventry Council-led lobby in support of random and static roadside breath testing policy. This policy operated in Finland, South Australia and some American states, still sadly unrealised 34 years later in the UK, although alcohol-related road accidents have declined greatly, and drinking and driving has long been consigned to socially unacceptable behaviour (Rollings et al., 1987). The Coventry Accident Prevention Group was active in road, home and occupational safety. They held multi-agency seminars on childhood accident prevention, produced a booklet on the epidemiology and life course of child accidents at different stages of child development, and supported children's car safety loans and sales scheme.

In our first revival of the Medical Officer of Health annual public health report entitled The Health of Coventry (Binysh et al., 1985), we used the World Health Organization (WHO) major determinants of health (WHO, 1978) and the newly published World Health Organization European Office 38 targets for Health for All in the European Region (WHOEURO, 1985) to set a framework and vision to achieve by the year 2000. We referenced crimes of violence, accidents and fires in the city.

Director of Public Health Sandwell and Work on Violence and Health

In my first annual public health report as Director of Public Health for Sandwell, 'Life and Death in Sandwell' in 1989, I was able to develop themes of peace, violence prevention and public health (Middleton et al., 1989). WHO had described peace as a positive sense of wellbeing and security for people in all countries, implying the opportunity to determine freely their own destiny and fully exploit their human potential. 'Freedom from violence' requires intervention at every level of the 'life course'—I was able to illustrate with local evidence on child abuse and overall crime statistics. We had no figures at the time on domestic violence, interracial violence or hate crime, and we needed to collect the data. In a comment that was somewhat ahead of its time, I floated the idea of institutional racism arguing that statutory organisations and other employers must recognise the part they may have played in the social violence of discrimination against ethnic minorities; they must look critically and positively at the employment opportunities and practices they operate as a means to improving community relations.

The Safer Sandwell Partnership

My 1995 annual report was entirely on the theme of 'Safer Sandwell' (Middleton et al., 1995). By this time, we were able to report extensively on the epidemiology of crime and violence. Police colleagues had rudimentary geographical data presented by police 'beats'; domestic violence and racial harassment were beginning to be reported albeit in crude counts of reported incidents. We sought to present a holistic picture of how adverse conditions in the economy, environment and education were the root causes of both ill health and poor safety. We developed the themes of the then newly published United Nations Development Programme idea of security as being more than military-economic, social, health and environmental (UNDP, 1994). Sandwell had just established a new voluntary crime prevention partnership. Using my report as a core resource, the partnership evolved rapidly into a community safety partnership called 'Safer Sandwell'. It is one of the communities of interest between health and law enforcement. The Safer Sandwell Partnership predated by about 4 years, and informed the national, statutory expectation that local authorities would lead community safety partnerships in their area. Drug and alcohol partnerships were also voluntary at this time; Sandwell produced its first 5-year partnership strategy in 1995. There was a gathering pace to partnership working in Sandwell and across the country. In part, this was stimulated by national policy drives on economic and social regeneration—which led to statutory and business agencies coming together to address local issues which required multi-agency action.

Evidence-Based or 'Evidence-Informed' Law Enforcement and Health

Crime Is a Public Health Problem: Early Work with the Campbell Collaboration

In 1998, I published a paper in the Journal of Medicine, Conflict and Global Security, which began my involvement in the development of evidence-based policymaking in the field of law enforcement and public health (Middleton, 1998). The paper covered themes of the epidemiology of crime and violence, and the assessment of effective interventions and implementation. Following this paper, alongside Sir Iain Chalmers, then Director of the Cochrane Collaboration,[1] and Professor Richard Lilford, we embarked on a review of papers in the Cochrane database which covered public health interventions and multi-agency approaches to

---

[1] The Cochrane Collaboration is an independent organization made up of a collection of members and supporters who seek to make globally accessible the highest level of research evidence to empower health and health care decisions. See https://www.cochrane.org/about-us.

health problems. This led to the York Centre for Reviews and Dissemination publishing national evidence for the 'wider public health agenda' (Sheldon, Chalmers & Roundings, 2000). Within this suite of documents, Anthony Petrosino contributed an extensive crime and public health review (Petrosino, 2000). At the same time, Sandwell was involved with the UK Public Health Association developing their landmark report on the involvement of health services in responding to and preventing crime (McCabe & Raine, 1997).

'CRIMEGRIP'

The Petrosino (2000) report became a platform for a West Midlands Home Office-funded project called 'CRIMEGRIP'—*getting research into practice on interventions which reduce crime and improve health* (Middleton et al., 2001; Middleton, 2006a). The purpose of this project was to take the best evidence from studies and systematic reviews and examine how to get them into practice to reduce crime and improve health. Our workshops asked a sequence of questions: did our local and regional professionals agree with the results? If they did, were they following the recommendations? If they were not, what were the barriers? Money? Training? Are senior managers and political decision-makers agreeing or blocking? If they did not believe the evidence, what more would they want to see? An extraordinarily wide range of different disciplines was involved—from nursery nurses in the early years interventions to highway engineers and security personnel in the CCTV and street lighting studies. CRIMEGRIP informed much of the argument in my 2003 public health annual report *What works for health in Sandwell* (Middleton, 2003). We held seminars on evidence-based policymaking for local politicians involved in council scrutiny, and we took our evidence into the Sandwell Community Safety Partnership in 2006 (Middleton, 2006b) to further inform strategy.

Unintended Consequences: Interventions That Cause Harm

The idea of unintended consequences was still barely appreciated—that things we can do can cause harm. The last item on our CRIMEGRIP reviews was Scared Straight. Scared Straight is the totemic example of an intervention that has the reverse effect than the one we expect. Young men were shown the inside of jails mainly in the USA, with the rationale that if they saw how bad these jails were, they would be scared into a 'straight' life. In reality, the outcomes of well-conducted randomised trials were the opposite—the young men so exposed were more likely to be involved in criminal acts subsequently. The mystery and fear of the unknown had been removed by showing the subjects what prison was like, and it was also observed that some of the young men found role models in the prison inmates they came across (Petrosino et al., 2013). We did not have 'Scared Straight' on offer to us in Sandwell, and we would have declined it. We also advised local schools against the similar scheme which was on offer in neighbouring areas 'Prison Me, No Way', in which ex-prison officers were allowed to take over schools for a day and run it like a prison. We observed some of the psychological processes at play in another central government initiative to address anti-social behaviour. Anti-social behaviour orders (ASBO) became a badge of honour for some of the young people who were placed under them. And some of the uses of the ASBOs were dubious also—like playing 'hopscotch' or playing the bagpipes. In Sandwell's work, extreme reservations were expressed about the negative impact of the government's dispersals of group orders in the Anti-Social Behaviour Act 2003. Other examples of the negative outcomes of some interventions that sound positive and well intentioned include Drugs Abuse Resistance Education (DARE) and other schools' education programmes delivered by uniformed personnel, such as nurses, priests and police, and teaching 16-year olds to drive cars prior to them being of road using age. In our review, we found CCTV to be ineffective in preventing crime (Middleton, 2003, Chap. 1). Now surveillance is so widespread, and CCTV plays a strong role in prosecuting crime; there is very little likelihood of CCTV going away. On the other hand, good-quality street lighting does seem to be strongly effective in preventing crime (Middleton, 2003, Chap. 5.7; Farrington & Welch, 2002).

Case Studies of Effective Interventions #1: Methadone Maintenance
The methadone maintenance key paper was the Marsch systematic review and meta-analysis showing substantial effect sizes for reducing drug-related crimes, blood-borne viruses and acquisitive crime/domestic burglary (Marsch, 1998). The CRIMEGRIP review found professionals in health, policing and social care readily aligned to the review findings, and so able to highlight shortfalls in funding services, setting up suitable facilities for treatment and expanding the pool of available and trained doctors and other primary care practitioners (Middleton, 2003, Chap. 5.7). The Sandwell Drug and Alcohol Team had become a statutory committee under the Safer Sandwell Partnership in the early 2000s. The new status came with a growing fund to support education, prevention, treatment and care of drug users. Teams were permitted to cover alcohol in their remit by local decision and we did. Building from the CRIMEGRIP review, our community drug team met with every GP practice in the borough, preparing the ground for wider understanding of harm reduction approaches including methadone maintenance, and a shared care protocol where possible. The Drug Interventions Programme (DIP) came in from the national Home Office permitting police officers to divert offenders to a drug treatment programme (DIP, 2004). In 2004, Sandwell doubled the number of opiate drug users in its methadone maintenance and harm-reducing programmes, and the accompanying result was a 33% cut in domestic burglary offences. It was possible to see from press reports how a few prolific offenders

(continued)

taken out into a drug programme could contribute substantially to the reduction in burglaries (Middleton, 2014), but there was also a more generalised reduction in opportunistic break-ins. The fall in domestic burglary continued, despite the financial crash and austerity measures through the early 2010s (Middleton, 2014). The fall has continued nationally as measured by the Crime Survey for England and Wales, but police recorded figures remain fairly even. Drug crimes recorded by the police nationally fell throughout the 2010s, from a high in 2007–2008 (Office of National Statistics, 2020). Is this a true and successful reduction of drug crime due to the reduction in the pool of drug users through treatment programmes, or stronger preventive policing? A reduction in police recording drug crimes, in favour of use of cautions, or a reduction in police numbers meaning drug crimes are not detected or highest priority for policing. Most worrying in the austerity years has been the rise in opiate drug-related deaths in the United Kingdom. We have attributed this to the politically motivated change to a methadone-reducing strategy with an emphasis on rewarding providers for abstinence and removal of clients from their lists. A generation of ageing opiate injectors are now falling back on poor quality street heroin, cocaine and crack with fatal consequences, in what is a public health emergency (Middleton et al., 2016).

Case Studies of Effective Interventions #2: Early Years Support
Sandwell Education Authority had sought to provide some nursery preschool education even from the time of 1980s austerity. It had extended the quality and comprehensiveness of this through its multi-agency centre programme (MAC) in the Tipton City Challenge programme (1992–1998) and its Family Education and Training Centres (FETC) programme in the single regeneration budget years 1994–2000. I was impressed by the 27-year outcomes of the American HighScope/Perry Pre-school Study. This had shown children from deprived African-American backgrounds, given family support and a HighScope educational programme between 3–5 years had done better in their education achievements and economic wellbeing; and they had not needed social welfare programmes, special education services or been perpetrators or victims of crime (Schweinhart, 2013). Indeed, most compelling in the cost–benefit analysis of the study was the benefit in terms of the five times reduction in crime levels compared with controls, by the age of 27 years. I was able to bring one of the researchers, Larry Schweinhart, to Sandwell in a Health Action Zone (HAZ) initiative in 1999. Sandwell's nursery schools were already piloting the HighScope approach to early years education, and the HAZ subsequently funded all 34 nursery schools to adopt HighScope

(continued)

pedagogy (Thomson, 2002). The Early years interventions were another of the case studies of CRIMEGRIP (Middleton, 2003, Chap. 5.7). This initiative as well as the National Sure Start programme for 0–3 year olds has had a major long-term inter-generational benefit to the children, now young adults of Sandwell, as witnessed in continuing growth of educational attainment, falling teenage pregnancy and a range of other health measures and falling crime (Middleton, 2014).

Communities of Interest: Young People's Services

In our 1998 annual public health report, Child Friendly Sandwell (Middleton, 1998), we devoted a chapter to prevention and response to bullying in schools. Teachers, and head teachers particularly, taking it seriously, is an essential requirement for an anti-bullying strategy. Any head teacher who says there is no bullying problem in their school should set our alarm bells running. Active involvement of pupils in putting together an anti-bullying strategy is also necessary. Even from a young age, children can be asked how they want to be treated in school and how they should expect to treat others. Active involvement and mutual respect were also evident in our CRIMEGRIP review of young people's services.

Our CRIMEGRIP review of drug education programmes had complemented these findings. Structured and prolonged programmes with a strong peer involvement, and teachers in supportive information-providing roles, were far more effective than single lectures from out-of-school presenters who offered no chance for communication and problem solving (Middleton, 2003; Tobler & Stratton, 1997). A West Midlands Home Office rapid review looking at implications for gang culture and gun crime reached similar conclusions (Butler et al., 2004). The main recommendations from these observations were that effective programmes should adopt a problem-solving approach and analyse the local problem rather than simply importing an intervention. They should have a strong management structure with clear leadership and take a collaborative approach with front line staff.

Programmes should target behaviour (gang violence) rather than affiliation (gang membership). They should offer both a 'carrot' by providing opportunities out of gang activity through employment, training, treatment and family support and a 'stick' through enforcement, prohibitions and sanctions. They should focus both on reducing incidence and reducing lethality. Programmes should exchange information both formally and informally and engage community groups and voluntary groups via existing networks. And they should market effectively. Once a strategy is agreed, it should be marketed to the target audience and the wider community. The enforcement elements of the strategy should be implemented consistently and as advertised. The approaches were widely applied in Scotland (see Chap. 9) in successful efforts to reduce knife crime based on the American models of Cure Violence and Boston and still hold true today as police authorities and politicians in

England recognise the urgent need to tackle knife crime (Braga et al., 2001; Braga & Weisburd, 2012; Younge & Barr, 2018).

The public health services developed peer education programmes in sex education, drugs and alcohol that worked alongside school nursing services (SRE Project, 2020). There were strong efforts by Sandwell Youth Services to develop the Youth Cabinet and the Young People's Parliament, involving young people in the decisions that affected their services and their lives. Despite the absence of hard scientific evidence for some youth intervention, I believe these principles were very sound. It was also a case of 'you don't know what you've got till it's gone', when the years of austerity cut savagely into these non-statutory services and young people were left unsupported to fend for themselves—with the disastrous but perfectly understandable and predictable recourse to gangs, knife crime and county lines of the late 2010s (Younge & Barr, 2018; Middleton & Shepherd, 2018).

Communities of Interest: Domestic Violence

Health services have had a long connection with voluntary services dealing with domestic violence including women's aid, refuges and rape crisis. But domestic violence did not have a statutory framework so it was always marginalised. Sandwell health services formalised a relationship with domestic violence voluntary services in one of ten priority programmes for the Sandwell Health Action Zone in 1998 (Sandwell HAZ, 1998). This was a developmental approach with local agencies that included a violence-free relationships education programme in schools between 1998 and 2002. In 2004, the Sandwell Organisation Against Domestic Abuse (SOADA) was established, bringing together all the partners with a multiagency team, supporting victims of domestic abuse. SOADA became members of the Safer Sandwell Partnership and domestic violence became a standing item. The high volume causes of violent crime in Sandwell, and probably many other communities, were domestic violence and alcohol-related violence. We developed joint protocols for recognition and intervention between domestic violence, police, alcohol agencies and child protection agencies. In 2011, the public health department developed a partnership intervention with the police that sought to use the best available evidence to determine the interventions required. Our evidence review concluded that interventions which involved the arrest of the perpetrator were more effective than those that did not; interventions in which there was an initial arrest and a support service for the abused person were more effective than those which did not, and those which involved arrest, support for the abused and intervention with the perpetrator had the best outcomes (Stokes, 2014; Heise, 2011). We found no evidence that anger management was an effective intervention with perpetrators; our conclusions mirrored more the polarised feminist view that domestic violence was less about anger, and more about controlling and power relationships (Domestic Abuse Intervention Programmes, 2020). We proposed intervention to complement existing services for victims of abuse with a perpetrator intervention (Stokes, 2014; Stokes et al., 2013).

However, finding a suitable provider of perpetrator services proved elusive. Funding became cut and key personnel close to the project left the authority. Pursuit of better responses to domestic violence should remain a major priority for all police and public health partnerships. It is a high-frequency offence with a high societal cost, damaging the lives of the abused, the abusers and the next generation (Heise, 2011).

Communities of Interest: Alcohol Services Strategy

Sandwell has sought to develop alcohol treatment services over many years. Unlike drug services, alcohol services have not been part of a statutory framework. The level of alcohol problems dwarfs those caused by illegal drugs. Many drug agency workers are active in dealing with alcohol problems and many drug users have multiple addictions. Multiagency and multi-professional working is necessary, and joint training should be essential. For these reasons, we called ourselves the Sandwell Drug and Alcohol Action Team.

Alcohol brief interventions were one of our CRIMEGRIP reviews (Williams, 2004, unpublished). We found them to be effective in terms of reducing the health harms of alcohol and concluded they should be more widely available at GP surgeries and hospitals (particularly A&E Departments). However, research evidence on the impact on crime was missing, and this remains largely the case today.

We highlighted the need for better evidence regarding alcohol arrest referral Schemes. A Home Office report of 10 pilot schemes found little evidence for reductions in offending although alcohol consumption was reduced (McCracken et al., 2012). There are legal provisions for offenders to be referred for alcohol treatment programmes and drink-driving education. However, the equivocal outcomes of the 2012 report discouraged widespread implementation of alcohol arrest referral schemes. Investment in alcohol-related brief interventions expanded through the community drug and alcohol team during the years 2000s. The Alcohol Community Prevention trial was a key informing study for the Sandwell Alcohol strategy (Holder et al., 2000). The five elements of the programme which had combined to reduce alcohol-related drinking driving harms in California had been: responsible beverage training for bar staff, restricted outlets and sales to minors, community and school education programmes, drunk driving controls, and labelling and point of sale information. The Sandwell Police Alcohol Licensing Officer was a major contributor to efforts to reduce alcohol-related violence. He had a central role in determining licences for local pubs. A last drink survey from victims of alcohol intoxication in the Sandwell Accident Department was a tool in addressing licence renewals for local pub owners introduced in 2011. Gradually, as in many parts of the country, local partnerships like Sandwell were starting to deliver the intelligent, data-sharing partnership able to respond effectively to alcohol and crime problems, as pioneered by Jonathon Shepherd in the iconic 'Cardiff model' (Florence et al., 2014).

Communities of Interest: Community Development and Involvement

The Safer Sandwell Partnership has been strongly committed to community involvement throughout its existence. Major council, police and health service resources were committed to community engagement. Some of this was consultative but much was at the higher end of the Arnstein ladder of community engagement with community involvement supported financially (Arnstein, 1969). In some cases, community resources were owned and managed by community representatives. The Sandwell Race Equality Council and Sandwell Voluntary Service Council were visible and active members. Sandwell Youth Parliament and 'Agewell' were also active participants in community development work. A platform of trust was established with community representatives that enabled successful responses to a number of potential community relations disasters to be made and civil unrest to be avoided. Among these was the media management of the return of the 'Tipton Taliban' from Guantanamo Bay (Branigan & Dodd, 2004), the murder by reckless driving of three young Muslim men in Winson Green (BBC News, 2011) and the bomb attack on a local mosque by a white supremacist (BBC News, 2013). The dialogue and support for local Muslim communities enabled a sensible approach to be adopted to the national 'PREVENT' initiative in its early stages. PREVENT had begun as a programme of community education and supportive actions within the Muslim community to prevent radicalisation and terrorism. Council and Health service financial support for the 'REWIND' anti-racism and anti-radicalisation programme was a key component of this (REWIND, 2020). This was a patient, long-term and respectful process, building trust between communities, helping to prevent radicalisation and building economic and social opportunities for all our communities. The years of austerity post-2010 brought major cuts in grants to community organisations and youth services. These programs were not statutory provision and so most vulnerable to being cut. These cuts, compounded by authoritarian and intolerant national policies fuelled by political dogma rather than evidence, led to disastrous outcomes in relation to PREVENT. Statutory agencies were required to refer anyone they suspected of having any tendency to radicalisation, without training in recognition and without any evidence that such a screening approach could detect radicalisation and actual intent to cause terrorist attacks. The generation of 'false positives' referred into the PREVENT system has created more community mistrust and alienation from using services (Middleton, 2016a; Aked, 2020). Most recently, Public Health Wales and the United Kingdom Faculty of Public Health (FPH) have reviewed the effectiveness of anti-terror policies and interventions on an international basis (Bellis et al., 2019).

Communities of Interest: Designing Out Crime

I had long been interested in ideas of 'defensible space' and using urban design which could reduce crime (Coleman, 1985; Newman, 1972). Appleyard's study of how major roads disconnect communities was another early influence (Appleyard & Lintell, 1972). We had pursued similar ideas in relation to health considering any issues which create physical barriers could damage mental and physical health, destroy social support networks and make access to services more difficult—as well as making unpoliceable crime more easy and likely. The creation of 'woonerven', the Dutch for 'living streets', was a model for health and human-scale domestic accommodation. By 2004, the ideas of designing out crime became mainstream with the Home Office Safer Places publication (Office of the Deputy Prime Minister and Home Office, 2004) and Sandwell Council subsequently produced supplementary planning guidance for community safety (Sandwell MBC, 2008). The Sandwell Healthy Urban Development Unit also led to planning guidance for healthy communities in 2012 (Local Government Association, 2016).

Partnerships of Necessity

Some joint working has always seemed to me to be essential—'partnerships of necessity'. In my role as a Director of Public Health, I have been required to be involved in emergency preparedness and response, safeguarding children and vulnerable adults, response to acute mental health problems, alcohol and problems of addiction, offender management and rehabilitation and preventing racial violence. All these have had, in the UK, some statutory framework in which the responsibilities of different agencies are defined and their actions working together are described. Except alcohol!

Safer Sandwell Partnership: A Partnership of Necessity

Community safety partnerships became statutory organisations in 1998 (NHS Data model and dictionary, 2020). Health organisations became responsible authorities within these partnerships in 2003. By 2006, the partnership was making strong use of local crime data and reviewing the best evidence. It was applying itself in large measure to 'volume crimes'—crimes of violence of which roughly one-third were alcohol related in town centres, and roughly one-third were domestic violence. The other volume crime was domestic burglary to which response by drug services was a major component. Anti-social behaviour was a major preoccupation, but the central government instruments given to the partners were considered blunt, unhelpful and not rooted in evidence. Neighbourhood tasking was developing throughout the years

2000s principally as a means to address reported crimes, antisocial behaviour and environmental damage. The Sandwell Drug and Alcohol Action team reported into the Safer Sandwell Partnership. There were major considerations about improving community relations through the representation of the Sandwell Race Equality Council and the voluntary services council. Partners also recognised their own roles in community safety, as major employers, landowners and participants in the local community.

The Safer Sandwell Partnership has remained as a successful and robust body in the 'performing' stage of organisational development. New areas of work have emerged in the 2010s including modern slavery and human trafficking (Safer Sandwell Partnership, 2020).

Child Protection

I was directly involved in the work of the Sandwell Area Child Protection Committee from 1988 to 1992, before I had colleagues of more expertise that I was able to delegate to. Much later Sandwell was judged to be inadequate in its child protection procedures and subject to external measures. Throughout good and bad times, it has always been clear to me that the problems of children's safeguarding are problems of inadequate communication and inadequate partnership working between agencies. I came into a system in 1988 in which all partners were completely committed, willing to share their problems, willing to accept the strong leadership from social services at the time and determined not to be found wanting as some parts of the country had with incidents such as the Cleveland child protection scandal (Anonymous, 1988). In the early 2010s when weaknesses of the Sandwell child protection were uncovered, all the agencies determined to turn it around. The desire to work together became enshrined in the co-location of police and social care staff in the Multi-Agency Safeguarding Hub (MASH) enabling real-time decisions about who would be the most appropriate first responder. There were commitments to improving information collection, effective responses and to early help. Appropriate responses and preventive measures were proposed by my team—most children's safeguarding issues were not the appalling physical abuse incidents which rightly invoke national horror (HM Government, 2003; Anthony, 2009), but physical and emotional neglect or abuse. Neglect requires a whole different approach in terms of prevention, through growing parenting skills and low-level community support. We argued for investment in parenting programmes such as those found to be successful in addressing mild to moderate behaviour disturbance in children (Solihull Approach to Parenting, 2020; Incredible Years Parenting Program, 2020; Triple-P Positive Parenting Programme, 2020). Children's safeguarding responsibilities have been most recently updated in 2018 (HM Government, 2018), and children's safeguarding is now overseen by the remodelled Sandwell Safeguarding Children's Partnership (Sandwell CSP, 2020). A range of parenting interventions are now offered by Sandwell (Sandwell MBC, 2020).

Mental Health: Diversion

In mental health we were faced with a different problem—an almost complete absence of a Sandwell service in 1988. We built up community mental health teams of social workers, community psychiatric nurses and psychologists over 4 years. By 1992, we were able to commit to Court diversion work with the police service. The principles of diversion have extended over the years—to drugs, alcohol and other areas of intervention (Vigurs & Quy, 2017). Over the years, Sandwell's diversion services have extended to liaison with criminal justice agencies as the Sandwell Criminal Justice Mental Health Team (Sandwell Criminal Justice Mental Health Team, 2020). With police forces reporting up to 80% of emergency calls being due to mental health emergencies, some forces have co-located community psychiatric nurses with police patrols (Nottingham Street Triage Team, 2020).

Emergency Preparedness

It had always been necessary for health and blue light agencies to work together with their local council on emergency preparedness. The strongest statutory framework for this was put in place with the 2004 Civil Contingencies Act. This had been prompted by fuel strikes, floods, foot and mouth disease in the early 2000s, and with a growing concern about terror threats. The Civil contingencies in question encompassed all risks therefore. Pandemic flu was almost from the start, at the top of national and local risk registers. Throughout my career, I have been active in emergency response. Many of Sandwell's concerns relate to its industrial legacy, mine shaft collapses, pollution episodes, industrial fires, localised floods. In 2002, I led the major incident team addressing a legionnaires disease outbreak located to a local industrial plant. In 2009, I led the pandemic H1N1 response with Sandwell and West Birmingham being the epicentre of the UK outbreak. In my later years as a DPH, I became chair of the Local Health Resilience Partnership and thereby the health representative on the Local Resilience Forum. We were confronted with a spate of major fires. It is absolutely essential that all the agencies work closely together at all times—planning and preparedness enables people to work together during incidents, who know each other, and do not have to start with ceremony. Understanding each other's roles, and respecting these is also essential. Procurement can be a major problem during an incident—whether it be requisitioning buses, graphite and nitrogen for the Chernobyl disaster, or getting enough chainsaws to deal with fallen trees in hurricanes, or getting ventilators and PPE for the current pandemic.

Blue light services and healthcare personnel often righty receive the plaudits on the immediate response. However, the disaster continues long after the ambulances have gone. There is a continuing need for effective handling of the press, securing of incident sites and recovery of services. The high drama of an incident can put people with life-threatening problems at risk if they are not in services' consciousness while dealing with the incident. There is also an insufficient attention to the long-term follow-up of health and social consequences of disasters. Community knowledge and involvement in emergency preparedness are also a potential strength. This was mandatory for us with a major industrial plant using chlorine and phosgene. It has also become apparent with the mutual aid movement mobilised during pandemic lockdowns.

National and International Work

In the second half of my career, I have been more involved in national and international developments related to law enforcement and public health and to violence particularly. For the public health community, violence has sometimes been neglected as a cause of ill health. The numbers of deaths from violence, even on a global scale, is dwarfed by the numbers of deaths from circulatory disease, cancers and infectious causes. This is well illustrated in the Global Burden of Disease (GBD) comparator presentations which consistently find more than 2/3rd of deaths and disease due to non-communicable, chronic disease and less than ¼ due to violence and injury (Institute for Health Metrics and Evaluation, 2020). However, whole lifetimes are affected by violent incidents and by the threat of violence. The lifetime impacts on families and individuals and the impacts in terms of public mental health are extraordinary and disabling. The causes of ill health and health inequality and the causes of crime and violence, and inequalities in violence, are in various cases identical. The WHO report on violence and health recognised the global inequalities in violence due largely to economic inequality, inequality in access to environmental resources and inequalities in opportunities for education (WHO, 2004). Since then, Mark Bellis and colleagues have elegantly described a life course of causes of violence and ill health and the need for partnership responses between police, public health and other agencies (Bellis et al., 2012). In my role as UK Faculty of Public Health President, we expanded these themes in our 2016 report 'The role of public health in preventing violence' (UK Faculty of Public Health, 2016). The public health approach to health problems can also be applied to crime and violence: measure the epidemiology of crime and violence, describe its causes and form hypotheses about ways to reduce it; review the scientific literature and critically analyse what works to prevent violence; advocate for intervention, implement effectively in the way the research says it should work, then monitor how effective it has been in real life. If there is no research evidence, plan your intervention based on your hypotheses, but build in the research that will enable you to know if it works. Addressing inequalities is a central tenet of public health practice and applies also to crime and violence prevention. A public mental health approach can also be insightful. Public mental health is not merely the absence of mental illness. Public mental health approaches seek to build positive mental attributes such as self-confidence, empathy, respect for others and searching for helpful solutions to problems. The outcome is often described by the idea of *emotional intelligence*, and the strength of this within individuals enables them to articulate their needs, communicate well, without anger, or threat, without recourse to violence, addiction or self-harming. Many of the roots of inadequate emotional intelligence come from adverse childhood experiences (ACEs). There is a growing interest in the neurophysiological pathways of the early human brain and how these negatively impact mentally and physically on the development of children, in the event of adverse incidents like the death or loss of a parent or domestic violence. The awareness of ACEs is now being adopted more widely, with police forces and emergency services seeking to respond to incidents and individual behaviours in an 'ACEs aware' or 'trauma-aware' manner (Hughes et al., 2017).

There has been a growing interest in the relationship between public health and law enforcement in the United Kingdom, most recently expressed in the accord between public health and police national authorities and the landmark report Public Health Approaches in Policing (Christmas & Srivastava, 2018). In the recent explosion of incidents of knife crime, particularly in England, there has been a growing awareness of the need for a public health approach to crime (Middleton & Shepherd, 2018). It is a deep and damning shame that policymakers in England have not responded in over 10 years to a problem for which there was evidence and experience that it could have been controlled (Butler et al., 2004; Braga et al., 2001; Braga & Weisburd, 2012; Younge & Barr, 2018; Middleton & Shepherd, 2018; please also see Chap. 9 for a discussion of the Northampton initiative). The 'County lines' drugs trafficking has grown up in England. It involves children being coerced or threatened into trafficking drugs to new markets in rural areas and small towns of England. The children undertake lonely and difficult tasks as 'mules' transporting drugs often for minor financial reward or a pair of trainers, or because they want to belong to the gang. It has grown up in the years of austerity, with the complete ignorance, or failure of recognition and neglect of parents, communities or young people's services (National Crime Agency, 2017).

Conclusion

There is clearly much to be done to develop the relationship between law enforcement and public health agencies. Policing and the public health community in the twenty-first century are confronted with a bewildering array of new challenges—being asked to regard climate change protesters as criminals, being asked to police the lockdowns of the pandemic, responding to major incidents against a background commentary from social media, having to consider fake news and disinformation in every domain from anti-vax to anti-terror and take a battering from cyber-crime, all in a context of populism, intolerance and growing inequalities. Our ability to work together as partners will be challenged and our partnerships will need to grow stronger. We will also need to widen our partnerships. Public health needs to embrace the disciplines of international law, political science, theology as well as climate science, ecology and economics (Middleton, 2016b). So too for law enforcement colleagues. In the post-pandemic era, we can brace ourselves for mass unemployment, civil unrest and a toughening of approaches to policing and health policy. Alternatively, we can set out a vision for evidence-informed policies that address underlying causes of ill health and violence, in the economy, in education, in the environment and in creating good community relationships. If we do this, we can see the possibility of improved health, reduced crime and fear of crimes, and satisfying roles for all our communities and individuals. We can also see a more satisfying role for police officers as well, as professionals and stewards for health, safety and well-being, rather than the pickers-up of the pieces when people fall off the cliff.

Acknowledgements   I would like to thank the following for their help and encouragement in the work of law enforcement and public health over many years: George Pollock, Sir Ian Chalmers, Richard Lilford, Trevor Sheldon, Anne Eisinga, Selena Ryan-Vig, Martin Burton, Merete Konnerup, the late great David Player, Angus McCabe, Jon Raine, Maggie Winters, Jacqui Reid, Gavin Butler, Mike Maher, Nick Price, David Pitches, Nick Crofts, Mark Bellis, Jonathon Shepherd, Helen Christmas, Justin Srivastava, Aphra Purkis-Garner and Susan Stokes, and to the editorial team—many thanks to you all.

References

Aked, H. (2020). *False positives: The prevent counter-extremism policy in healthcare*. MEDACT.
Anonymous. (1988). *Summary of the Cleveland inquiry BMJ News report, 297:190–191*. https://www.ncbi.nlm.nih.gov/pmc/articles/PMC1834212/pdf/bmj00295-0046.pdf
Anthony, A. (2009, August 16). Baby P: Born into a nightmare of abuse, violence and despair, he never stood a chance. *The Observer*. https://www.theguardian.com/society/2009/aug/16/baby-p-family
Appleyard, D., & Lintell, M. (1972). The environmental quality of city streets: The residents' viewpoint. *Journal of the American Institute of Planners, 38*, 84–101. https://doi.org/10.1080/01944367208977410
Arnstein, S. R. (1969). A ladder of citizen participation. *Journal of the American Planning Association, 35*(4), 216–224.
BBC News. (2011, August 10). Three killed protecting property during riots. *BBC West Midlands*. https://www.bbc.co.uk/news/uk-england-birmingham-14471405
BBC News. (2013, October 25). Mosque bomber Pavlo Lapshyn given life for murder. *BBC West Midlands*. https://www.bbc.co.uk/news/uk-england-birmingham-24675040
Bellis, M., Hardcastle, K., & Middleton, J. (2019). Preventing violent extremism: Time for a public health approach? *BMJ*. https://blogs.bmj.com/bmj/2019/05/02/preventing-violent-extremism-time-for-a-public-health-approach/
Bellis, M., Hughes, K., Perkins, C., & Bennett, A. (2012). *Protecting people, promoting health - A public health approach to violence prevention in England* [online]. Department of Health. Resource document. https://assets.publishing.service.gov.uk/government/uploads/system/uploads/attachment_data/file/216977/Violence-prevention.pdf
Binysh, K., Chishty, V., Middleton, J. D., & Pollock, G. T. (1985). *The health of Coventry* (p. 1985). Coventry Health Authority.
Braga, A. A., Kennedy, D. M., Waring, E. J., & Piehl, A. M. (2001). Problem-oriented policing, deterrence, and youth violence: An evaluation of Boston's operation ceasefire. *Journal of*

Research in Crime and Delinquency, 38(3), 195–225. https://doi.org/10.1177/0022427801038003001

Braga, A. A., & Weisburd, D. L. (2012). The effects of "pulling levers" focused deterrence strategies on crime. *Campbell Systematic Reviews, 8*, 1–90. https://doi.org/10.4073/csr.2012.6

Branigan, T., & Dodd, V. (2004, August 4). Afghanistan to Guantánamo Bay - the story of three British detainees. *The Guardian*. https://www.theguardian.com/world/2004/aug/04/afghanistan.usa

Butler, G., Hodgkinson, J., Holmes, E., & Marshall, S. (2004). *Evidence based approaches to reducing gang violence: A rapid review of the evidence for the Aston and Handsworth Operational group.* https://lemosandcrane.co.uk/resources/REA%20-%20gang%20violence.pdf

Sheldon, T., Chalmers, I., & Roundings, C. (2000). *Evidence from systematic reviews of research relevant to implementing the 'Wider Public Health Agenda'.* University of York: NHS Centre for Reviews and Dissemination. https://uk.cochrane.org/our-work/resources/archive

Christmas, H., & Srivastava, J. (2018). *Public health approaches in policing.* Resource document. College of Policing and Public Health England. https://www.college.police.uk/What-we-do/Support/uniformed-policing-faculty/Documents/Public%20Health%20Approaches.pdf

Coleman, A. (1985). *Utopia on trial: Vision and reality in planned housing.* Hillary Shipman.

DIP. (2004). *Drug interventions programme.* Home Office. https://assets.publishing.service.gov.uk/government/uploads/system/uploads/attachment_data/file/118069/DIP-Operational-Handbook.pdf

Domestic Abuse Intervention Programmes. (2020). *Duluth model for domestic violence intervention.* https://www.theduluthmodel.org/what-is-the-duluth-model/

Farrington, D. P., & Welch, B. C. (2002). *Effects of improved streetlighting on crime: A systematic review.* Home Office Research Study 251. London: Home Office Research, Development and Statistics Directorate.

Florence, C., Shepherd, J., Brennan, I., & Simon, T. R. (2014). An economic evaluation of anonymised information sharing in a partnership between health services, police and local government for preventing violence-related injury. *Injury Prevention, 20*, 108–114. https://doi.org/10.1136/injuryprev-2012-040622

Heise, L. (2011). *What works to prevent partner violence: An evidence review.* Strive Research Consortium. http://strive.lshtm.ac.uk/system/files/attachments/What%20works%20to%20prevent%20partner%20violence.pdf

HM Government. (2003). *The Victoria Climbie inquiry (report of an inquiry by Lord Laming).* Resource document. HM Government, https://www.gov.uk/government/publications/the-victoria-climbie-inquiry-report-of-an-inquiry-by-lord-laming

HM Government. (2018). *Working together to safeguard children.* Resource document. HM Government. https://assets.publishing.service.gov.uk/government/uploads/system/uploads/attachment_data/file/779401/Working_Together_to_Safeguard-Children.pdf

Holder, H. D., Gruenewald, P. J., Ponicki, W. R., Treno, A. J., et al. (2000). Effect of community-based interventions on high-risk drinking and alcohol-related injuries. *JAMA, 284*(18), 2341–2347. https://doi.org/10.1001/jama.284.18.2341

Hughes, K., Bellis, M. A., Hardcastle, K. A., Sethi, D., Butchart, A., Mikton, C., Jones, L., & Dunne, M. P. (2017). The effect of multiple adverse childhood experiences on health: A systematic review and meta-analysis. *The Lancet. Public Health, 2*(8), e356–e366. https://doi.org/10.1016/S2468-2667(17)30118-4

Incredible Years Parenting Programme. (2020). Website available at: http://www.incredibleyears.com

Institute for Health Metrics and Evaluation (IHME). (2020). *Global burden of disease study. GBD comparators, 2019. Table diagrams of cause of global causes death.* https://vizhub.healthdata.org/gbd-compare/

Local Government Association. (2016). *Sandwell healthy Urban development unit (SHUDU).* https://www.local.gov.uk/sandwell-sandwell-healthy-urban-development-unit

Marsch, L. A. (1998). The efficacy of methadone maintenance interventions in reducing illicit opiate use, HIV risk behaviour and criminality: A meta-analysis. *Addiction, 93*(4), 515–532. https://doi.org/10.1046/j.1360-0443.1998.9345157.x

McCabe, A., & Raine, J. (1997). *Framing the debate: The impact of crime on public health.* Public Health Trust.

McCracken, K., McMurran, M., Winlow, S., Sassi, F., & McCarthy, K. (2012). *Evaluation of alcohol arrest referral pilot schemes (phase 2).* Resource document. Home Office. https://assets. publishing.service.gov.uk/government/uploads/system/uploads/attachment_data/file/116267/ occ102.pdf

Middleton, J. (1998). Crime is a public health problem. *Medicine, Conflict and Survival, 14*(1), 24–28. https://doi.org/10.1080/13623699808409369

Middleton, J. (2003). What works? For health in Sandwell. The 14th annual public health report for Sandwell, 2002. Sandwell PCTs.

Middleton, J. (2006a). The West Midlands Crimegrip project case study. In J. Popay (Ed.), *Moving beyond effectiveness in evidence synthesis: Methodological issues in the synthesis of diverse sources of evidence* (p. 108). National Institute for Clinical and Health Effectiveness, NICE. www.publichealth.nice.org.uk (Available via Google search & ResearchGate) https://www. google.com/url?sa=t&rct=j&q=&esrc=s&source=web&cd=&ved=2ahUKEwjA_ fiV6ODtAhVRUcAKHYjpAzMQFjAAegQIBBAC&url=https%3A%2F%2Fwww. researchgate.net%2Fprofile%2FPetya_Fitzpatrick%2Fpost%2FI_need_a_guideline_in_qualita tive_systematic_reviews_please_help_me_Thanks%2Fattachment% 2F59d61d9579197b8077978061%2FAS%253A271739735478273%25401441799209644% 2Fdownload%2FPopay%2Bsynthesis%2B2006.pdf&usg=AOvVaw3AChsvjV4Dz_ NX3raFaWGD

Middleton, J. (2006b). *Evidence based crime reduction and plausibility: Presentation to Safer Sandwell Partnership.* https://www2.slideshare.net/johnmiddleton7965/evidencebased-crime-reduction-and-plausibility

Middleton, J. (2014). *Public health: A life course. The 24th annual public health report for Sandwell, for the year 2013.* Sandwell Metropolitan Borough Council, March 2014. https:// betterhealthforall.org/2014/05/13/sandwell-public-health-my-life-course/

Middleton, J. (2016a). Preventing violent extremism: The role of doctors. *Lancet.* http://www. thelancet.com/journals/lancet/article/PIIS0140-6736(16)31902-X/

Middleton, J. (2016b). ISIS, crop failure and no anti-biotics: What training will we need for future public health? *European J Public Health.* https://eurpub.oxfordjournals.org/content/26/5/735

Middleton, J., McGrail, S., & Stringer, K. (2016). Drug related deaths in England and Wales. *BMJ, 355*, i5259. http://www.bmj.com/content/355/bmj.i5259

Middleton, J., Reeves, E., Howie, F., Hyde, C., & Lilford, R. (2001). The Campbell collaboration. *BMJ, 323*, 1252. https://www.bmj.com/content/323/7323/1252.2

Middleton, J., & Shepherd, J. (2018). Preventing violent crime. *BMJ, 361*, k1967. https://doi.org/ 10.1136/bmj.k1967

Middleton, J., et al. (1995). *Safer Sandwell: The seventh annual report of the director of public health.* Sandwell Health Authority.

Middleton, J. D., Srivastava, N. K., Donovan, D., Rao. J. N., & Douglas, J. (1989). *Life and Death in Sandwell.* First Annual Report of the Director of Public Health, Sandwell Health Authority.

National Crime Agency. (2017). *County lines violence, exploitation and drug supply.* http://www. nationalcrimeagency.gov.uk/publications/832-county-lines-violence-exploitation-and-drug-sup ply-2017/file

Newman, O. (1972). *Design guidelines for creating defensible space.* National Institute of Law Enforcement and Criminal Justice. https://thecrimepreventionwebsite.com/garden-boundaries-fences-and-defensive-plants/619/personal-and-defensible-space/

NHS Data Model and Dictionary. (2020). https://datadictionary.nhs.uk/nhs_business_definitions/ community_safety_partnership.html

Nottingham Street Triage Team. (2020). *NHS Mental health case studies*. https://www.england.nhs.uk/mental-health/case-studies/notts/

Office of National Statistics. (2020). *Crime in England and Wales: Year ending March 2020*. https://www.ons.gov.uk/peoplepopulationandcommunity/crimeandjustice/bulletins/crimeinenglandandwales/yearendingmarch2020#long-term-trends-in-theft-offences

Office of the Deputy Prime Minister and Home Office. (2004). *Safer places: The planning system and crime prevention UK government*.

Petrosino, A. (2000). Crime, drugs and alcohol review. In T. Sheldon, I. Chalmers, & C. Rounding (Eds.), *Evidence from systematic reviews of research relevant to implementing the 'wider public health agenda'*. University of York: NHS Centre for Reviews and Dissemination. https://uk.cochrane.org/our-work/resources/archive; https://uk.cochrane.org/sites/uk.cochrane.org/files/public/uploads/7crim.pdf

Petrosino, A., Turpin-Petrosino, C., Hollis-Peel, M. E., & Lavenberg, J. G. (2013). Scared straight and other juvenile awareness programs for preventing juvenile delinquency: A systematic review. *Campbell Systematic Reviews, 9*(1). https://doi.org/10.4073/csr.2013.5

REWIND. (2020). *Website available*. https://rewind.org.uk

Rollings, T., Middleton, J. D., Purser, R., Hoyland, M., Warren, J., & Pollock, G. T. (1987). Coventry - a no drinking driving city by the year 2000? *British Medical Journal, 295*, 71–72.

Safer Sandwell Partnership. (2020). *Safer Sandwell Partnership website*. https://www.sandwell.gov.uk/info/200208/crime_prevention_and_emergencies/662/safer_sandwell_partnership

Sandwell Criminal Justice Mental Health Team. (2020). *homepage*. https://wmmeritvanguard.nhs.uk/crisis-care/sandwell-criminal-justice-team

Sandwell CSP. (2020). *Sandwell Children's Safeguarding Partnership home page*. https://www.sandwellcsp.org.uk

Sandwell Health Action Zone. (1998). *Programme of action*. Sandwell Health Partnership.

Sandwell MBC. (2008). *Supplementary planning guidelines on community safety*. Sandwell MBC.

Sandwell MBC. (2020). *Parenting courses*. Sandwell Schools and Learning. https://www.sandwell.gov.uk/info/200295/schools_and_learning/3440/parenting_courses

Schweinhart, L. (2013). Long term follow up of a pre-school experiment. *Journal of Experimental Criminology, 9*, 389–409. https://doi.org/10.1007/s11292-013-9190-3

Solihull Approach to Parenting. (2020). https://solihullapproachparenting.com

SRE Project. (2020). *The APAUSE programme SRE website*. http://www.sreproject.org/apause

Stokes, S. (2014). *Evidence-based policing developing a response to domestic violence: A summary of evidence using the Campbell Collaboration Systematic review*. Presented to Sandwell Health and Wellbeing board, March 2014.

Stokes, S., Middleton, J., Bramley, G., & Veigas, H. (2013). Evidence review study of public health interventions in policing: An example of translating evidence into practice for implementation of effective interventions for crime reduction. *Lancet*. Public Health Science. p. 92. https://www.researchgate.net/publication/273724933_Evidence_review_study_of_public_health_interventions_in_policing_an_example_of_translating_evidence_into_practice_for_implementation_of_effective_interventions_for_crime_reduction

Thomson, R. (2002). *Highscope: Time to choose*. Nursery World. https://www.nurseryworld.co.uk/news/article/high-scope-time-to-choose

Tobler, N. S., & Stratton, H. H. (1997). Effectiveness of school-based drug prevention programs: A meta-analysis of the research. *Journal of Primary Prevention, 18*(1), 71–128.

Triple-P Positive Parenting Programme. (2020). https://www.triplep.net/glo-en/home/

Tuckman, B. (1965). *Forming, storming, norming, performing: Stages of group development*. https://en.wikipedia.org/wiki/Tuckman%27s_stages_of_group_development

UK Faculty of Public Health. (2016). *The role of public health in preventing violence*. Resource document. https://www.fph.org.uk/media/1381/the-role-of-public-health-in-the-prevention-of-violence.pdf

UNDP. (1994). *Human Development report 1994*. UN library. https://www.un-ilibrary.org/content/books/9789210576550/read

Vigurs, C., & Quy, K. (2017). *What works: Crime reduction systematic review series. NO. 6: Police responses to people with mental health needs: A systematic map of the literature*. The EPPI Centre, University College.

WHO. (1978). *Alma Ata declaration*. https://www.euro.who.int/__data/assets/pdf_file/0009/113877/E93944.pdf

WHO. (2004). *World report on violence and health*. WHO. (update 2014) https://www.who.int/violence_injury_prevention/violence/world_report/en/full_en.pdf?ua=1

WHOEURO. (1985). *Targets for health for all in the European region*. WHOEURO.

Williams, N. (2004). *Brief interventions for alcohol problems. A Crimegrip review*. Sandwell Primary Care Trust (Unpublished).

Younge, G., & Barr, C. (2018, December 3). How Scotland reduced knife deaths among young people. *Guardian* https://www.theguardian.com/membership/2017/dec/03/how-scotland-reduced-knife-deaths-among-young-people

Chapter 3
Defund, Dismantle, or Define

James Clover

Introduction

In the wake of societal reaction to the death of African-American George Floyd, on May 25, 2020, and similar incidents of violent interactions between police and racialized communities, a growing call to defund or dismantle the institution of law enforcement emerged as people reflected on the health and wellbeing of their communities. The police institution as a positive actor within the overall human service system was no longer recognized, if ever it was, and within certain communities, the potential engagement with police officers was an experience of fear and real negative health consequences. Yet the reality is police have always shared certain space within public health. Perhaps not immediately apparent and not necessarily space in a physical or even philosophical sense, but for decades police have reported that a significant portion of their work was not related to the enforcement of laws but rather to social welfare and health demands (Punch & James, 2017, p. 254; Neusteter et al., 2019a; Bartkowiak-Theron & Asquith, 2017, p. 279).

Despite efforts to strengthen police–health collaborations, including partnered response to mental health crisis calls, drug programs, violence interruption and injury surveillance, law enforcement as a discipline remains a distinct entity with distinct corporate objectives, performance measurements, budgets, and even language that prevents legitimate and sustained interoperability with health (van Dijk et al., 2019, p. 287). Properly evaluating the health and wellness value of these partnered responses, such as Crisis Intervention Teams (CIT), requires continued evaluation and separate from the prominent lens of how these partnerships reflect at an officer level (Kane et al., 2018; Compton et al., 2008).

J. Clover (✉)
Faculty of Health and Community Studies, MacEwan University, Edmonton, AB, Canada
e-mail: jamesbclover@gmail.com

Law enforcement is the primary way many people have intimate contact with the government (Campeau et al., 2020, p. 3), often related to some crisis, and the contact is frequently highlighted on the evening news and ultimately on the collective memory (Desmond et al., 2016) particularly when use-of-force is applied. Systemic racism and the violence, broadcast for mass consumption, not only inform the community but also create reluctance, albeit not sustained, of impacted communities to engage with police for assistance (ibid, p. 870). And recall that the laws being enforced, or applied, are the codified behaviors that society has deemed criminal, and the alternative conduct that police respond to is social disorder—behaviors outside of our collective comfort or pleasure. Not every social disorder is a crime, but it is arguable that all crimes can be social disorders. Therefore, police are asked to respond, or choose to respond, to social disorder that may or may not be a crime. Police officers are by their nature problem solvers, and they have been asked to prevent future crime and victimization, and so begins "policification" or the varied responses by police organizations into areas that are reasonably better managed by social agents with the suitable training, capacity, and legitimacy (Millie, 2013).

Academia and practitioners continue to explore and strengthen a collective understanding to the root causes of social disorders including crime and respond to the missing social determinants of health (SDOH) and adverse childhood experiences (ACEs). If we consider these social disorders as symptomatic evidence of unaddressed health needs for people and communities, the role of a police officer is revealed as one of many agents charged with and who inevitably influence the health and overall wellness outcomes—positively and negatively—of people and communities they come into contact with. The interconnectedness of health, wellbeing, and efforts to respond to social disorder perhaps reveal friction of role expectations placed upon organizations that were socially constructed and tasked with the enforcement of laws to maintain societal security.

A retrospect into the genesis of what some consider modern democratic policing might reveal the connectedness to health and wellbeing. We will need to ask the difficult question of whether policing, in its current state and design, complements an overall objective of public health; or whether the mission of law enforcement as currently defined conflicts with improving collective wellbeing. If an institution is purported to inflict harm, fear, and racial divide, it may be time to ask what is expected of this institution from the patient, the client, the community, and all of society. If that same institution is conducting work that conflicts with other social agents charged with improving the health and wellbeing of us all, it may be time to explore what a new version of the institution would be. And finally, the physical and emotional impact the men and women of law enforcement are experiencing, including moral distress and disorientation, might not be the exclusive result of their exposures, but the disconnect in their role identification and their place within the overall system of health and wellness.

If we remedy within ourselves that policing is like any construct, open to adaptation based on communal needs, and we rethink the emphasis placed upon the strict ethos of enforcement as the primary function and look more holistically to how police can occupy the same space and contribute to the broader mission of public health and wellness, we might define a new paradigm of policing. A model that reflects, first and foremost, the primary mission of contributing to the health and wellness needs of the community. What we want the police to be, or not be, is as important as what we want the police to do or not do.

Language Is Important to Consider When Having Any Discussion

Before exploring how some believe the modern democratic policing was cast, and how we might collectively define and develop an institutional 'replacement' for policing as expressed in the Foreword, we need to acknowledge that our use of language can empower or limit any discussion depending on whether we are exercising a shared vernacular. This is particularly important when our desire is to bridge organizations, or dare we say cultures, to positively contribute in one direction. And in furtherance to the Foreword, if any country including the United States of America wishes to converse on this topic of police reform, there will need to be careful attention to the words, phrases, and the beliefs we hold to positively contribute at this critical juncture.

Paramount to this collection is the interchangeable expressions of 'law enforcement' and 'policing'. In an effort of consistency for the readers and contributors, 'law enforcement' can be considered the non-negotiable application of legislation and police powers. Or in another way, "the organized and legitimate effort to produce or reproduce social order – evident in rules and norms – to enhance the safety and security of society" (van Dijk et al., 2019, p. 288). As described previously, when society codifies certain behaviors as criminal, someone or something needs to be appointed to monitor and enforce the criminal conduct. It is articulated within legislations that the police are traditionally the sole public body to exclusively conduct those responsibilities. Alternatively, the term "policing"[1] incorporates all the same responsibilities described as "law enforcement," but in addition includes a variety of negotiated, consultative, community-oriented, and self-imposed initiatives. These initiatives are sometimes described as the soft side of policing and may include initiatives such as crime prevention through community engagement. As Coyne and Meurant-Tompkinson (2018) describe: "law enforcement – jailing people for breaking the law – is one aspect of policing."

To use these terms interchangeably without some level of clarity and agreement might promote certain risk in misunderstanding. There are further influences at play that will change or amend the definition of "policing" or "law enforcement"— including established and changing policing paradigms (Punch & James, 2017,

---

[1] The term policing could also speak to a broader social concept of overarching control and authorities. For the discussion in this chapter, the focus is placed on the organizational needs and expectations that the public expects and the institution believes.

p. 252; see also Chap. 15), politics, expectations placed onto police due to geography, economics, active war or civil unrest, and in certain times involvement in responding to health crises like transmission of HIV or containment of COVID-19. The terror attacks in the United States in 2001, and the reintroduction of concerns of domestic radicalization towards extreme violence, created a response void that was filled primarily with the law enforcement community. The dramatic spike in the global movement of people, a result of unmet health and security demands (Punch & James, 2017, p. 258), introduced to the police new clients with unique needs as captured in Chap. 13 in this collection.

Policing as a profession is not static, and the paradigms and other influences that assist to define the accepted and expected role and responsibilities of police complements with what Chap. 2 described—partnerships of necessity versus communities of shared interest—so who is being served and for what purpose may dictate how they are being served. With a nod to the most basic principle for architecture, form must follow the intended function. Efforts to establish a common language on a global scale will require significant, careful, and continual thought. Not only does the reader need to remain mindful of the breadth of these roles, in particular what we call policing, the function, it will become increasingly difficult when trying to direct join-up activities and partnerships to complement the equally dynamic mission, mandates, and language within the public health arena.

The Genesis of "Modern" Policing

During times of crisis and vocal disapproval of police, we tend to see resurgence in agreement in what has been popularly described as the genesis of the tenants of modern democratic policing—*Sir Robert Peel's Nine Principles of Law Enforcement*. A scan of police organization websites continues to reveal what has become a certain gospel for many police administrators.[2] Primary to these principles is that police are to prevent crime and disorder, and the test of police efficiency is the absence of crime and disorder and not the presence of police dealing with it. Police are the people and people are the police, and the privilege to conduct their policing duties is rooted in the approval and cooperation of the people, preserved by the commitment to remain equitable, impartial, and professional in their role. Police use the minimum force necessary to secure the good order and should only be used once other persuasive measures have failed.

Despite a rich history of conflict among historians about who Sir Robert Peel was and his contributions and intentions, generally uncontested is his stewardship that led to the creation of the Metropolitan Police Force in 1829—long cited as when "modern public policing had been born" (LaGrange, 1993, p. 31). Whether Sir

---

[2] As example, see Ottawa Police Service https://www.ottawapolice.ca/en/about-us/Peel-s-Principles-.aspx.

Robert Peel actually penned these principles as part of the efforts to design the Metropolitan Police Act, or these principles are the product of twentieth-century interpretations by historians or police practitioners (Lentz & Chaires, 2007), these tenants of "police are the people and the people are the police" continue to resonate for police in many countries beyond the UK including the United States, Canada, New Zealand, and Australia.

England in the 1700s and early 1800s saw significant change, largely based on the industrialization of manufacturing. Rapid population growth in London and similar cities saw increases in adverse health consequences and related social disorder (Williams, 2003, p. 98). Mechanization in factories and strengthening trade led to job availability. People driven by the opportunity for employment migrated to the industrial centers, lending to growing negative health impacts such as overcrowding, poor sanitation, reduced water and air quality, and certain toxicity from coal and other introduced materials. This newly formed poor industrial class created another mouth to feed and group to manage, in the eyes of the upper and middle class, and societal tensions rose. Riots and general social disorder, including crime, needed to be addressed, but the appetite by the government-in-power to utilize the standing military was lacking due to likely use of violence by soldiers and the negative reflection such conduct would have.

The Peelian movement towards policing leveraged data purporting that crime and social disorder had risen (Gaunt, 2010, p. 68) and an administrative response was required, and so the path to create a single government-controlled policing institution of paid constabulary (ibid, 69) was plotted. Critics at the time remained suspicious of the political motivations in the interpretation of the data, they were concerned that the messaging being used intentionally struck fear to secure the movement's success, and lastly there remained the unaddressed risk of creating an extension of the government that would be charged with maintaining order through significant powers. The government would need to be convinced, in essence sold the concept, that a body separate from the military was required to prevent lawlessness, address disorder, and secure peace. Even with data (Williams, 2003, p.99), this social contract of sorts was required to address the concerns held by the administration that policing would not complement the health of the people. So now in retrospective review through the lens of the concerns that were held about the creation of a police force, the Peel's Principles of Policing is possibly revealed as more of a contract of identity rather than a prescriptive list of mandates or organizational responsibilities.

This new construct of policing[3] was a singular body struck by the government, with the implied but contractual consent of the people, and charged with a broad mandate, enormous powers, but seriously cautioned to the use of force. It was the

---

[3] The reader may wish to explore the means and methods of the establishment of policing in other countries, and how those police institutions have evolved into their modern versions. For example, Canada created the North West Mounted Police (NWMP) in 1873 in response to the expansion of territory for settlement, the necessity to secure trade routes for commodities like alcohol, and make contact with Indigenous communities to strike treaties.

diminishing social and physical health of the community, and the resulting social disorder including crime, that secured that consent. The enforcement of laws was only one aspect of this new institution, and there was a strong decree that the service provided by the police would be friendly, courteous, without regard to race or social standing, and in the positive benefit to protect and preserve "the lives," or perhaps "the health," of everyone.

Global Mission, Corporate Objectives, and Unintended Consequences

A scan of police organization websites will reveal mission statements, adopted values, and descriptors of what that particular organization subscribes to be and do. These statements of principles can reveal how the organization fits, or believes they fit, within the overall human services system, and possibly how the organization justifies how they may direct resources and activities to meet those objectives. Some examples include:

> The mission of the **New York City Police Department** is to enhance the quality of life in New York City by working in partnership with the community to enforce the law, preserve peace, protect the people, reduce fear, and maintain order.[4]
> **Victoria Police**'s role is to serve the Victorian community and uphold the law so as to promote a safe, secure, and orderly society.[5]
> The **Ghana Police Service** exists to deliver services in crime prevention, detection, apprehension, and prosecution of offenders consistent with the expectations of Ghana stakeholders for maximum protection, safe, secure, and peaceful Communities.[6]
> The **Ottawa Police Service** is committed to protect the safety and security of our communities.[7]
> **[Police Scotland]** Our purpose: To improve the safety and wellbeing of people, places, and communities in Scotland.[8]

If an effort is to be made to define what we expect from our police, what we want them to be, then as suggested it may start with the language we use to describe what police are expected to be and how they will contribute to the mission of health and wellbeing. What do we wish our defined contract for policing to be in the twenty-first century. If one was to propose that a healthy community, with efforts to secure and maintain equitable wellbeing for all, is more likely to be a safe community, then

---

[4] Retrieved November 3rd, 2020 from: https://www1.nyc.gov/site/nypd/about/about-nypd/mission.page.

[5] Retrieved November 3rd, 2020 from: https://www.police.vic.gov.au/about-victoria-police.

[6] Retrieved November 3rd, 2020 from: https://police.gov.gh/en/index.php/vision-mission/.

[7] Retrieved November 3rd, 2020 from: https://www.ottawapolice.ca/en/About-Us.aspx#Our-Mission-Vision-and-Values.

[8] Retrieved November 3rd, 2020 from: https://www.scotland.police.uk/about-us/our-purpose-focus-and-values/.

efforts to improve the overall health of society would seem like a viable addition to the mission statements, corporate objectives, policies, and procedures to secure a "long-term pledge to the public's health and the needs of the least well-off" (Gostin & Powers, 2006, p. 1057).

At several places in this collection, readers will be challenged to explore the context and efforts when bringing two disciplines together, public health and law enforcement, to tackle "wicked problems." Wicked problems are those very complex matters that have linkages to a number of disciplines, and often have persistent and potentially catastrophic impacts on the health of humans and the world (Walls, 2018); climate change, exponential population growth with resource sustainability, poverty, and food insecurities, and interconnectedness of global security and threats are only a few examples. National and global responses to COVID-19 reveal how a potential wicked problem is interconnected to politics, economics, racial disparity, and equal access to necessary resources such as protective equipment or vaccines. To effectively address wicked problems, leadership and functional collaboration requires proper role definitions in how and what each actor will contribute. But most importantly the parties need to be aligned and committed to addressing the same problem, and amending their contributions when there is evidence that the activities of one party are conflicting with collective mission.

Caution is required when collaborating to address the wicked problem, as evidence exists that: (1) the mission of law enforcement will at times, and perhaps as an unintended consequence, conflict with the mission of public health, and (2) internal conflict between the role of enforcing laws and the rapidly expanding duties in policing causes further disruption. This conflict may be connected to how we define the role of police, and the mission distortion or mission creep that can occur when competing organizational objectives are brought together. If police are the first contact with the community when crisis occurs, and that crisis is primarily social disorder suggesting a breakdown in access or possession of those required determinants of health, having a clear role definition in and among the broader health realm is paramount.

Research has looked into the effectiveness of a variety of partnerships that police have undertaken, such as the shared space within community corrections (Corbett, 1998; Murphy & Worall, 2007). Murphy and Worall (2007) explored how police and probation collaboration within community correction initiatives in Spokane Washington might experience mission creep or mission distortion—when the collective goal of the partnership deteriorates as one partner's formal identity begins to supersede that of the other partner. Or similarly, how the formation of a shared space amends the focal mission of each respective partner, which leads to discrediting the value, credibility, and possibly the objectives that were originally intended.

In Murphy and Worall (2007), the study explored distortions such as elevated abuse of authority, leveraging authorities outside an officer's respective discipline to achieve their agenda, and liability issues in conducting work in a quasi-organized collaboration. For example, a probation officer may have the authority to enter a dwelling without a warrant, and evidence can be collected to use in a hearing, but those same privileges are not present for the accompanying police officer and the threshold for a criminal court (Murphy & Worall, 2007, pp. 144–145). Beyond the concerns of one discipline superseding another, and the risk of liability when the conduct of the collaboration ebbs and flows between competing policies, which institutional mandate has priority? When institutions of different mandates come together, how can the competing priorities be managed so that the person and the public is best served?

Recognizing that joining-up has issues of identity, mission creep, and mission distortion, joining-up may still be attractive but not necessarily possible. There may be other factors of disruption such as temperamental funding, leadership continuity, negative press, and other factors (Punch & James, 2017, p. 255). If the corporate objectives that exist within each party are not clearly defined, and more importantly a shared global mission for what the collaboration was struck to achieve is not distinct, the collaboration is set up for probable conflict and eventual failure. Equally noted is that certain partnerships may never work if there exist negative consequences to that partnership from the onset. It has become relatively accepted that police officers continue to operate in a mental health interventionist role (Wood et al., 2020), again traditionally being the first touch-point with the community during crisis, despite the mounting evidence of adverse mental health consequences as a result of these police encounters (Bowleg et al., 2020; Geller et al., 2014). Even without personal experience of negative contact with police, a person may adopt preconceptions or stereotypes of the potential threat—being judged or treated unfairly by the police—causing the person increased anxiety, frustration, and possibly adapting strategies that further the disconnect of positive interaction with police (Najdowski et al., 2015). Fear and harm, whether actual or perceived, clearly mitigate any positive and sustainable outcomes during encounters with police and conflicts with efforts by other social actors to improve the lives of people.

Without a defined and relevant police paradigm, the conflict or distortion in the mission of policing can equally occur exclusively within the organization, which further highlights the spectrum of responsibilities that law enforcement and policing have adopted. An officer from a West African police service described his role as an AIDS Control Officer (Clover, 2018, p. 91). He revealed that as a result of prostitution being an illegal behavior in his country, police officers in his organization are trained to look for indicia of prostitution including the possession of condoms. As a result, sex workers were less likely to carry sexual protection to avoid police detection, which encouraged unprotected sexual transactions and risk of further disease transmission. So which mission within the police service is more important? This example is a rather blunt portrayal of the conflict that can occur, but should provide caution that similar distortions can be occurring subtly.

In the first wave of response to countering violent extremism (CVE) in the United States after 9/11, there was both an increase in the militarization of police organizations and the targeted engagement by police within communities that were thought to be the feeder groups for both domestic and external terrorism. This duality of roles causes conflict, to both the police officers and the community being engaged. If police are advised by a mother or an Imam that a young person is watching beheading videos in the darkness of their basement, who responds to that call will absolutely dictate the response and ultimately the trajectory of that young person within the systems. Depending on which "hat" the responding police officer will be wearing will have an influence on the type of engagement and response. The mother or Imam might not know the risk of role duality, which again begs the consideration to which mission within the police mandate is more important or appropriate.

Attending to unintended consequences first requires awareness, by leveraging and honestly assessing qualitative and quantitative feedback to understand the impact policing activities are having on the community. As example, knowledge generated from CVE research suggests that police-led CVE engagement reduces willingness of that targeted community to collaborate and actually provokes community resistance (Weine et al., 2016, p. 208). That source of feedback does not come from established policing performance indicators or what might be intuitively assumed to be good work, but directly from the client, the community, and the community partners. Once police receive the feedback, they need to be authentic in their response to undo the unintended consequences of their policing activities. Feedback may suggest that in certain cases taking a police minimalist approach, or no approach at all, is what is best for the community. The 'join-up' agenda is not free of controversy, and as shown in this reading, both the application of law and poorly coordinated partnerships can create as much harm as what was initially intended to be addressed. The join-up agenda will inevitably extend the reach of the criminal legal system in the lives of people when other responses are better suited, having a real or perceived association with law enforcement as a response partner might prevent safe and effective engagement with the intended client or community. Without an improved and shared definition on the expected core duties of the police, the described conflicts will continue.

Case Study
Prostitution, the transactional relationship of sexual services, is not exclusively illegal in Canada. To deter prostitution, the Criminal Code of Canada made the act of communicating for the purposes of selling sex in public places an illegal act, citing that certain deprivations of constitutional freedoms of expression and security held by a sex worker are reasonable deprivations of rights in order to protect the community and deter this public nuisance (Greene & McCormick, 2019, p. 115). Police were afforded the authority to manage prostitution in a number of ways, including criminalizing the conduct of both sellers and consumers, and pushing the practice to areas within the community where the public would not see prostitution. The activities of law enforcement were for the most part driven by response to community pressure to make this conduct disappear and away from the public's eyes.

In 2008, several sex workers brought forward legal arguments that the restrictions in the Criminal Code were violations of their rights—specifically the right to life and security of person. Social science evidence was now heard

(continued)

and ultimately accepted by the courts that the laws as written and ultimately applied by the criminal justice system including police (Matthews, 2005; Lowman, 1992; Shannon et al., 2008), with respect to prostitution, were having negative health and safety implications for those people selling sex (Greene & McCormick, 2019, p. 114). Chief Justice Beverley McLachlin of the Supreme Court of Canada noted the previous laws were "arbitrary, overboard or grossly disproportionate" (Government of Canada, 2013, para. 127), and clearly identified the health implications that sex workers were subject to:

"The prohibitions at issue do not merely impose conditions on how prostitutes operate. They go a critical step further, by imposing dangerous conditions on prostitution; they prevent people engaging in a risky – but legal activity taking steps to protect themselves from the risks" (ibid, para. 60–64).

A successful legal battle led to the creation of Bill C-36 (Government of Canada, 2014), which recognized that chartered rights and freedoms do extend to sex workers, and essentially made selling sex and the activities required to safely conduct that transaction lawful. Policing the public space to deter consumption around schools and parks, in contrast to activities behind closed doors and on the Web, would still remain a priority and disproportionate enforcement and criminalization would impact only those people forced to sell their bodies on the street as a means of survival. Police would now need to rethink their response to this issue and manage the longstanding bias police officers have held towards prostitution, now having full awareness and legal direction that those people selling their body had the same protections and status as other citizens. The law had changed, as did the status of those in the sex industry, but the (de)application of law by police would need time to properly respond. Even the use of language, such as prostitute or VICE, would require reconsideration.

Police engage with sex workers, escorts, and those working in body rub businesses, hoping that those being exploited and trafficked will willingly file a complaint. Most investigations relating to sexual exploitation and human trafficking require the testimony of the victim. Sex workers and the community organizations that support them remain reluctant to fully engage with police, knowing that many sex workers have had difficult experiences with law enforcement, they fear the possible prosecution of their consumers of the sexual services, they hold a real or perceived opinion about police bias to their lifestyle, or are perhaps worried that an eventual agreement to a prosecution of an exploiter would require their testimony of profoundly personal accounts often becoming re-victimized without knowing if the prosecution would even be successful.

Void on many policing radars are the homosexual boys and men who operated in the shadows and often within the drug community. A deep distrust of police, the stigma of illegal drug use, paired with the fact that these sexual

(continued)

exploitations often occurred outside of the public view or concern, prevent any intervention or collaboration between police, these people, and the groups supporting their clients. Many of these boys and men manage significant health issues, including substance abuse and mental illness, but avoid detection or engagement with police and as a result become less likely to access appropriate health services (Platt et al., 2018). Imagine a young man kicked out of his home, after disclosing his questions of sexuality and without support groups or safe places to access, uses the Internet to seek guidance and assistance such as temporary accommodations only to become sexually exploited at the hands of consumers who value their anonymity.

What We Want the Police to Be, or Not to Be Is as Important as What We Want the Police to Do or Not to Do

There has been sufficient attention in policing research, in particular what police do (van Dijk et al., 2015; Punch & James, 2017), but we are now at the place where we are being asked by the public to explore what police are for (Millie, 2014). Why police were originally formed may declare institutional legitimacy, and at one time, we drafted a social contract and bestowed consent, and still there remains evidence of an intrinsic belief held for "a promise of law" and "potential for justice and transformation" (Campeau et al., 2020, p. 14). But we have come to a point in our societal growth that we need to explore what we cannot allow the institution of policing to be. Finding consensus on what we do not wish our policing efforts to be, aligned with our new understandings on how police can complement the mission of health, we might be able to redefine the role and rewrite the social contract in an effort to create the type of society we wish to live in (Punch & James, 2017, p. 259).

Police should not blindly contribute as a source of racism, as no institution that serves within the human services system should. Contact with police has become the litmus test to bluntly reveal the systems of racism that exist, and the conduct that occurs between police and community continues to amplify inequalities, disproportionate treatment, and fear. Dismantling or defunding the police institution fails to address the systemic racism that exists, and only prolongs future dismantling or defunding of other institutions that provide essential services. To address "discriminatory policing," what is needed is for the law to remove the need for police to make moral judgements (Johnson, 2012, p.35), and re-establish a clearly defined place for policing among our collective health efforts.

Police cannot be a source of unreasonable harm, and the contributions that police make to the overall human systems services, including the use of harm, must complement the global mission of health and not conflict with it. Friedman (2020, p.1) articulates that "harm is not collateral to policing, it is innate to it," but what needs to remain upfront is that harm is to be viewed as a spectrum of both conduct and impact. A physician's mantra for patient care, such as the Hippocratic Oath, remains conscious of the possibility that certain harm may be necessary to provide certain care. As made clear within the tenants of Peel's Principles of Policing, the use of force can only be as proportionate to the allowance of that force the public will tolerate. With our increasing knowledge of causes of social disorder and crime as rooted in missing determinants of health, our tolerance as a society has perhaps responsibly shifted towards alternative approaches to crisis management.

An extension to unreasonable harm is fear. Police cannot be a source of unreasonable fear, and we need to explore the root causes of that fear and make change a priority. We have been unable to resolve the truth that segments of society have a genuine fear of the police. Fear as deterrence, as a consequence to maintain lawful obedience, is far different than real fear of contact with a police officer. Police cannot remain a viable social actor unless they become relevant to the mission of health, and fear of police, real or perceived, deprives any opportunity for trust, reconciliation, or a legitimate and sustainable opportunity for partnerships. Despite the paradox that contact with police may bring a negative health consequence, particularly if that contact is within communities of color, seeking help from police remains an institutional reflex that we need to recognize and respond to. It is our job to adapt the support systems, and not expect the public to initiate change in how or when they seek assistance.

Police cannot be exclusively responsible for the trajectory of a person's overall wellbeing. Police cannot arrest their way out of the issues of the day, and yet they are the "gatekeepers" to the justice system (Neusteter et al., 2019b) but do not have the keys to open doors to positive health opportunities. Discretion by young police officers and the autonomy police have held serves certain benefits, but can pose irresponsible power in a single touch point between the State and the citizen at a time of crisis. It is the application of the law, the enforcement, and not the actual law that has shown to create a certain impact on the future health and wellness of people (Johnson, 2012, p. 23). And while the laws may be amended and adapted, as we better understand SDOH and ACEs, it will remain in the application of those laws and how we define the new modern policing that triggers future consequences. Further police should not be the sole institution responsible for social control and security (Fleetwood & Lea, 2020, p. 27). The safety and security of our communities can be improved through a number of alternative agents, such as the use of family workers to engage with victims and perpetrators of domestic violence, community mobilization to restore use of public spaces and instill sense of communal care, or the corporate commitment to design and support traffic calming measures to reduce road injury. Measures to maintain and improve safety and security can be a shared responsibility.

Lastly, policing as an institution needs to remain cognoscente to the physical and emotional impact men and women of law enforcement are experiencing, including moral distress and disorientation. These occupational injuries might not be the exclusive result of their exposures, but to the disconnect in their role identification, the changing social and legal accountability that is being applied faster than police culture can adapt, and their questionable place as a positive actor within the overall system of health and wellness. Efforts to constructively engage with the community can be difficult when role confusion exists; gaining and sustaining public trust is draining when there remains a baseline of fear; adding increasingly complicated curriculum relating to SDOH and ACEs to police recruit training, on all facets of social ill they might come into contact, while still expecting both clear exercise of discretion when necessary and sufficient use of force when required creates a predisposition to become an emotional causality.

Evidence exists that communities who face negative health implications through being policed still maintain a belief that police have a purpose. This belief may be attributed to a lack of alternatives (Campeau et al., 2020, p. 3), a "situational trust" and learned ability to navigate the system for benefit or protection (Bell, 2016, p. 338), or the hope that an institutional promise of safety and security for all does exist (Campeau et al., 2020, p. 1). Even when the police grossly wrong a community, the community will return to accessing the police in times of need (Desmond et al., 2016). There may be merit to suggest that as a society we still see the potential for a social contract with police, such was purportedly desired by Sir Robert Peel.

As captured in the case study on sex work in Canada, social science and health research can educate the justice system to the harms that exist in both the law and the application of the law. Despite maturity in the Court's understanding of the health consequences, there still exists significant gaps in servicing and support to that community because police remain a threat to health and wellbeing. The real or perceived policing paradigms that target drug consumption or prostitution, the criminalization or devaluing that occurs for those who have health issues, or a simple but sad realization that queer sex workers feel they are not worth protecting, will push people into the shadows to actively avoid contact and thereby adopting lifestyles with increased risk to health (Burris et al., 2004; Mimiaga et al., 2010). The case study is a reflection of only one specific community, but potentially represents any marginalized community that police will likely engage.

Policing for the public health—or *public health policing*—may be the start to realize a replacement institution. Reducing the autonomy and deference provided to police at the time of crisis contact, with the decision-making on the trajectory of the client or community falling to health agencies and consultation with the community. This approach will require radical restructuring of the current system, and reconsidering the distinct mandates we place on each social agency. Business hours can no longer be a barrier to accessing partnerships in the moment, technology needs to be leveraged to create real-time engagement for client care, data collected by police needs to be freely shared with health authorities for non-investigative purposes, and we need to re-establish a renewed appreciation and social expectation to the value and necessity that professional crisis intervention plays as part of our response to social ills.

As forecasted, the primary mission in a new police paradigm is positive crisis intervention, which is making any situation safer than it was. There exists an institutional reflex to contact police when social support and natural means to manage crisis have collapsed, and we as social designers need to recognize that reflex as what the community does when they need help. Therefore, police response to crisis needs to be measured on their responsible approach to make any scenario safe by doing the least amount of harm. The opportunity to problem-solve and engage supports will occur later, and the crisis response, like triage at the hospital, needs to make the client safe before any further interventions can possibly occur. It is not such a radical notion to expect that we can strive towards a time and place when police arrive on scene and a sense of fear is replaced by a sense of security.

Criminal investigations, and in particular the application of law, are conducted only when they are in the greatest interest of the public, and that activity complements the shared efforts to safeguard the community by reducing future victimization. Paramount is that the application of law becomes a separate role than that of crisis response. The fear of criminalization, linked to historical weight placed on specific and general deterrence, prevents police in managing the first priority of positive crisis intervention. If we opt not to make a change in the way we determine when to apply the laws, and ultimately how the public perceives the role of the criminal justice system, fear of contact will remain and we will continue to forgo constructive opportunities to engage with those that need our help.

And finally, public campaigns to improve safety, health, and wellness need to be driven by all institutions, particularly those that have legitimacy in health, and police would become servants to those campaigns if and when practical to that mission. Injury prevention such as road safety, domestic violence, and homelessness are three important examples where sensitive consideration of directed police intervention is necessary. To manage mission creep, prevent "policification," suspend fear of criminalization, and start to reimagine policing as an effort to contribute to our collective health, we need to reserve the use of police and safeguard the institution's integrity as an agent that supports, and not controls, the wellbeing of the citizenry.

Conclusion

If we opt to dismantle or significantly defund police, an institutional void will be created that will need to be carefully filled (El-Sabawi & Carroll, 2020, p. 8). This discussion on defining the institution of policing needs to remain rooted in a wider effort of structural reform to place sufficient attention to overall wellness for everyone. To track towards "the just distribution of health" (Marmot, 2015, p. 346), each and every touch-point that all institutions have with the community will require rethinking both within and among one another. Significant budget reductions, without dialogue, will force police to adapt to what we have erroneously come to believe is their core contribution—enforcement of laws and criminalization of people. Our incentive to remain in silos is based on bureaucratic comfort and a dated social construct, so we need to take time to reconsider what we want the police to be, or not be, in the society we wish to create.

References

Bartkowiak-Theron, I., & Asquith, N. (2017). Conceptual divides and practice synergies in law enforcement and public health: Some lessons from policing vulnerability in Australia. *Policing and Society, 27*(3), 276–288.

Bell, M. (2016). Situational trust: How disadvantaged mothers reconceive legal cynicism. *Law & Society Review, 50*(2), 314–347.

Bowleg, L., Maria Del Río-González, A., Mbaba, M., Boone, C. A., & Holt, S. L. (2020). Negative police encounters and police avoidance as pathways to depressive symptoms among US black men, 2015–2016. *American Journal of Public Health, 110*(1), 160–166.

Burris, S., Blankinship, K. M., Donoghoe, M., Sherman, S., Vernick, J. S., Case, P., Lazzarini, Z., & Koester, S. (2004). Addressing the "risk environment" for injection drug users: The mysterious case of the missing cop. *The Milbank Quarterly, 82*, 125–156.

Campeau, H., Levi, R., & Foglesong, T. (2020). Policing, recognition, and the bind of legal cynicism. *Social Problems, 68*(3), 658–674.

Clover, J. (2018). Unintended consequences as evidence to mission distortion: Reconsidering the intended contributions of policing to the public health. *Journal of Community Safety & Wellbeing, 3*(3), 91–92.

Compton, M. T., Bahora, M., Watson, A. C., & Oliva, J. R. (2008). A comprehensive review of extant research on Crisis Intervention Team (CIT) programs. *The Journal of the American Academy of Psychiatry and the Law, 36*(1), 47–55.

Corbett, R. (1998). Probation blue: The promise (and perils) of probation-police partnerships. *Correctional Management Quarterly, 2*(3), 31–39.

Coyne, J., & Meurant-Tompkinson, A. (2018). *Police, public servants and law enforcement: A contested domain?* Australian Strategic Policing Institute. https://www.aspistrategist.org.au/police-public-servants-law-enforcement-contested-domain/

Desmond, M., Papachristos, A., & Kirk, D. (2016). Police violence and citizen crime reporting in the black community. *American Sociological Review, 85*(1), 184–190.

El-Sabawi, T., & Carroll, J. (2020). *A model for defunding: An evidence-based statute for behavioral health crisis response.* Elon University Law Legal Studies Research Paper Forthcoming, https://ssrn.com/abstract=3683432 or https://doi.org/10.2139/ssrn.3683432.

Fleetwood, J., & Lea, J. (2020). *De-funding the police in the UK.* British Society of Criminology Newsletter, No. 85, Summer 2020, ISSN 1759-8354.

Friedman, B. (2020). *Disaggregating the police function.* Public Law and Research Paper Series, Working Paper no. 20–03. New York University School of Law.

Gaunt, R. (2010). *Sir Robert Peel: The life and legacy.* I.B.Tauris.

Geller, A., Fagan, J., Tyler, T., & Link, B. G. (2014). Aggressive policing and the mental health of young urban men. *American Journal of Public Health, 104*(12), 2321–2327.

Gostin, L. O., & Powers, M. (2006). What does social justice require for the public's health? Public health ethics and policy imperatives. *Health Affairs, 25*(4), 1053–1060.

Government of Canada. (2013). Canada (Attorney General) v. Bedford, 2013 SCC 72.

Government of Canada. (2014). *Prostitution criminal law reform: Bill C-36, the protection of communities and exploited persons act.*

Greene, I., & McCormick, P. (2019). *Beverley McLachlin: The legacy of a supreme court chief justice.* James Lorimer & Company Ltd..

Johnson, P. (2012). The enforcers of morality. In Johnson & Dalton (Eds.), *Policing sex* (pp. 23–37). Routledge.

Kane, E., Evans, E., & Shokraneh, F. (2018). Effectiveness of current policing-related mental health interventions: A systematic review. *Criminal behaviour and mental health: CBMH, 28*(2), 108–119. https://doi.org/10.1002/cbm.2058

LaGrange, R. L. (1993). *Policing American society.* Nelson–Hall.

Lentz, S., & Chaires, R. (2007). The invention of Peel's principles: A study of policing 'textbook' history. *Journal of Criminal Justice, 35*, 69–79.

Lowman, J. (1992). Street prostitution control: Some Canadian reflections on the Finsbury Park experience. *British Journal of Criminology, 32*, 1–17.

Marmot, M. (2015). *The health gap: The challenge of an unequal world.* Bloomsbury Press.

Matthews, R. (2005). Policing prostitution ten years on. *British Journal of Criminology, 45*, 877–895.

Millie, A. (2013). The policing task and the expansion (and contraction) of British policing. *Criminology & Criminal Justice, 13*(2), 143–160.

Millie, A. (2014). What are the police for? Re-thinking policing post-austerity. In J. M. Brown (Ed.), *The future of policing.* Routledge.

Mimiaga, M., Safren, S., Dvoryak, S., Reisner, S., Needle, R., & Woody, G. (2010). We fear the police, and the police fear us: Structural and individual barriers and facilitators to HIV medication adherence among injection drug users in Kiev, Ukraine. *AIDS Care, 22*(11), 1305–1313.

Murphy, D., & Worall, J. (2007). The threat of mission distortion in police-probation partnerships. *Policing: An International Journal of Police Strategies & Management, 30*, 132–149.

Najdowski, C., Bottoms, B., & Goff, A. (2015). Stereotype threat and racial differences in citizens' experiences of police encounters. *Law and Human Behavior, 39*(5), 463–477.

Neusteter, R., Mopolski, M., Khogali, M., & O'Toole, M. (2019a). *The 911 call processing system: A review of the literature as it relates to policing.* Vera Institute of Justice. https://www.vera.org/publications/911-call-processing-system-review-of-policing-literature

Neusteter, R., Subramanian, R., Trone, J., Khogali, M., & Reed, C. (2019b). *Gatekeepers: The role of police in ending mass incarceration.* Vera Institute of Justice. https://www.vera.org/publications/gatekeepers-police-and-mass-incarceration

Platt, L., Grenfell, P., Meiksin, R., Elmes, J., Sherman, S., Sanders, T., Mwangli, P., & Crago, A. (2018). Associations between sex work laws and sex workers' health: A systematic review and meta-analysis of quantitative and qualitative studies. *PLoS Medicine, 15*(12), e1002680. https://doi.org/10.1371/journal.pmed.1002680

Punch, M., & James, S. (2017). Researching law enforcement and public health. *Policing and Society, 27*(3), 251–260.

Shannon, K., Kerr, T., Allinott, S., Chettiar, J., Shoveller, J., & Tyndall, M. W. (2008). Social and structural violence and power relations in mitigating HIV risk of drug-using women in survival sex work. *Social Science and Medicine, 66*, 911–921.

van Dijk, A., Herrington, V., Crofts, N., Breunig, R., Burris, S., Sullivan, H., Middleton, J., Sherman, S., & Thomson, N. (2019). Law enforcement and public health: Recognition and enhancement of joined-up solutions. *Lancet, 393*, 287–284.

van Dijk, A., Hoogewoning, F., & Punch, M. (2015). *What matters in policing? Change values and leadership in turbulent times.* Policy Press.

Walls, H. L. (2018). Wicked problems and a 'wicked' solution. *Globalization and Health, 14*(34). https://doi.org/10.1186/s12992-018-0353-x

Weine, D., Eisenman, D. P., Kinsler, J., Glik, D. C., & Polutnik, C. (2016). Addressing violent extremism as public health policy and practice. *Behavioral Science of Terrorism and Political Aggression, 9*(31), 208–221.

Williams, K. (2003). Peel's principles and their acceptance by American police: Ending 175 years of reinvention. *The Police Journal, 76*, 97–120.

Wood, J., Watson, A., & Barber, C. (2020). What can we expect of police in the face of deficient mental health systems? Qualitative insights from Chicago police officers. *Journal of Psychiatric and Mental Health Nursing, 28*(1), 28–42.

Chapter 4
Law Enforcement, Public Health, and Vulnerability

Isabelle Bartkowiak-Théron and Nicole L. Asquith

Introduction

The widespread scholarly and practice agreement that vulnerability is at the very core of law enforcement and public health (LEPH) partnerships is fundamentally embedded into the realities of the field. Practitioners agree that 'clients' are the same across sectors: police encounter people who have been receiving the care of (public) health practitioners[1] or, at the very least, been on the radar of these practitioners. Calls for collaboration across sectors has also remained a pillar for the whole of government strategies in problem-solving for more than 20 years across the world (Julian et al., 2017). Despite such overwhelming agreement by those at the frontline, legislation and policy disciplinary and practice collaborations in the field remain hesitant (Asquith & Bartkowiak-Théron, 2012). As a result, siloed practice remains the norm; but it is quickly becoming outdated in terms of efficiency of service delivery and appropriate care. This chapter will identify the reasons why seeking a better integration of practice across all sectors is a worthwhile pursuit. We will argue that the debates around disciplinary specificity and fenced-in budgets are to the detriment of better-targeted, holistic service delivery for vulnerable people.

Collaborations across law enforcement and public health may appear costly and time-consuming in the short term; however, in the longer term, multidisciplinary practice can elicit significant return on investment and timely recuperation of costs (Julian et al., 2017). Our argument is strengthened in the context of the COVID-19 crisis, which has unveiled the glaring undeniability of human fragility, and precipitated new modes of working that have forced collaborations across sectors. Our

---

[1] Or, more likely, who are subject to a public health intervention from their general or clinical health practitioner.

I. Bartkowiak-Théron (✉) · N. L. Asquith
Tasmanian Inst. Law Enforcement Studies, University of Tasmania, Hobart, TAS, Australia
e-mail: isabelle.bartkowiaktheron@utas.edu.au

© The Author(s), under exclusive license to Springer Nature Switzerland AG 2022   53
I. Bartkowiak-Théron et al. (eds.), *Law Enforcement and Public Health*,
https://doi.org/10.1007/978-3-030-83913-0_4

vulnerability is irrefutable, and a robust response to this vulnerability is sited at the intersection of law enforcement and public health.

Background

We have spent the better part of the past 10 years arguing two things. First, that vulnerability is universal, and that law enforcement agencies cannot afford to ignore its ubiquity in policing (Bartkowiak-Théron & Corbo Crehan, 2010; Bartkowiak-Théron & Asquith, 2019). Second, that any police work that assumes this ubiquity of vulnerability necessitates that practitioners work within a multidisciplinary field and according to a universal precautions model (appropriated from public health; Bartkowiak-Théron & Asquith, 2012a).

Across the years, the categorisation of people as 'vulnerable' or 'at risk' has done little other than normatively designate particular types of people as being more prone to becoming victims or offenders (Bartkowiak-Théron & Corbo Crehan, 2010; Stanford, 2012). In legislation and policy, this exercise has translated into a 'tick-in-the-box' approach, fed by long-winded lists of vulnerability attributes, which have proven difficult to actualise in practice. From a more paradigmatic point of view, however, many disciplines—particularly, health and philosophy—have considered the topic of vulnerability holistically (Herring & Henderson, 2011; Misztal, 2011; Fineman, 2008). Central to these other conceptualisations of vulnerability have been social determinants of health (Karpati et al., 2002; Wood et al., 2015; Asquith & Bartkowiak-Théron, 2017), which are

> ... the conditions in which people are born, grow, live, work and age. These circumstances are shaped by the distribution of money, power and resources at global, national and local levels. The social determinants of health are mostly responsible for health inequities – the unfair and avoidable differences in health status seen within and between countries. (World Health Organization, 2020)

Social determinants of health manifest in a number of ways, and specifically in our (in)ability to navigate the complexities that life throws at us. There are occasions where these determinants manifest in ill-health and criminal behaviour, which requires responses from both health practitioners and the justice system. Some of the most obvious examples of this need for interdisciplinary responses are incidents where mental illness may manifest into a crisis resulting in violent behaviour, or behaviours which may be considered dangerous or 'anti-social'. Similarly, the misuse of drugs (even licit drugs) may also lead to offending or abuse.

Policing practice is rife with altercations with people whose determinants of health—associated with their identity—have been at the centre of over policing, or police abuse of powers (Cunneen, 2001; Body-Gendrot, 2011; Bartkowiak-Théron & Asquith, 2019). Race is a salient example of such, with ethnic minorities over-represented in policing and criminal justice more generally. Similarly, disability is disproportionately represented in policing statistics. We have discussed these matters in detail elsewhere (see, for example, Bartkowiak-Théron & Asquith, 2012a,

2012b; Asquith & Bartkowiak-Théron, 2017; Bartkowiak-Théron & Asquith, 2015; Bartkowiak-Théron & Asquith, 2019) and argued that rather than the aforementioned tick-in-the-box approach to vulnerability, practitioners should consider vulnerability as a fundamental trait of being human. As a core human characteristic that is heightened in some situations (such as policing), vulnerability cannot be captured in a checklist of vulnerability attributes (Bartkowiak-Théron & Asquith, 2019).

The fundamental characteristics of vulnerability are that it can be transient (like unemployment), permanent (e.g. Down syndrome or autism), incremental (e.g. an escalation of legal or illegal drug use), or cross-sectional (in the case of co-, tri- or multiple morbidities). As such, the only way to properly address vulnerability is to expect it as a norm, rather than an exception. The universal precaution model that we started developing in 2012 advocates that police officers need to be forewarned and prepared to consider vulnerability in any context, situation, or event (Bartkowiak-Théron & Asquith, 2012a). This includes their own fragility as police officers, constantly working in dangerous settings, and likely to be physically or mentally injured throughout the course of their career (Kamkar et al., 2019; Papazoglou et al., 2020). This extends to the vulnerability of their case in court. We also argue that working according to a universal precaution model, stemming, more fundamentally, from trauma-informed practice, fosters empathy, and invites respectful, careful engagement with vulnerable communities, as per well-documented community policing agendas.

More and more, practitioners and policymakers have been considering our framework (Enang et al., 2019; Coliandris, 2015; Keay & Kirby, 2018; Ford et al., 2020). While a minimalist perspective on vulnerability (the current UK approach) has been the flavour of most policy and legal work, the maximalist approach that we propose stems from the reality that the policing remit has expanded in the past decades (Millie & Herrington, 2014) and now includes work that in the past was addressed by practitioners better prepared for specific forms of vulnerability (e.g. addiction, homelessness, mental illness). The relentless continuation of budget cuts worldwide and the legacy of austerity measures have meant that public health agencies have faced limitations to their service capacity. With the addition of well-intentioned, but ill-informed and ill-conceived, public policies (like the de-institutionalisation of the mentally ill in the 1960s; see Bittner, 1967; Teplin & Pruett, 1992; Burris et al., 2010; Asquith & Bartkowiak-Théron, 2017) police have, by default, become the first port of call for matters they are often ill-prepared to address, including non-criminal and safeguarding matters.

It is now well-documented that rather than crime, most police work relates to welfare matters, calls for concern, and the facilitation of other organisations' business (Punch, 1979; Asquith & Bartkowiak-Théron, 2017; Ratcliffe, 2016). As we have noted previously, at least 75% of police work relates to vulnerable people, and as documented by the UK College of Policing, 84% of calls to police are not crime-related (College of Policing, 2015). For the most part, everyday policing is focussed on activities that seek to safeguard vulnerable people, or respond to calls concerning matters that may be better addressed by other practitioners. It is a consequence of both the dominance of law and order in political campaigns, and the assignment of work to one of the few services available 24/7, that police are now Jack-and-Jill-of-all-trades (Bartkowiak-Théron & Julian, 2018).

We have explored most of these arguments previously and have already focused some of our work on the necessary interaction between law enforcement and public health (Asquith & Bartkowiak-Théron, 2017; Bartkowiak-Théron et al., 2017). In this chapter, we expand our arguments to propose that anything other than collaboration and integration is ill-advised policy. We make this claim in the context of increasingly thoughtful and considered initiatives across multiple areas of practice, the perfunctory nature of some police–health collaborations across the world, and the constant and increasing public scrutiny under which police action is placed. The time is ripe for calling for action in collaboration and engagement, and reconsider what police do, on a daily basis. While the policing remit is an important factor in our consideration of these issues, our arguments stem from the lived reality of everyday policing and its impact on vulnerable people.

Positioning Vulnerability at the Centre of LEPH: Year 2020

The year 2020 will remain in the universal psyche as one that exposed our undoubted fragility as human beings. If there is one thing that the COVID-19 pandemic has revealed, it is that everyone is vulnerable in the face of a contagious disease. Deniers aside, most under locked-down measures watched the disease spread like wildfire, with horror and despair at the inability to help sick family members or friends. Similarly, and almost at the same time, the resurgence of Black Lives Matter, and the associated #DefundthePolice movement helped revive and give renewed vigour to questions asked in the past about the role of police, its remit, and police communication with vulnerable people. These questions about role, remit, and communication are contextualised not only by the graphic and virtually disseminated images of police abuse of powers and injuries to the public, but also the denial or dismissal of vulnerability by some governments. In this section of our chapter, we pay our respect to those who have died during this difficult time in human history. We also argue that there are also several opportunities facilitated by the pandemic, the #Defundthepolice and Black Lives Matter movements on which we can build.

Increased, Necessary Cross-Agency Collaboration

Health and law enforcement agencies, as well as other essential workers, saw a significant increase in the amount of work they are doing together, by virtue of quarantine or forced isolation guidelines imposed by governments. The idea of 'police as public health interventionists' has often been illustrated by police intervention in mental health crisis, response to suicide attempts, or enforcement of drug laws (Wood et al., 2015; Asquith & Bartkowiak-Théron, 2017; Bartkowiak-Théron

& Asquith, 2017). The protection of the health of the public in the case of COVID-19 saw health and police practitioners work together, at times, in a very specific context of the health continuum, which sought to confine the public to private quarters to avoid community contagion. In this case, any movement or action that could potentially transmit a disease became criminalised in some jurisdictions. The monitoring of people's whereabouts, within their own neighbourhood or across districts or state lines, became highly scrutinised by law enforcement authorities, with any unauthorised or unjustified movement immediately sanctioned, most commonly by fines. Multidisciplinary attention was also placed on the likely impact of the pandemic on the increased risk of domestic violence, amongst already victimised families, and in regional and rural areas further isolated by quarantine rules (Campbell, 2020; Hansen & Lory, 2020).

Spotlight on (Not Forgotten) Vulnerabilities and Elevated Communication

The pandemic gave rise to the need for increased communication between governments and their people. It also put in the spotlight the need for alternative communication strategies, which were not considered in the early days of the pandemic, but led to a scurry of activity, including the use of sign language during government briefings on televised media. Similarly, in Australia, audio-supported shows have been boosted across a number of programs (including kids' program), which were unavailable for sight-impaired people prior to the pandemic. Suddenly, forms of disability that were never really forgotten, but had often been considered too hard to integrate, were foregrounded, and people with disability were being (re-)invited to the public sphere. In some respects, these developments brought about by the pandemic have 'flattened the curve' on the 'competition of suffering' (Mason-Bish, 2013) and provided alternative means for vulnerable people to make informed decisions about their health, wellbeing, and safety. Yet, our cynicism leads us to believe that if these developments are not embedded as standard practice, it is likely that the cyclical nature of policy will see some of these efforts, arguably necessary and essential for the wellbeing of all community members, disappear.

Visibility of Police Action in Vulnerability Matters

Video footage of George Floyd's death is one of those most graphic examples of police abuse of power that has been relayed by the media recently. The public's response to this homicide also indicates that public scrutiny (and distrust) of police is at an all-time high. This new reality, facilitated by access to technology and social media, means that there are now new accountability mechanisms that police need to take into account. As we type these words, new incidents of police malpractice emerge daily in the media, especially in the USA (see, for example, the case of Elijah McClain's death, who died in the same way as George Floyd 3 months later; Fausset & Dewan, 2020). Many of these incidents have highlighted the unequal application of both policing resources and sanctions within what can be dubbed 'health enforcement' policy. These incidents also highlight the gaps that have emerged in the absence of collaboration, more astute training, and better accountability mechanisms.

The case of Victoria Police officers severely brutalising 'John', a disabled pensioner in 2017, recently led to the conviction and dismissal from the police force of three out of the six police officers attending what initially started as a concern from welfare, called in by a health practitioner (Percy, 2020). The police were called to support the work of ambulance officers and were never meant to lead the encounter. Instead, they chose to send in the most junior officer present to negotiate with John, who was perceived by the officers as being aggressive and threatening (Percy, 2020). In this case, despite being advised by the man's practitioner to gently handle him, the attending officers refused to accept the man's own assessment of his wellbeing and needs. After he refused to exit his home, he was physically assaulted, held pinned on the ground by four officers and subjected to sustained attack by police using both physical force and capsicum spray (Knight, 2018). Rather than address this man's obvious distress, the attending police officers began videoing the encounter and laughing at his response to the police action. They also decided that rather than approach the man with water to rinse his face, they would use a high-pressure garden hose, which sprayed all over him as he laid on the front lawn of his house (Knight, 2018). In the video footage of this encounter, officers can be heard giggling at his distress and took the time to spray him again to take pictures. John was devastated by the way he was treated by the police at the most vulnerable moment of his life. His treatment by the police will stay with him and shape future encounters with the police (Percy, 2020). As a consequence of this horrendous encounter with the police, John has since been diagnosed with PTSD.

How this incident was managed, and the sheer ill-advised manpower deployed to "safeguard" John, was observed again in August 2020 when police officers of the Boulder Police forcefully evicted four homeless people who were squatting at an alleged abandoned house (Safe Access for Everyone (SAFE), 2020). Despite the City of Boulder, Colorado, having a housing-first lens to most of its government services (Castle, 2020), and during the significant restrictions imposed by COVID-19, the Boulder Police responded by deploying over 14 vehicles and 14 highly apparelled officers. At least one detained person was charged with felony trespassing, which could lead to up to 3 years imprisonment, and in the process of detaining another disabled man, removed his service support dog, who was sent to Animal Control (SAFE, 2020). This approach was far from being trauma-informed; nor was it collaborative.

The longer-term consequences of addressing a public health issue as a felony are significant. During a pandemic, homelessness is to be avoided at all costs, especially homelessness under the shadow of a felony conviction. Not only will those people have to manage the short-term consequences of being without shelter, the police decision to violently arrest them also means they are likely to experience ongoing house insecurity, and with a felony charge, unlikely to secure employment to enable housing security in the future. The loss of a service support dog is also costly to both the individual (particularly in terms of psychological support) and the disability service who spent significant money in training that support dog.

If the police actions were informed from the beginning by the high likelihood of trauma and vulnerability, much of this damage could have been avoided. While too little information on this incident has come to light, we suggest that even the interests of the homeowner could have been met if a coordinated response to the housing crisis was considered. Abandoned houses are more likely to be trashed, and in the absence of a paying tenant, even squatters can have pride in their homes and protect them from further damage (Herbert, 2018; Spelman, 1993). The path forward for these four individuals has been well-traced in the past: they will re-enter the criminal justice system, and because they will be unable to pay any fine imposed, they will be given a gaol sentence. Upon existing, their houseless/rough sleeping status will remain, in addition to possible associated poverty crimes.

Engaging with the issues of housing insecurity and psychological wellbeing from a siloed policing perspective is unlikely to result in either the reduction in crime, or the security and safety of residents. As Anderson and Burris (2017) rightly point out, at times, policing is just not the right medicine, and attempts to move upstream to address the issues that create the conditions for crime may in fact eliminate the need for police actions on public health issues. Upstream preventative work is difficult, costly, and hard to evaluate, and the results may take generations to come to fruition. Yet, upstream strategies are cheaper in the long term, and more likely to address the underlining trauma and vulnerability that often lands downstream on the desks of police officers incapable or unwilling to properly address the aetiology of these social problems. In the case of both of our case studies, we wonder, in comparison to the outcomes noted above, what would have been the cost of police doing nothing (at worse), referral ideally, and conferring with other agencies on these vulnerable people's safety collaboratively, in best practice approaches? Too often we reach out to police perfunctorily to address issues that are better managed upstream, by public health agencies, before they come to the attention of the police.

The criminalisation of vulnerabilities that have nothing to do with actual deviance, but everything to do with health, is a serious issue that needs to be redressed. In many cases, police interaction with individuals in crisis is ill-advised, as it may aggravate the situation. Too often the resourcing of police is increased to manage these incidents, when limited resources may be better directed to enhance public and primary health services. Police commonly reject the construction of their work as 'street psychiatrists', yet rarely seek more appropriate health services when they are called to respond to situations of medical crisis that require specialist knowledge and training around trauma and mental illness. Arguably, responding to health crises is not a matter for policing, and while police should have some knowledge about how to respond collaboratively to these incidents, their training, remit, and function do not prepare them to do this work in isolation.

Similarly, public stigma around vulnerability needs to be considered, as ill-informed perceptions of vulnerability by members of the community often trigger unfounded calls for police. However, police remain the first port of call, and as with the public, they may make assumptions about the dangerousness and criminality of vulnerable people. This is most obvious in both the public and police responses to homelessness, which often brings homeless people in contact with police and, in turn, diverts homeless people away from the public health services critically important in avoiding criminalisation.

Conclusion

The recent worldwide events that have marked 2020, while most certainly heartbreaking, are useful for us to consider, once again, but with more salience, the futility of siloed interventions. Increased collaboration in the public health sphere, enhanced communication strategies between agencies and towards the public are all phenomena that government, with political leadership and will, can harness to strengthen approaches to vulnerability. Currently, however, most of these initiatives seem to be just one-way, and do not consist of real participatory democracy, which should be our next aim. Vulnerable people can have a voice in policy, and influence practice for the better. At this stage, however, vulnerable people are just being given information in a form that is accessible. The only logical next step is to make such collaborative and consultative practice (and communication) accessible.

In a way, the current calls to #Defundthepolice may help achieve such aims. More than a rally cry, the movement not only calls for a more educated allocation of resources from police onto public health agencies (like housing, education, drug education programs, etc.). Because there is an appetite (however sparse) for such a reinvestment of resource, with police agencies inviting all to the negotiation table, there has never been a better time to examine the role of police and reframe in a context of holistic, trauma-informed practice.

Learning to say no, to delegate, and to consider police work as an extension of public health strategies may avert the criminalisation of vulnerability and trauma in policing. Calls to defund or abolish the police will only resolve the issues police confront on a daily basis when the divestment from policing is actualised in addressing the real problems that facilitate or create criminal behaviours. This is not to say police are irrelevant or not needed in addressing vulnerability. Utopian goals of a world without police cannot be met when the causes of crime continue to be ignored, minimised, or dismissed. In working collaboratively, the aetiology of crime may become clearer to those working on the frontline. Calling for the simplification of vulnerability definitions is futile. Vulnerability is intricate, as it can be generated from individual characteristics, social processes, institutional practices, or even the ontological fragility of being human. Yet, intricacy should not be a reason for inaction. Vulnerability, after all, is any circumstance or condition that is likely to create or exacerbate harm (Watts & Bohle, 1993), without a mechanism to mitigate that harm. The mitigation of harm is best achieved by systems of wellbeing and primary health support rather than police squads in riot gear.

References

Anderson, E., & Burris, S. (2017). Policing and public health: Not quite the right analogy. *Policing and Society, 27*(3), 300–313.

Asquith, N. L., & Bartkowiak-Théron, I. (2012). Vulnerability and diversity in policing. In I. Bartkowiak-Théron & N. L. Asquith (Eds.), *Policing vulnerability* (pp. 3–9). Federation Press.

Asquith, N. L., & Bartkowiak-Théron, I. (2017). Police as public health interventionists. In N. L. Asquith, I. Bartkowiak-Théron, & K. Roberts (Eds.), *Policing encounters with vulnerability* (pp. 145–170). Palgrave.

Bartkowiak-Théron, I., & Asquith, N. L. (2012a). Vulnerable people policing: A preparatory framework for operationalising vulnerability. In I. Bartkowiak-Théron & N. L. Asquith (Eds.), *Policing vulnerability* (pp. 278–292). Federation Press.

Bartkowiak-Théron, I., & Asquith, N. L. (2012b). The extraordinary intricacies of policing vulnerability. *Australasian Policing: Journal of Professional Practice and Research, 4*(2), 43–49.

Bartkowiak-Théron, I., & Asquith, N. L. (2015). Policing diversity and vulnerability in the post-Macpherson era: Unintended consequences and missed opportunities. *Policing: A Journal of Policy and Practice, 9*(1), 89–100.

Bartkowiak-Théron, I., & Asquith, N. L. (2017). Conceptual divides and practice synergies in law enforcement and public health: Some lessons from policing vulnerability in Australia. *Policing and Society, 27*(3), 276–288.

Bartkowiak-Théron, I., & Asquith, N. L. (2019). *Policing vulnerable people*. TILES Briefing Paper, 14 (July).

Bartkowiak-Theron, I., & Asquith, N. L. (2019). Policing ethnic minorities: Disentangling a landscape of conceptual and practice tensions. In S. Ratuva (Ed.), *The Palgrave handbook of ethnicity* (pp. 1–24). Palgrave.

Bartkowiak-Théron, I., Asquith, N. L., & Roberts, K. (2017). Vulnerability as a contemporary challenge for policing. In N. L. Asquith, I. Bartkowiak-Théron, & K. Roberts (Eds.), *Policing encounters with vulnerability* (pp. 1–23). Palgrave.

Bartkowiak-Théron, I., & Corbo Crehan, A. (2010). The changing nature of communities: Implications for police and community policing. In J. Putt (Ed.), *Community policing: Current and future directions for Australia – Research and public policy*. Australian Institute of Criminology.

Bartkowiak-Théron, I., & Julian, R. (2018). *Collaboration and communication in police work: The 'jack-of-all-trades' phenomenon.* https://connect42.org/collaboration-and-communication-in-police-work-the-jack-of-all-trades-phenomenon/

Bittner, E. (1967). Police discretion in emergency apprehension of mentally ill persons. *Social Problems, 14*(3), 278–279.

Body-Gendrot, S. (2011). Police marginality, racial logics and discrimination in the banlieues de France. In P. Amar (Ed.), *New racial missions of policing* (pp. 82–99). Routledge.

Burris, S., Wagenaar, A. C., Swanson, J., Ibrahim, J. K., Wood, J., & Mello, M. M. (2010). Making the case for laws that improve health: A framework for public health law research. *Milbank Quarterly, 88*(2), 169–210.

Campbell, A. M. (2020). An increasing risk of family violence during the Covid-19 pandemic: Strengthening community collaborations to save lives. *Forensic Science International: Reports, 2.* https://doi.org/10.1016/j.fsir.2020.100089

Castle, S. (2020, July 10). Boulder boards, staff split on homeless response, *The Boulder Beat.* https://boulderbeat.news/2020/07/10/boulder-boards-staff-split-on-homeless-response/

Coliandris, G. (2015). County lines and wicked problems: Exploring the need for improved policing approaches to vulnerability and early intervention. *Australasian Policing: A Journal of Professional Practice and Research, 7*(2), 5–36.

College of Policing. (2015). *College of policing analysis: Estimating demand on the police service.* www.college.police.uk/News/College-news/Documents/Demand%20Report%2023_1_15_noBleed.pdf

Cunneen, C. (2001). *Conflict, politics and crime: Aboriginal communities and the police.* Allen and Unwin.

Enang, I., Murray, J., Dougall, N., Wooff, A., Heyman, I., & Aston, E. (2019). Defining and assessing vulnerability within law enforcement and public health organisations: A scoping review. *Health Justice, 7*(2). https://doi.org/10.1186/s40352-019-0083-z

Fausset, R., & Dewan, S. (2020, June 30). "Elijah McClain died after he was detained. Now he's being remembered. *The New York Times.*

Fineman, M. A. (2008). The vulnerable subject. *Yale Journal of Law & Feminism, 20*(1), 1–23.

Ford, K., Newbury, A., Meredith, Z., Evans, J., Hughes, K., Roderick, J., Davies, A. R., & Bellis, M. A. (2020). Understanding the outcome of police safeguarding notifications to social services in South Wales. *The Police Journal, 93*(2), 87–108.

Hansen, J. A., & Lory, G. L. (2020). Rural victimization and policing during the COVID-19 pandemic. *American Journal of Criminal Justice, 45*, 731–742. https://doi.org/10.1007/s12103-020-09554-0

Herbert, C. W. (2018). Like a good neighbor, squatters are there: Property and neighborhood stability in the context of urban decline. *City and Community, 17*(1), 236–258.

Herring, C., & Henderson, L. (2011). From affirmative action to diversity: Toward a critical diversity perspective. *Critical Sociology, 38*(5), 629–643.

Julian, R., Bartkowiak-Théron, I., Hallam, J., & Hughes, C. (2017). Exploring law enforcement and public health as a collective impact initiative: Lessons learned from Tasmania as a case study. *Journal of Criminological Research, Policy and Practice, 3*(2), 79–92.

Kamkar, K., Edwards, G., Hesketh, I., McFee, D., Papazoglou, K., Pedersen, P., Sanders, K., Stamatakis, T., & Thompson, J. (2019). Dialogue highlights from the LEPH2019 panel on police mental health and Well-being. *Journal of Community Safety and Well-Being, 5*(1).

Karpati, A., Galea, S., Awerbuch, T., & Levins, R. (2002). Variability and vulnerability at the ecological level: Implications for understanding the social determinants of health. *American Journal of Public Health, 92*, 1768–1772.

Keay, S., & Kirby, S. (2018). Defining vulnerability: From the conceptual to the operational. *Policing: A Journal of Policy and Practice, 12*(4), 428–438.

Knight, B. (2018, 3 April). Melbourne police captured on video taking down disability pensioner. *ABC Online.* https://www.abc.net.au/news/2018-04-03/melbourne-police-on-video-taking-down-disability-pensioner/9591006

Mason-Bish, H. (2013). Conceptual issues in the construction of disability hate crime. In A. Roulstone & H. Mason-Bish (Eds.), *Disability, hate crime and violence* (pp. 11–24). Routledge.

Millie, A., & Herrington, V. (2014). How wide or narrow should the police's remit be? *Public Safety Leadership Research Focus, 2*(4), 1–10.

Misztal, B. (2011). The challenges of vulnerability. In *Search of strategies for a less vulnerable social life.* Palgrave Macmillan.

Papazoglou, K., Blumberg, D. M., Kamkar, K., McIntyre-Smith, A., & Koskelainen, M. (2020). Addressing moral suffering in police work: Theoretical conceptualization and counselling implications. *Canadian Journal of Counselling and Psychotherapy, 54*(1), 71–87.

Percy, K. (2020, July 24). Victoria police officers Brad McLeod, John Edney and Florian Hilgart found guilty of 2017 assault on disability pensioner. *ABC Online.* https://www.abc.net.au/news/2020-07-24/police-officers-guilty-unlawful-assault-on-disability-pensioner/12488008

Punch, M. (1979). The secret social service. In S. Holdaway (Ed.), *The British police* (pp. 102–117). Edward Arnold.

Ratcliffe, J. (2016). *Intelligence-led policing* (2nd ed.). Routledge.

Safe Access for Everyone. (2020, August 30). Boulder Police evicted four people from an abandoned house today. *Facebook post.* https://www.facebook.com/SAFEboco

Spelman, W. (1993). Abandoned buildings: Magnets for crime? *Journal of Criminal Justice, 21*(5), 481–495.

Stanford, S. (2012). Critically reflecting on being 'at risk' and 'a risk' in vulnerable people policing. In I Bartkowiak-Théron & N.L. Asquith (Eds.), Policing vulnerability (pp. 20–32). Federation Press.

Teplin, L. A., & Pruett, N. S. (1992). Police as streetcorner psychiatrist: Managing the mentally ill. *International Journal of Law and Psychiatry, 15*(2), 139–156.

Watts, M. J., & Bohle, H. G. (1993). The space of vulnerability: The causal structure of hunger and famine. *Progress in Human Geography, 17*(1), 43–67. https://doi.org/10.1177/030913259301700103

Wood, J. D., Taylor, C. J., Groff, E. R., & Ratcliffe, J. H. (2015). Aligning policing and public health promotion: Insights from the world of foot patrol. *Police Practice and Research: An International Journal, 16*(3), 211–223.

World Health Organization. (WHO). (2020). *Social determinants of health.* https://www.who.int/social_determinants/en/

Chapter 5
Challenges and Opportunities in Educating Law Enforcement Officers: 2020 and Beyond

Richard F. Southby and Brandon del Pozo

It is difficult to suppress the suspicion that the high-school level of entrance into the police is retained not for any realistic reasons, but because those who set the standards, those who do the recruiting, and those who run the police departments, do not wish to be educationally outranked by their subordinates and risk all sorts of disciplinary problems on that account.
—Egon Bittner, The Functions of the Police in Modern Society

Introduction

Since the 1970s, there has been rapidly growing global interest in revising and expanding the content and quality of training and educational opportunities for law enforcement personnel (Saunders, 1970). The working theories are numerous: police with more formal education are more likely to use communication and problem-solving skills in their work than adherence to rote procedure, less apt to use excessive force, and may have more employment options, so their decisions to join the profession are well-considered rather than out of perceived necessity. It can result, research suggests, in an increase in the perceived legitimacy of the agency concerned (Thompson & Payne, 2019). This chapter reflects the combined law enforcement and academic experiences of the authors in relating the current landscape and the potential for improving the profession of policing through stronger linkages with institutions of higher learning.

R. F. Southby (✉)
Milken Institute School of Public Health, The George Washington University,
Washington, DC, USA
e-mail: southby@gwu.edu

B. del Pozo
Miriam Hospital/Warren Alpert Medical School of Brown University, Providence, RI, USA

© The Author(s), under exclusive license to Springer Nature Switzerland AG 2022   65
I. Bartkowiak-Théron et al. (eds.), *Law Enforcement and Public Health*,
https://doi.org/10.1007/978-3-030-83913-0_5

We have observed a number of common themes based on our US and international perspectives. Old attitudes of negativity towards enhancing educational opportunities for police, from recruits to senior police members, were based on the idea that policing was a working class refuge for people of modest educational attainment, and that a facility with scholarship was at odds with the skills and abilities required of police officers. These outlooks are being replaced with encouragement and support for establishing educational requirements for recruits and law enforcement members throughout their careers, as the scope and complexity of policing continues to grow, and as the interventions it requires to become increasingly interdisciplinary. Currently, we are witnessing seismic changes in the recruitment, selection, and recruit training and professional development programs in police departments worldwide. In many European nations, police are required to attend years-long university-style academies, and in the United States, even in jurisdictions with modest formal requirements, the typical educational level of police recruits is on the rise. Many police departments are reaching out to local academic institutions and establishing formal relationships to improve the quality of training and education programs and to build research programs, especially those with an applied emphasis.[1] The old "rote learning" approach used by many police academies is being replaced with critical thinking, problem-solving, and scenario-based learning.

There is also a growing awareness of the need for properly conducted applied research in all areas of law enforcement as the prerequisite for evidence-based policy development and practice protocols. The American Society of Evidence-Based Policing is an example of a professional organization that strives to promote original research that yields findings or hypotheses which can be translated into practical solutions. George Mason University's Center for Evidence-Based Crime Policy is based on the premise that research into policing and crime control is of limited value unless it fosters translation and implementation.

Societal Expectations of Law Enforcement Personnel

In parallel with the changing attitudes towards training and education, society's expectations of police are also evolving. This has been strongly influenced by the evolving patterns of crime and social behaviors which now include the increasing prevalence of cybercrime, domestic violence, drugs, gangs, homelessness, mental health, and truancy.

A further driving force for far-reaching changes across the entire spectrum of law enforcement in modern society, including recruiting, training, education, and professional development, as well as the mission and organizational alignment of police

---

[1] See, for example, the New York City Police Department's formal arrangement with the John Jay College of Criminal Justice for both undergraduate and master's-level coursework: https://www.jjay.cuny.edu/NYPDProgram.

departments, is the reaction to the numerous examples of police brutality in the United States. Most recently, this includes the murder of George Floyd by a police officer in Minneapolis, Minnesota, and the nation-wide "Black Lives Matter" demonstrations and protests.

Inappropriate police behavior all too often results in unjustified injuries and deaths. The reporting of these incidents is facilitated by witnesses recording what has occurred with cell phones and the greater use of body-worn cameras by police.

It is appropriate to ask whether these incidents of police violence reflect poor recruitment and selection practices, inadequate or ineffective training and education, and the lack of proper supervision and accountability. Does the increased stress experienced by police in their daily work lead to inappropriate behaviors in their interactions with the public and even within their own families and social networks?

Police in many countries have traditionally been expected to focus on law enforcement as their primary role, but they are increasingly being utilized as the "first contact" for an increasing number of societal problems, simply because they are the default government agency available and poised to respond in many crisis situations. In many of these instances, police are not adequately prepared to identify these untoward signs, symptoms, and behaviors or to know which agency in the community would be a better resource to deal with these complex situations. Arrest is usually the typical police response, but this is not always the most appropriate course of action. In fact, it may only exacerbate existing problems. Police should not be viewed as "heavily armed" social workers or mental health professionals; however, their training should prepare them to make appropriate assessments of situations and coordinate with the more appropriate community services. It must be acknowledged, however, that these 'more appropriate' services are usually not readily available or even viewed by local governments as necessary. Even where their value is recognized, availability of personnel and funding may be major barriers.

Better training and education for law enforcement members is one positive factor in helping them to deal with today's social problems. This preparation needs to be supplemented by improvements in police management, leadership, and mentoring. Senior police leaders should lobby their local political leaders to emphasize that investing in the development of collaboration among police, mental health, and social work professionals will result in a "win-win" situation for those members of the community needing these services and those responsible for ensuring public safety in its broadest sense.

The "Militarization" of Law Enforcement

Another factor that has harmed police–community relationships in the United States has been the very noticeable trend towards the "militarization" of law enforcement. While riot-control gear and armored personnel carriers are clearly needed when police are called to school shootings, hostage situations, and terrorist incidents, all too often police assigned to routine patrols, peaceful protests and community policing programs look more like military personnel going to war. These images are not viewed positively by the general public, and the resulting loss of respect for law enforcement is not easy to reverse, especially when the militarized look is accompanied by excessive use of force incidents. The US federal government agencies have not helped in this regard. They have often been the major source of donations of surplus military equipment, vehicles, and money to many police departments throughout the country, thereby establishing police para militarism as a norm, and helping to perpetuate it (Radil et al., 2017).

This increased militarization of policing has sadly almost obliterated the "Norman Rockwell" image of local police officers being regarded as trustworthy, friendly, and supportive sources of help for all age groups in small and large communities.

Challenges for Law Enforcement to Develop and Sustain Improved Education and Training Programs

Identifying high-quality tertiary education institutions that have a strong interest in, and commitment to, law enforcement education and applied research is a challenge for police academies and departments. There are over 17,000 police agencies in the United States, and their officers are recruited and trained in myriad ways that make consistent linkages with higher education difficult to develop and sustain at the local level. This may be compounded by the arrogance and hostility exhibited by too many academic staff refusing to accept law enforcement personnel as genuine colleagues, and this has extended into refusing to be involved in law enforcement teaching and research programs. Some members of the public health community have asked public health academics to sign a pledge of non-collaboration with law enforcement. Carleton University in Canada as of 2021–2022 will no longer offer the opportunity for their undergraduate students to do placements with either police or correctional organizations.

These unhelpful attitudes and behaviors, however, are not a one-way street. In the past, it has been common for police, at all levels, to view the academic community as being too theoretical, impractical, and essentially irrelevant and unhelpful to the law enforcement agencies.

To move forward, these attitudes cannot persist. There is much to be gained through greater collaboration between police academies and tertiary education institutions. Faculty members can assist police academy staff in modifying and developing intellectually rigorous courses, both at police academies and within the university and college environments, and especially where the course content is relevant to improving police practices.

An additional gain from such collaboration could be the awarding of academic credit for some police academy courses towards Associate and Baccalaureate degrees for police members. Certain accredited academic programs, many of them part time or online with the goal of facilitating enrollment by active police officers, already accept such credits.

The ever-increasing costs of tertiary education in the United States pose major challenges for police departments, resulting in significant barriers for their personnel, sworn and civilian, to gain tertiary educational degrees and qualifications.

This problem is exacerbated by police agencies that implement academic graduation requirements for promotion but, at the same time, make it difficult for their employees to pursue these qualifications because of restrictive work schedules and lack of scholarships and financial aid. Flexible work schedules, which accommodate class schedules, have been established by some police departments, but this needs to become the norm rather than the exception. At present, the more attractive options are limited to evening and midnight shifts that come with their own collateral concerns.

There should be strong encouragement from the senior police leadership for their members to aspire to being able to pursue higher education qualifications, not just at the baccalaureate level but all the way through to doctoral studies.

There are examples where academic institutions have helped to address these issues by offering significant tuition discounts and access to financial aid for law enforcement students, but research suggests that only one agency in the United States has developed something akin to an internal command staff college for the academic development of its leadership (Martin, 2017).

An Illustration of Two Educational Initiatives

Two examples of educational initiatives undertaken by one of the authors illustrate the possibilities of a deliberate partnership between a police agency and an institution of higher learning. When the Police Science program was launched at The George Washington University in 2004, it was based on three "stackable" certificates which, along with general education requirements, leads to an Associate degree and then a Bachelor's degree in Professional Studies. The certificates also serve as free standing qualifications for those who do not desire to complete the formal degree requirements.

Since its inception, this program has provided opportunities for many local law enforcement members to receive an excellent tertiary education at reduced cost to the individual and the agency and feasible with a full-time occupation. The George Washington University generously provided 50% tuition scholarships to full-time law enforcement employees admitted to the academic program. The certificate aspect of the program provided officers who were not ready to commit to a full course of study the opportunity to case back into education in a way that provided the benefits of structure with fewer demands and a lower level of commitment. Many of the officers who enrolled in the certificate programs transitioned to the degree-granting course of study. In recent years, the Police Science Program has evolved into a Police and Security Studies program with the addition of numerous master's degrees in specialist areas.

The second illustration is the development of a carefully designed Graduate Certificate in Strategic Management and Executive Leadership as a collaborative arrangement between The George Washington University and American University in Washington, DC. This graduate certificate was developed especially for mid-to-senior level sworn and civilian members of police departments in the metropolitan area, especially to include the District's Metropolitan Police Department. It was designed for cohorts of 15–20 students who upon completion would receive a "double-badged" diploma from both universities. Faculty were to be drawn from both universities and students would be granted a 50% tuition discount in line with the earlier Police Science program discussed earlier. Provision was also made for graduates to be able to apply the credits from the graduate certificate to a master's degree at either participating university.

Regrettably, this program was cancelled upon the withdrawal of promised scholarship support from the Metropolitan Police Department as the agency contended with budget concerns. The model, however, remains a very viable option for creative approaches by police departments and academic institutions. The Metropolitan Police Department has subsequently participated in a smaller, seminar-based course of instruction offered by the Georgetown University Law Center that takes an interdisciplinary approach but does not grant degrees or certificates. Until the distant time when American police academies become long-term training and education environments that culminate in the conferral of an academic degree and have opportunities for postgraduate education, these hybrid models of academic institutions partnering with police agencies offer the best alternative.

Additional Opportunities for Collaboration and Partnerships: Joint Faculty Appointments, Expansion of Applied Research, and Evidence-Based Policing

As academic institutions and police departments work together more closely to their mutual advantage, a high priority should be to recruit instructors with the knowledge, skills, experience, and commitment to teach across their respective sectors. The establishment of "joint faculty appointments" would help strengthen these relationships for the mutual benefits of the education and police environments. Criminology, sociology, and anthropology are related fields with overlapping methods that would benefit from cross-pollination with the scholarship being produced in the fields of police science, public administration, and law. These fields could further be informed by behavioral science and public health (van Dijk et al., 2019), and actively serving police leaders with the appropriate level of training and education could serve as needed voices in the translation and implementation of the related scholarship. Such faculty linkages between study and practice are critical, since an increased emphasis on applied research and its translation are essential for the quality and usefulness of academic collaboration (Fyfe, 2019). This will be attractive to dedicated researchers who hope to influence practice and provide evidence-based findings which can be translated into policy and programmatic options for police leadership.

An additional bonus will be the ability for evaluations of programs and policies to be included as an ongoing activity meant to fulfill the recommendations of the twenty-first-century policing.

An additional opportunity to ensure that these new collaborations between policing and academia are sustained and developed—as well as produce research that can be effectively implemented—is through the creation of an Academic Advisory Group, comprising senior police officials and members of the agency's wider academic community. Such an entity has recently been established within the Metropolitan Police Department in Washington, DC. Its purpose is to assist the Police Academy, and the broader Department, in reviewing existing training and education programs; developing new educational offerings; strengthening professional development for all levels of police personnel; implementing a collaborative research agenda; and producing a strategic plan for the Police Academy.

A Perspective from the UK

In various parts of the UK, there has been a growing connection between police and academia. In England and Wales for example, the introduction of the Police Education Qualifications Framework through the College of Policing has encouraged and formalized an already existing relationship with higher education establishments. The reason behind this approach was linked to increasing concerns about the complexities and vulnerabilities that police officers were increasingly having to deal with, as well as a desire to further professionalize the police service (Neyroud, 2011). Green and Gates (2014) suggest that higher education and an emphasis on life-long learning are two of the core components in creating a more professional police service. While the PEQF focuses on the educational intentions across ranks, the main priority has been developing initial entry routes into the police through the introduction of degree apprenticeships. The most common form of apprenticeship available is the Police Constable Degree Apprenticeship which allows those who enter the program for a 3-year period of work-based learning combined with academic study where officers spend time at a Higher Education Institution. A key part of the new degree apprenticeship is to ensure that recruits are equipped with the skills, knowledge, and ability to serve the public in a way that enables them to demonstrate critical thinking and reflection in the way they approach their duties.

The Scottish Institute for Policing Research

A notable partnership between the police and academia is the Scottish Institute for Policing Research (SIPR). It may be the model that subsequent partnerships draw from.

The SIPR model of police–academic partnership was established following the Hedderman Review into police research in Scotland in 2005. The review identified that while there was some evidence of high-quality research on policing in Scotland, it was ad hoc and infrequent, and the results of the research were not being fed into police practice (SFC, 2017). This overview led to the development of SIPR in 2007. With a dispersed network organized around different themes, SIPR has been deemed particularly successful in formalizing police research partnerships in the Scottish context (SFC, 2017). A key aim has been the development of a dynamic approach to knowledge exchange and use where engagement with policing research has been a significant part of SIPR's development (Fyfe & Wilson, 2012). Another important aim is to maintain a sustained engagement process which goes beyond a series of one-off events that typify knowledge exchange partnerships (Fyfe & Wilson, 2012; Engel & Henderson, 2014). Engel and Henderson noted that SIPR is the best example of "a fully collaborative police academic partnership" which over time can facilitate "incremental change on police practice based on research." While a primary focus for SIPR continues to be research, it currently engages in a range of activities to support evidence-informed policing and develop a strong research community through supporting postgraduate activity and development. SIPR has also had a role in stimulating international police partnerships and works with a range of other police academies and research groups.

Conclusion

This chapter has highlighted some of the many opportunities for law enforcement agencies and academic institutions to work more closely together to advance the collaboration between these two important sectors of society.

The outcomes will be better-educated law enforcement professionals at every level and increased opportunities for the academic community to contribute through teaching and research to safer communities. These two outcomes will further professionalize policing, and if they are consistently pursued, the result will likely be a shift in police culture that both emphasizes the benefits of formal education and attracts recruits who value them as well. There is also tremendous potential to expand these collaborative activities to many related disciplines, including security, public health, and leadership development—locally, nationally, and globally.

As these programs develop and expand throughout the world, it is vital that the emerging ideas and findings be shared by police professionals and academics on a regular basis at relevant international conferences and through publishing articles in high-quality journals. At present, the main consumer of the research in these journals is other researchers, and this needs to change. When Egon Bittner wrote his monograph on the role of the police in society, it was a National Institutes of Health-funded study. In it, he called for a mandatory 2-year college education as the basic training for police officers, and for bachelor's degrees as a welcome complement. He saw it as a critical way to overcome policing's more harmful and reactionary practices. The year was 1970.

The fundamental and important message then, and now, is that a better-educated officer will be a better officer, and these better officers will improve the department as a whole. The entire society will be the ultimate beneficiary.

References

Engel, R., & Henderson, S. (2014). Beyond rhetoric: Establishing police-academic partnerships that work. In J. Brown (Ed.), *The future of policing*. Routledge.

Fyfe, N. R. (2019). Evidence-based policing: Translating research into practice. *Policing and Society, 29*(9), 1126–1127. https://doi.org/10.1080/10439463.2019.1678621

Fyfe, N. R., & Wilson, P. (2012). Knowledge exchange and police practice: Broadening and deepening the debate around researcher-practitioner collaborations. *Police Practice and Research: An International Journal, 13*(4), 306–314.

Green, T., & Gates, A. (2014). Understanding the process of professionalisation in the police organisation. *The Police Journal, 87*(2), 75–91. https://doi.org/10.1350/pojo.2014.87.2.662

Martin, R. H. (2017). Military, university, and police agency command and staff colleges in the United States. *Journal of Education and Training Studies, 5*(2), 215–222.

Neyroud, P. (2011). *Review of police leadership and training*. Home Office.

Radil, S., Dezzani, R., & McAden, L. (2017). Geographies of U.S. police militarization and the role of the 1033 program. *The Professional Geographer, 69*(2), 203–213. https://doi.org/10.1080/00330124.2016.1212666

Saunders, C. B. (1970). *Upgrading the American police: Education and training for better law enforcement*. Brookings Institution.

SFC. (2017). *Impact review: The Scottish Institute for Policing Research*. Scottish Funding Council, Research and Innovation Directorate, SFC/CP/01/2017.

Thompson, J., & Payne, B. (2019). Towards professionalism and police legitimacy? An examination of the education and training reforms of the police in the Republic of Ireland. *Education Sciences, 9*(3), 241. https://doi.org/10.3390/educsci9030241

van Dijk, A. J., Herrington, V., & Crofts, N. (2019). Law enforcement and public health: Recognition and enhancement of joined-up solutions. *The Lancet, 393*(10168), 287–294.

Chapter 6
Historical and Conceptual Issues: Community Voices

Dan Jurman, Denise Martin, and Shelley Turner

Introduction

Denise Martin

Reflections from lived experiences are critical to our understanding of vulnerability and practitioners who have worked extensively with trauma, and those who experience it can help us appreciate the challenges for those with seldom heard voices. The community voices in this edited collection provide us with important insights about how we understand inequalities from the perspective of those that experience them. They also highlight that the solutions to address trauma is much broader and beyond a singular approach, solution of agency. Like other chapters in the book, these contributions remind us that in order to try and resolve adverse experiences, collaboration and connective thinking are necessary. This does not simply refer to connections between agencies but across existing and previous divides that could potentially create situations of mistrust or suspicion between agencies like the police and young people as outlined by Shelley Turner in a forthcoming section. Building relationships across agencies and within communities need to be embedded to effectively address vulnerability.

D. Jurman (✉)
Pennsylvania Office of Advocacy and Reform, Office of the Governor, Lancaster, PA, USA
e-mail: djurman@pa.gov

D. Martin (✉)
School of Business, Law and Social Science, Abertay University, Dundee, UK
e-mail: D.Martin@abertay.ac.uk

S. Turner (✉)
School of Primary and Allied Health Care, Monash University, Frankston, VIC, Australia
e-mail: shelley.turner@monash.edu

The contribution from Dan Jurman reminds us of the universality that trauma plays amongst efforts to address health inequities. Not only do we need to respond to poverty, crime, physical and behavioural unwellness, we must also remain vigilant to the lingering impacts of situational and generational trauma. This piece equally provides optimistic insight into the potential positive impact that public policy can have, when new policy is informed in cooperation with champions that have worked within and among the communities we wish to better serve.

In her contribution from the field of social work, Turner approaches several crucial issues in our discussion of law enforcement and public health synergies in regard to young people. The first one is that of police as a portal or as brokers of public health services. Then for services to be accessible and for support systems to properly unfold for young people, an analysis of police–youth interaction indicates procedural justice is an essential element of good law enforcement and public health integration. However, for this to happen, sophisticated skills in communication and communication adaptation are necessary to establish a dialogue in which young people are allowed to have a voice and to become agents within the process.

The Impact of Trauma and the Response from Public Health

Dan Jurman

My career has taken me to many places where people struggle because of poverty and the vulnerabilities that come with it. I worked with at-risk youth in places like Camden, Newark, and Atlantic City, New Jersey. I worked with people with extremely low incomes, many of them made more vulnerable by their undocumented status as well, in a community near the University of South Florida known as 'Suitcase City' because of the transitory nature of its substandard, slum housing. That community had 25 times the violent crime rate of the rest of the United States, an HIV rate similar to that of Somalia, the infant mortality rate of Malaysia, and the overall health outcomes of El Salvador. All this in a community surrounded by the wealth of Tampa and New Tampa; a community intentionally cut off from that wealth, in fact, as the City of Tampa annexed the land for New Tampa by going around this impoverished neighbourhood. I had the privilege to lead the Community Action Partnership of Lancaster, and the City of Lancaster's 'Mayor's Commission to Combat Poverty'. There I served a city with a poverty rate higher than that of Pittsburgh or Philadelphia, and with a 'south side' that had the same poverty rate as Detroit (40%), with some census tracts as high as 70%. Over three states, there were lots of common themes. I saw crime, violence, lack of opportunity, slum housing, single parents, predatory businesses, underfunded education systems, overzealous policing and horrible physical and behavioural health outcomes that led to shorter life expectancies. Most of all, though, over and over again, I saw trauma, and the way that trauma creates a feedback loop that feeds and drives all of these issues. A child was traumatised by abuse, the violence in their neighbourhood, and poverty itself through the toxic stresses of hunger, homelessness and scarcity. Their parents were traumatised by the same forces, trapping them in the cycle. The children could not focus at school, because they were hungry, or triggered by something their teacher does, limiting their future prospects to the same cycle within which their parents were trapped.

Because of their Adverse Childhood Experiences (ACEs), the child's brain is regularly sending out alarm signals along with chemicals like adrenaline and cortisol, not only making it harder to learn or function in society, but also taking a toll on their cardiovascular system. The more ACEs they have the more likely they are to suffer from heart disease, strokes, cancers (including cancers that have nothing to do with smoking), substance abuse, and suicide.

Dig deeply into the lives of the people I served in any of those three, very different states, and you will find the same thing: trauma—poverty and trauma, crime and trauma, substance abuse and trauma, behavioural health issues and trauma, poor physical health outcomes and trauma, child abuse and trauma, domestic violence and trauma. One feedback loop after another where the common denominator is trauma. So, what do we do about it?

In my career, I have also been lucky enough to connect to people who have shown me the power of public health. The University of South Florida College of Public Health was a huge resource to me while I worked in 'Suitcase City' and was launching interventions in poverty through an epidemiological lens. That was where I began the journey to look for upstream core causes that could be disrupted instead of constantly fighting never-ending symptoms downstream. I have now served for 5 years on the Community Advisory Board of the Penn State Hershey College of Public Health where I am also a guest lecturer for them and their School of Medicine. Both the institutions have taught me that you can move big community indicators and solve big problems by attacking core causes and working with multidisciplinary teams using the Social Ecological Model as a template for designing big campaigns.

The Social Ecological Model forces us to focus on more than what one organisation can do, because it requires us to consider five strata of change and leveraging strengths for any issue. You need to work at the individual, interpersonal, organisational, community and policy levels all at the same time to make meaningful progress. This is how the United States changed habits around seatbelt usage and drunk driving, and I believe strongly that it is how we can break cycles around trauma, like poverty, child abuse, crime, poor health outcomes, and even racism just for a start. In the City of Lancaster, after the first year of implementation of our plan to reduce poverty by 50%, we saw the largest single-year reduction of poverty in the city's history; 9% in 1 year. Change is possible, but it requires changes in our paradigms first.

For Lancaster, that meant non-profits, local government and business all working together towards the same end. It meant using the social ecological model to make sure we were working at all five levels. Finally, it meant being relational with people living in poverty instead of transactional; walking alongside them on the journey out of poverty instead of giving them things that just make them more comfortable in poverty. Relationships and healing traumas are the secret ingredients.

Now I am working in the Governor's Office in Pennsylvania, and I have launched an initiative to make Pennsylvania a Trauma-Informed and Healing-Centered State. We will be attacking trauma head on as the lynchpin within these tragic cycles. The key to creating better outcomes for people living in poverty, or struggling with behavioural health challenges, will be working in multi-generational ways to help parents and their children heal from trauma, and taking steps to prevent trauma and toxic stress in the first place.

Because of the COVID-19 pandemic, we will be moving away from the debate over universal screening for trauma and moving to a philosophy of universal healing from trauma, providing tools to parents and high-touch providers like teachers, social workers and paediatricians. We also need to change the nature of children and youth services, policing and the justice system while also fighting for a living minimum wage and universal health care, all issues that create trauma for families when we fail. This will not be easy, but given what is at stake, and what is possible, it is a cause worthy fighting for, regardless of the odds.

'Giving Voice': Communicating with Young People to Enhance Police Legitimacy and Compliance

Shelley Turner

Police are typically the first contact children and young people have in their lives with the criminal justice system. Young people are more likely than adults to come into direct contact with police, as perpetrators or victims of crime, or simply as citizens (Murphy, 2015). The majority of direct police contact with young people occurs on the 'street'—on a footpath or in a public space, like a shopping centre (White, 1994, p. 103). Indirect police contact includes observation or accounts of police encounters from family, friends and the media. Whether the contact occurs directly or indirectly, the police are, in effect, the 'receptionists' of the criminal justice system. That is, they 'welcome' and orient young people to the justice system, explicitly and implicitly setting norms and expectations; the 'rules of the game'. How police behave can influence young people's perceptions of police legitimacy, which impacts their willingness to comply with police directives (Hough, 2021; Ugwudike & Raynor, 2013). Young people's lived experiences of encounters with police are likely to be translated into trust—or distrust—of police (Hough, 2021 p. 20). This matters, as police play a critical role in promoting and protecting public health, and the success of both public health and law enforcement measures is heavily reliant on voluntary compliance (van Dijk et al., 2019; Richards et al., 2006).

Research suggests that young people typically hold less favourable views of the police and police behaviour than adults (Fagan & Tyler, 2005; Hurst & Frank, 2000; Leiber et al., 1998; Piquero et al., 2005). Particular attention should be given to these findings and young people's perceptions of police legitimacy, given their impressionability, vulnerabilities, and the potential for their formative views to cement into adulthood (see Asquith & Bartkowiak-Théron, 2012; Bartkowiak-Théron & Corbo Crehan, 2012; Richards, 2011). Colwell and Huth (2010, p.89) argue that every police–citizen contact offers an opportunity to build community partnerships, but police with '[c]ondescending, contemptuous, and disrespectful attitudes' sour these interactions and generate 'a "self-fulfilling prophesy" that affirms and hardens the contemptuousness of law enforcement'. Similarly, harsh, punitive or coercive strategies employed by police typically generate perceptions of unfairness (Ugwudike & Raynor, 2013), and young people who mistrust the police are more likely to defy law enforcement and public health directives.

A substantial body of research finds that when police behaviour embodies procedural justice, it improves people's perceptions of police legitimacy and compliance with police authority (see Jackson et al., 2013; Mazerolle et al., 2012; Paternoster et al., 1997; Tyler, 1990). Mazerolle et al. (2014, p. 3) summarise the four principles of procedural justice as: 'dignity and respect, trustworthy motives, neutrality, and voice'. This entails treating people with dignity and respect, explaining the reasons for police actions, adopting a non-judgemental approach and listening to and taking fully into account what people have to tell them—or 'playing by the rules' (Tyler, 1990, 2003; Ugwudike & Raynor, 2013). While only a handful of studies have examined the impacts of procedural justice in policing with young people, each provides support for using procedural justice to enhance police legitimacy in the eyes of young people (see Hinds, 2007; Murphy, 2015; Piquero et al., 2005; Reisig & Lloyd, 2009; Reisig et al., 2012; Saarikkomäki, 2016). Notably, an Australian survey of 513 young people and 2611 adults concludes that procedural justice is even more important to young people than it is to adults (Murphy, 2015). So, how can police best apply procedural justice with young people?

The four principles of procedural justice are almost entirely reliant on the actions and attitudes of the individual police officer. However, the fourth principle—*voice*—entails listening to and fully taking into account what young people have to say and this, to a large degree, is dependent on a young person's communication skills. Australian research raises concerns about the poorer than average oral language skills (see Bartels & Richards, 2013; Snow & Powell, 2002, 2004, 2005, 2008, 2011, 2012) of justice-involved young people. Snow and Powell (2002, 2008) compared the oral language skills of male youth justice clients to their non-offending peers. They found that a significant number of the justice-involved males are 'language impaired'; with low expressive vocabulary, poor auditory processing skills, limited understanding of abstract language and difficulties constructing logical and coherent narratives. Snow and Powell (2004, p. 223) conclude that 'young offenders are disadvantaged with respect to their ability to "tell their story"—a task which is fundamental to the police and courtroom interactions required of them'. This has important implications for how police should communicate with young people to achieve the procedural justice principle of 'voice'.

Police need to ensure that, wherever possible, they use short, grammatically simple sentences and modify the complexity of their language, especially to minimise the use of figurative or abstract language (Snow & Powell, 2004). This includes explaining common, abstract legal and public health terms such as 'conditional bail', 'curfew', 'community transmission', 'essential activities' or 'quarantine'. Police also need to be aware that feelings of shame or embarrassment may cause young people to try to cover up their language impairments, by feigning comprehension and using minimal responses like 'yep', 'nup', 'dunno' and 'maybe' (Snow & Powell, 2011). This can be misinterpreted as untrustworthiness, disrespect or caginess (Snow & Powell, 2012). Police should use clarifying strategies to continually and sincerely check the young person's level of understanding, such as asking the same question in different ways, using open-ended questions and paraphrasing content (Snow & Powell, 2004). They should also let a young person know when parts of their story are unclear, inconsistent or lacking in detail. To allow for any reduced processing capacity, police need to provide young people with ample time to respond to questions or directives, particularly since feeling pressured can exacerbate young people's oral communication difficulties (Snow & Powell, 2004, 2012). These approaches can assist police to communicate effectively with young people and to better recognise when a young person may be experiencing language difficulties or require additional support.

The strategies outlined for communicating effectively with young people may not always be feasible in emergency or high-risk situations, where police may need to shout commands and make quick assessments with limited information. Notably, research suggests that young people are able to take such contextual factors into account when assessing the appropriateness of police behaviour and their overall legitimacy (see Saarikkomäki, 2016). However, police must resist adopting a professional persona that constantly operates in a pro-active 'crime-fighter' mode (Dick, 2005; Colwell & Huth, 2010). Instead, police should adopt a more genuine and friendly approach to young people that embodies procedural justice and builds trust. Such a reception for young people can encourage trust and compliance and ultimately may divert young people away from the criminal justice system. These principles are consistent with the consensus that effective communication with young people is characterised by respect, fairness and mutual understanding, as well as participatory approaches that encourage young people to develop agency, autonomy and respect for self and others (see Adler et al., 2016).

References

Adler, J. R., Edwards, S. K., Scally, M., Gill, D., Puniskis, M. J., Gekoski, A., & Horvath, M. (2016). *What works in managing young people who offend? A summary of the international evidence*. Ministry of Justice Analytical Services. https://assets.publishing.service.gov.uk/government/uploads/system/uploads/attachment_data/file/498493/what-works-in-managing-young-people-who-offend.pdfs

Asquith, N., & Bartkowiak-Théron, I. (2012). *Vulnerability and diversity in policing, policing vulnerability*. The Federation Press.

Bartels, L., & Richards, K. (2013). Talking the talk: Therapeutic jurisprudence and oral competence. *Alternative Law Journal, 38*(1), 31–33.

Bartkowiak-Théron, I., & Corbo Crehan, A. (2012). For when equality is given to unequals, the result is inequality: The socio-legal ethics of vulnerable people. In Bartkowiak-Théron & Asquith (Eds.), *Policing vulnerability*. The Federation Press.

Dick, P. (2005). Dirty work designations: How police officers account for their use of coercive force. *Human Relations, 58*(11), 1363–1390.

Colwell, J., & Huth, C. (2010). *Unleashing the power of unconditional respect: Transforming law enforcement and police training*. CRC Press, Taylor & Francis Group.

Fagan, J., & Tyler, T. R. (2005). Legal socialisation of children and adolescents. *Social Justice Research, 18*(3), 217–242. https://doi.org/10.1007/s11211-005-6823-3

Hinds, L. (2007). Building police—Youth relationships: The importance of procedural justice. *Youth Justice, 7*(3), 195–209. https://doi.org/10.1177/1473225407082510

Hough, M. (2021). *Good policing: Trust, legitimacy and authority*. Policy Press.

Hurst, Y. G., & Frank, J. (2000). How kids view cops the nature of juvenile attitudes towards the police. *Journal of Criminal Justice, 28*(3), 189–202. https://doi.org/10.1016/S0047-2352(00)00035-0

Jackson, J., Bradford, B., Hough, M., & Murray, K. (2013). Compliance with the law and policing by consent: Notes on police and legal legitimacy. In A. Crawford & A. Hicklesby (Eds.), *Legitimacy and compliance in criminal justice*. Routledge.

Leiber, M. J., Nalla, M. K., & Farnworth, M. (1998). Explaining juvenile attitudes toward the police. *Justice Quarterly, 15*(1), 151–174. https://doi.org/10.1080/07418829800093671

Mazerolle, L. G., Bennett, S., Antrobus, E., & Eggins, E. (2012). Procedural justice, routine encounters and citizen perceptions of police: Main findings from the Queensland community engagement trial (QCET). *Journal of Experimental Criminology, 8*, 343–367. https://doi.org/10.1007/s11292-012-9160-1

Mazerolle, L. G., Sargeant, E., Cherney, A., Bennett, S., Murphy, K., Antrobus, E., & Martin, P. (2014). *Procedural justice and legitimacy in policing*. Springer.

Murphy, K. (2015). Does procedural justice matter to youth? Comparing adults' and youths' willingness to collaborate with police. *Policing and Society, 25*, 53–76. https://doi.org/10.1080/10439463.2013.802786

Paternoster, R., Bachman, R., Brame, R., & Sherman, L. R. (1997). Do fair procedures matter? The effects of procedural justice on spousal assault. *Law and Society Review, 31*(1), 163–204.

Piquero, A. R., Fagan, J., Mulvey, E. P., Steinberg, L., & Odgers, C. (2005). Developmental trajectories of legal socialisation among serious adolescent offenders. *The Journal of Criminal Law & Criminology, 96*, 267–298.

Reisig, M. D., & Lloyd, C. (2009). Procedural justice, police legitimacy, and helping the police fight crime results from a survey of Jamaican adolescents. *Police Quarterly, 12*, 42–62. https://doi.org/10.1177/1098611108327311

Reisig, M. D., Tankebe, J., & Mesko, G. (2012). Procedural justice, police legitimacy, and public cooperation with the police among young Slovene adults. *Journal of Criminal Justice and Security, 14*, 147–164.

Richards, K. (2011). What makes juvenile offenders different from adult offenders. *Trends and issues in crime and criminal justice*, 409.

Richards, E., Rathbun, K., Brito, C. S., & Luna, A. (2006). *The role of law enforcement in public health emergencies: special considerations for an all-hazards approach*, September 2006, Police Executive Research Forum, Bureau of Justice Assistance, Office of Justice Programs, U.S. Department of Justice. https://www.ncjrs.gov/pdffiles1/bja/214333.pdfs

Saarikkomäki, E. (2016). Perceptions of procedural justice among young people: Narratives of fair treatment in young people's stories of police and security guard interventions. *British Journal of Criminology, 56*(6), 1253–1271. https://doi.org/10.1093/bjc/azv102

Snow, P., & Powell, M. (2002). *The language processing and production skills of young offenders: Implications for enhancing prevention and intervention strategies*. Report to the Criminology Research Council.

Snow, P., & Powell, M. (2004). Interviewing juvenile offenders: The importance of oral language competence. *Current Issues in Criminal Justice, 16*(2), 220–225.

Snow, P., & Powell, M. (2005). What's the story? An exploration of narrative language abilities in male juvenile offenders. *Psychology, Crime & Law, 11*(3), 239–253.

Snow, P., & Powell, M. (2008). Oral language competence, social skills and high-risk boys: What are juvenile offenders trying to tell us. *Children & Society, 22*(1), 16–28.

Snow, P., & Powell, M. (2011). Oral language competence in incarcerated young offenders: Links with offending severity. *International Journal of Speech-Language Pathology, 13*(6), 480–489.

Snow, P., & Powell, M. (2012). Youth (In)justice: Oral language competence in early life and risk for engagement in antisocial behaviour in adolescence. *Trends & Issues in Crime and Criminal Justice, 435*, 421–440.

Tyler, T. (1990). *Why people obey the law*. Yale University Press.

Tyler, T. (2003). Procedural justice, legitimacy, and the effective rule of law. In M. Tonry (Ed.), *Crime and justice: A review of research* (pp. 431–505). University of Chicago Press.

Ugwudike, P., & Raynor, P. (2013). *What works in offender compliance: International perspectives and evidence-based practice*. Palgrave Macmillan.

van Dijk, A. J., Herrington, V., Crofts, N., Breunig, R., Burris, S., Sullivan, H., Middleton, J., Sherman, S., & Thomson, N. (2019). Law enforcement and public health: Recognition and enhancement of joined-up solutions. *The Lancet, 393*(10168), 287–294. https://doi.org/10.1016/S0140-6736(18)32839-3

White, R. (1994). Street life: Police practices and youth behaviour. In E. White & C. Adler (Eds.), *The police and young people in Australia*. Cambridge University Press.

Part II
Law Enforcement and Public Health: Partnerships and Collaborations in Practice

Chapter 7
Improving Community Outcomes and Social Equity Through Leveraged Police Leadership

Norm Taylor, Cal Corley, Dale McFee, and Matthew Torigian

Introduction

We were recently parties to a conversation among some well-placed policing authorities about an upcoming search and selection process to fill the vacancy for a new Chief of Police in a major Canadian city. We readily agreed that across the country, there may be as few as a half-dozen genuinely suitable candidates. Such conversations are not new to us, and we were immediately reminded of similar ones that came to similar conclusions, occurring not more than 10 years ago. It is striking that in a country with over 68,000 highly trained police officers any such candidate stream could be so narrow, then or now. But what really struck us is how different are the reasons that the stream is so narrow today, in contrast to the reasons we had discussed in those similar conversations only a decade ago.

The common narrowing factor in both instances is that among the most senior levels of police leadership, the most sought-after candidates are truly easy to spot. By this stage in their careers, they will have distinguished themselves, much more so

N. Taylor (✉)
Global Network for Community Safety and Journal of Community Safety and Well-being, Toronto, ON, Canada
e-mail: norm@globalcommunitysafety.com

C. Corley
Community Safety Knowledge Network, Ottawa, ON, Canada
e-mail: ccorley@cskacanada.ca

D. McFee
Edmonton Police Service, Edmonton, AB, Canada
e-mail: dale.mcfee@edmontonpolice.ca

M. Torigian
Munk School for Global Affairs and Public Policy, Toronto, ON, Canada
e-mail: matthew.torigian@utoronto.ca

© The Author(s), under exclusive license to Springer Nature Switzerland AG 2022
I. Bartkowiak-Théron et al. (eds.), *Law Enforcement and Public Health*,
https://doi.org/10.1007/978-3-030-83913-0_7

than their peers. They will have exhibited a consistent combination of reliable character traits supported by strategic command choices, alongside policy and operational decisions that grant them almost mythical status, relevant to their times.

What has changed is that those distinguishing decisions and choices, as demanded by today's context, have become vastly different in their nature. Simply put, the star candidates of a decade ago were often hailed as "the cop's cop," a loaded descriptor to be sure. We could devote another chapter entirely to what that has come to mean. In short for now, their myth was mostly constructed on achievements native to and mostly respected by those in their own sector. Today, the short supply of names clearly evident in our recent conversation have each earned their position on this high-prized succession list for the respect they have gained from the communities they serve, and from the ground-breaking work they have done reaching outside of the police sector, as much as within it.

A lot of people can lead an operational crime-fighting command, comprised of loyal members deeply rooted in a paramilitary structure and culture, especially when their leadership chops are ably supported by a recognized rank. Very few, it seems, have the ability to be recognized as a community leader, a leader for all of society, a leader committed to and laser-focused on achieving the broadest community safety and wellbeing outcomes. Progressive police leaders are emerging as those ready to mobilize and help to guide every human service sector, including their own, toward that cause. The mission has changed. Policing today and in the years ahead must be as much about public health as it is about enforcing the law. And with this change in mission, also changed are the requisite character, skills, knowledge, and attitudes for those who are to be invested with unique powers and state authorities and to effectively lead a police organization, today.

In this chapter, we delve into some of those distinguishing leadership characteristics. To be clear, this is not a chapter on "leadership theory." We leave it to others, scholars and practitioners alike, who continue that long respected quest to research and define those general and multi-faceted dimensions that separate success from failure, distinction from mediocrity, and healthy from unhealthy workplaces. Our focus is decidedly on policing, but also on its interfaces and collaborations among other human services. Most apparent to us are the emerging differences in the most vital requirements for police leaders, in all functions of their organizations, amid sweeping social challenges in the post-2020 communities they must serve, protect, and support.

We also recognize that leadership in policing is neither synonymous with nor confined to executive ranks. At current rates of turnover and succession in most developed nations, including Canada, the essential leadership that will guide policing through urgent internal reforms and toward new community relationships is currently being nurtured and applied at every rank level, and among both sworn police officers and a growing proportion of civilian policing professionals. Thus, we have chosen not to limit this discussion to executive police commanders alone, but rather, to learn from evident differences in both the nature and the locus of distinguishing leadership characteristics that are already making a significant difference to police practices while also reshaping police, community, and multi-sector dynamics.

Finally, as evident in the careers of the authors, and reflected in the profiles of our featured case study examples, these changes have not just appeared in the wake of the intersecting crises of 2020, or in direct response to the most recent calls for reform. Rather, the new forms of leadership we examine here have been emerging for more than a decade, and in many ways we will showcase, the calls for reform being amplified today reflect the very initiatives and passions that have defined the careers of all of our profile subjects.

To put somewhat of a base under our observations on change, we begin this chapter with a section that traces and examines the more traditional pathways to leadership in policing that have dominated the past few decades, not only in our home country of Canada, but in many similar policing systems around the world. In addition to the patterns themselves, we also examine the parallel systemic changes that have put increasing tension upon them.

We then take a personal approach to tabling what is different today, departures from those traditional patterns, as each author offers reflections on how new trends and notable distinctions have become evident to them in practice over recent years. We conclude and summarize these reflections by zeroing in on three "distinguishing leadership characteristics" that most clearly depart from those past patterns, and we devote subsequent sections to exploring the meaning, the evidence, and the significance of each.

Alongside these three middle sections we showcase four featured profiles, none of which is limited to a single individual, but rather, permits us to examine the evidence of distinctive characteristics in action, and in the interactions among like-minded and mutually reinforcing teams. Each and every one of these teams has our unbridled respect, and our deep gratitude for their willingness to be held up to the light of our own discussions in this chapter.

We close this chapter by linking back to the general fields of leadership and policing research, education and development. Here, we offer some observations on how these fields may need to recognize and better prepare for the emergence of the distinguishing characteristics we expose, and the growing implications of the social conditions that are increasingly driving them to the surface.

Historical Pathways to Senior Police Leadership

As policing continues to be shaped in response to its evolving operating environment, so too does police leadership. But the dynamic nature of environmental forces, together with the rapid nature of change, is outpacing the abilities of many organizations to adapt. Never before has leadership mattered more. Police leaders today are facing issues and dynamics that could not have been imagined even a decade ago.

This section explores the dominant pathways to senior leadership roles over recent decades. Because many of the vestiges of leadership culture from one era to the next can remain intact for years, we set context with brief depictions of the traditional law enforcement era (also known as the "professional model"—early 1900s to 1970s) and the community policing era which followed and remains the dominant organizing philosophy in policing today.

Context

With its emphasis on patrol, timely response to calls for service and the investigation of crime, the traditional model positioned the police as the "community's professional defense against crime and disorder," with citizens cast as "relatively passive recipients" of services (Kelling, 1988). The traditional model relied on top-down hierarchical management structures supported by command and control systems, policies and procedures. There was distance between the police and communities.

Community policing was borne out of a growing dissatisfaction with the "professional model." The model centers on community and police collaborating to solve local safety problems. Other strategies such as problem-oriented policing, intelligence-led policing, evidence-based policing have fit within this philosophy.

As community policing evolved, new technologies and innovations were transforming how we communicate, supervise, investigate crime and solve complex problems. During this time, societies also began directing more attention to police legitimacy—demanding greater accountability, transparency, and responsiveness from the police.

In Canada, and elsewhere around the world, much of day-to-day policing relates to social problems—not crime. Most of these problems cross the mandates of multiple human service agencies. They are *adaptive problems*. In other words, fixing one part of the problem won't make much difference unless there are corresponding changes in other related areas. There is a growing recognition that integrated multidisciplinary responses are necessary—that organizations focusing only on their perceived part of the problem are ineffective and often counter-productive (Nilson, 2018).

The community policing era—and today's further evolution—require decentralized and flattened organizational structures to support sophisticated adaptation and innovation in collaborating with others to solve complex adaptive problems. This called for new leadership approaches: "The voices for parochial interests are usually much stronger than those for collective responsibility. It requires efficacious, inspiring leadership to create unity within diversity" (Bandura, 1998, p. 68).

Pathways to Senior Leadership: Looking Back and Forward

Among other things, the traditional policing model's rigid paramilitary leadership culture served to:

- impede the quality of problem-solving and decision-making
- promote risk-aversion
- discourage innovation and creativity
- encourage inauthenticity in leaders
- promote low tolerance for ambiguity
- demand unequivocal loyalty to the individual leader
- encourage a common worldview and discourage diverse thinking
- value action over reflection and analysis
- censure internal critics (Stamper, 2006)

Notwithstanding the incongruence with modern requirements, many elements of this leadership culture remain intact today.

While today's most effective senior police leaders are respectful of the past traditions, in our view they are also more forward thinking, innovative and results-oriented leaders who thrive in the discomfort of ambiguity. They flourish in the integrated human services arena—right at the intersection of policing and public health. They understand that sustaining and improving these integrated approaches requires:

- organizational cultures that support higher intersectoral performance
- police leaders with broad strategic perspectives
- trust relationships across partnering agencies
- a respect for—and ability to work with—each other's values, perspectives, and capacities

These leaders are adept at working with others to develop shared visions for change, challenge assumptions and traditional ways of thinking, and influence others across systems to address complex issues. They also foster organizational learning. Finally, they understand the power of organizational culture. In short, these leaders possess exceptional transformational leadership talents (Aust & Laporte-Aust, 2013; Batts et al., 2012; Corley, 2009; Council of Canadian Academies, 2014; Flynn & Herrington, 2015; Guyot, 1991; Lunney, 1988; Schneider, 2000; Senge et al., 1994; Stamper, 2006; Stone & Travis, 2011; Wigfield et al., 1998; Yammarino, 2013).

Why so few? According to Schein (1992, p. 313), "Leaders create cultures, but cultures, in turn, create the next generation of leaders." He notes that a key challenge is how to break the cycle wherein senior leaders define organizational culture, yet the current culture defines the next generation of leaders. Little wonder that nearly 40 years into the community policing era, there are still significant elements of paramilitary command and control culture alive and well. We offer a couple of thoughts.

First, too often in the past, the basic assumptions relied upon as to what made a good leader, combined with a lack of rigor in staffing processes, led to many unqualified people being appointed to senior roles. Often, loyalty was valued much more than competence or anticipated contribution. Today, most police agencies have adopted structured competency-based approaches to recruiting, professional and leadership development, succession, and other human resource processes.

Second, the present context calls for skills and levels of awareness not required (nor developed) in the past. Often, police leaders have lacked a diverse enough background of experience and depth of knowledge to provide quality transformational leadership so necessary today. Until recently policing was a closed system, with limited transparency and public accountability. There was little impetus to seek outside knowledge. Until recently most senior leaders spent their entire careers in one organization. They were managed and promoted through a maze of systems, culture, and internal politics. In certain respects, this limited their perspectives and capacities to change these very organizational elements. Many of today's exemplar leaders have benefited from working outside of their "home" organization—either in another sector or by transferring to another police agency. These opportunities can provide perspectives on policing and police leadership culture they could seldom obtain otherwise.

Finally, today's emphasis on advanced education at all levels of police organizations is providing a strong foundation for improving the depth and breadth of leadership perspectives required for the present context for policing and community safety and wellbeing. Part of the ongoing development of leaders must provide them a more in-depth understanding of organizational culture and its implications during times of change. Such knowledge is important to establishing effective pathways to break the *leadership—culture—future leaders* cycle.

See Table 7.1 for a concise summary of differences in the ongoing evolution of police leadership.

Table 7.1 Comparing then and now in police leadership

Successful senior police leaders (Sources: Aust & LaPorte-Aust, 2013; Lunney, 1988; Stamper, 2006)	
Contemporary	Traditional
Low focus on formal hierarchy	High focus on formal hierarchy
High degree of self-awareness	Not so much
Challenge assumptions and status quo	Respect established orthodoxy—Compliance
Understand organizational culture	Have little understanding of organizational culture
Character-based leadership	Authority-based leadership
Principle driven	Rules bound
Inspire others	Motivate others
Relationship builders	Paternalistic—Silo-oriented
Value diversity	Accept diversity
Evidence and data-informed decisions, involving collective efforts where appropriate	Leader-centered decisions—Often based on personal experience and instinct
"Mistakes are a normal part of learning"	"There is no tolerance for mistakes."
Organizational learning—Everyone a leader	Leadership as a hierarchy with corresponding power
Model desired behaviors	"Do as I say"
Results through teamwork	Results through command
Balance reflection and analysis with action	Action-oriented

The Rapidly Evolving Twenty-First Century Context: Renewing the Policing Mission

In this section, we introduce ourselves as co-authors of this chapter, and in Part I of the section we first set the stage for the discussions to follow by sharing our own personal perspectives and reflections on the changes we have witnessed throughout our respective careers, up to and including the current and complex challenges of 2020, and beyond. We then consolidate these observations and in Part II, where we introduce three distinctive characteristics, each a compilation of traits, attitudes, choices and behaviors, to introduce our more in-depth discussion of each of these in subsequent sections of the chapter.

Our Personal Reflections on Three Decades of Leadership Change

Dale McFee

McFee served for 27 years with the Prince Albert Police Service in central Saskatchewan, Canada, achieving a national profile to become President of the Canadian Association of Chiefs of Police before retiring to become the Deputy Minister of Corrections and Policing for the Saskatchewan provincial government. After 7 years as DM, where he gained global recognition as a game-changing innovator, Dale moved to re-enter policing as the Chief of Police for the Edmonton Police Service in Alberta, where he continues to serve today.

For over 30 years, I have been humbled to have served and to continue to serve within many capacities in the fields of policing, justice, and business. Several years ago, while participating in the Governor General's Leadership Cohort, I had the opportunity to meet Indra Nooyi. Her words, simple yet effective, still resonate with me today: "Being a leader is leaving the team a little better off than if you were not there."

I believe the true measurement of oneself is not simply what you do with your own time and talent, but rather the impact you have on people's development and growth. A leader without followers is simply someone out for a long walk. There is great satisfaction in seeing your people excel, and in many cases, take what you have started to the next level. Invest in people and inspire within them the confidence to fail and learn, and you will receive significant return on your investment.

However, a leader's call to action does not end there. Today's leaders must be adept at both identifying problems and remaining persistent in finding their root cause. Understanding the full value and impact of our actions in turn drives the innovation needed to change the status quo: something that is not possible without partnership. Human services, including policing, rely on external partners to achieve greater success in relation to community safety and wellbeing. Knowing who constitutes your consortium of the willing—the team working with you toward collective outcomes—breaks down silos, begins conversations and gets results. In turn, their voices of influence will ultimately amplify your own, and together, will further the cause of helping those within your community who are most in need of our support and services.

Matt Torigian

Torigian had a successful 29-year career with the Waterloo Regional Police, including seven years as Chief of Police before taking on the role of Deputy Minister of Community Safety for the province of Ontario, Canada. In that role between 2014 and 2018, Matt helped to introduce the first-of-its-kind legislation to mandate collaborative CSWB planning in municipalities across the province, also launching the first major reform of the Police Act in a generation. He now serves as a Distinguished Fellow at the Munk School for Global Affairs and Public Policy.

On many occasions throughout my tenure as a senior police leader, including as Chief of Police, new acquaintances would often remark how surprised they were to hear of my vocation. "You don't act or sound like a chief of police," would be the refrain. I was taken aback as I thought I was "acting" precisely like a chief of police, and thus began my ritual of leadership through reflection. As I reflect back on the role models in my previous police organization, I realize what had happened. A unique mix of innovation, principles, and the professionalization of advocacy was the emerging recipe for effective police leadership. I had great role models and the good fortune of learning within a progressive environment. Failure was accepted because those leaders of the day were confident in the community's support and in their own ability to course correct without losing public credibility. They were viewed as professionals that possessed the visionary principles of community innovators and early adopters.

To abate any criticism of being more politician than cop, some past leaders aligned themselves with the more traditional police colleague, shoring up internal credibility crucial to their success. Many of the core competencies for leadership remained, such as communication skills, strategic thinking, political acuity, and financial literacy. However, it was the introduction of community policing as the overarching ethos for service delivery that helped shape the characteristics for today's leaders. A focus on community can be either a legitimate business practice, or merely an empty, catch-phrased marketing strategy. The difficulty that remains for today's police leaders is breaking free from the capture of parochial structures and a culture that grips at the ankles of progressive change. The evolution from community engagement, community mobilization, through to collaborative community planning and interventions has been slow. The innovations are clear and evident. The professionalism required for today's contemporary police leader is non-negotiable. Still, the principles of multi-agency collaborations, the humility of outcomes-based results, and the value of community impact have yet to be institutionalized in many police services worldwide.

Cal Corley

Corley served with the Royal Canadian Mounted Police for over 35 years, retiring at the rank of Assistant Commissioner in 2014. In his final years he led the Canadian Police College and was the RCMP Senior Envoy to Mexico and the Americas. He has since operated as a strategic advisor in private practice, including overseas supporting policing reform. Cal has also served since 2015 as the first Chief Executive Officer of the Community Safety Knowledge Alliance (CSKA).

These are immensely challenging times for all human services agencies, including the police. Among the environmental shifts currently taking shape I note two important trends. First, broad-based calls for social change are intensifying expectations that the police sector will improve transparency, responsiveness, and accountability, while bringing greater attention to social inclusion and social justice. Secondly, extraordinary levels in government stimulus and other pandemic-related expenditures will bring unparalleled pressure on all public services to dramatically reduce costs. All told, the present situation offers a new launchpad for leaders to fundamentally reorient how policing and community safety and wellbeing are organized and delivered.

As a self-confessed progressive regarding the future of community safety, I have spent many years working with colleagues in the trenches of reform ... my once unbridled optimism tempered by a healthy dose of pragmatism. Notwithstanding, I remain optimistic that we are closer than ever to the tipping point of change. Many of the progressive leaders I know well have developed highly refined transformational leadership skills that they are using to collective advantage. While many of their peers remain struck by inertia, these leaders are driving reform. By extension, they are also building greater change-readiness in their organizations.

Broad adoption of such reforms across the policing sector will not happen by chance. Reflecting upon major police transformations over the past 25 years reminds us that virtually all were introduced from the outside. It took those few progressive and open-minded police leaders who embraced new ideas and led the way, just as the leaders profiled later in this chapter have done. Moving beyond this point will require a critical mass of senior police leaders with transformational leadership competence, diversity of experience, and perseverance to renovate the way policing is conceived. We must continue to encourage these pathfinders and early adopters by continuing to challenge the status quo along with the assumptions that underpin leadership development and succession. The window of opportunity is here for the taking. As progressive leaders respond and show the way, others will follow. Now more than ever, that tipping point is in plain sight.

Norm Taylor

Taylor has practiced as an independent executive advisor and educator for over 40 years, with a concentration in policing for the past 25. In 2002 he co-founded and continues to serve as Program Director for the CACP Executive Global Studies, leading over 200 police leaders into research studies in 50 countries to date. Since 2016 he has also served as the Editor-in-Chief of the peer-reviewed Journal of Community Safety and Well-being. He holds an Honorary Commission in the Ontario Provincial Police.

I consider it a privilege to have shared spaces with senior police executives for 25 years. I have advised a lot of them, coached some through pre-retirement planning, and helped prepare many others both prior to their succession to their highest career ranks and onward into their second careers. I have witnessed the authority they cast in the presence of those under their direct command, along with the influence they wield and the deference they are granted in the company of their peers and others.

In prior decades, such deference was most often evident for the leader who was the most strident defender of his own sector (usually "his" with some notable exceptions), secondary only to his defense of his own agency. Pride in the shoulder flash combined with an evident "own-the-room" attitude to reinforce the paramilitary tradition that, "Here stands the smartest person in the room. Challenge at great risk." The mission with which these leaders identified was equal parts clear and compelling, imbued with the absolute authority of the state, and tightly framed under the "core functions of policing." Those who held most tenaciously to those tenets were the ones to follow and emulate. And, so went the peer pressure to do so.

During the most recent decade, such power-by-rank has rapidly yielded to evident knowledge, insight, and innovation. The wider the scope of the innovation, and the more it carried policing outside of its own remit, and the more it expanded the essential mission to broader social outcomes, the more that whole conference rooms of admirers would seek to join the movements being led by any such leader today. In fact, the term "leader" may even have been replaced. Today's followers tend to align most behind true "champions of change."

Three Distinctive Characteristics that Will Define Police Leadership for a Renewed Mission

From our own combined reflections, we are able to see and highlight the most evident changes in leadership that we have experienced, observed, and tracked toward early and promising successes in leadership that we consider essential to a post-2020 world for policing. Of course, we anchor these in an assumption that successful and influential leaders in policing will continue to draw upon the best of the broader qualities featured prominently in the extant literature on leadership. And, we take as a baseline that they will be transformational in their approach, at every level of the organizations they serve. They will be those who build internal coalitions, craft a shared vision, and inspire others toward it with urgency (Kotter, 1995).

Beyond this, however, in the following sections we condense a number of traits into three distinguishing leadership characteristics that we have come to regard as exceptional and central to success in the current and still-emerging post-2020 era of policing. We devote some discussion to each of these, as follows:

- Leaders with the courage and passion to expand the mission
- Leaders able to shift their focus from positional power to multi-sector influence
- Leaders who develop, serve, and support their own members

Alongside our discussions on each of these characteristics, we also feature four illustrative Profiles in Distinctive Leadership. Each is centered on an innovating team of leaders who have already given proof to these traits as they have successfully embraced a broader upstream-focused mission for policing, operated outside of traditional policing structures, and helped to guide and coach their colleagues through new ways of thinking about the services police must provide to achieve the better outcomes required for individuals, families, and communities amid today's global and local realities.

Leaders with the Courage and Passion to Expand the Mission

Cheryl is a leading figure in her community today. She was also an exceptional high school student in the late 1970s, so much so that the local Rotary Club awarded Cheryl by inducting her as a Rotary Medalist, an honor bestowed upon those that exemplified community service. Cheryl's forward-thinking School Principal of the day worked diligently at trying to convince Cheryl not to accept the award, as a protest against a misogynistic club that didn't allow women to join. Cheryl gave this careful consideration, only to decide instead to accept her well-deserved recognition. Cheryl's award, her acceptance and, frankly, her courage, exemplified transformational leadership, the tenets of which hold true to this day.

Cheryl's decision, and her subsequent actions to change the very system that recognized her, reveal three necessary conditions for courageous leadership. The first is a form of leadership whose journey includes a directional change from long held conventions and policy. An outside-in perspective can at times be intimidating to any culture, and at once also liberating to those caught inside where organizational inertia typically pushes back against the tides of change. In many organizations, culture can be an invisible shield to change. There, meaningful and sustainable change must come from within, even if at times discovered first through an outsider's lens. Such is a tall order for those simply yelling at the castle from the other side of the moat. What a perfect infiltration by Cheryl, one that involved an invitation and a partial lowering of the drawbridge.

Profiles in Distinctive Leadership: Team Scotland

We lead off our case studies in this chapter pretty much where it all began for us. In a decade filled with pivotal moments in change and innovation, our initial and subsequent encounters with Scotland's John Carnochan and Karyn McCluskey have, since the autumn of 2010, inspired and guided our own work across Canada and beyond. As with all our profile subjects, we are certain both Karyn and John would wish to name countless others who have contributed to the sweeping innovations in policy and practice with which they are closely identified. But, the powerful symbiosis this duo achieved while launching the Violence Reduction Unit (VRU) in 2004 remains in clear evidence even in our most recent conversations. Interestingly, both of them insisted that we include one name as their own early champion: then Chief Constable Willy Rae of the Strathclyde Police, where they were both employed at the time. As Karyn put it, among the Chief's many qualities, it was the one thing he lacked that set him apart and set them in motion . . . he did not have "the terror of error."

Since receiving that early encouragement, and still today, Karyn and John have forged ahead tirelessly and broadly, applying their personal and professional insights and influence well beyond the original remit of the VRU. For many of us working to advance collaborative CSWB and LEPH models around the world, these two pioneers have come to be synonymous with those concepts, starting out long before such language was in wide usage. When we asked for their reflections on the new forms of leadership that drove them forward in their cause, here are a few highlights that they generously credited to each other, and also to others who have helped along the way.

The first they cited was the courage to lead "outwith their authority" (a notably Scottish phrasing). The close second was to quickly enlist others in a newly understood mission. For both of these, this necessitated a bold departure for long-serving police leaders, raised up in a strongly prevailing culture of command, control, and stay-in-your-own-lane traditions. The circumstances affecting Scottish communities, particularly those in their Glasgow jurisdictions, while often manifesting as crime and disorder, owed their true origin to socioeconomic conditions. As such, mobilizing new ways to address them immediately took them outside any policing and criminal justice comfort zones.

As John describes from his background perspective as "a straightforward crimefighter," you cannot just show up at a school or an A&E unit and ask the teachers or the doctors to suddenly commit to reducing gang violence. You cannot simply invite them to give their time to advancing your own mandate. Rather, you need to work together, and to begin by asking them what success might look like for Scotland, for their local communities, and for their pupils, patients and their families. They both recalled engaging in such efforts through literally hundreds of presentations and meetings. They considered it a growing

(continued)

success if about 5–10% of those other professionals got on board. As Karyn observed, your role becomes much less about commanding, and much, much more about convincing. They report that over the past 16 years, they have never wavered from that understanding of their role.

By focusing on violence as "a topic to which everyone in Glasgow could easily relate", and as John notes, with Karyn bringing in new forms of data and analysis to bear on its origins and patterns, their growing coalition approach gained early momentum. As just one example, when they could show others, and also show their own policing colleagues, that A&E admissions indicated triple the extent of injuries from violence over what a simply crime-centered approach revealed, every human service sector began to see themselves as part of the required solutions. New language followed closely behind, as a widened public health lens more easily engaged everyone from mental health and child-protection officials to midwives, dentists, and veterinarians.

As for any unique implications for currently servicing police members considering embracing such different leadership roles, they observe that police leaders may in fact possess a certain "swagger" that peer leaders raised up in differing workplace cultures may not. Anyone who has ever had the privilege of meeting John and Karyn, or even just attending one of their presentations, will know immediately what that means.

Once inside, the opportunity to lead comes only with consequential credibility. Recognition from others can often be an immediate validation. In some police organizations, this can be accompanied by a rank or position. In others, it is more discerning and meritorious, similar to a rotary medal. For too many it rests with cliques, or groups formed through bias and parochialism. The mettle to stand firm, armed with a "right to belong," cements a foundation upon which some can begin to build the momentum for change. Some describe this as nurturing followership. Inspiring those around you to walk together toward a new destination touches on the many types of power that scholars and theorists have often cited. Police organizations and members of police services are not homogeneous environs, and there is a danger in viewing all leaders as a single type. The diversity of power bases can stimulate leadership credibility from many parts of the organization. However, many police organizations have also been known to be "closed-shops" where an outside view is met with suspicion and circumspection. Hence, an outside-in dissection, buoyed by internally sanctioned credibility, is the more fertile ground for leading a directional shift.

Many ask why one would enter the castle at all if the reception runs such risk of being cold, frustrating, or worse, even dangerous? Here, Cheryl again provides insight into the weightiest characteristic yet: the power of principles, beliefs, and values. Not everyone walks into an organization, police or otherwise, with the intention of making dramatic or significant change. What may be indisputable is the importance of a nexus between authenticity and sustainability. Cheryl gained more visibility into the world of chauvinism after her acceptance of the medal. Cheryl's voice could be heard within the discriminating walls of Rotary only through her much-earned credibility. Now, once inside, Cheryl's values set about to guide the rest of her journey. Who wouldn't follow?

There are many contemporary police leaders of the day whose stand against discrimination and injustice is borne from their own lived experiences. Their rightful quest is not up for dispute, as society has rallied around and marched forward in unison. The pace of change may be too slow, but the destination remains clear and compelling in its own right. More difficult is a redirection associated with culture and mission. As we have witnessed over the years, and read through many passages, the evolution of policing has travelled along a variety of roads and endured a myriad of iterations. The emerging era for policing is perhaps the most difficult yet to sustain. It requires moving outside of itself and embracing a collective approach to issues of community safety, security, and quality of life, best described as community safety and wellbeing. The antecedent to this is arguably community mobilization, predated by community engagement and enveloped by the overarching era of community policing. At the core, in all its manifestations, is policing-beyond-crime. More pointedly, it is policing-beyond-policing, the internal resistance to which continues to this day.

Profiles in Distinctive Leadership: Two Among Many Upstream Pioneers in Chelsea, MA, USA

A little over 5 years ago, the tiny City of Chelsea, Massachusetts, held the unwelcome honor of topping the list of American cities with the highest per capita incidents of violent crime. At just over 2 square miles, and populated by about 35,000 residents, this dense and charming community looks south across the Mystic River to the City of Boston, and east to Logan International Airport. Today, the community leaders of Chelsea take enormous pride, as they should, in no longer seeing their city on that top 100 list at all. This is no accident of fate. It is the result of non-stop innovations in local civic administration and the adoption of a comprehensive community safety and wellbeing approach that has since been replicated in many other communities across that state and beyond.

Needless to say, there have been many leaders, champions, and committed front-line operators who have driven such rapid success, despite facing continuing factors of marginalization, a relentless spike in opioid overdoses, other ravages of substance use and homelessness, and most recently, a pandemic that has hit this community harder than most. Here, we center our attentions on just two such champions, both members of the Chelsea Police Department, one with a long and diverse operational career, Captain Dave Batchelor, and the other, a civilian with the dual title Community Engagement Specialist and Hub Coordinator, Dan Cortez.

(continued)

In an earlier section, we highlighted the need for progressive police leadership to reach outside of itself to engage sectoral and community partners. Both Dave and Dan credit their Chief Brian Kyes for going one better. By bringing Dan, along with his past successes in grass-roots community mobilization and similar work in health institutions, directly into the department and establishing an ongoing funded position with a clear "engagement" mandate, an ideal synergy was formed with Dave's deep operational credibility and his "in-the-system" range of influence. The passion part, well, that came from both of them as individuals.

Dan and Dave also credit two City Managers, the first being Jay Ash who had the foresight to support their early leadership in the adoption of the Hub, a rapid triage and intervention model imported from central Canada, adapted there from its origins in Glasgow, Scotland, and now in operation in well over 100 communities on both sides of the 49th parallel. And the second is the currently serving Tom Ambrosino, who continues to move the necessary pieces into place to enable the Downtown Task Force, just one among many collaborations that have gained momentum from the early successes of the Chelsea Hub.

To further highlight the distinctive leadership applied in Chelsea outside of policing, they also offer a lot of credit to Roca Inc., and to its founder and CEO Molly Baldwin, for the role that non-government agency has played in the community's adoption of the Hub, among other new and successful public health and restorative approaches to crime and gang violence, improving many other composite health, social, education, and justice indicators in their path.

Both Dave and Dan note that despite a lot of the successes they have helped to drive in Chelsea and beyond, the work never stops. Reflex responses from some local leaders who revert to their siloes are still too evident, especially when a new crisis like COVID arrives, and downstream, pure-enforcement thinking is still very hard to change among their own colleagues in policing. Dave offers, "If I ran the academies, I would introduce upstream thinking at the basic training level." Dan adds, "You have to show your colleagues, inside and outside your own sector, that this thinking will make a positive difference in their own duties, their own workloads, and their own stressors."

These two influencers have continued to refine and tap their own distinctive talents to help many others to better recognize and realize upon that positive difference, inside and well outside of Chelsea.

Any interesting study of leadership might reveal a consistent set of conditions that determines the successful implementation of multi-agency collaborations, designed to address the root causes of crime and social disorder, involving among others, the police. Further, it might reveal a shift in leadership mantra, where local police chiefs advocate for community solutions with a belief that early intervention equates to reduced demand on the justice system, and thus reduced reliance on police services.

In the revelations of any such study, albeit anecdotally, we will no doubt find a not surprisingly similar set of characteristics. The champions of change in almost every instance include police chiefs and selective other significant police leaders, not in isolation, and importantly, not without both. The significance of their leadership influence is in almost all situations cut from the cloth of the successful criminal investigator. And where it is not, police chiefs wisely tap experienced "cops" and present them with a new problem to solve; read: "problem-oriented policing." The inside hears about a new strategy emanating from outside. With positional power as the only brace, two scenarios are then likely to follow. Either the new paradigm will become simply another program within the old ways, or worse, its lifecycle will last only as long as the championing police leader. A second condition is also required.

A sustaining element is the well-cited notion of internal credibility, especially if also well-supported by credibility external to the organization. The leveraging of inspiring leadership, with success and humility, has proven prior transformations and vivid examples of progressive change. An inclusive leader who empowers others, accepting the opinions and wisdom of those around, and focused squarely on the mission at hand. One not focused on the conventional mission of yesterday, but on the new mission, developed as a collective, supported by others, and consistent with this new era of policing. Yet, all this is still not enough.

Finally, the authenticity of a leader, or the absence thereof, will almost always be revealed in a police organization. Change for the sake of change becomes either purely political, or worse, a public relations exercise. Neither can generate sustainable momentum. Neither builds trust or legitimacy. Neither can inspire the necessary cohort of followers that will take the torch and build upon its success. The successful implementation of community safety and wellbeing, and the courage displayed by the innovators and early adopters, is rooted in a principled belief that policing must work in collaboration with community leaders and others for a common good. Heroism (or often, mere egoism) no longer wins the day. This new style of police leader has transformed into a community leader, one among many, firmly ascribing to the adage that it matters not who leads, but more importantly, *who leads when*, a value and belief that must intrinsically reside within.

Cheryl did not win her award for changing the constitution of Rotary Clubs around the world. The change to allow women as members, and today as Club Presidents, was a long-fought battle. But, what Cheryl and others like her started back then, grew into an unstoppable movement toward social equity and inclusion.

The mission shift from reactive "law enforcement" to a more community collaborative on safety and community matters is still underway. What has not changed is the need for Cheryl's type of leadership. This is leadership that requires openness to an outside-in lens, one that demands credible and passionate leaders capable of shifting the mission, and leadership that has *principled values* as a non-negotiable trait.

Leaders Able to Shift from Positional Power to Multi-Sector Influence

A successful police leader's career may be best measured in the number of ah-ha moments that inspire change and innovation. It is such moments through the years that many have credited for driving their pursuit of transformation within the policing world, specifically in the area of community safety and wellbeing. These moments compound in the realization that great leaders have the foresight to look outward, beyond their immediate position, and use their influence across a wider network to share the stage with their counterparts in other sectors. Though these moments may translate into career-defining moments for individual leaders in unique ways, there are a handful of common ingredients worth examining as essential to leveraging leadership across entire systems: forging multi-agency partnerships; the pairing of public and private sector thinking; reverse engineering solutions; and strengthening outcomes through collective data and research.

A decade ago, while at a 3-week police leadership course in Boston, McFee was encouraged by professors from the University of Boston and Harvard to identify the driving force behind increased calls for police service in his home city of Prince Albert, Saskatchewan (PA). This led both McFee and Taylor to lead a multi-agency site visit to Scotland where all of those local PA partners learned about the Violence Reduction Unit (VRU) and its coalition approach to applying a public health lens to that country's then growing crime rate, amid multiple other "indicators of deprivation." Based on that experience overseas, the PA partners established Canada's first "Hub" where they gathered human service agencies together to place those individuals most in need of assistance in their community directly in the middle. They developed a truly human-centered approach that leveraged their collective multi-disciplinary knowledge and resources to prevent such individuals from becoming entrenched and returning again and again to the criminal justice system. With all of the partners at the table working proactively to address initial and repeat contact with the justice system, they soon discovered an ability to fundamentally change the driving forces behind calls for police service, and to provide much better-aligned services with closer-to-real-time responses to people in need (McFee & Taylor, 2014).

Further to the importance of partnership is the advantage of pairing public and private sector institutions together to solve complex and pressing problems. Having been involved with Entrepreneurs International for nearly a decade, McFee recalls the opportunity to work alongside and learn from many influential business colleagues. They challenged him to ensure his own actions as a leader focused on creating value and impact—or as it goes in the business world, the relationship between net dollars versus gross expenditures. In policing, this translates into focusing on balance and connectivity to truly make a difference. Instead of simply doing things because it is how they have always been done, the entrepreneurial mindset calls on leaders to challenge norms, seek innovation, and look for solutions that truly work. This bolder form of leadership looks at the whole picture and examines the available data, research, and historical patterns to work smarter instead of simply working harder.

Equally as important is the concept of reverse engineering, which requires leaders to examine issues from a macro-level rather than becoming fixated on individual, sector-specific aspects. When both McFee and Torigian left their respective positions as police chiefs to join their provincial governments as Deputy Ministers responsible for policing and corrections, they both recognized their new mandates were to lead broader transformational change. However, they each soon discovered that complete transformation is not possible without deconstructing the issues at hand, and thoroughly examining the parts that make up the whole. For example, to fully understand those over-represented groups within the correctional system, and alongside other Federal-Provincial-Territorial counterparts, they identified and analyzed the pathways that had led people there. They found that with those pathways in mind, the entire system could more easily identify how and where interventions could take place to reduce the over-representation of marginalized populations in the system.

Profiles in Distinctive Leadership: Toronto's FOCUS Coordinators, Leading from the Front Lines of Collaboration

We introduced earlier in this chapter Schein's (1992) observations on the *leadership—culture—future leaders cycle* and its tendency to impede change while perpetuating stubborn cultural patterns in policing organizations. The three police leaders we profile here offer an encouraging argument that such a predictable cycle can indeed be broken, and historical and cultural leadership artifacts can yield to new and innovative ways of doing business.

In the spring of 2012, then-Sergeant and now Acting Superintendent Gregory Watts represented the Toronto Police Service (TPS) as part of a small delegation that travelled to Prince Albert, Saskatchewan, to examine the early success and promise of their Community Mobilization model, one that combines a risk-driven collaborative intervention with data-driven systemic change, operating in that small city for just over a year at that time (McFee & Taylor, 2014). Anyone familiar with Toronto's country-wide epithet as "the center of the universe" will recognize the courage it took for Greg and his colleagues to even consider suggesting the big-city adoption of any solution conceived and led by a small-town prairie police service. But within weeks, Toronto had launched its first neighborhood FOCUS Table (an acronym for Furthering Our Communities Uniting Services). Greg served as the first TPS FOCUS Toronto Coordinator, sharing an entirely new *lead-from-the-front-lines* mobilization role with two partner-agency colleagues in similar roles, Scott McKean (City of Toronto) and Jamie Robinson (United Way Toronto).

A year or so later, Greg passed the TPS torch to Sergeant Donovan Locke, and in turn, it passed again in 2016 to Detective Brian Smith who continues in

(continued)

the Coordinator role today. In the intervening 8 years, these three leaders have helped to grow FOCUS into a city-wide multi-sector community collaborative with the active participation of 130 agencies and with triage and intervention "tables" serving 8 distinct police divisions across Canada's largest city. The FOCUS team also played a leading role in nation-wide adaptations to the model necessary to include upstream action on countering violent extremism (CVE).

When asked how three Sergeants have been able to achieve such outcomes, Greg offers, "From the very beginning, and not just for me in policing but also for Scott and Jamie, we knew our job would be to 'manage-up' every single day." In other words, if there were to be barriers to adoption and success, their instincts and experience told them they would come from the higher-placed authorities in every sector. They learned early, he added, that they could actually leverage each other to avoid direct vertical confrontations in their respective sectors. And, where community agencies might be uncomfortable taking guidance from a police sergeant, some responded very well to a leader like Jamie, coming from an influential community-based organization (CBO). Others benefited from the municipal government levers that Scott had at his disposal, with strong connections right into the Office of the Mayor.

Subsequently, Donovan and then Brian led the ongoing expansion to other active tables. Brian notes, "People tend to think of policing as a top-down structure. We discovered that when it comes to innovation, it is much more bottom-up in reality. We brief the multi-sector Steering Committee, and if they like the directions we are proposing and the evidence we are bringing them, the higher ranks in each organization tend to listen as well. Once in a while you need the power of your Superintendent or Deputy Chief to dislodge something, but that is required much more rarely than one might think." Truly good ideas tend to derive a lot of support, it seems, especially when they are working to the satisfaction of corresponding executives in 120 different agencies across the city. But, Donovan also notes, "It won't happen without tireless, collaborative efforts from those closest to the innovation, applied together, and working simultaneously across multiple organizational frontiers."

All three leaders agree that getting yourself and others to see people's challenges outside of their police lens has been vital to the success of the collaborative model. Supported by the profile of FOCUS, TPS has engaged about 100 of its neighborhood community officers, deployed across 21 neighborhoods, who now form part of the forward face of 60–70% of the composite risk situations triaged at the tables. Or as Brian puts it, "They are our rock stars that the other agencies trust and with whom they enjoy collaborating." In other words, they might just be another 100 front-line police leaders who will help to break Schein's cycle.

Central to making informed leadership decisions is the power of using data and research to create connections across larger systems. Years of police collaboration with the Canadian Centre for Justice Statistics (CCJS) at Statistics Canada have demonstrated how data—when used for the right purposes—can strengthen solutions and outcomes by demonstrating clear ties between areas of health and justice where marginalized populations are involved. In fact, it builds a strong case that the social determinants of health and the social determinants of criminal justice are one and the same. When examined through multiple lenses, the available datasets also show a distinct difference between those who drive the majority of initial calls for police service, and those who disproportionately drive re-contact with the justice system.

Sheldon Kennedy, our colleague and a widely respected advocate for violence and abuse prevention programs, has often said, "To know better is to do better." The world of policing finds itself in a unique time where mounting death inquests, economic downturn, the COVID-19 pandemic, and the tragedy of George Floyd (among too many others) have highlighted a need for agencies to come together in addressing community safety and wellbeing as a larger systemic change. We have an opportunity and considerable promise to bring greater balance into policing and public health outcomes through partnerships with a "collective outcomes" focus. Police leaders can no longer remain tied to the status quo that has historically functioned to separate our interests and to keep conversations inside our respective siloes. The time for change is long-past due and it is incumbent upon leaders of today and tomorrow to not only call their structures into question, but to completely rearrange them where necessary. This opportunity can be seized by developing a "consortium of the willing": a broader leadership group that will take the necessary calculated risks knowing that we may not always get it right. Our own character will show in the humility it takes to step outside of our comfort zones—the individual corners of the system we have come to know so well—and to connect with those beyond our immediate surroundings who can further our common cause. Such actions will reflect a solid and shared investment in community safety and wellbeing by prioritizing demand reduction and working ourselves out of a job, versus protecting our jobs. What we can most look forward to is the potential that such current and future police leaders will hold, not solely in their own hands, but together in the hands of many others.

Leaders Who Develop, Serve, and Support Their Own Members

Anyone who has ever coached elite athletes, will readily explain that the role of the coach is to elicit, guide, nurture, and support the native talents of those athletes, such that the athletes can consistently deliver and execute the best version of themselves to the game. This may require the coach to apply strategic and tactical direction, and to impose and monitor discipline. It will also require that the coach watch and listen constantly, to pay exacting attention to the needs, strengths, weaknesses, and stressors of each and every athlete on the team. What it never requires is fealty to the coach, nor fealty to earlier stars of the sport.

Imagine a coach of a sports team whose response to any and every criticism of the team's performance was to say, "Don't worry team, I won't ever let these critics get away with saying our offense is outdated, our passing is clumsy, our running is slow, and our kickers cannot hit the net on a good day." The athletes might adore such a protective coach for a short while, but they will most likely, and very soon, grow weary of never winning the game.

Ultimately, in discussions about progressive leadership, we find an emerging story about evident humility. And in that, it is a story for our times from which today's most promising and ultimately successful police leaders will learn. No other single trait is more essential, and yet so scarce, among too many of the leaders who have continued to grab the brass rings in succession to the power ranks in policing, even today. To meet the demands for service, the calls for reform, the inevitable new pressures on resources and budgets, and to regain the public trust that has been too casually presumed and thus greatly eroded, will require policing as a sector, and everyone courageous enough to lead, to think and act with evident humility like never before.

It is encouraging to see the concepts of servant leadership taking a more prominent place on the menus of police leadership development programs. Sylven and Crippen (2018) note that at its core, the premise of servant leadership is that a leader's focus is first and foremost on serving the highest order needs of his or her followers.

They go on to cite Van Dierendonck (2011) who summarized servant leadership models into six overarching characteristics that are repeatedly perceived from the point of view of followers (pp. 1232–1234). These were: (a) empowerment and development of others; (b) humility; (c) authenticity; (d) interpersonal acceptance; (e) providing direction; and (f) stewardship.

In his own early essays, Greenleaf (1977/2002) asked of leaders, "Do those served grow as persons? Do they, while being served, become healthier, wiser, freer, more autonomous, more likely themselves to become servants? And, what is the effect on the least privileged in society? Will they benefit or at least not be further deprived?" (p. 27) These questions seem prescient as police continue to navigate and adjust their roles and relationships amid a troubled society almost a half century later. In a more recent assertion, Baldomir and Hood (2016) offer that only when leaders fully accept their role as stewards of their organizations, will followers have what they need to successfully navigate the difficult changes they must face.

Thus more than ever before, for the sake of the health and wellbeing of their members, successful police executives will be those who quickly recognize and abandon the folly of continuing to model a defensive reflex in the face of community-driven demands for long-overdue changes in policy, practice, and in the essential culture of the policing profession. For the sector as a whole and for any single police agency to truly rise to meet the challenges of a post-2020 society, police leaders will be ready to respond with maturity and with the ethical responsibility to finally confront and dismantle the intractable traces of colonialism and systemic racism that plague their communities, and yes, which also infect their organizations.

They will also be ready to amplify others' voices, and to mobilize the entire state-led and community-based system to work collaboratively to reduce the broader factors of marginalization that truly drive the disproportionate demands upon their service delivery to many of those same communities. It is these same relentless demands that have led police members to distrust the communities whose wellbeing they are meant to serve. Trust is fragile, and to thrive, it must be reciprocal (CACP, 2017). Instead, lingering adherence to simplistic notions of "law enforcement" and "crime prevention," with their attendant "catch and release" and "revolving door" approaches to criminal justice, all relics of the "professional policing" era from decades ago, have driven a wedge between police and those who need them most, while driving frustration and stress levels to a breaking point for far too many police professionals.

Thus, successful leaders will also be ready to dedicate themselves, with frank honesty and compassionate expression, to serve and support the new learning, listening, and adapting that all their members will be required to undertake. At the same time, they will steadfastly direct their organizational systems and supports toward building "authentically inclusive" workplaces (CACP, 2018), and to the continued mental health, wellbeing, and resilience of those dedicated members who join and serve in the policing profession to the continuing benefit of an inclusive, healthy and prosperous society. In 2019, Ontario's Office of the Chief Coroner examined not only the most tragic outcomes, but the full scope of upstream mental health issues that are in growing evidence in police organizations. That report argues for "a new policing culture . . . where the full cycle of prevention, recognition, appropriate disclosure, care and treatment, recovery and reintegration can occur with greater openness, greater success, and without repercussion to anyone facing mental health challenges whether due to operational or organizational stressors, *or from any other cause inside or outside of work*. [emphasis added]" (Ontario, 2019).

In short, tomorrow's police leaders will rise to great influence both within and well beyond the narrow concept of "law enforcement." They will be those that have recognized that, like charity, "public health" starts at home.

Some Concluding Observations

We made a conscious choice to direct the foregoing discussions in this chapter toward the distinctive characteristics of police leadership that most closely align with emerging collaborative approaches to community safety and wellbeing (CSWB). And, we acknowledge that our narrative leans very much toward the intersections among law enforcement and public health (LEPH). We regard the former (LE) as a proxy term for the full criminal justice apparatus, and the latter (PH) encompassing a broader system of public policy and related infrastructure designed to respond to both immediately evident and underlying health, social, economic, environmental, education, employment and early childhood development factors among others.

In no way do we intend to ignore the very real demands for the operational leadership that more directly connects policing to national security and criminal justice concerns, and which guides successful police actions in many ongoing functions including criminal investigations, traffic enforcement, cybercrime, public order, emergency response, and assistance to victims of crime. Rather, our view is that policing systems in Canada and in many other countries already invest heavily in developing such leadership capacities, and as a result, can with few exceptions take continuing pride in those operational achievements.

We also note that some of the emerging collaborative practices and specific CSWB models that helped to shape this chapter have yet to receive the full benefit of study and validation they may require, and we encourage researchers to continue to seek ways of developing a solid evidence-base that will ensure confidence in their adoption and sustainability in their execution. However, that such practices have already met the threshold of promising practice is undeniable in our own view, and this is also reflected in the committed global engagement among a growing community of CSWB and LEPH scholars and practitioners.

Thus, while firmly anchored in decades of literature that will no doubt continue to guide leadership development in policing, our foregoing discussion intentionally steps off into what is different today, and what we believe to be essential to tomorrow. Over the past decade, in Canada and elsewhere, governments, community-based organizations, the private sector, and academia already have been thinking differently about how policing and related human services are organized and delivered to achieve improved outcomes for at-risk individuals, families, and communities.

Now, as we enter a post-2020 world, we can see more than ever before that most of the vexing problems that will face our communities will not fit nicely within the mandate or realm of any single organization, and traditional structures will not easily align with most of the pressing issues affecting at-risk individuals, families, and communities. The clear consensus is that more integrated, multi-disciplinary approaches focused both in the present and upstream are essential if real improvements are to occur.

It should not be surprising that policing—and community safety more broadly—must enter a period of significant transition—perhaps to Community Policing 3.0. History has shown that such periods of transition are marked by considerable experimentation and a challenging of traditional ways of doing things (Kempa, 2014). The progressive leaders we have profiled in this chapter are challenging the status quo and shaping new approaches for working across disciplines and sectors to markedly improve community safety and wellbeing outcomes, and to set the foundations for further and long-overdue social reforms. Such leadership during such transitionary times is not for the faint of heart. We are inspired by the leadership these and others have shown. We hope their stories will inspire our readers to have the courage to move forward in similar fashions.

Without question, we remain optimistic that by bringing its own leadership into closer alignment with an updated worldview, policing can do much to realign our collective public investments and to better harness state and community-based efforts in response to the most urgent health, economic, wellbeing, and social equity challenges facing communities around the world, in the current circumstances and in the decades to come.

References

Aust, A., & Laporte-Aust, T. (2013). *Reflections on police independence and culture.* (unpublished manuscript). Submission to Canadian Association of Chiefs of Police, 15 January 2013.

Baldomir, J., & Hood, J. P. (2016). Servant leadership as a framework for organizational change. *International Leadership Journal, 8*(1), 27–41.

Bandura, A. (1998). Personal and collective efficacy in human adaptation and change. In J. G. Adair, D. Bélanger, & K. L. Dion (Eds.), *Advances in psychological science* (Social, personal, and cultural aspects) (Vol. 1, pp. 51–71). Psychology Press/Erlbaum Taylor & Francis.

Batts, A. W., Smoot, S. M., & Scrivner, E. (2012). Police leadership challenges in a changing world. *New Perspectives in Policing.* https://www.ncjrs.gov/App/Publications/abstract.aspx?ID=260382

CACP. (2017). *Trust matters: A summary report on the proceedings and outcomes of the 10th cohort of CACP Executive Global Studies.* Canadian Association of Chiefs of Police.

CACP. (2018). *Diversity is a Canadian reality: Inclusion is a choice. A summary report on the proceedings and research outcomes of the 11th cohort of CACP Executive Global Studies.* Canadian Association of Chiefs of Police.

Corley, C. (2009). Police executive development: Leadership matters. *Canadian Association of Chiefs of Police Journal, 2009,* 14–16. https://www.securitepublique.gc.ca/lbrr/archives/cnmcs-plcng/cacp-cpcm-rcpc-2009f.pdf

Council of Canadian Academies. (2014). *Policing Canada in the 21ˢᵗ Century: New policing for new challenges.*

Flynn, E. A., & Herrington, V. (2015). *Toward a profession of police leadership.* New Perspectives in Policing. Harvard Kennedy School.

Greenleaf, R. (2002). *Servant-leadership: A journey into the nature of legitimate power and greatness.* Paulist Press.

Guyot, D. (1991). Bending granite: Attempts to change the rank structure of American police departments. *Journal of Police Science and Administration, 7,* 253–284.

Kelling, G. (1988). *Police and Communities: The Quiet Revolution.* Perspectives on Policing. Harvard Kennedy School.

Kempa, M. (2014). *Understanding the Historical Relationship between Economics and Change in Policing: A Policy Framework.* Ottawa (ON): Canadian Police College.

Kotter, J. P. (1995). *Leading change.* Harvard Business Review Press.

Lunney, R. F. (1988). Police management: The past twenty years and the next twenty. *Canadian Police College Journal, 12*(1).

Nilson, C. (2018). Community safety and Well-being: Concept, practice, and alignment (LEPH2018). *Journal of Community Safety and Well-Being, 3*(3), 96–104. https://doi.org/10.35502/jcswb.81

McFee, D. R. & Taylor, N. E. (2014). *The Prince Albert Hub and the Emergence of Collaborative Risk-Driven Community Safety.* Ottawa (ON): Canadian Police College.

Ontario. (2019). *Staying visible, staying connected, for life.* Report of the Ontario Chief Coroner's expert panel on police officer deaths by suicide. Queen's Press.

Schein, E. H. (1992). *Organizational culture and leadership*. Jossey-Bass.

Schneider, W. E. (2000). Why Good Management Ideas Fail: The neglected power of organizational culture. *Strategy and Leadership, 28*(1), 24–29.

Senge, P., Kleiner, A., Roberts, C., Ross, R., & Smith, B. (1994). *The fifth discipline fieldbook: Strategies and tools for building a learning organization*. Penguin Random House.

Stamper, N. (2006). *Breaking rank: A top cop's exposé of the dark side of American policing*. Bold Type Books.

Stone, C., & Travis, J. (2011). *Toward a new professionalism in policing*. New Perspectives in Policing. Harvard Kennedy School.

Sylven, L., & Crippen, C. (2018). First to serve and protect, then to lead: Exploring servant leadership as a foundation for Canadian policing. *Journal of Community Safety and Well-Being, 3*(2), 22–26. https://doi.org/10.35502/jcswb.77

Van Dierendonck, D. (2011). Servant leadership: A review and synthesis. *Journal of Management, 37*. https://doi.org/10.1177/0149206310380462

Wigfield, D., Burton, C., Aitchison, D., & Knill, L. (1998). Developing leaders in the police service. *The Police Journal, 71*(2), 99–108. https://doi.org/10.1177/0032258X9807100202

Yammarino, F. (2013). Leadership: Past, present and future. *Journal of Leadership & Organizational Studies, 20*(2), 149–155.

Chapter 8
Law Enforcement and Mental Health: The Missing Middle

Stuart Thomas, Chris White, Nadine Dougall, and Inga Heyman

Introduction

Over the last 30 years there has been increasing global recognition of the high prevalence of mental health conditions and the impacts this can have on individuals, communities and economies. Stigma, public attitudes, economic constraints, service availability and public policy all impact on the level of mental health treatment available within societies and, in turn, on people's inclinations and ability to access services. One group that is beginning to receive more attention have been termed the 'missing middle'; people who have mild to moderate levels of mental health need who commonly fall between the gaps of health services delivery. This is a group in need of more help and support than they can readily access in the community, but their level of need does not routinely or consistently reach the threshold of going to hospital.

This chapter starts by considering what mental distress is and how it can manifest, then explores the associations between social determinants of health and the experience of distress. Next the chapter navigates how, why and to what extent the police find themselves involved in responding to people in mental distress, focussing on the interface with the emergency department (ED). Finally, the chapter examines the challenges experienced by people navigating this space and questions whether, in light of the significant downfalls of the current health responses, a different service response if required to better meet the needs of this missing middle. A lived

S. Thomas (✉)
RMIT University, Melbourne, Australia
e-mail: stuartdm.thomas@rmit.edu.au

C. White
Mental Health Foundation, Edinburgh, UK

N. Dougall · I. Heyman
Edinburgh Napier University, Edinburgh, UK

experience reflection is provided at specific junctures of the chapter to bring to life some of the challenges experienced when interfacing with our health and justice system when experiencing mental distress.

What Is Mental Distress?

There are various ways of measuring the prevalence of mental illness across populations. Estimated rates reported include that 1 in 4 people will experience a mental health condition at any one time, around 1 in 8 people will actually receive mental health treatment at any one time (at least in economically developed countries), and as many as 1 in 2 people will experience mental illness at some point in their lives. While the majority of people will access mental health-related treatment through planned primary care pathways, such as their local General Practitioner, others will experience a significant mental health crisis or a level of distress that can lead them to need to access services in an unplanned way.

Broadly speaking, it can be argued that there are three main 'groups' of people who experience mental distress. There are those who access/receive specialist mental healthcare or treatment, those who receive support from primary care services, and those who fall somewhere in between; in this chapter we refer to the latter group as the 'missing middle'. Attempts to quantify the size and scale of these groups is actually not a straightforward task. What we do know, however, is that mental distress varies in severity and duration; and further that only somewhere between a third and a half of those eligible to receive mental health-related supports do so in any given year (AIHW, 2020, p. 5).

Distress has been defined as 'a state of emotional suffering associated with stressors and demands that are difficult to cope with in daily life'; individuals may have symptoms of distress in relation to 'everyday life struggles', 'feeling inferior to others', or 'losing a grip on life' (Arvidsdotter et al., 2016). Conversely, people can feel that their 'whole world is caving in' (Geraghty et al., 2016), with acute psychological distress directly associated with a perceived helplessness to cope with serious life stressors. However, symptoms of psychological distress may also occur independently of stressful life events.

Symptoms of distress are also highly variable, and their causes are unique and complex; frequently they stem from significant life events and social causes such as failed relationships, unemployment, perceived lack of mobility, work and family conflicts (Horwitz 2007). Psychological distress may persist, with worsening symptoms that may become enduring and clinically significant, sometimes to the extent that they interfere with activities of daily living. Some individuals are pre-disposed to being more vulnerable, and less resilient to life events in adulthood, contributing to the distress they experience (Masten, 2011).

For some, the experience of mental distress is a one off or short-term occurrence, although the severity of distress can still vary; others will experience more than one, and often several episodes of distress over a prolonged period of time. How people find themselves accessing crisis services is also highly variable; some may self-refer, or health or emergency services may be alerted by a friend/family member or a concerned member of the public. These referral routes may all indicate a different service response and need. There is increasing acknowledgement that frequent presentation to the ED is associated with both socioeconomic disadvantage and a significant burden of disease (Kahan et al., 2016). While presentation at an ED can lead to psychiatric referral and then admission to mental health services, for the vast majority this is not an available pathway with high admission thresholds precluding many from receiving this service response. There can be very good reasons to try to keep people out of acute psychiatric care, with admissions doing more harm than good (e.g. VLA, 2020). However, for many who present to the ED in mental distress, there may not be a timely or appropriate support available.

We know that people who experience mental distress may present to the ED for emergency treatment and support, or also as a point of access to other service pathways (Minshall et al., 2020). Evidence gleaned from research studies internationally also indicates that a small number of people account for a disproportionate number of emergency presentations (Wise-Harris et al., 2017); many of these presentations represent the 'missing middle'. While this group are heterogeneous, they commonly perceive and/or experience significant stigmatising attitudes and behaviours, as well as structural discrimination from the very health services they are seeking help and support from (Perry et al., 2020). This next section explores factors related to why some people can and do lead more complex lives, why they experience more distress and why they may be perceived as additionally vulnerable by the various agencies they come in contact with.

Multiple Disadvantage and the Social Determinants of Health

Within recent decades, the role of social inequalities and their detrimental effect on health outcomes has grown in increasing prominence. Strong relationships have been demonstrated between poverty and health inequalities, with the conditions that people grow, live and work known as the social determinants of health (e.g. Marmot & Wilkinson, 2000).

Studies of early life adversity and its impact on later adulthood have been well documented. In a landmark study, Felitti et al. (1998) reported that four or more adverse childhood experiences (ACEs) were reported to be linked to 4- to 12-fold increases in alcohol misuse, drug abuse, depression and suicide attempts. Multiple studies published since have confirmed the relationship between ACEs and a wide range of negative health outcomes in adulthood (Hughes et al., 2017). In short, these studies suggest that neglect, sexual, physical and emotional abuse in childhood are related to an increase in depression, anxiety, drug use, suicidal behaviour and attempts in adulthood. Robust international evidence also adds that adulthood mental distress is exacerbated by the extent and types of childhood adversity experienced.

Poorer socioeconomic status and inequality have been found to at least partially explain poorer health outcomes, with around 15–20% of the association of poor health risks in adulthood for those with high numbers of ACEs being explained by (poor) socioeconomic circumstances in adulthood. The three ACEs of domestic violence, parental divorce, and living with someone once incarcerated, are almost entirely explained by socioeconomic circumstances (Font & Maguire-Jack, 2016). However, ACEs characterised as physical, emotional and sexual abuse have been reported to be associated with many adult health risks not adequately explained by socioeconomic status alone. Cohort studies, tracking people prospectively over time, have found ACEs associated with lower educational attainment, and higher risk of depression, substance use and use of tobacco; while those with four or more ACEs reported 2.4 times more diagnoses of depression, and 3.1 times more substance-use that persisted, after taking into account the effects of various family and socioeconomic factors (Houtepen et al., 2020). A recent systematic review and meta-analysis of 37 published studies confirmed that having multiple ACEs was a major risk factor for many adverse health outcomes, noting that the strongest associations were for problematic drug use, interpersonal and self-directed violence (Hughes et al., 2017); sexual risk-taking, mental ill-health and problematic alcohol use also featured prominently.

Many susceptible individuals with multiple ACEs, living in disadvantaged communities, exposed to social inequality, can face particularly challenging circumstances that make them more likely to be exposed to our health and justice systems. This necessitates a public health approach to health and justice, with attention paid to prevention of harm, and addressing the panoply of complex social issues present in people's lives. Cumulatively, what we now know is that the people who frequently present to EDs, and those who have ongoing unmet healthcare needs due to a lack of access to these services are, on the whole, the same people from the same communities as those who become justice involved (Crofts & Thomas, 2018). The next section considers how, and in what contexts, people who experience mental distress come into contact with the police and how the nature and extent of these encounters can lead to potentially very different health and/or justice pathways.

The Role of the Police in Responding to Mental Health-Related Incidents

It has long been recognised that the police are pivotal in determining the health and criminal justice trajectories of people they come into contact with (Lamb et al., 2002); in this way, some have described the police as providing the 'gateway to appropriate care' (Adebowale, 2013, p. 6). In recent years, there has been increased recognition that mental health should be considered core business for the police (Thomas & Watson, 2017). At the same time, policing services report that the demands being placed on them in responding to mental health calls are at an 'intolerable' level (HMICFRS, 2018, p. 3). A good part of the reason that the police remain centrally involved in responding to mental health-related situations is that it is their legal obligation to respond to calls for assistance and provide services 24 h a day, 7 days a week. Because of this, they are often the first and, more often than not, the only community response available (Lamb et al., 2002).

Despite this, the true extent of mental health-related calls that the police respond to remains difficult to ascertain (McGeough & Foster, 2018); international research estimates, based on official records or frontline officer estimates, suggests that this part of their role consumes somewhere to up to 20% of police time (Thomas & Kesic, 2020). The actual figure is likely to be much higher. The fundamental question about whether police should be involved at all in mental health-related matters remains moot here; police contacts-based statistics clearly demonstrate the significant role policing services have had, and continue to have, in responding to mental health-related calls. However, it is well-established that the police statistics do not adequately capture contemporary police functions and tasks (Davis et al., 2015). For example, a significant area of police work is said to involve conducting 'welfare checks' on people in the community; these checks require police to locate a person to make sure they are safe (e.g. Department of Health and Human Services [DHHS], 2016, p. 15) and can be requested in response to a wide range of concerns that community members (or health workers) may have about the personal safety of an individual. While, anecdotally speaking, police suggest that this forms a significant part of their role, there has been very little written about it, nor attempts to quantify or otherwise measure the extent of this type of policing work. Piecing together the available anecdotal evidence and commentary, it suggests that a significant proportion of this involves responding to situations where the person is experiencing mental distress and presenting as a risk to their own safety.

What does appear clear is that, due to the complex, multidimensional and inter-generational histories and presenting challenges of people who experience mental distress, no one service is adequately equipped to respond (van Dijk et al., 2019). Indeed, for some time now, many agree that both the policing and emergency mental health system need to work in partnership to adequately respond to people experiencing a mental health crisis (Lamb et al., 2002). One area of particular (vexed) focus has been on the nature and extent of their role in transporting people to the ED. It is now generally accepted that the police should only be used as a means of transportation for a person experiencing a mental health crisis as a last resort, when all other options have been considered and ruled out. This stance is based on basic principles of basic dignity and human rights (Boscarato et al., 2015). What is especially worrying, in this respect therefore, are (now dated) estimates that suggest that up to 30% of mental health presentations to EDs are the result of police referral (Lee et al., 2008); either with police escorting an ambulance, or directly transporting the person when an ambulance isn't available or where safety issues preclude an alternative response. An Australian study (Short et al., 2014) found that despite the last resort mantra, once police were involved, they were most commonly the ones used to transport the person for further assessment. Another Australian-based study reported a substantial increase in the proportion of mental health-related presentations brought in by police, comparing rates recorded in 2003 to those in 2013 (Alarcon Manchego et al., 2015).

There is also a connected resourcing issue here with limited numbers of ambulances being available, coupled with high demand in densely populated areas. Those patients assessed as being in serious critical need are prioritised, which can lead to long wait times in accessing supports for people experiencing mental distress. Furthermore, there is also evidence that people living in more regional and rural areas are also more likely to transported to ED by police due to a lack of availability of ambulances (VLA, 2020). While this may simply be a pragmatic decision, aimed at getting the person to care and treatment, it also, in part, criminalises mental distress.

While people are not always transported to an ED for assessment and can find themselves being taken directly to a psychiatric service or into police custody (Short et al., 2014), one of the more practical challenges reported by police has been the wait time at ED and substantial knock-on effect of having less police resources to respond to subsequent incidents. Some jurisdictions have developed agreements between police and health services so that there are no delays in handover by police to health at the ED (Steadman et al., 2001), but this is uncommon. Most jurisdictions require police to remain with the person in the ED until they have been assessed by ED staff; indeed, their release from police custody and formal handover to ED staff needs to be based on the mutual agreement of the police and health staff present that there are 'no significant safety risks or concerns for themselves or others' (DHHS, 2016, p. 11). Essentially, the person remains in police custody until the ED staff accept the custody of that person. A perennial problem reported by police in these matters is that the low priority given to these cases in the triage process leading to protracted delays for police at the ED precluding them from responding to further calls for assistance. However, from an ED clinician perspective, the high rates of intoxication found among those brought in by the police impedes thorough assessment of wellbeing and risk (Zisman & O'Brien, 2015); nursing staff also commonly report being concerned about the person absconding and committing another act of self-harm, as well as feeling uneasy around people who could be violent, aggressive or unstable (Doyle et al., 2007).

In a number of jurisdictions, there is a four-hour limit imposed or aspired to; reports from Scotland and Australia suggest that the majority of those referred to the ED by police are seen within 2 h (McGeough & Foster, 2018; Short et al., 2014); the Scottish report notes that the target is for 95% of ED patients to be either admitted, transferred or discharged in 4 h. International reviews have frequently commented on the need to expedite the transfer of care. The Iacobucci Report (2014, p. 12) noted wait times in Toronto, Canada of up to 8 h, and speaks of the lengthy procedures as being 'an obstacle to efficient care for people in crisis, and symptomatic of the uncoordinated relationship between the police and the mental health system' (p. 101).

In distress I was always scared of what would happen. Sometimes I would drink in the hope that it would dampen the distress. But then either I would make a drunken call or a member of the public would be so concerned about me they would call. The police would take me to

ED. I would be told I wouldn't be assessed until I was sober. I was never aggressive towards staff, but the police would remain until i was assessed, which could be hours later.

Another significant frustration reported by police relates to the threshold for admission to public mental health services; this threshold being so high as to exclude the vast majority of those who present to services in need of assistance. While some jurisdictions have developed an 'accept all' policy for police referrals (Steadman et al., 2001), this is certainly not the norm. The Short et al. (2014) study noted that one in five mental health transfers was deemed inappropriate for admission, while statistics from a Scottish Government report (McGeough & Foster, 2018) reported that as many as 61% of police referrals to the ED for mental health assessment were allowed to go home. Related Australian-based research reported people being told they were 'not sick enough' or 'not in crisis' so could not access services (Olasoji et al., 2017, p. 407).

A substantial proportion of people referred to in the McGeough & Foster report had self-harm or suicide-related concerns, which resonates with earlier findings internationally that reported 'situational crises' as a common precursor to ED presentations (Meadows et al., 1994). Other research has found that people who have substance-use related disorders (Tran et al., 2020) and those attracting a personality disorder label, particularly borderline personality (Martin & Thomas, 2015) are frequent presenters to ED services. As noted by Iacobucci (2014), while hospitals should seek to connect the person with appropriate community services when they don't meet admission thresholds, their efforts may not be sufficiently robust, or the person may refuse. Iacobucci notes that this means that police 'may encounter the person in the community after a few days – or even after only a few hours, once again in need of help' (p. 84–85). A longstanding concern reported here is that these groups do not routinely access voluntary services (McNiel et al., 1991; Burgess et al., 2009), and receive little or otherwise sub-optimal care and support from community services.

I frequently found myself in distress. The more I presented in crisis, the harder it seemed to be able to access help. I found myself turned away from EDs, I was told by psychiatric wards they would not admit me again. On one occasion I was outside and crying. I'd been trying to cut myself, but only managed some superficial scratches. I remember the police officer talking to me, saying let's go to hospital where i could get help. It must have been late afternoon, by early evening I had been sent home. That's when I really hurt myself. It was the same officers that had attended earlier in the day.

A recent UK-based HMICFRS report (2018, p. 3) went as far as to say that the mental health system was broken. While this report recognises that the failure of health services to adequately respond to levels of mental health need in the community has directly contributed to ongoing tensions between police, health, justice and welfare services (Thomas & Watson, 2017), it has also paved the way for the development of some innovative partnerships. These partnerships acknowledge that, due to the breadth of the presenting needs of a population, any response needs to span multiple disciplines and agencies (Christmas & Srivastava, 2019) in a 'joined-up' fashion (van Dijk et al., 2019). Such sentiments for a shared, common, agenda involving multi-agency commitment require a sustained significant investment in time and energy.

The Impact of Gaps in the System and Human Responses to People's Experiences of Being Kept Safe

> Many times I was picked up in crisis, accessed ED or was admitted to hospital I always felt alone, fighting for support, judged. There was no planning. It felt like a roundabout, each crisis we all just went around again looking for something that just was not there.

As already mentioned, compelling international evidence indicates that most people who are brought into the ED by the police are not viewed as time critical. This represents a double-edged sword. From a service-based partnerships perspective, as noted by Iacobucci (2014), the ongoing de-prioritisation of mental health-related referrals by police inevitably contributes to an increasing disincentive for police members to bring people to the ED for assessment and treatment. It is broadly acknowledged that the ED environment is not conducive to good mental healthcare (Clarke et al., 2014); quite fundamentally, EDs are not set up to adequately treat or respond to mental health-related incidents (Innes et al., 2013). There is accumulating evidence that people will actively avoid the ED given the significantly negative prior experiences but, at the same time, see ED attendance as inevitable due to the lack of 'alternative accessible destinations' (Wise-Harris et al., 2017). When people do present to ED in distress, all too commonly, they are left waiting too long for initial assessment and/or treatment without adequate information or reassurance (Morphet et al., 2012); this can lead to a panoply of negative consequences including dissatisfaction and frustration with healthcare services/providers, as well as, in some cases, agitation and aggression; the latter being commonly associated with substance intoxication (Alarcon Manchego et al., 2015).

Unfortunately, people can and do have poor experiences, with pejorative views of ED staff negating or minimising the distress being reported. Clarke et al. (2014) noted that people who present to ED feel that their concerns can be trivialised; some studies have reported people with mental distress have felt ritual humiliation in EDs, feeling like they were being punished as a result of their self-harming or suicidal behaviours. This lived experience directly resonates with the 'why bother attitude' reported by some ED staff (e.g. Hadfield et al., 2009), especially in response to frequent ED attenders. Of note, Clarke et al.'s review noted that negative attitudes of ED staff were associated with a lower likelihood of wanting to help the person in distress. Worryingly, one study (Doyle et al., 2007) reported that nursing staff based their response on the perceived 'genuineness' of presentations. Given the established links between repeat presentations and subsequent harm (Stanley et al., 2015), this kind of ill-informed approach is hugely problematic.

A recently published report by Victoria Legal Aid simply describes the system as broken; based on the experiences of 34 lived experience experts, it describes a system that harms instead of helping (VLA, 2020, p. 2). While there are certainly strong arguments supporting the position that the traditional ED environment is not the right place for a person experiencing mental distress, the question arises as to safe and viable available alternatives? Currently this missing middle is shunted between health and social welfare services; this is both dehumanising and undignified and does little to build trust, rapport or faith that engaging with services can lead to positive change and outcomes. Given the common co-occurrence of comorbid mental health, substance use and physical health concerns, a viable alternative is challenging, but arguably increasingly necessary (Wise-Harris et al., 2017). Currently there is a real conflict at play—the police are trying hard to keep people out of the criminal justice system, but healthcare workers are also working hard to keep people out of hospital to prevent medicalising mental distress and long-term harm caused by inpatient care. It is of perhaps little surprise, therefore, that the current pathways and models of response are failing many of those experiencing mental distress.

Summary and Conclusions

The available evidence suggests the need for a system that is responsive to distress stemming from social factors. Rosenberg (2017, p. 1) posits that continued priority needs to be given to increasing the availability of secondary clinical and non-clinical mental health services to act as a 'glue to bind primary and acute systems and create a more durable continuum of care'. The author describes the need to better integrate physical and mental health services in primary care settings, as well as forming cohesive partnerships between primary, secondary and tertiary mental health services, and also providing provision for access to and support from other wraparound health and social welfare services. As noted by Bywood et al. (2015, p. 3), something as simple as a 'no wrong door' approach that can help the person navigate the system to get the support they need could go a long way towards addressing a good deal of this current unmet healthcare need. Weaver and Coffey (2017) importantly re-emphasise the need to prioritise the patient's views and experiences of care when considering a continuity of (integrated) care, noting the core differences between what professionals and service users see as priorities with respect to healthcare delivery.

Peer-led, peer-driven services have been proposed as both an adjunct to existing services and an alternative altogether. An early US-based study of peer support programme set up in the psychiatric service of an ED reported that a sustained, well-supported programme led to consumers feeling supported, respected and understood (Migdole et al., 2011). The viability and practicalities of providing a peer support service in the ED setting have more recently been explored by Minshall et al. (2020) who reported strong support for the peer support workers from consumers, support persons and also from ED staff; of note, the peer workers provided what was considered to be much needed support for the support persons as well as the person presenting in distress. Their report also cautions about the infrastructure and supports that are necessarily required to foster and enable successful peer support programmes. Based on this, and other cognate research, it is evident that a significant proportion of the ongoing barriers in responding to mental distress in the ED are structural; they are based around the built environment of the ED providing limited space and being/feeling overcrowded. While these kinds of challenges have the potential of being ameliorated by changing the built environment, this does not overcome the challenge of time pressures that ED staff operate under. This is further compounded by increasingly complex and, at times, challenging presentations that stem from entrenched social inequalities (Dombagolla et al., 2019).

In conclusion, it is clear that the current binary systems of health and criminal justice are simply not working; we have a missing middle and a missing system. There is a need for bold reform and arguably a need for a new third system: a system that is responsive to people's needs; a service that does not unnecessarily criminalise or medicalise mental distress; and a service that serves to reduce structural issues within what is currently a severely over-stretched system. As a new service, it will be incumbent upon all involved to actively facilitate lived experience peer workers' roles to help facilitate best practice responses to people experiencing mental distress.

References

Adebowale, V. (2013). Commission on mental health and policing report. Independent Commission on Mental Health and Policing.

Alarcon Manchego, P., Knott, J., Graudins, A., Bartley, B., & Mitra, B. (2015). Management of mental health patients in Victorian emergency departments: A 10-year follow-up study. *Emergency Medicine Australasia, 27*, 529–536. https://doi.org/10.1111/1742-6723.12500

Arvidsdotter, T., Marklund, B., Kylén, S., Taft, C., & Ekman, I. (2016). Understanding persons with psychological distress in primary health care. *Scandinavian Journal of Caring Sciences, 30*, 687–694. https://doi.org/10.1111/scs.12289

Australian Institute of Health and Welfare. (2020). *Mental health services in Australia.* AIHW. https://www.aihw.gov.au/reports/mental-health-services/mental-health-services-in-australia/report-contents/summary-of-mental-health-services-in-australia/prevalence-impact-and-burden

Boscarato, K., Lee, S., Kroschel, J., Hollander, Y., Brennan, A., & Warren, N. (2015). Consumer experience of formal crisis-response services and preferred methods of crisis intervention. *International Journal of Mental Health Nursing, 23*, 287–295. https://doi.org/10.1111/inm.12059

Burgess, P. M., Pirkis, J. E., Slade, T. N., Johnston, A. K., Meadows, G. N., & Gunn, J. M. (2009). Service use for mental health problems: Findings from the 2007 national survey of mental health and wellbeing. *Australian & New Zealand Journal of Psychiatry, 43*, 615–623. https://doi.org/10.1080/00048670902970858

Bywood, P. T., Brown, L., & Raven, M. (2015). Improving the integration of mental health services in primary health care at the macro level. In *PHCRIS policy issue review*. Primary Health Care Research and Information Service.

Christmas, H., & Srivastava, J. (2019). *Public health approaches in policing. A discussion paper.* College of Policing Ltd..

Clarke, D., Usick, R., Sanderson, A., Giles-Smith, L., & Baker, J. (2014). Emergency department staff attitudes towards mental health consumers: A literature review and thematic content analysis. *International Journal of Mental Health Nursing, 23*, 273–284. https://doi.org/10.1111/inm.12040

Crofts, N., & Thomas, S. (2018). Law enforcement and public health: Finding common ground and global solutions to disparities in health and access to criminal justice. *Journal of Community Safety & Well-being, 2*(3). https://doi.org/10.35502/jcswb.56

Davis, R. C., Ortiz, C. W., Euler, S., & Kuykendall, L. (2015). Revisiting "measuring what matters:" developing a suite of standardised performance measures for policing. *Police Quarterly, 18*, 469–495. https://doi.org/10.1177/1098611115598990

Department of Health and Human Services. (2016). *Department of Health and Human Services – Victoria police protocol for mental health: A guide for clinicians and police*. DHHS. https://www.health.vic.gov.au/mental-health/practice-and-service-quality/service-quality

Dombagolla, M. H. K., Kant, J. A., Lai, F. W. Y., Hendarto, A., & Taylor, D. M. (2019). Barriers to providing optimal management of psychiatric patients in the emergency department. *Australasian Emergency Care, 22*, 8–12. https://doi.org/10.1016/j.auec.2019.01.001

Doyle, L., Keogh, B., & Morrissey, J. (2007). Caring for patients with suicidal behaviour: An exploratory study. *British Journal of Nursing, 16*, 1218–1222. https://doi.org/10.12968/bjon.2007.16.19.27362

Felitti, V. J., Anda, R. F., Nordenberg, D., Williamson, D. F., Spitz, A. M., Edwards, V., et al. (1998). Relationship of childhood abuse and household dysfunction to many of the leading causes of death in adults: The adverse childhood experiences (ACE) study. *American Journal of Preventive Medicine, 14*, 245–258. https://doi.org/10.1016/S0749-3797(98)00017-8

Font, S. A., & Maguire-Jack, K. (2016). Pathways from childhood abuse and other adversities to adult health risks: The role of adult socioeconomic conditions. *Child Abuse & Neglect, 51*, 390–399. https://doi.org/10.1016/j.chiabu.2015.05.013

Geraghty, A. W., Santer, M., Williams, S., Mc Sharry, J., Little, P., Muñoz, R. F., et al. (2016). You feel like your whole world is caving in: A qualitative study of primary care patients' conceptualisations of emotional distress. *Health (London, England), 21*, 295–315. https://doi.org/10.1177/1363459316674786

Hadfield, J., Brown, D., Pembroke, L., & Hayward, M. (2009). Analysis of accident and emergency doctors' responses to treating people who self-harm. *Qualitative Health Research, 19*, 755–765. https://doi.org/10.1177/1049732309334473

HMICFRS. (2018). *Policing and mental health. picking up the pieces*. Her Majesty's Inspectorate of Constabulary and Fire & Rescue Services. www.justiceinspectorates.gov.uk/hmicfrs

Horwitz, A.V. (2007). Distinguishing distress from disorder as psychological outcomes for stressful social arrangements. Health: *An Interdisciplinary Journal for the Social Study of Health, Illness and Medicine, 11*, 273–289. https://doi.org/10.1177/1363459307077541

Houtepen, L. C., Heron, J., Suderman, M. J., Fraser, A., Chittleborough, C. R., & Howe, L. D. (2020). Associations of adverse childhood experiences with educational attainment and adolescent health and the role of family and socioeconomic factors: A prospective cohort study in the UK. *PLoS Medicine, 17*, e1003031. https://doi.org/10.1371/journal.pmed.1003031

Hughes, K., Bellis, M. A., Hardcastle, K. A., Sethi, D., Butchart, A., Mikton, C., et al. (2017). The effect of multiple adverse childhood experiences on health: A systematic review and meta-analysis. *The Lancet Public Health, 2*, e356–e366. https://doi.org/10.1016/S2468-2667(17)30118-4

Iacobucci, F. (2014). *Police encounters with people in crisis. An independent review conducted by the Honourable frank Iacobucci for chief of police William Blair, Toronto police service*. June 2014.

Innes, K., Morphet, J., O'Brien, A. P., & Munro, I. (2013). Caring for the mental illness patient in emergency departments – An exploration of the issues from a healthcare provider perspective. *Journal of Clinical Nursing, 23*, 2003–2011. https://doi.org/10.1111/jocn.12437

Kahan, D., Poremski, D., Wise-Harris, D., Pauly, D., Leszcz, M., Wasylenki, D., & Stergiopoulos, V. (2016). Perceived case management needs and service preferences of frequent emergency department users: Lessons learned in a large urban Centre. *PLoS One, 11*(12), e0168782. https://doi.org/10.1371/journal.pone.0168782

Lacobucci, F. (2014). Police encounters with people in crisis. An independent review conducted by the Honourable frank Iacobucci for chief of police William Blair, Toronto police service. June 2014.

Lamb, H. R., Weinberger, L. E., & DeCuir, W. J. (2002). The police and mental health. *Psychiatric Services, 10*, 1266–1271.

Lee, S., Brunero, S., Fairbrother, G., & Cowan, D. (2008). Profiling police presentations of mental health consumers to an emergency department. *International Journal of Mental Health Nursing, 17*, 311–316. https://doi.org/10.1111/j.1447-0349.2008.00553.x

Marmot, M., & Wilkinson, R. (2000). *The social determinants of health.* Oxford University Press.

Martin, T., & Thomas, S. (2015). Police officers' views of their encounters with people with personality disorder. *Journal of Psychiatric and Mental Health Nursing, 22*, 125–132. https://doi.org/10.1111/jpm.12099

Masten, A. S. (2011). Resilience in children threatened by extreme adversity: Frameworks for research, practice, and translational synergy. *Development and Psychopathology, 23*, 493–506. https://doi.org/10.1017/S0954579411000198

McGeough, E., & Foster, R. (2018). *What works? Collaborative police and health interventions for mental health distress.* Scottish Government.

McNiel, D. E., Hatcher, C., Zeiner, H., Wolfe, H. L., & Myers, R. S. (1991). Characteristics of persons referred by police to the psychiatric emergency room. *Psychiatric Services, 42*, 425–427.

Meadows, G., Calder, G., & Van Den Bos, H. (1994). Police referrals to a psychiatric hospital: Indicators for referral and psychiatric outcome. *Australian and New Zealand Journal of Psychiatry, 28*, 259–268.

Migdole, S., Tondora, J., Silva, M. A., Barry, A. D., Milligan, J. C., Mattison, E., Rutledge, W., & Powsner, S. (2011). Exploring new frontiers: Recovery-oriented peer support programming in a psychiatric ED. *American Journal of Psychiatric Rehabilitation, 14*, 1–12. https://doi.org/10.1080/15487768.2011.546274

Minshall, C., Roennfeldt, H., Hamilton, B., Hill, N., Stratford, A., Buchanan-Hagen, S., Byrne, L., Castle, D. J., Cocks, N., Davidson, L., & Brophy, L. (2020). *Examining the role of mental health peer support in emergency departments.* Melbourne Social Equity Institute, University of Melbourne.

Morphet, J., Innes, K., Munro, I., O'Brien, A., Gaskin, C. J., Reed, F., & Kudinoff, T. (2012). Managing people with mental health presentations in emergency departments - a service exploration of the issues surrounding responsiveness from a mental health care consumer and carer perspective. *Australasian Emergency Nursing Journal, 15*, 148–155. https://doi.org/10.1016/j.aenj.2012.05.003

Olasoji, M., Maude, P., & McCauley, K. (2017). Not sick enough: Experiences of carers of people with mental illness negotiating care for their relatives with mental health services. *Journal of Psychiatric and Mental Health Services, 24*, 403–411. https://doi.org/10.1111/jpm.12399

Perry, A., Lawrence, V., & Henderson, C. (2020). Stigmatisation of those with mental health conditions in the acute general hospital setting. A qualitative framework synthesis. *Social Science and Medicine.* https://doi.org/10.1016/j.socscimed.2020.112974

Rosenberg, S. (2017). Shangri-La and the integration of mental health care in Australia. *Public Health Research & Practice, 27*(3), e2731723. https://doi.org/10.17061/phrp2731723

Short, T. B. R., McDonald, C., Luebbers, S., Ogloff, J. R. P., & Thomas, S. D. M. (2014). The nature of police involvement in mental health transfers. *Police Practice and Research, 15*, 336–348. https://doi.org/10.1080/15614263.2012.736717

Stanley, B., Brown, G. K., Currier, G. W., Lyons, C., Chesin, M., & Knox, K. L. (2015). Brief intervention and follow-up for suicidal patients with repeat emergency department visits enhances treatment engagement. *American Journal of Public Health, 105*, 1570–1572. https://doi.org/10.2105/AJPH.2015.302656

Steadman, H. J., Stainbrook, K. A., Griffin, P., Draine, J., Dupont, R., & Horey, C. (2001). A specialized crisis response site as a core element of police-based diversion programs. *Psychiatric Services, 52*, 219–222. https://doi.org/10.1176/appi.ps.52.2.219

Thomas, S. D. M., & Kesic, D. (2020). International models of police response to mental illness. In J. McDaniel, K. Moss, & K. Pease (Eds.), *Policing and Mental Health: Theory, Policy and Practice.* Routledge.

Thomas, S., & Watson, A. (2017). A focus for mental health training for police. *Journal of Criminological Research Policy and Practice, 3*, 93–104. https://doi.org/10.1108/JCRPP-01-2017-0005

Tran, Q. N., Lambeth, L. G., Sanderson, K., de Graff, B., Breslin, M., Huckerby, E. J., Tran, V., & Neil, A. L. (2020). Trends of emergency department presentations in Australia by diagnostic group, 2004-5 to 2016-17. *Emergency Medicine Australasia, 32*, 190–201. https://doi.org/10.1111/1742-6723.13451

van Dijk, A. J., Herrington, V., Crofts, N., Breunig, R., Burris, S., Sullivan, H., Middleton, J., Sherman, S., & Thomson, N. (2019). Law enforcement and public health: Recognition and enhancement of joined-up solutions. *The Lancet, 393*, 287–294. https://doi.org/10.1016/S0140-6736(18)32839-3

Victoria Legal Aid. (2020). Your story your say. In *Consumers' priority issues and solutions for the Royal Commission into Victoria's Mental Health System*. Victoria Legal Aid. https://www.legalaid.vic.gov.au/law-reform/building-better-justice-system/access-to-justice-for-people-with-mental-illness-and-disability/roads-to-recovery-building-better-system-for-people-experiencing-mental-health-issues-in-victoria/your-story-your-say

Weaver, N., & Coffey, M. (2017). & Hewitt, J. (2017). Concepts, models and measurement of continuity of care in mental health services: A systematic appraisal of the literature. *Journal of Psychiatric and Mental Health Nursing, 24*, 431–450. https://doi.org/10.1111/jpm.12387

Wise-Harris, D., Pauly, D., Kahan, D., de Bibiana, J. T., Hwang, S. W., & Stergiopoulos, V. (2017). "Hospital was the only option": Experience of frequent emergency department users in mental health. *Administration and Policy in Mental Health and Mental Health Services, 44*, 405–412. https://doi.org/10.1007/s10488-016-0728-3

Zisman, S., & O'Brien, A. (2015). A retrospective cohort study describing six months of admissions under section 136 of the mental health act; the problem of alcohol misuse. *Medicine, Science and the Law, 55*, 216–222.

Chapter 9
The Challenges of Sustaining Partnerships and the Diversification of Cultures

Denise Martin and William Graham

Introduction

Previously perceived as two separate disciplines, Public Health and Law Enforcement have different approaches and priorities towards reducing vulnerability (see Chap. 3). However, increasingly, there is recognition that partnership working and the willingness of different services to collaborate is critical to the success of Law Enforcement and Public Health (LEPH) initiatives. Collaborative working draws together institutions and actors from different sectors, spheres, and even countries who may have different traditions, different governance structures, and different values and priorities. While partnership approaches are not new and can operate successfully, there are continued challenges around sustaining partnerships in the longer term (Crawford & Cunningham, 2015). These include short-term planning cycles, limited resources, shifting priorities and political pressures. These pressures often contribute to the re-enforcing of siloed approaches and retreatism back into organisational cultures and norms as a way of managing hurdles that these challenges raise. Examining two programmes based on initiatives focused on collaborative working to prevent crime and violence, this chapter discusses the benefits of partnerships to resolve challenges faced by vulnerable communities. It also raises some of the difficulties to maintain these partnerships in the longer term.

D. Martin (✉)
School of Business, Law and Social Science, Abertay University, Dundee, UK
e-mail: d.martin@abertay.ac.uk

W. Graham
Abertay University, Dundee, UK

The Importance and Emerging Nature of Collaboration

Collaboration as a way to resolve complex and challenging societal problems has existed for some time. The extension of collaboration and its use in the realm of public policy connects to broader shifts in governance where the emergence of neoliberalism in the 1970s changed the nature and role of the state. Governments in many western jurisdictions were trying to reduce their dominant role in delivery of services and increasingly devolve more responsibility towards communities, individuals and markets. This was partly due to a failure of the state to effectively manage the cost of services where it was believed that introducing new partnerships, for example, private providers could encourage a more competitive and effective systems of delivery and enhance the quality of the service. Collaboration has not just expanded due to changes in states dominance, but changing demands and expectations of public services are relevant too. Newman and Clarke (2009) suggests that recent agendas for public services stress the importance on their role in the remaking of community and civil society through building capacity of communities and working in partnerships. Successful partnerships can be effective in addressing a broader range of problems that might lead to or be responsible for the engagement of individuals in negative behaviour such as criminal activity or anti-social behaviour. Often different agencies have the expertise to look at the same issue but in different ways that viewed collectively can create wider and more holistic approaches to the issue at hand meaning a better resolution for both the individual and communities.

However, Newman and Clarke (2009) also discuss what they refer to as assemblages where different policies, personnel, practices and governance structures are brought together as a way to resolve societal issues. They argue the assumed coherence of different elements misses the sometimes incompatibility and instability of these assemblages. In the field of Law Enforcement and Public Health, it is these fragilities that can lead to disruption for progress and an ability for partnerships to succeed particularly in the longer term and when resources are precious and limited.

The purpose of this chapter is to examine two programmes where the key aim was working in partnership to reduce violence and anti-social behaviour while focusing on addressing the individual issues faced by those engaged with them. By examining these programmes, it demonstrates the potential benefits in collaborative working in the Law Enforcement and Public Health area. It also addresses the challenges and questions that emerged from these programmes, critical for any initiatives that aim to work across disciplinary spaces.

Prevention First: A New Local Partnership to Prevent Crime and Anti-Social Behaviour

The Prevention First model was introduced as an Operating Model in Policing utilised in New Zealand. Its introduction was not by accident, but emerged due to earlier strategic changes to the way that public services were being delivered across the country (Den Heyer, 2018). Driven by a desire to reduce the cost of public services and create more effective services, the main feature of this and a previous change management programme was to shift from a reactive to preventative model of police work. A core part of this was to change the mind-set towards New Zealand Police understanding the demand for their resources, what the drivers were behind crime and to ensure that victims and prevention were central (Den Heyer, 2016). There was a requirement to understand that a range of factors influenced crime including of social issues and vulnerabilities. Indeed, the strategy for the New Zealand Police from 2013 onwards was to demonstrate an awareness of and leverage community services and networks to protect vulnerable people, particularly repeat offenders, act with urgency against prolific offenders and develop innovative and sustainable, practical solutions using problem-solving approaches to manage crime hotspots and priority locations (New Zealand 2011c cited in Den Heyer, 2016, p539). The approach in New Zealand was underpinned by a broader shift in the Ministry of Justice to improve performance and cut crime by setting ambitious crime reducing targets, which required a joined-up approach by agencies. A critical step towards achieving these targets was a structured framework that ensured the effective management of demand and resourcing to efficiently and effectively tackle issues that arose.[1]

This specific case study discussed here takes into account the introduction of a programme concerned with trying to reduce anti-social behaviour and violence in the west coast of Scotland. One of the authors was part of a team that conducted an evaluation of the scheme (Smith et al., 2018). A Chief Superintendent who was divisional commander was keen to consider ways to reduce crime and violence in her local area particularly where part of the county had continued to experience high levels of violence and anti-social behaviour and increasing demand on local service provision. It was believed that the existing operational model has shifted the focus away from preventative strategies and community policing to one which was very reactive. Partners from local agencies expressed their disappointment that there had been a loss of effective community policing and partnership working in the area. Prevention First was suggested as a way to re-establish this community style police and re-engage the skills of community officers with the intention of trying to:

> '...prevent crime, reduce victimisation and reduce locations where offending takes place, through a partnership early intervention approach which gets to the heart of issues and

---

[1] For a fuller outline of the approach in New Zealand, see Den Heyer (2016, 2020), and for the approach in Scotland, see Smith et al., 2018.

identifies the best way to solve problems and tackle community concerns' (Prevention First Proposal Document, 2014 cited in Smith et al., 2018).

The Scottish Model of Prevention First

Scotland, like many other countries, was experiencing crime decreases but the demands and pressures on police and other services were continually raising and concentrated in particular areas. Other drivers meant that this type of policy made sense. It drew on recommendations from the Christie Commission (2011) which outlined a number of core principles focused on creating safer communities in Scotland through more prevention-focused activities to reduce inequalities. The main aim of Prevention First in the Scottish context was that violence is preventable, not inevitable, and that crime, violence and anti-social behaviour are driven by underlying social conditions.

How the Prevention First Model Worked in Scotland

A key approach in Scotland was to ensure the management of data and monitor demands coming in; this was achieved via intense daily scrutiny of incidents, crime reports and patterns of concern. This enabled partners to identify areas of common concern including victims, offenders, repeat callers, problematic locations and emerging crime trends. Information sharing and timely referral to partners was then enacted and ongoing dialogue and agreed actions taken forward. Daily communication with partners, backed up by weekly/fortnightly meetings to discuss progress, also took place.

Findings from the Prevention First Initiative

Overall, the evaluation of Prevention First in Scotland demonstrated success across a range of outcomes. Initial strong leadership and existing relationships were key to driving the initiative forward and gaining buy-in from the partners. The focus and responsibilisation of middle managers in the shape of Community Inspectors meant an emphasis on local leadership and ability to manage the initiative. In relation to reducing violence and anti-social behaviour, figures suggested that crime did decline in the local authorities' areas, where the Prevention First Initiative was introduced. However, it was hard to disaggregate this data from other potential impacts which could have had a reducing effect, meaning it is difficult to fully attribute the fall in incidents of crime and anti-social behaviour (see Smith et al., 2018).

The qualitative data suggested that Prevention First was successful in a number of ways, in particular, enhancing partnership approaches to resolve issues of victimisation and address vulnerability issues. To illustrate the

(continued)

types of cases that came to the attention of the Prevention First Teams, the following outlines a couple of incidents.

Incident 1—Drug dealing and anti-social behaviour: This referral related to low-level anti-social behaviour. The initial referral was for a noise complaint, but it became apparent that it was a drug-dealing case. A large volume of callers to the door caused anxiety to neighbours. It transpired that the tenant was being manipulated by friends, and had no gatekeeping skills. The tenant was arrested after one incident and was bailed back to his address. Social work involvement was arranged and the tenant was placed on a methadone and rehabilitation course. He has followed advice and now has his home to himself. There is no anti-social behaviour in the street now.

Wellbeing and mental health: This referral related to a male who reported petrol being poured through his letterbox. Police who attended found no evidence or smell of petrol. The tenant made 2 or 3 similar calls complaining of neighbours trying to kill him. A joint visit with the council established that the man had barricaded himself into the house in apparent fear for his life. He only removed the barricades once he was convinced that it was the police. It was apparent that most of his rooms were empty and that he was sleeping on the floor. He was armed with a knife and visibly paranoid. It became obvious that mental health issues were in play. Interventions with NHS, Mental Health and his GP were arranged. It was learned that he had presented at his doctors several weeks earlier with a mass on his neck which caused pressure on his brain. It is believed that this resulted in his delusional behaviour. He was admitted to hospital and sectioned and received appropriate medical treatment. He is now back living at home and no further issues have occurred. This partnership approach led to a letter of commendation from the Social Work Department.

Focused Deterrence Strategy

The Community Initiative to Reduce Violence (CIRV) approach, pioneered in Boston, Massachusetts; Cincinnati, Ohio; and Glasgow, Scotland, applied a focused deterrence strategy (see Kennedy et al., 1996; Braga et al., 1999; Braga et al., 2001), with the aim of reducing the frequency of street violence. CIRV brings together various statutory and voluntary agencies to work in partnership using a public health approach and coordinates law enforcement, service providers and community members to ensure that those who participate in violent gangs receive due consequences and those who choose transition to a non-violent lifestyle, receive the appropriate support in the most effective, efficient, and respectful manner possible.

The concept of focused deterrence strategy (FDS) is closely aligned with Problem Oriented Policing (POP) (see Eck & Spelman, 1987) developed in Boston in the mid-1990s by a team of academics and Boston Police Department to deal with the problem of youth and gun violence associated with gangs in the city. Braga et al. (1999) reported that from the mid-1980s continuing until the early 1990s, there was an increase in firearm homicides involving youths and in particular, young black males. They noted that between 1984 and 1994 the homicide rate for young black males, under the age of 18 years, increased by 418% involving handguns while the rates for the use of other guns in the same category also increased by 125%. They also realised that a small number of individuals involved in gangs or groups were responsible for a majority of crimes (Braga et al., 1999).

In order to address the high homicide rates, academics and police practitioners developed interventions, known as the Boston Gun Project, or Operation Ceasefire (Kennedy et al., 1996; Kennedy, 1997; Braga et al., 1999; Braga et al., 2001). The Boston Gun Project adopted a focused deterrence strategy (FDS) to tackle gang-related violence and a 'pulling levers' strategy, described as 'using every means available to target gangs as a whole, including individual members' (Kennedy, 1997: 462) to first identify at-risk gang members and thereafter communicate the consequences of continued violence to them. Such was the success of this approach, that Boston saw a reduction of 63% in youth homicides (Braga et al., 2001).

Given the success of this project, other American cities adopted the FDS to address rising violence and homicides, across the USA, including Oakland and Los Angeles (California), Cleveland and Dayton (Ohio) and Detroit (Michigan) (National Network for Safer Communities, 2014). The city of Cincinnati also adopted a FDS in 2007, following a recognition that something should be done about the high levels of shootings and gang-related homicides in the city. This Cincinnati Initiative to Reduce Violence (CIRV) recorded a 34% reduction in homicides in Cincinnati over the following 2 years (see Engel et al., 2013) and it was this approach that the police in Glasgow sought to copy to deal with the levels of gang-related violence in the city.

The city of Glasgow has long been associated with gang-related violence and by the mid-2000s Glasgow had been named not only the murder capital of Britain, but also of Western Europe, largely as a result of knife crime, blamed on both alcohol consumption and Glasgow's long association with gang/group violence. Many researchers have discussed the fact that Glasgow has suffered for generations from a 'gang problem' along with the associated violence and territorialism issues (see Patrick, 1973; Davies, 2007; Davies, 2013; Kintrea et al., 2010). In 2007, police intelligence determined that there were 55 gangs in the east end of the city, known by particular names, including the 'Parkhead Rebels', the 'Dentoi' and the 'Calton Tongs'. Gang members tended to be young males typically in their teens, but can range from ages 12 to mid-20s. The issue of territoriality or as Suttles (1972) describes it, 'defended territory', regularly led to large-scale fights and instances of violence, including serious assaults and murders (homicides) (see Kintrea et al., 2010).

Glasgow embarked on a process of policy transfer (Dolowitz & Marsh, 1996 & Dolowitz & Marsh, 2000) and initially attempted to copy the Cincinnati model in full. However, it quickly became apparent that this was not possible due to the local context and legal constraints. They thereafter engaged in a process of emulation of the Cincinnati model and established the Glasgow Community Initiative to Reduce Violence (Glasgow CIRV). The Glasgow model relied heavily on a partnership approach with multiple agencies coming together to deal with the violence problem. The Glasgow CIRV team comprised of Police, Social Work, Education, Housing and City Council officers co-located and working together in an obvious attempt to break down barriers and prevent working in 'silos', an often cited problem with partnership approaches that attempt to reduce crime (Crawford & Cunningham, 2015).

Public Health Approach in Glasgow

A major difference to the approaches taken in Cincinnati and the USA, in general, was the public health approach adopted by the authorities in Glasgow, which treats violence as a social malaise and seeks to address the key risk factors that may increase the likelihood of violent behaviour (Krug et al., 2002). This approach attempts to deal with the root causes of the violence by endeavouring to engage with young people involved in violence and gangs. Thereafter, to devise a strategy to identify the social and health factors that may lead a person to become involved in gangs and the violence associated with them and offer support and advice to those that needed them.

One of the main differences was the case management process developed by Glasgow CIRV, which was distinctly different from that operated in Cincinnati. In Cincinnati, case management was provided by an external partner, a non-profit organisation 'Cincinnati Works', which only dealt with adult 'clients' and focused on employability, reflecting the perceived needs of the target population (adult gang members involved in serious violence). In contrast, in Glasgow the target audience encompassed a wider range of young people, who had not necessarily come to the attention of the criminal justice system, but nonetheless wished to engage with the initiative. The in-house case management team thereafter addressed their needs, allocated appropriate services, and monitored their progress. By signing a pledge that they would cease their violent offending behaviour, they were able to access a range of services offered under the 'whole systems approach' (Glasgow CIRV Case Management Practice Note, 2010a, 2010b), where the focus was not just on employability, but included life skills, wellbeing and health, personal development and skills, and anti-violence and knife awareness courses.

Glasgow CIRV launched in June 2008 and ran for a period of three years, with some success in reducing violence among those who engaged with the project. Evaluation indicated that there was an average of 46% reduction in violent offending by those who engaged with the project, a 73% reduction in gang fighting and a reduction of 85% for weapons offences. Violent offending in the area where CIRV operated also saw a reduction of 56% (Williams et al., 2014).

Northampton: Community Initiative to Reduce Violence (CIRV)

Over a period of a few years from 2015, Northamptonshire County, an area in the East Midlands of England and an hour north of London, experienced a surge in violence associated with gangs and associated crime (drug dealing, acquisitive crime and county lines). In an effort to tackle the growing problem, police staff visited the Scottish Violence Reduction Unit in Glasgow and there learned of the Glasgow Community Initiative to Reduce Violence (Glasgow CIRV), that had been established in the city in 2008, to tackle gang violence. The CIRV concept had, in turn, been 'borrowed' from Cincinnati by the Strathclyde Police force in Glasgow police and over a period of 3 years saw dramatic drops in gang violence and weapons offences (Williams et al., 2014).

In July 2018, Northamptonshire Police employed as a consultant one of the co-authors, Dr. William Graham, to consult and advise on the formation of a multi-agency and community-centred project designed to deliver significant reductions in violence and drug related criminality among gang members across Northamptonshire, the Northamptonshire Community to Reduce Violence (CIRV). Dr. Graham is a former senior police officer from Strathclyde Police and was the Deputy Manager of Glasgow CIRV from 2008 until his retirement from the police in 2010.

The leaders of the proposed initiative recognised that the approach in Glasgow did not address the 'county lines' issues that was prevalent within Northamptonshire and so the programme was adapted to meet the needs of the local context. Partnership working is a central tenet of this type of approach and collaboration was established between agencies and the community to deliver a clear message to violent street gangs: the violence must stop.

Northamptonshire CIRV officially launched in February 2019, and by the time of writing had received over 1000 referrals since the beginning of the project. There is a wealth of anecdotal evidence indicating a drop in violent crime across the county associated with the drugs trade. An independent evaluation of the project carried out by the College of Policing in England and Wales found reduced level of violence and in numbers of gang members (College of Policing forthcoming). CIRV was having a positive impact on programme participants' relationships, health and outlook. It also helped in changing perceptions of the police and support services among young people/adults.

Northampton CIRV

As noted earlier, Northamptonshire experienced a significant rise in violence, associated with the illegal drugs market and 'county lines' operating out of London and other major conurbations in the surrounding areas from 2015. Indeed, police intelligence revealed that there were in excess of over 300 people on the intelligence systems with 'warning markers' to alert police officers and staff to risks associated with those individuals for various crimes, including the possession and use of weapons, violence, drugs and mental disorders, etc. The growing issues of violence, associated with the drugs market, prompted the police to look at new, innovative practices to target the growing problem. This search for new ideas led to a visit to the Scottish Violence Reduction Unit in Glasgow, where staff learned of the work of Glasgow CIRV that had operated in the east end of Glasgow from 2008 to 2011 and saw reductions in violence and weapons offences.

On returning to Northampton, work began on building partnerships with relevant agencies and funding secured to create a similar approach to that in Glasgow. Northampton CIRV is police-led and is supported by a variety of agencies, including the Police and Crime Commissioner, local authorities, statutory agencies and local businesses. This approach is designed to break down barriers and prevent working in 'silos', facilitating sharing of information and ensuring that appropriate services are accessed for those engaged (clients) in the project.

One of the main issues that Glasgow CIRV discovered on trying to implement the FDS, was that the borrowing body, in that case, Glasgow, could not directly copy the approach followed elsewhere, i.e. Cincinnati, but must look to emulate the approach instead (see Dolowitz & Marsh, 1996 & Dolowitz & Marsh, 2000) and adapt it to fit the local context. Therefore, following on from the lessons learned in Glasgow, it was incumbent on the Northampton CIRV team to adapt the approach taken in Glasgow to fit the local circumstances and cultures in Northamptonshire to ensure that the approach would be relevant to the local context.

The Northamptonshire team needed to consider contextual differences between their county and Glasgow, in terms of demographics, local culture and type of gang violence and associated criminal activity. For example, gang violence in Glasgow at the time was based on territorial issues with a large number of gangs involved in activities such as casual violence and alcohol abuse (Kintrea et al., 2010). This was in contrast to Northamptonshire, where there are a smaller number of gangs and associated crime is more likely related to drug supply and county lines. The approach designed for Northamptonshire was unique because there was an absence of street-based gang activity.

(continued)

The identification of appropriate 'clients' is important in order to make a difference to the problems being experienced. Potential clients came to the attention of the CIRV team through two different routes.

- Referral by a professional (e.g. a local school) member of the community, parent or self-referral.
- Use of police or partner intelligence and crime data and by proactively searching for cases that may be suitable for inclusion in the programme.

The primary criteria for access to the CIRV programme included those individuals deemed to be at risk of criminal exploitation or already involved in or at risk of being recruited into gangs. However, there are many different definitions of a 'gang', which raises issues for academics, police and policy-makers on what actually constitutes a gang. The term 'gang' and who is a member of a 'gang' is a highly contestable and debatable subject with no recognised consensus and has produced much debate over the years (see Curry & Spergel, 1990; Ball & Curry, 1995; Esbensen et al., 2001; Bennett & Holloway, 2004; Spergel et al., 2004; Bradshaw, 2005; Bradshaw & Smith, 2005).

The Northampton CIRV team used a tool developed by Northamptonshire County Council (the Signs of Gang Involvement Screening—SIGS) that provides two overarching indicators of gang involvement:

- Strong signs of gang involvement, for example possession with intent to supply class A drugs; associating with pro-criminal peers who are involved in gang activity; multiple mobiles/changing phones frequently.
- Moderate signs of gang involvement, for example sudden change in appearance; interest in music which glorifies weapons/gang culture; and whether the person had committed robbery offences.

Case Management

Northampton CIRV adopted a similar case management system to that operated in Glasgow, with a dedicated case manager, the CIRV Deputy, using their professional experience and judgement to assess the best possible outcomes for the clients. This reflected the bespoke and individualised nature of CIRV where all decision-making and management of programme participants was guided by three principles or 'golden rules'. These were developed by the Northamptonshire management team to help inform decision-making around allocation, delivery and deselection from the programme in recognition of the complexity of cases, where the matters considered together, provide a rich context for making a decision rather than arbitrary thresholds.

(continued)

This public health approach reflects the Glasgow model by seeking to address the causes of gang membership, violence and drug misuse to make a difference in the young person's lives. A suite of options was developed for the use of the case manager and to allocate appropriate interventions for the clients. Furthermore, in a new development in Northampton that had not been utilised elsewhere, was the addition of a business development mentor to engage with businesses and help ensure that CIRV would not only provide a model of support but also facilitate progression into training and employment.

The main method that Glasgow CIRV used to communicate the key messages to the gangs in the target area of the city was the 'Self-Referral Session' while in the US CIRV this was named a 'Call-In' session, which was also adopted by the Northampton CIRV team. The 'Call-In' approach was a major departure from routine policing and law enforcement in both Cincinnati and Glasgow.

The session was designed to suit the local context in Northampton with the main focus being to demonstrate the availability of services for those choosing to get out of 'gang life', the expectations of the community and the consequences for them should the violent acts continue.

The session speakers asked to take part in Northampton came from a variety of backgrounds to reflect the local community. The session followed a similar pattern as set out in Glasgow, to ensure that the North-ampton CIRV key messages were communicated to those attending the session. It was the stated expectation in the session that those in attendance would pass on those messages to their peers. The key messages delivered in the session focused on emphasising that this was a new law enforcement strategy intended to target subsequent violence through effectively apply-ing and using police powers if necessary, the community had had enough of the violence and finally that there was support and help available to move people away from involvement in crime (see Glasgow CIRV Self-Referral Session Practice Note, 2010, for a full description of the process).

Discussion and Lessons from the Case Studies

While both the outcomes of these programmes were positive, a number of challenges also emerged. One challenge often cited in cross partnership working is the division of work cultures that can have an impact on the ability of initiatives to succeed. While the overall sense was one of positive partnerships relationships throughout the evaluation of Prevention First, there was some mention of the sometimes more challenging relationship with social work in the partnership. Overall partners were supportive and praised colleagues from social work but commented that they were the partner less likely to attend meetings regularly. There was recognition that this was probably as a result of demands already on social work. One or two participants noted that the physical separation of social work teams meant they had developed their own autonomy and work practices. One council respondent commented that, historically, there has been institutional resistance from the Social Work Department to exchanging information, because they believe it to be private and sensitive and that to share such information would be breaking client confidentiality (Smith et al., 2018, p. 95).

Despite the success of Prevention First and the positive creation of genuine partnership working, there was real concern for the longevity of the project. A similar evaluation has also been made of the model used in New Zealand (Den Heyer, 2020). There are a couple of issues that are critical here; first, the programme did involve a lot of dedication of those working at a local level particularly who invested a substantial amount of effort and time into identifying local issues and working hard with partners to resolve community and individual cases. Second, the amount of resources utilised to make the approach work particularly when other police priorities also need attention. Den Heyer's (2020) evaluation of the New Zealand approach suggested that while the project initially worked and there seemed to be a demonstrable decline in crime occurrence in key areas being measured, this was only temporary; longer-term, the impact police were having on prevention eventually reaches a point of diminishing returns. This is not to say that prevention should not be seen as ineffective but programmes such as Prevention First may have to be adapted and changed or combined with other responsive forms of policing. It has the potential to be effective but only if aligned as part of an overarching strategy. This is important for longer-term planning and success.

Like the Prevention First Project described earlier, one of the key challenges experienced in Glasgow and Northampton was the breaking down of barriers and cultural differences between the various agencies involved in the programmes. In Glasgow and Northampton, this was achieved through an Information Sharing protocol that was agreed on where all agencies undertook to work together. Even though the police took on the lead role, incorporating key workers from the other agencies in the joint teams ensured partnership working. The sharing of information by police, especially with Social Work and Education, in both Glasgow and Northampton, was believed to be a breakthrough, as all agencies saw the benefits of working together in the public health approach to help young people. However, this was not the case in Cincinnati, where the police tended to retain information. This can often act as a barrier to effective partnership working where one partner dominates potentially undermining the development or trust and reciprocity. Glasgow CIRV ceased to operate in July 2011 due to various factors, not least in the change of direction for the initiative away from establishing the programme in existing city structures. This failure led to a lack of funding and a cessation of the programme. However, this approach has continued to be utilised in Scotland with the establishment or a Scottish Violence Reduction Unit that follows a similar public health approach.

From both of the case studies, what was relatively clear was that each area adopted parts of different initiatives and not the precise system or programme. In the Prevention First project this meant that each local authority involved in the police area slightly adapted the approach to account for their circumstances. Similarly, in the CIRV project, Northampton Police recognised that their county lines issues meant that the focus and context was different for them. One critical issue that often emerges when policies are transferred from one area to another, is the need to consider why a programme works somewhere may be determined by specific local and cultural context. Graham's (2017) analysis of the transfer of the CIRV programme was the need to adapt the project in Scotland as a result of different legal systems and powers of the police. Often in adopting programmes these differences are forgotten and programmes are deemed a failure even though they have been successful elsewhere potentially undermining their potential. In the era of 'what works' and evidence-based policing, the need to remember adaptability and context are critical for those adopting innovative ideas from elsewhere. Added to this is the challenges of appropriate evaluation of programmes, as pointed out by Graham (2017) the outcomes of the CIRV programme were nor fully evaluated meaning that when it came to funding cuts it proved difficult to justify the demonstrable positive outcomes it was having. This might have been likely to add to the decisions to cut the funding for the programme.

An analysis of both these case studies shows that great effort and resources are required to enable these approaches to be successful. It also demonstrates that this is possible in the short- to medium term. Longer-term success of these partnership approaches is harder to establish. For example, examining the longer-term impact of Prevention First in New Zealand Den Heyer (2020) commented that eventually after the first few years there was no evidence from the data that the Prevention First initiative had ongoing impact. The Glasgow CIRV did come to an end, but was a legacy for the establishment of a similar approach being adopted throughout Scotland and as a case study it demonstrates the success of partnership working. It has not stopped violence completely but has reduced particular forms of violence and reduced weapon carrying that meant a reduction in homicides overall. One obvious challenge for partnerships and public health initiatives that adopt the types of model discussed here is the ongoing challenge of resources. Both programmes often rely on a small number of dedicated staff members, which places them under stress with high workloads. Also, if one person leaves a programme or moves roles (as incidentally happened in both of these initiatives), the partnerships developed can be lost. The Cincinnati initiative demonstrated that what is critical for the longevity of the project is attention to organisational structures is as important as focusing on reductions in crime and violence. In their evaluation of the programme, Engel et al. (2013) argue that in the early phases of the project, strategic planning was critical to address institutionalisation and accountability challenges that inevitably arise with turnover in key leadership positions. Often crime reduction approaches are seen as failing when the reality is that more holistic structural mechanism also needs consideration.

One strong theme that was evident in analysing these programmes was the continued dominance of the police as a key agency in leading preventative programmes. This is not to undermine the role of police in supporting prevention activities but when prevention is followed up by enforcement or the threat of enforcement there is a potential for undermining the development of trust leading to the reinforced Police strategy development: the New Zealand police prevention strategy of dominant roles of particular agencies. Den Heyer (2020) notes other social agencies may well be better placed to resolve vulnerability and community problems. This is also supported by the current 'defund' the police movement which has become more prominent since the death of George Floyd in the summer of 2020. This view is supported by academics like Vitale who discusses the End of Policing and suggests 'any real agenda for police reform must replace police with empowered communities working to solve their own problems' (Vitale 2017: 30). However, while the sentiment that we need to reduce police responses to social problems and instead shift resources to other more socially equipped agencies is relevant, a requirement for police services is likely to remain. These police services would look significantly different to the one witnessed in the killing of George Floyd and would encourage effective partnership with other services with police in a supportive rather than enforcement role (Fleetwood & Lea, 2020). It would also see the rebalancing of funds away from criminal justice towards improving health, education and wellbeing across society. Both cases we discussed have elements of this caring role embedded in them and need to be viewed as longer-term solutions rather than initiatives adopted to resolve issues in the short term. Additionally, who leads on these programmes and the distribution of power might be other considerations that need further thinking. Police tend to dominate and lead many of these initiatives primarily due to cuts elsewhere and as a result of other organisational factors such as their availability as a 24-hour social service (Punch & Naylor, 1973) or the only response available out of hours. This refers back to the point made by Clarke and Newman that often it is broader structures and embedded organisational routines that create challenges to enabling better partnership initiatives to work effectively.

Conclusions

It is clear that partnership working can be successful. What both these initiatives indicate is that successful partnerships that focus on reducing crime applying a broader preventative framework that focus not on the misdeeds of people but that construct people as vulnerable are more likely to have an ongoing impact on people's life. Additionally, outcomes both for the individual and for their communities are likely to be better with more productive solutions, for example, people not being evicted from their property or reducing the likelihood of gang violence. The police can effectively engage in preventative programmes that support a shift away from enforcement towards support. While enforcement is still applied as a mechanism for security purposes and still see as a core aspect of the police role, moving more towards a preventative space can and does occur. Despite this optimism, what we have also learned is that pre-existing organisational cultures and structures can create a barrier to reform. Funding and cuts to services can also have a negative impact. We would argue that rather than embedded in some programmes, prevention needs to be embedded as part of collaborative endeavour over the longer term. Currently in Police Scotland where both the programmes discussed were ran, the strategic approach (SPA 2020) has shifted away from enforcement towards improving the safety and wellbeing of people, places and communities in Scotland. This feels like a refocusing and a step in the right direction towards embedding a more public health approach into organisational thinking. This is critical if the ambition of intersecting Law Enforcement and Public Health is to be fully realised.

References

Ball, R. A., & Curry, D. G. (1995). The logic of definition in criminology: Purposes and methods for defining gangs. *Criminology, 33*(2), 225.

Bennett, T., & Holloway, K. (2004). Gang membership, drugs and crime in the UK. *British Journal of Criminology., 44*(3), 305–323.

Bradshaw, P. (2005). Terrors and young teams: Youth gangs and delinquency in Edinburgh. In S. H. Decker & F. M. Weerman (Eds.), *European street gangs and troublesome youth groups: Findings from the Eurogang research program* (pp. 241–274). Alta Mira Press.

Bradshaw, P., & Smith, D. J. (2005). Gang membership and teenage offending. In *The Edinburgh study of youth transitions and crime* (Vol. 8). University of Edinburgh.

Braga, A., Kennedy, D., & Piehl, A. (1999). *Problem-oriented policing and youth violence: An evaluation of the Boston gun project.* Unpublished Report to the National Institute of Justice.

Braga, A. A., Kennedy, D. M., Waring, E. J., & Piehl, A. M. (2001). Problem-oriented policing, deterrence, and youth violence: An evaluation of Boston's operation ceasefire. *Journal of Research in Crime and Delinquency, 38*, 195–225.

Christie, C. (2011). 'Commission on the future delivery of public services'. *Scottish Government.* http://www.gov.scot/Publications/2011/06/27154527/18, Acessed 10/01/2021.

Crawford, A., & Cunningham, M. (2015). Working in partnership. In *Police leadership–rising to the top* (pp. 71–94).

Curry, D. G., & Spergel, I. (1990). Strategies and perceived agency effectiveness in dealing with the youth gang problem. In C. R. Huff (Ed.), *Gangs in America.* Sage.

Davies, A. (2007). Glasgow's 'Reign of Terror': Street gangs, racketeering and intimidation in the 1920s' and 1930s. *Contemporary British History, 21*(4), 405–427.

Davies, A. (2013). *City of gangs; Glasgow and the rise of the British gangster.* Hodder and Staughton.

Den Heyer, G. (2016). Ghosts of policing strategies past: Is the New Zealand police 'prevention first' strategy historic, contemporary or the future? *Public Organization Review, 16*(4), 529–548.

Den Heyer, G. (2018). Policing excellence and prevention first: A model for transforming police service delivery. *European Journal of Police Studies, 5*(4), 90–108.

Den Heyer, G. (2020). Police strategy development: The New Zealand police prevention strategy. *Police Practice and Research, 22*(1), 127–140. published online July 2020.

Dolowitz, D., & Marsh, D. (1996). Who learns what from whom? A review of the policy transfer literature. *Political Studies, 44*, 343–357.

Dolowitz, D., & Marsh, D. (2000). Learning from abroad: The role of policy transfer in contemporary policy-making. *Governance, 13*, 5–24.

Eck, J. E., & Spelman, W. (1987). *Problem-solving: Problem-oriented policing in Newport News.* Police Executive Research Forum.

Engel, R., Tillyer, S. M., & Corsaro, N. (2013). Reducing gang violence using focused deterrence: Evaluating the Cincinnati initiative to reduce violence (CIRV). *Justice Quarterly, 30*, 1–38.

Esbensen, F., Winfree, L. T., He, N., & Taylor, T. J. (2001). Youth gangs and definitional issues: When is a gang a gang and why does it matter? *Crime and Delinquency., 47*, 105.

Fleetwood, J. & Lea, J. (2020). De-funding the Police in the UK. *British Society of Criminology Newsletter*, p. 25.

Glasgow CIRV Case management practice note (2010a). http://www.actiononviolence.co.uk/content/cirv-case-management-practice-note

Glasgow CIRV Self-referral session practice note (2010b). http://www.actiononviolence.co.uk/sites/default/files/CIRV_practice_note.pdf

Graham, W. (2017). Global concepts, local contexts: A case study of international criminal justice policy transfer in violence reduction. *The Police Chief, 84*(7), 16–17.

Kennedy, D., Piehl, A., & Braga, A. (1996). Youth violence in Boston: Gun Markets, serious youth violence, and a use-reduction strategy. *Law and Contemporary Problems., 59*(1), 147–196.

Kennedy, D. M. (1997). Pulling levers: Chronic offenders, high-crime settings and a theory of prevention. *Valparaiso University Law Review, 31*, 449–484.

Kintrea, K., Bannister, J., & Pickering, J. (2010). Territoriality and disadvantage among young people: An exploratory study of six British neighbourhoods. *Journal of Housing and the Built Environment., 25*, 447–465.

Krug, E., Dahlberg, L. L., Mercy, J. A., Zwi, A. B., & Lozano, R. (2002). *World report on violence and health*. World Health Organisation.

National Network for Safer Communities. (2014). http://nnscommunities.org/impact/cities

Newman, J., & Clarke, J. (2009). *Publics, politics and power: Remaking the public in public services*. Sage.

Patrick, J. (1973). *A Glasgow gang observed*. Neil Wilson Publishing.

Punch, M., & Naylor, T. (1973). Police-social service. *New society, 24*(554), 358–361.

Smith, R., Frondigoun, L., Martin, D., Campbell, R., & Thomas, L. (2018). *An independent assessment of the 'prevention first' crime prevention strategy in Ayrshire: Full report.* Police Scotland.

SPA. (2020). *Joint Strategy for Policing; Policing for a safe, protected and resilient Scotland.* https://www.spa.police.uk/strategy-performance/strategic-police-plan/, Acessed 10/01/2021.

Suttles, G. (1972). *The social construction of communities*. University of Chicago Press.

Vitale, A. (2017). *The end of policing*. Verso.

Williams, D. J., Currie, D., Linden, W., & Donnelly, P. D. (2014). Addressing gang-related violence in Glasgow: A preliminary pragmatic quasi-experimental evaluation of the community initiative to reduce violence (CIRV). *Aggression and Violence Behaviour., 19*(6), 686–691.

Chapter 10
Using Public Health Concepts and Metrics to Guide Policing Strategy and Practice: The Case for an Academic Center for Policing and Public Health

Brandon del Pozo

Introduction

Amidst loud and sustained calls for sweeping reform both at home and abroad, American policing would be well-served by conceptually and operationally aligning itself with the nation's pursuit of improved population health outcomes. The intersection between the fields of policing and public health is a natural one; both sectors respond to the same critical issues in our communities, ranging from the drug crisis and gun violence, to community mental health and both natural and human-caused disasters. However, a present set of institutional and cultural differences prevent them from joining efforts in advancing joint research, innovation, advocacy, and practice (van Dijk et al., 2019, p. 293). This chapter argues that the congruence between these sectors, and the advantages of collaboration, merit the effort needed to overcome any institutional and cultural obstacles to such an alignment. To better develop the evidence base for conjoined practice, and to bring the two sectors to the table, proponents of such an alignment should consider creating an academic center for policing and public health at a major university as a joint endeavor between the practitioners and faculty of both disciplines, with the goal of attracting a broad international audience of researchers, professionals, and students. Such a center would cultivate a lasting and widespread relationship between these two fields, both in their theoretical grounding and in practice.

The project could start with executive sessions that introduce police leaders to the ways in which public health concepts and practices can be used to shape and inform their work. The sessions would give public health practitioners and scholars better insight into the ways policing can contribute to their goals, and provide an

B. del Pozo (✉)
Miriam Hospital/Warren Alpert Medical School of Brown University, Providence, RI, USA
e-mail: bdelpozo@lifespan.org

opportunity to test and refine the pedagogic approaches to fostering collaboration. At present, however, public health seems to evince a hostility to policing, and policing doesn't quite understand its public health partners. This is to the detriment of both fields.

The Call for Reform

The public and elected officials in many communities have sought a departure from the dominant methods of policing (Jackson, 2019), because "the police are not delivering what is expected of them, including protecting vulnerable and at-risk populations" (van Dijk et al., 2019, p. 293). Of their own volition, due to prosecutorial reform, or because they see the writing on the wall, many police agencies are moving away from traditional strategies that rely on criminalization, prosecution, conviction, and incarceration, but the resulting reforms been varied and disjunctive: some agencies use more traditional hot spot policing, others have relied on real-time data to make strategic decisions (Hollywood et al., 2019). Many have focused on behavioral health interventions as alternatives to arrest and enforcement, with considerable variations in approach (Trautman & Haggerty, 2019).

These variations can be attributed to a lack of foundational research about what interventions work best (Engel et al., 2018). As a result, a range of alternatives to traditional enforcement methods has not been systematically developed, evaluated, and integrated into the practice of policing (van Dijk et al., 2019). One of the reasons why this is the case is that these alternative approaches lack a conceptual framework—and a corresponding research program—that coalesces them into a unified and effective approach to defining problems, solving them, and evaluating the results. This has left the profession in a state of uncertainty about policing goals and mission alignment with other government sectors.

This lack of clarity has had other consequences: police officers are frustrated about the unclear or shifting expectations placed on them, how they ought to perform their work, the standards they will be held to, and the ways in which their outcomes will be evaluated. It is becoming increasingly difficult to recruit qualified candidates to become police officers, putting a strain on the profession: "fewer people are applying to become police officers, and more people are leaving the profession, often after only a few years on the job," while "the skills, temperament, and life experiences needed to succeed as an officer are becoming more complex" (Mostyn, 2019, p. 7), and policing itself has become politically polarized, not only in the United States but notably in the United Kingdom and France as well (BBC, 2020). A Center for Policing and Public Health would drive the alignment of the policing and public health sectors in ways that are effective and sustainable, while better realizing the values and expectations of the communities that police departments serve.

A Nascent Collaborative Approach

An international cadre of researchers has recently begun to explore the opportunities presented by merging the practices of policing and public health (A. van Dijk & Crofts, 2017). Nearly all of the research on the explicit intersection of public health and policing is less than 6 years old, with a notable increase that generally coincides with the establishment and growth of an annual Law Enforcement and Public Health (LEPH) conference, which has been held in several international locations since 2012. The research has also been largely conceptual, noting the opportunities for collaboration and the merging of approaches, while commonly citing the fact that practical intersections are in their infancy and that the systems in place in the various institutions will require significant cultural and bureaucratic changes before they can operate together effectively (van Dijk et al., 2019).

It is important to note, however, that the idea that policing has a role in community health is not new. Before the broken windows approach to policing (Kelling & Wilson, 1982) was taken as license for a zero-tolerance approach to enforcing laws and maintaining order (Kohler-Hausmann, 2018), prioritizing arrests and citations above other interventions, much of policing was about solving risk behavior-related problems in other ways. Egon Bittner, perhaps the most prominent early sociologist of policing, remarked that "when one looks at what policemen actually do, one finds that criminal law enforcement is something that most of them do with the frequency located somewhere between virtually never and very rarely" (Bittner, 1990, p. 240). During his field research, Michael Banton found that "the most striking thing about patrol work is the high proportion of cases in which policemen do *not* enforce the law" (Banton, 1964, p. 127). In some ways, then, the intersection of policing and public health can be conceived of as the modern construal of an older strain of police work that focused on community problem solving and peacekeeping rather than law enforcement per se, which has always been a part of their mission and features prominently in accounts of the role and ethics of policing (del Pozo, 2020a; Kleinig, 1996).

The intersection of policing and public health may also be considered the revival of a political philosophy developed by Georg Hegel 200 years ago. As Alan Wood writes in the notes on his translation of Hegel's *Elements of the Philosophy of Right*, "the 'police' in [Hegel's] sense includes all functions which support and regulate the activities of civil society with a view towards the welfare of individuals. . . only later in the nineteenth century was the meaning of *Polizei* limited to the maintenance of peace and order, 'law enforcement' in a narrower sense" (Hegel, 1821/1991, p. 450). Policing, in Hegel's view, was one of the principal regulatory functions of a cameralist state that employed a wide range of interventions to stabilize communities and ensure the welfare of citizens. We may therefore consider the possibility that there is a philosophical precedent for an idea of policing that is broader in its functions, and aspires to positive outcomes beyond the boundaries of criminal justice through the regulation of everyday life and its common spaces. Although Hegel does not invoke the idea of public health, this is because it would have been anachronistic, not because doing so was inappropriate on its face. It is also not as foreign an idea as it might seem: the American Public Health Association's (2019) *Public Health Code of Ethics* identifies health and safety as "essential conditions for human flourishing. Public health practitioners and organizations have an ethical responsibility to... promote and protect public safety, health and wellbeing" (p. 5), and the authority officials use to undertake various coercive measures to improve population health is referred to as their "police power" (Kass, 2001).

An Alignment of Policing and Public Health

The relationship between policing and public health should be genuinely intersectional, rather than of one approach supplanting or subsuming the other. Harm reductionists cite the negative consequences of police interventions (Wood et al., 2015), such as the use of force (Bui et al., 2018) and the effects of incarceration (Alexander, 2010), or the politicizing law order maintenance (Thacher, 2014) for oppressive political ends (Fassin, 2011). Arrests are often made for their own sake, without regard to a legitimate state interest (Harmon, 2016). Policing that concentrates on the enforcement of minor offenses and that sustains social stigmas regarding addiction have led to negative outcomes in stopping the spread of infectious diseases (Beletsky et al., 2011). Many therefore advocate for measures that reduce those harms by employing police interventions less frequently, or replacing them with non-police interventions, or decriminalizing acts in order to deprive the police with the ability to intervene in the first place (Husak, 2009).

Delimiting the police role is a valid approach in some cases, but it should be considered as one among many approaches to aligning policing and public health. In some ways, we can conclude that police officers are public health interventionists by default (Asquith & Bartkowiak-Théron, 2017) and some approaches, for example, use occupational safety training to better equip police to promote public health goals (Beletsky et al., 2011). Depending on the jurisdiction, their work could center on policing when appropriate, promote collaborative efforts whenever possible, and be replaced by interventions with non-police actors responding in lieu of the police whenever necessary (Fleetwood & Lea, 2020). Such work would hopefully come as the product of a cautious and evidence-informed approach, rather than a rapid and deep defunding of police departments before alternative arrangements can be effectively implemented (del Pozo, 2020b). Shifting policing towards public health can, therefore, be guided by the following intersectional principles:

- The goal of policing is to protect a community and promote the safety of its residents by reducing morbidity and mortality at the jurisdictional level; this makes it naturally congruent with the overall goals of public health (Shepherd & Sumner, 2017), which distinguish between the health of individuals and that of an entire population (Rose, 1985).

- Successful police interventions are the ones that result in improved population health and safety outcomes rather than simply lower crime rates or increased enforcement statistics (Christmas & Srivastava, 2019), which are inadequate surrogate endpoints.
- Police interventions should be formulated and evaluated based on how well they accomplish this goal, and traditional criminal justice methods centering on law enforcement and arrest are but one of the means of meeting the goals of policing (Burris & Koester, 2013).
- Every intervention has possible collateral consequences and iatrogenic effects (Anderson & Burris, 2017, p. 3), policing should acknowledge this, and seek to both measure and minimize them (del Pozo, 2020a, p. 343).
- Policing is one of the means by which particular interpersonal conflicts are solved and our duties to citizens as victims of crime and misfortune are acknowledged. These interventions are "clinical" in nature because they aim for specific individual outcomes apart from community-level implications. They are an important part of policing, but when pursued as exclusive ends they can be at odds with population health goals, with the order of precedence open to debate (Redmond, 2019). Police should strike the appropriate balance between these two goals, as should public health officials.

The flow of innovation and reform that these principles yield should not be represented by an arrow that only points from public health to policing. The best value will come from arrows that point in both directions; policing also has something of value to offer traditional public health interventionists. Such value is despite the sometimes intense hostility that public health acolytes have towards police agencies, in great part due to the politicization of the police role, which in the United States has placed it in the crucible of racial oppression. But this does not diminish the immense utility of the police role: police officers are generalists who are both summoned to a wide range of situations where people believe their interventions are necessary, and they proactively seek to intervene in situations that implicate their roles and powers. Population health interventions heavily favor a recasting of the structural determinants of health and wellbeing, but in doing so, they invoke the very difficult, long-term task of restructuring society and its most complex institutions (Dasgupta et al., 2018).

Policing, for its part, specializes in quickly employing partial solutions that can make a real community-level difference in the interim. Sometimes the harms the police impose are with the clear intention of averting even greater ones, such as when they use force to intervene in a dangerously violent act between people (del Pozo, 2018), and this is another way in which the practices complement each other, since public health interventions can have collateral consequences as well. For example, the economic and social restrictions imposed to limit the spread of the COVID-19 pandemic caused severe emotional distress, contracted economies in ways that imposed severe hardships on people, some which undoubtedly reduced health or caused mortality, and led to a severe resurgence in opioid overdose deaths (Katz et al., 2020). At the very minimum, they severely restricted the liberty of people under the premise that it was necessary to protect health at the population level. For their part, police agencies have developed complex systems for quickly and safely intervening at any time and place within a jurisdiction, with little predictability, and under a very wide range of circumstances. Public health could benefit from better understanding and employing such speed, breadth, and flexibility in its work when it is called upon to intervene in proximate threats to health that can have an aggregate effect at the population level.

The work police do is controversial, but its features and dynamics are often not well understood outside of the realm of its practitioners (Greenberg & Frattaroli, 2018). Both policing and public health have coercive elements to their work: they both use laws, norms, mechanisms of social control to regulate and influence behavior. Public health interventions can be seen as overly paternalistic (Turcotte-Tremblay & Ridde, 2016), as can those of policing. By confronting these concerns across both practices as they intersect, we can come to a better understanding of how coercive measures best fit into a plan for public safety and population health, when they soon reach important moral and practical limits, and when we ought to defer to tailored "clinical" interventions (such as a detailed domestic violence plan or an intervention to provide a person with treatment for substance use disorder) at a level that better acknowledges the specific needs of individual people.

A Public Health Approach to Policing Practically Defined

There are two broad categories of police work that seek the ends of population health: regimes that regulate objects and practices that produce public health risks, and interventions that seek to deter and abate risk behavior. In both cases, policing affords the opportunity to shape the social ecologies and structural determinants that affect population health, provided that practitioners understand the relationship between their work and population health outcomes. Some of the common ground in these two broad categories are as follows:

- *Risk behavior* related to community safety, violence, mental illness, homelessness, sex work, and substance abuse.
- *Regulatory regimes* concerning alcohol, tobacco and nicotine, medicines and controlled substances, and vehicular travel.

Moving away from public health as an alternative in opposition to policing towards an understanding of the ways in which it can shape police work to better achieve its acknowledged ends in the aforementioned categories requires offering an account of how public health would define, conceptualize, solve, and evaluate the problems policing seeks to address. An intersectional approach between policing and public health would:

- *Define* the problems policing seeks to address as issues of morbidity, mortality, harm, and community resilience rather than exclusively as law and order violations best suited for the criminal justice system. Policing is expected to protect a community with the collective goal of helping it thrive, improving not only physical, but also mental and social wellbeing.

- *Conceptualize* these problems using perspectives and language of public health: for example, epidemiology and its epi-triangle of agents, hosts and vectors; incorporating an understanding of the structural/social determinants of disruptive/violent behavior.
- *Solve* these problems by using evidence-based interventions, and by recognizing that solving complex problems requires a collaborative, interdisciplinary approach. Public health solutions identify and seek to minimize collateral consequences and iatrogenic effects (APHA, 2019, p. 8). They do not presuppose that one agency has the right solution or can act alone.
- *Evaluate* the success of police interventions in terms of public health's goals of lower community harm indices, and longer, healthier more resilient lives at the community level rather than raw number changes in crime numbers or police productivity statistics (Cloud & Davis, 2015, p. 19).

Policing, Public Health, Harms, and Racial Justice

If a public health approach to policing intends to be practical and useful in a way that improves the profession and the communities it serves, it will have to tackle the issues of racism and racially disparate outcomes of law enforcement. Policing has long been relied upon as the principal means of reducing community violence and securing public safety, producing racially disparate outcomes even in cases where minorities had the political influence necessary to formulate interventions themselves (Forman Jr., 2017). This is apart from instances in which policing has been explicitly used as a tool of political oppression (Shelby, 2007), in ways and subjugate vulnerable communities (Soss & Weaver, 2017), or for political gain at the expense of vulnerable demographics (Barkow, 2019). All of these concerns speak to the idea that policing—as part of an equally culpable criminal justice system as a whole—can produce undesirable collateral consequences and iatrogenic effects that disparately impact racial minorities even when it is conducted in good faith. The United States has a long and consistent history of political regimes that diminish the health and wellbeing of minority communities (Galea et al., 2011), from slavery and lynching through segregation and excessive incarceration (Laqueur, 2018). Policing has also had a negative effect on the ability of minority adolescents to participate in the civic life of their communities (Weaver & Geller, 2019). One of the goals of justice must be to undo these effects and ensure that civic institutions no longer create or exacerbate them.

One of the ways in which a public health approach to policing can contribute to racial justice is by ensuring that outcomes are measured by means that accurately reflect the condition of a community rather than the traditional metrics of criminal justice, such as enforcement statistics, crime volume and rate, and the amount of contraband seized (Burris & Koester, 2013; Cloud & Davis, 2015). These latter measures are more susceptible to political manipulation because they are surrogate endpoints that offer an incomplete picture of the lived and felt experiences of a community; they can be touted while masking the iatrogenic effects of the interventions that produced them (such as, for example, the mental trauma that results from being party to a police use of force (DeVylder et al., 2018)). As an alternative, researchers have proposed using indices of community harm to measure the outcomes of policing (Ratcliffe, 2015). Christmas and Srivastava (2019) observe that "a key element of public health approaches is skilled use and interpretation of data and the evidence base to ensure that interventions are designed, tailored and delivered to be as effective as possible" (p. 5). These approaches, if adhered to, would go far in limiting the implementation of police interventions that have harmful racial justice outcomes. In that way, they would hew closely to Pawson and Tilley's realist approach (1997), where the outcome of an intervention is not only a product of its mechanism but its cultural and political contexts. Measures of morbidity, mortality, and wellbeing are within the reach of police interventionists and analysts, and they are close enough to being true endpoints of the condition of a community that achieving them would mean that the practice of policing has contributed to achieving racial justice: health and equality are firmly linked in the lived experience of a community, and especially a vulnerable or underserved one (Voigt & Wester, 2015).

An Institutional Center for Policing and Public Health

Taking an evidence-based approach to policing using the methods of public health means conducting research, synthesizing the evidence, translating it into practice, and implementing the resulting pilots, programs, and policies in scalable, sustainable ways that can be evaluated for effectiveness. This endeavor, which is in its infancy, requires a dedicated research program that combines the various disciplines implicated by the intersection of policing and public health, while remaining in close contact with practitioners during all stages of research, implementation, and evaluation. It would also benefit from education and advocacy, since while there is much in common between the overall goals of policing and public health, the methods and paradigms of public health are not yet well understood by most police practitioners, especially when explicitly using them to describe ways to police a population.

A university-based center dedicated to this work would address these concerns. Worldwide, there are few research centers specifically dedicated to advancing the conjoined practice of policing and public health, and no notable ones in the United States. A. J. van Dijk et al. (2019) see such as center as an opportunity to provide evaluative rigor and an evidence base to such a partnership, doing so with an approach that would strike a neutral balance between the bureaucratic and cultural interests of the two practices. They observe that:

This model is interesting because rather than create an overarching bureaucratic structure to bring different interests under one agency, university researchers provide an intermediary and hopefully neutral platform. For example, if law enforcement and public health were to jointly fund and manage a university based research center, university-based researchers could provide the rigor for research evaluation and the so-called outsider perspective to assist law enforcement and public health agencies to rise above bureaucratic constraints (ibid, 2019, p. 292).

Creating a center would fill two gaps, which together would increase the quality of public safety and population health outcomes of the nations that embrace its work. In the United States, it would bridge the research gap that exists in this field domestically, and it would help operationalize research findings in the specific context of American policing and propagate the results widely. The goal would be to do so in a rigorous but practical and accessible way that ends the "dialogue of the deaf," in which research and practice operate on disparate tracks that talk past each other (Bradley & Nixon, 2009). Accordingly, a Center for Policing and Public Health should:

- Develop a unified approach to policing and public health as a concept and in practice.
- Educate government leaders about the planning and performance expectations they should have of police leaders and their police departments if they expect them to take a public health approach to policing. Show them how to evaluate police leadership based on the success of their public health-driven policing strategies and practices.
- Educate police leaders about the principles of public health and how they can be used to shape policing in practice. Equipping them with the strategic skills necessary to lead a police department committed to the collaborative pursuit of public health.
- Devise particular policing strategies and interventions that achieve the goals of policing using the means and methods of public health.
- Create an analytical suite that allows police department data and policy analysts to devise and evaluate police interventions using the methods and metrics of public health.
- Train police analysts to use the analytical methods of public health to evaluate police interventions.
- Inform the public about the opportunities that integrating police and public health affords in the pursuit of community and individual health, wellbeing, and justice.

The center would be well-versed in the employment of observational studies, quasi-scientific experiments, and the iterative cycle of evidence informing practice, and then practice subsequently informing research design, one of the key ways to generate innovation and reform in a practitioner environment (Ogilvie et al., 2019). There is a consensus that foundational research gaps exist in policing generally (Friedman, 2017). In response to such gaps in evaluating alternatives to arrest, Engel et al. (2018) argue that "scholars should engage in more natural experiments and case studies, which could provide opportunities for comprehensive exploration of the impact of changes in laws or policies on the decision to arrest," because "reestablishing this research foundation is critical to the subsequent success of alternative to arrest initiatives" (2018, p. 86).

A center for policing and public health would therefore confer the additional benefit of refining experimental methodologies that are well-suited to the complexities and demands of the policy and practice environments of policing. Such a center would be an institution that leads the profession of policing, as Green (2008) envisions for clinical practices, towards "a future in which we would not need to ask the question of how to get more acceptance of evidence-based practice, but one in which we would ask how to sustain the engagement of practitioners, patients and communities in a participatory process of generating practice-based research and program evaluation" (p. i24), brought about through "the training of practitioner students in use of evidence and methods of evaluation that would predispose and enable them to participate more actively in the appropriate adaptation of received evidence and the critical evaluation of their own practices and programs" (p. i24). In other words, a center for policing and public health would be instrumental to the furtherance of evidence-informed policing.

The First Step: An Executive Session Pilot

The first step in this endeavor could be executive sessions for police practitioners, to be held on an academic campus and led by an interdisciplinary team of faculty. It would be used to test the basic concept of the center, help refine its research agenda, develop the corresponding curriculum, and test the pedagogical methods that best convey its research to the intended audience. It would consist of:

- Read-ahead assignments on the fundamentals of public health and its intersection with policing.
- An introduction to the concepts and methods of public and population health generally.
- The ways in which these concepts and methods can be applied to policing.
- Techniques used to demonstrate the relationship between policing and public health within an agency and to the public and elected officials.
- The means by which public health metrics can be used to evaluate policing outcomes.
- Case studies in the intersection of public health and policing.
- Exercises in which participants develop public health-informed strategies to solve policing problems.
- Exercises in which participants evaluate police interventions using public health metrics.

The pilot would be developed with the input of police practitioners who have experience in administration, strategic planning, and the evaluation of police work. A handful of United States police practitioners are in the process of seeking advanced degrees in public health, and their contributions would be especially valuable. Partnership with one or more research organizations in policing would ensure that the pilot does not get out too far ahead of policing norms at the start and would allow the program to recruit participants using the existing communication channels these organizations have developed. Upon the conclusion of the pilot, participants would be invited to frame, address, and evaluate a particular police problem in their jurisdiction using the concepts they have learned and developed during the week. Joint work between a school of public health and an academic criminal justice department or institution with a notable commitment to research into evidence-based police interventions and influence over police administration would ensure that initial programming and an ultimate center would be able to leverage the proper expertise and influence in these two fields to ensure high quality research, program development, and the reach necessary to conjoin the two fields in practice.

Conclusion

At present, when mayors, city managers, and city councils interview prospective chiefs of police, they are likely to ask them what they will do to promote community policing in their jurisdiction. The question is as broad and indeterminate as the concept of community policing itself, and the answers can be everything and nothing at once: more police-community events, more community input into policing, or a focus on problem-solving rather than law enforcement per se. It would be more insightful to ask a candidate what she would do to align a city's policing efforts with its public health goals. This would commit the respondent to a discussion about public safety, violence reduction, and concerns about drug use, mental health and homelessness, but in a way that invokes the present concerns about the profession: its harmful collateral consequences, the need to collaborate and rely on evidence, and the need for equity in the outcomes across communities and demographics. Until this line of questioning becomes commonplace, researchers and public health practitioners have an obligation to at least give the nation's police leaders an opportunity to answer its question correctly. A university center that takes up the concerns of policing and public health is an important first step, and the need for one is as apparent and urgent as ever.

Acknowledgments I would like to thank Leo Beletsky and Jennifer Wood for reviewing this manuscript and making valuable suggestions, and Nick Crofts for his insights and support. I would also like to thank the editors of this volume for their valuable insights and feedback.

References

Alexander, M. (2010). *The new Jim crow*. The New Press.

American Public Health Association. (2019). *Public health code of ethics*. American Public Health Association. https://www.apha.org/-/media/files/pdf/membergroups/ethics/ethics_brochure. ashx

Anderson, E., & Burris, S. (2017). Policing and public health: Not quite the right analogy. *Policing and Society, 27*(3), 300–313. https://doi.org/10.1080/10439463.2016.1231188

Asquith, N. L., & Bartkowiak-Théron, I. (2017). Police as public health interventionists. In *Policing encounters with vulnerability*. Palgrave Macmillan.

Banton, M. (1964). *The policeman in the community*. Basic Books.

Barkow, R. (2019). *Prisoners of politics: Breaking the cycle of mass incarceration*. Belknap Press of the Harvard University Press.

BBC. (2020). *France's macron calls for 'urgent' police reform following protests*. BBC News. https://www.bbc.com/news/world-europe-55229428

Beletsky, L., Agrawal, A., Moreau, B., Kumar, P., Weiss-Laxer, N., & Heimer, R. (2011). Police training to align law enforcement and HIV prevention: Preliminary evidence from the field. *American Journal of Public Health, 101*(11), 2012–2015.

Bittner, E. (1990). *Aspects of police work*. Northeastern University Press.

Bradley, D., & Nixon, C. (2009). Ending the dialogue of the deaf: Evidence and policing policies and practices. An Australian case study. *Police Practice and Research, 10*(5–6), 423–435. https://doi.org/10.1080/15614260903378384

Bui, A. L., Coates, M. M., & Matthay, E. C. (2018). Years of life lost due to encounters with law enforcement in the USA, 2015–2016. *Journal of Epidemiology and Community Health, 72*(8), 715–718. https://doi.org/10.1136/jech-2017-210059

Burris, S., & Koester, S. (2013). Investigating the intersection of policing and public health. *PLOS Medicine, 10*(12), 1–2. https://doi.org/10.1371/journal.pmed.1001571

Christmas, H., & Srivastava, J. (2019). *Public health approaches in policing: A discussion paper*. Public Health England & College of Policing.

Cloud, D., & Davis, C. (2015). First do no harm: Advancing public health in policing practices. https://www.prisonpolicy.org/scans/vera/public-health-and-policing.pdf

Dasgupta, N., Beletsky, L., & Ciccarone, D. (2018). Opioid crisis: No easy fix to its social and economic determinants. *American Journal of Public Health, 108*(2), 182–186. https://doi.org/10.2105/AJPH.2017.304187

del Pozo, B. (2018). An intervention, not an accident: Research into use of force by police requires understanding its context and counterfactuals. *Journal of Epidemiology and Community Health, 72*(8) https://jech.bmj.com/content/72/8/715.responses#an-intervention-not-an-accident-research-into-use-of-force-by-police-requires-understanding-its-context-and-counterfactuals

del Pozo, B. (2020a). The police and the state. (PhD). City University of New York Graduate Center.

del Pozo, B. (2020b, November 11). The way forward on police reform *New York daily news*. https://www.nydailynews.com/opinion/ny-oped-the-way-forward-on-police-reform-20201118-vd6rcixvafdwdmervdh6zraebm-story.html

DeVylder, J. E., Jun, H., Fedina, L., et al. (2018). Association of Exposure to police violence with prevalence of mental health symptoms among urban residents in the United States. *JAMA Network Open, 1*(7), e184945. https://doi.org/10.1001/jamanetworkopen.2018.4945

Engel, R. S., Worden, R. E., Corsaro, N., McManus, H. D., Reynolds, D., Cochran, H., et al. (2018). Deconstructing the power to arrest: Lessons from research. Resource document. International Association of Chiefs of Police. https://www.theiacp.org/sites/default/files/2018-08/CPRP_Deconstructing%20the%20Power%20to%20Arrest_FINAL.PDF.

Fassin, D. (2011). Enforcing order: An ethnography of urban policing (R. Gomme, Trans.). Polity Press.

Fleetwood, J., & Lea, J. (2020). De-funding the police in the UK. *British Society of Criminology Newsletter, 85*, 25–35.

Forman, J., Jr. (2017). *Locking up our own*. Farrar, Straus & Giroux.

Friedman, B. (2017). *We spend $100 billion on policing. We have no idea what works*. Washington Post.

Green, L. W. (2008). Making research relevant: If it is an evidence-based practice, where's the practice-based evidence? *Family Practice, 25*(suppl_1), i20–i24. https://doi.org/10.1093/fampra/cmn055

Greenberg, S., & Frattaroli, S. (2018). What police officers want public health professionals to know. *Injury Prevention, 24*(3), 178–179. https://doi.org/10.1136/injuryprev-2017-042675

Harmon, R. (2016). Why arrest? *Michigan Law Review, 115*, 307–364.

Hegel, G. W. F. (1821/1991). Elements of the philosophy of right (H. Nisbet, Trans.). Cambridge University Press.

Hollywood, J. S., McKay, K. M., Woods, D., & Agniel, D. (2019). *Real-time crime centers in Chicago: Evaluation of the Chicago police Department's strategic decision support centers*. RAND Corporation. https://www.rand.org/pubs/research_reports/RR3242.html

Husak, D. (2009). *Overcriminalization: The limits of the criminal law*. Oxford University Press.

Jackson, L. (2019, June 1). Change Agents: A new wave of reform prosecutors upends the status quo. *American Bar Association Journal*. https://www.abajournal.com/magazine/article/change-agents-reform-prosecutors

Kass, N. (2001). An ethics framework for public health. *American Journal of Public Health, 91*(11), 1776–1782.

Katz, J., Goodnough, A., & Sanger-Katz, M. (2020, July 15). *In shadow of pandemic, U.S. drug overdose deaths resurge to record*. The New York Times.

Kelling, G., & Wilson, J. (1982, March). Broken windows: The police and Neighborhood Safety. *The Atlantic Monthly*, 29–38.

Kleinig, J. (1996). *The ethics of policing*. Cambridge University Press.

Kohler-Hausmann, I. (2018). *Misdemeanorland: Criminal courts and social control in an age of broken windows policing*. Princeton University Press.

Laqueur, T. (2018). Lynched for drinking from a White Man's well. *London Review of Books, 40*(19), 11–15.

Mostyn, S. (2019). *The Workforce Crisis, and What Police Agencies are doing About it*. https://www.policeforum.org/assets/WorkforceCrisis.pdf

Ogilvie, D., Adams, J., Bauman, A., Gregg, E. W., Panter, J., Siegel, K. R., . . . White, M. (2019). Using natural experimental studies to guide public health action: Turning the evidence-based medicine paradigm on its head. *Journal of Epidemiology and Community Health*. https://doi.org/10.1136/jech-2019-213085

Pawson, R., & Tilley, N. (1997). An introduction to scientific realist evaluation. In E. Chelimsky & W. R. Shadish (Eds.), *Evaluation for the 21st century: A handbook* (pp. 405–418). Sage Publications, Inc..

Ratcliffe, J. (2015). Towards an index for harm-focused policing. *Policing: A Journal of Policy and Practice, 9*, 164–182.

Redmond, H. (2019). *Grappling with the "promise and perils" of public health*. Filtermag.org.. https://filtermag.org/public-health-promise-perils/

Rose, G. (1985). Sick individuals and sick populations. *International journal of epidemiology, 14*(1), 32–38. https://doi.org/10.1093/ije/14.1.32

Galea, S., Tracy, M., Hoggatt, K. J., Dimaggio, C., & Karpati, A. (2011). Estimated deaths attributable to social factors in the United States. *American Journal of Public Health, 101*(8), 1456. https://doi.org/10.2105/AJPH.2010.300086

Shelby, T. (2007). Justice, deviance, and the dark ghetto. *Philosophy & Public Affairs, 35*(2), 126–160. https://doi.org/10.1111/j.1088-4963.2007.00106.x

Shepherd, J., & Sumner, S. A. (2017). Policing and public health—Strategies for collaboration. *JAMA, 317*(15), 1525–1526.

Soss, J., & Weaver, V. (2017). Police are our government: Politics, political science, and the policing of RaceClass subjugated communities. *Annual Review of Political Science, 20*(1), 565–591. https://doi.org/10.1146/annurev-polisci-060415-093825

Thacher, D. (2014). Order maintenance policing. In M. Reisig & R. Kane (Eds.), *The Oxford handbook of police and policing* (pp. 123–147). Oxford University Press.

Trautman, L., & Haggerty, J. (2019). Statewide policies relating to pre-arrest diversion and crisis response. https://www.rstreet.org/wp-content/uploads/2019/10/Final-187.pdf

Turcotte-Tremblay, A.-M., & Ridde, V. (2016). A friendly critical analysis of Kass's ethics framework for public health. *Canadian Journal of Public Health, 107*(2), e209–e211. https://doi.org/10.17269/cjph.107.5160

van Dijk, A., & Crofts, N. (2017). Law enforcement and public health as an emerging field. *Policing and Society, 27*(3), 261–275.

van Dijk, A. J., Herrington, V., Crofts, N., Breunig, R., Burris, S., Sullivan, H., & Thomson, N. (2019). Law enforcement and public health: Recognition and enhancement of joined-up solutions. *The Lancet, 393*(10168), 287–294. https://doi.org/10.1016/S0140-6736(18)32839-3

Voigt, K., & Wester, G. (2015). Relational equality and health. *Social Philosophy and Policy, 31*(2), 204–229. https://doi.org/10.1017/S0265052514000326

Weaver, V. M., & Geller, A. (2019). De-policing America's youth: Disrupting criminal justice policy feedbacks that distort power and derail prospects. *The Annals of the American Academy of Political and Social Science, 685*(1), 190–226. https://doi.org/10.1177/0002716219871899

Wood, J. D., Taylor, C. J., Groff, E. R., & Ratcliffe, J. H. (2015). Aligning policing and public health promotion: Insights from the world of foot patrol. *Police Practice and Research, 16*(3), 211–223.

Chapter 11
Law Enforcement and Public Health Partnerships and Collaborations in Practice: Community Voices

James Clover, Emily Craven, Donna Maree Evans, Wayne Helfrich, Liz Komar, Miriam Aroni Krinsky, and Michael Peters

Introduction

James Clover

It was imperative for the Editors of this collection to both access and showcase the voices of practitioners, and we fully acknowledge the tremendous value these perspectives can have in thoughtfully reminding us of the complexities in the shared roles and relationship charged with serving the people we intend to support. When we have an opportunity to learn from practitioners outside our personal or

J. Clover (✉)
Faculty of Health and Community Studies, MacEwan University, Edmonton, AB, Canada
e-mail: jamesbclover@gmail.com

E. Craven (✉)
Sex Worker Education & Advocacy Taskforce (SWEAT), Cape Town, South Africa
e-mail: emilyc@sweat.org.za

D. M. Evans (✉)
RMIT University, Melbourne, VIC, Australia
e-mail: donnaevans999@gmail.com

W. Helfrich (✉)
Key Population Advocate, Pretoria, South Africa
e-mail: Wayne.helfrich@gmail.com

L. Komar (✉) · M. A. Krinsky (✉)
Fair and Just Prosecution, Los Angeles, CA, USA
e-mail: lkomar@fairandjustprosecution.org; mkrinsky@fairandjustprosecution.org

M. Peters (✉)
YMCA of Northern Alberta, Edmonton, AB, Canada
e-mail: michael.peters@northernalberta.ymca.ca

professional sphere, we become enriched with a fuller understanding of what our clients and communities need. Through these dialogues we also reveal the ways our personal and organizational efforts can both complement and conflict with the activities of others, which at times can have dire health consequences for the people that look to us for essential care and support.

Michael Peters speaks to an important truth that is often underappreciated when considering a more responsive system of health and wellness delivery. Timing is a crucial factor when we engage with respective clients or the community-at-large; it is vital that engagement and support be provided when the recipient is amicable, in whatever state they present, and not when convenient for the institutions that provide the service and support. As the reader explores within this collection the shared space that law enforcement and public health occupy, we can consider Peters' professional priority to strive to meet the client "where they are at geographically, emotionally, and mentally."

The contributions from Donna Evans, Emily Craven, and Wayne Helfrich transport the reader to South Africa, specifically within the sex work community. Evans and Craven describe a number of initiatives including the Positive Policing Partnership—a non-confrontational and relationship-focused effort directed at police officers to humanize the sex worker. Evans and Helfrich provide a parallel description to the negative health consequences sex workers face when being policed, including violence, criminalization, and dehumanization as a result of drug addiction, health status, or their station as a sex worker. The evidence put forward in these contributions appear to reveal a common theme captured within this collection, specifically the negative health consequences marginalized communities face when in contact with law enforcement.

The final piece by Miriam Krinsky and Liz Komar eloquently demonstrates the position that punitive approaches to drug users is a false endeavor, and provides certain inspiration that supportive health strategies can be effective despite political opposition. Equally important is the recognition that any discipline which has a touchpoint to serve people, including the longstanding institution of prosecutorial services in the United States, can purposefully reflect and reform their intended contributions, learn and adjust from the unintended consequences that have proven harmful, and align themselves with others' efforts toward a shared global mission of improving the overall public health wellness.

The Power of Collective Practices

Michael Peters

Throughout my career, I have had the opportunity to work with many individuals, primarily children, youth and their families who have had varying experiences with many aspects of the health and law enforcement systems. Meeting them where they are at geographically, emotionally, and mentally has always been my top priority.

Working with children and youth has helped me understand the need for *all* of the supports in their life to take a harm reduction approach. People come from diverse backgrounds, family dynamics, and lived experiences. The need to continually be there to pick an individual up when they stumble is absolutely imperative for both their short-term and long-term success. Like all of us, having someone who cares for you "unconditionally" creates an environment of trust and mutual respect. This level of unconditional support can be provided through many areas of an individual's life—from the police officer who stops by to play a game of basketball or a doctor or nurse who spends that extra minute with them to truly hear their concerns and help find a solution. When we look at the person instead of the problem, we can create a more inclusive and connected community.

The true opportunity to positively intersect law enforcement and public health or mental health support requires a bigger conversation around systemic change. Currently the system is not set up for law enforcement and public health to naturally work together to support individuals who would benefit from such collaboration. Both systems meet the individual needs they historically have, however, due to the policies and procedures each system has in place, they lack agility to meet the needs of all individuals they interact with. When the system is ready and when the individual is ready, buy-in increases as well as the chance of success, resulting in the right level of support at the right time.

If we were to broaden the academic definition of "public health" to the many community agencies striving to meet individuals where they are at on a daily basis, the chance for intersection is more likely. Surrounding an individual with the supports they select, such as mentors, cultural supports, community agencies, and faith leaders empowers them to play an active role in the direction of their life. It also ensures that these supports remain consistent as needs vary. Looking to define public health as both the system as a whole and the more specific, individualized approach, truly meets the public need.

We know law enforcement is necessary to keep the community safe. When you use the same approach to broaden the definition of "law enforcement" to include the same community agency supports, it can not only reduce recidivism but decrease negative interactions that lead to individuals becoming involved with the justice system. The common denominator here is the need to broaden these definitions to include the natural and community supports the individual identifies.

I had the opportunity to work with a young man named James[1] who was incarcerated at an early age. James and a number of his peers took part in a group workshop on self-esteem offered by the YMCA Youth Transition Program. This workshop was designed to introduce the group of young males to the importance of building healthy self-esteem and surrounding themselves with positive people. When the workshop concluded, James expressed a desire to continue learning

---

[1] All names and other personal identifiers in this case have been changed to protect privacy and confidentiality.

about ways to develop himself. We set up bi-weekly meetings that continued regularly for nearly 5 years.

During our time together, I grew to understand that a number of key determinants of health were not currently present for this young man to develop. He expressed his desire to have a positive future. As we worked through multiple workbooks and took part in many conversations, it became very clear that James was able to self-reflect on what he needed to do to become successful. More importantly, he was able to identify for himself which social supports he needed around him to succeed.

As James grew up and was relocated throughout the province, I was able and willing to continue to connect with him. When he had a rough day at school or in court, he would give me a call just to talk. The pinnacle of his success came when he was awarded the Gold Level Duke of Edinburgh award for his work academically, and as a peer mentor and leader. With consistent guidance and individualized support, James found the internal motivation to help him achieve this honor. He ensured I was invited to the ceremony where he was awarded this honor.

James continues to connect to this day with a holiday greeting or a quick text or call to check in.

By working together, law enforcement and public health systems have the opportunity to positively impact the lives of some of our community's most vulnerable citizens. When working in collaboration to address the individual's concerns, these systems have the opportunity to be more effective in their treatment and care. This requires a basic human action: empathy. When workers from these systems take the time to understand what the individual needs are and are backed by the systems they work within to offer wrap-around services, real change is possible for those who need it.

Looking at all of the determinants of health and developmental assets can be daunting for anyone, however, if all of the support systems for individuals in need can support the development of one item at a time it acts as a building block. Over time these blocks create a strong foundation that enables and empowers the individual to begin living a more positive life that they can take ownership of. It requires that the public systems they encounter develop a seamless collaboration and openness to work together.

We may not be able to change the system overnight, but we can work together, communicate and support each other to meet the needs of the individuals we serve. This will in-turn open the door for policy-makers to see a more collaborative way of supporting people, which will ultimately lead to the systemic change required.

Contested Spaces: South African Sex Worker and Operational Policing Interactions

Case Study 1: The Sex Worker Education & Advocacy Taskforce

Donna Maree Evans and Emily Craven

The sex work environment in South Africa is challenging, with laws criminalizing all aspects of adult consensual sex work (Sexual Offences Act, 1957; Criminal Law (Sexual Offences and Related Matters) Amendment Act, 2007). South Africa also experiences high rates of inter-personal violence, including gender-based violence and femicide (Stats, 2020; South African Police Service, 2019; Africa Check, 2019). While sex workers experience violence from clients and other community members, there is substantial evidence of violence perpetrated by law enforcement officers against sex workers including rape and sexual assault, physical assault, torture, unlawful arrest and detention, harassment and intimidation, bribery and corruption; together with policing neglect such as refusing to take complaints or open investigations for sex workers when they attempt to report crimes like rape (Human Rights Watch & SWEAT, 2019; Evans & Walker, 2018; Evans, 2017; Manoek, 2017; South African Women's Legal Centre, 2016; Scorgie et al., 2013; Gould & Fick, 2008; Fick, 2006a; Fick, 2006b; Pauw & Brener, 2003).

SWEAT (Sex Worker Education & Advocacy Taskforce) has a 20-year history in organizing, advocating for and delivering services to South African sex workers. It has birthed two social movements: the South African Sisonke Sex Worker Movement (Sisonke), and the African Sex Worker Alliance (ASWA) now based in Kenya. SWEAT programming embraces a concept of sex worker wellness which goes beyond merely the absence of disease—it includes physical, mental, and social wellbeing. To combat the detrimental health and social impacts of negative policing behaviors, SWEAT adopts an evidence informed human rights-based approach to catalyze change in this difficult context. SWEAT's policing partnership work takes place across two streams: the Sex Worker Empowerment & Enabling Environment Programme (SWEEP) which mobilizes sex workers advocating for service delivery; and the Advocacy & Law Reform Programme (ALRP) which strives to reduce violence, improve access to rights and to enable sex workers to actively claim their rights and advocate for law reform. The ALRP includes a sex worker legal defense center with lawyers and peer-based paralegals who provide advice, representation, and emergency responses for sex workers in contact with the criminal justice system.

In 2018, the South African sex work sector launched the Positive Policing Partnership (PPP) initiative to improve the health and safety of South African sex workers. The PPP approach requires a move away from the more traditional adversarial and complaint-based strategies to focus on relationship- and capacity-building partnerships, forward-focused dialogue, policy interventions, and solution-based actions. The aim of the PPP is to catalyze change through embedding an understanding of the human rights experiences of sex workers across law enforcement, government and society; and to generate and promote opportunities for positive engagement on policing issues through publishing and advocacy on evidence-based research. The origins, tenets, and learnings to date from the PPP approach have been documented in the Journal for Community Safety & Well-Being (Evans, Richter, & Katumba, 2019). The PPP and South African sex work sector continue to convene public events, create dialogue opportunities, and publish reports to ensure the human rights experiences of South African sex workers remain in the government and society's consciousness. Recent events include the Positive Policing Practices & Sex Work Roundtable Discussion (Sonke Gender Justice & SWEAT, 2019), #SayHerName Report 2014–2017 (SWEAT, 2019), and Asijiki Coalition Sex Work & COVID-19 Webinar on Unlawful Policing (Asijiki Coalition, 2020).

A core strategy for SWEAT and Sisonke to catalyze change is their engagement in an extensive sex worker sensitization training strategy with the South African Police Service, effectively "humanizing" the stereotyped "sex worker" through individuals relating their lived experience. The resourcing for this training has primarily been funded through HIV programming which targets frontline staff interacting with sex workers, particularly law enforcement and health providers. It therefore generally has a public health focus such as ensuring sex workers do not default on their medications and treatment plans when in police custody. At a strategic level, Sisonke members participate in the large-scale harm prevention Dignity, Diversity & Policing Project conceived and funded through COC Netherlands (COC) which focuses on promoting and protecting human rights, dignity, and safety for all (Katumba, 2018). This COC project has successfully embedded sensitization training on marginalized groups within the South African Police Training College curriculum and established a delivery program for national rollout to operational police. Sisonke peer educators also deliver sensitization training at the community level, in locations where sex workers may be experiencing difficulties with a local police station. Where required, SWEAT's lawyers and paralegals will also intervene to assist sex workers in contact with police. Very few people are actually charged or prosecuted for sex work; they are more likely to be fined for petty offences such as loitering or nuisance. In many cases, sex workers are simply unlawfully arrested and detained for extended periods without charge or fine, or are subjected to bribery demands in order to avoid arrest or secure release from custody.

One broadly anecdotal observation from this sensitization and training work is that when both sex workers and police participate in the workshops, police often gain a better understanding of the lived experience of the sex worker and some of the commonalities across their lives—they come from the same communities, and they perform underpaid and perilous work in difficult conditions. Many come to understand their personal beliefs and morality are separate from their role and responsibilities as law enforcement officers, and to view sex workers as community members rather than just stereotyping them negatively as "sex workers." In some localities, SWEAT has observed change where sensitized police now champion the rights of sex workers and go out of their way to ensure due process occurs during the criminal justice processes.

On the negative side, there are still far too many instances of sex workers experiencing violence from police or dying in police custody without adequate investigation or accountability. Robyn was a 39-year-old South African sex worker and LGBTQI+ advocate who died in a Cape Town police cell in April 2020. Her death was referred to the Independent Police Investigative Directorate, which to date has declined to make public the findings of its investigation. This stonewalling despite sustained advocacy by the sex work sector for transparency on the circumstances and investigation of Robyn's death reflects the lack of recourse for sex workers even when specialist police accountability mechanisms are appropriately utilized. For many South African sex workers, police are still the one thing they fear the most.

Case Study 2: The Grass Roots Practitioner

Donna Maree Evans and Wayne Helfrich

This case study focuses on the work of advocate and activist Wayne Helfrich, whose qualifications lie in disease management. Wayne has a long-term association with a South African non-governmental organization (NGO) which delivers group community health clinical services to key populations including sex workers, people who use drugs, the homeless and undocumented foreigners. The NGO is based in a large metropole serviced by both the South African Police Service (SAPS), and a Metropolitan Police Department (Metro Police) attached to the municipality. Originally clinical services were offered to community members who could not access government-funded services because the law would not permit it, or because they feared the stigmatizing conduct directed at them by staff in mainstream services.

With funding from PEPFAR (President's Emergency Plan for AIDS Relief), the NGO expanded to become a large-scale community clinic focusing on HIV, initially through harm reduction and later through harm prevention. It quickly became clear that HIV was only one of a range of critical issues affecting their clients. As sex workers and drug users were less likely to access the NGO building for service delivery, the program called Community Orientated Primary Care was developed where the clinic would conduct "home" visits to overcome this barrier. The program concept was based on a South African Research Council study of children who were presenting with HIV symptoms yet were not sexually active and were not receiving treatment. The NGO started looking for these children in order to provide services, only to discover many children were being marginalized due to their parents' status as sex workers, drug users, homeless persons, or undocumented foreigners. The NGO was able to respond agilely to meet these newly discovered community needs through their mobile service delivery strategy. Where the client's "home" was a park bench, staff would provide the clinical services at that park bench. Where the sex worker operated from bushland, the clinical services staff would deliver services in that bushland setting.

Over the years, the NGO has been in continual contact with law enforcement concerning the negative impacts of operational policing behaviors on both clients and clinic staff. One of the very first engagements arose from sex worker complaints that after the mobile clinic staff left the site, police were destroying the condoms and antiretroviral (ARV) medications the clinic had just supplied by setting them on fire, as well as beating and harassing the sex workers. The NGO contacted the local police station and arranged a meeting. This proved to be a very unsuccessful strategy as once SAPS realized the clinic was providing services at various mobile sites, the police would then attend the locations to harass both the sex workers and staff. The NGO obtained a letter for the National Department of Health explaining the staff were providing clinical services which were approved by the Department. When the clinic's peer educators would produce a copy of the letter to police on the scene, the letter would often be ripped up and thrown to the ground, with police then arresting the NGO's Peer Educators and holding them without charge at the station for extended periods of time. The NGO then convened a further multidisciplinary meeting with Metro Police and various NGOS including SWEAT, Sisonke Sex Worker Movement, Homeless Forum, Drug Users Forum, etc. The training focused on human rights compliant policing and sensitization on key populations. At the conclusion of the workshop it was clear little progress had been achieved, when a police official commented that as long as there were whores in this city, (we) will arrest them.

The NGO then changed strategy and began documenting the harassment through videos and photographs of the offending police behavior. At a subsequent meeting with the local Police Station Commander attended by both SAPS and Metro Police, agreement was reached to meet monthly to discuss incidents on a case-by-case basis. After three such meetings the Police Station Commander was transferred, with the police harassment of the clients and clinic staff immediately resuming. This frequent rotation of police officers and station commanders means NGOs routinely have to re-establish relationships and protocols to maintain fundamental legal protections and rights for their clients and staff, a process which continually drains scarce NGO resources from direct clinical services. Police are often focused on meeting arrest targets, with key populations offering high reward for little effort in this endeavor. The connections between health, police, and social development are simply not understood and crimes against sex workers often remain un-investigated. It is no surprise that at a site close to this same police station, a serial rapist and suspected murderer has been preying on sex workers over years. Despite local sex workers identifying who the suspected offender is, efforts to report information and provide witness statements to police have only resulted in threats to arrest the sex workers themselves. Three sex workers have now lost their lives, with at least five more sex workers raped and a confirmed case of HIV transmission from one assault. A clear and enforceable national policing directive and training on the rights of key populations in contact with law enforcement may provide some relief from these recurring issues of non-rights compliant policing and refusal to act on sex worker crime reports.

Disillusioned with the possibilities of effecting change through NGO advocacy, Wayne had approached many politicians for assistance over the years; however, in conservative South African society sex work is a sensitive topic and sex workers simply do not vote. Only through becoming active in the country's political space was he able to effect more sustainable change. With a human rights focus to the advocacy, politicians from the municipality held a roundtable event and established two units within Council, one to provide sensitization to police on sex worker issues and the other being a drug unit which sensitizes police on drug use as a form of disease. These specialist units promote strategies such as police assisting sex workers and drug users by conveying them to appropriate clinics to access services rather than to a police cell. Over time a good informal working relationship has developed where sex workers in particular locations now voluntarily report suspicious activities to police involving crimes such as theft of copper cables and hot water systems from houses—in effect, sex workers act as strategic assets for police to detect crime. Trust has been established between specific sex workers and specific police, but the relationship is ad hoc and dependent on the individuals involved. In some cases, a sex worker who feels he or she is in danger might contact the police officer on their personal cell phone, and that officer will arrive to assist even they are off duty. While there will always be rogue behavior, success can be difficult to achieve and we should celebrate these incremental changes as steps along the pathway to a fairer, safer and more inclusive South Africa.

From Prosecuting Overdoses to Preventing Them: Overdose Prevention Sites, Harm Reduction, and Prosecutorial Culture Shift

Miriam Krinsky and Liz Komar

The Current Landscape

Three epidemics have collided in the United States over recent months producing tragic consequences: a growing demand for reckoning with systemic racism, the novel coronavirus, and the escalating opioid overdose crisis. Prior to the COVID-19 pandemic, the USA was already besieged by deadly overdoses—over 50,000 people died from opioid overdoses in 2019 (American Hospital Association, 2020, July 16). In the wake of the pandemic, 40 states have reported increased overdose deaths and overdose deaths nationally are on track to reach an all-time high (American Medical Association, 2020). In many cities, those increases in fatalities have disproportionately been borne by the Black community (Haley & Saitz, 2020; Whelan, 2020; Bogan, 2020), echoing the health disparities made visible by COVID-19 (Centers for Disease Control and Prevention, 2020).

Philadelphia, Pennsylvania has felt these losses particularly acutely and has become the stage for the United States' first battle in the courts over the legality of overdose prevention sites (OPSs), and elected prosecutors have become unlikely allies in that fight. The movement to open OPSs in the United States, led by harm reduction activists and people who use drugs, has historically been met by opposition from local and federal law enforcement. But as a new generation of reform-minded prosecutors takes office (Bazelon & Krinsky, 2018) and works to undo regressive drug policies that drive mass incarceration, the fight over overdose prevention sites has become emblematic of a broader shift. These prosecutors are not simply moving away from carceral approaches to drug use—they have become active proponents of preventative public health approaches, reflecting a fundamental shift in the role and values of elected prosecutors in the United States.

The Benefits of Overdose Prevention Sites

Overdose prevention sites, also called supervised consumption sites, provide a location to use drugs under the supervision of people trained to immediately reverse overdoses. They can also serve as harm reduction outreach centers where people can receive medical care, access social services, and explore treatment if desired—but they are designed and centered around saving lives (Fair and Just Prosecution, 2019).

OPSs are a proven means of decreasing fatal overdoses, and they have other beneficial outcomes that make them attractive to reform prosecutors. Research shows that they reduce the transmission of infectious diseases, public injections, and discarded syringes, and increase the number of people entering treatment programs (Singer, 2018). As of 2019, 118 OPSs operated in 12 countries, without recording a single fatal overdose in an OPS (Harm Reduction International, 2018).

Promoting OPSs Amidst the Current National Crises

In the context of the broader movement in the United States to reduce police shootings and over-policing of marginalized communities, OPSs offer a way not simply to save lives, but also to reduce police contact with the community. Police officers are often the first to respond to overdoses in US communities, creating the potential for escalation and incarceration. OPSs offer a path where people can access care rather than risk police contact, while reducing the cost and risk to police officers as well.

Given the intense focus among many taking to the streets calling for a redoubling of efforts to address racial inequity, markedly disparate overdose rates form another powerful rationale to embrace OPSs. Despite the perception that the USA's overdose epidemic is a crisis primarily in its white rural areas, overdose rates have skyrocketed in its Black communities. From 2016 to 2017, the mortality rate among Black people rose by 25%, compared with the 11% increase among white individuals (Centers for Disease Control and Prevention, 2019). OPSs offer a means to save some of the most vulnerable Black lives.

Reform Prosecutors Rallying around the Need for OPSs and Harm Reduction Strategies

Around the USA, reform elected prosecutors are using their bully pulpit and credibility to support efforts to open OPSs in their community. In Burlington, Vermont, State's Attorney (SA) Sarah George convened a commission of law enforcement officials, medical professionals, and local leaders to study whether to recommend OPSs after the state saw an increase in opioid-related deaths. The commission ultimately supported legislation to establish an OPS in the state (Murray, 2017). King County (Seattle, Washington) Prosecuting Attorney Dan Satterberg publicly endorsed plans to open OPSs in that city. Then-District Attorney (DA) George Gascon (who has since been newly elected as District Attorney in Los Angeles, California) endorsed efforts to open an OPS in San Francisco, saying, "Sometimes when the law hasn't caught up with the need of the community, we have to be bold and we have to act in a different direction" (Stremple, 2019). His successor, District Attorney Chesa Boudin, continued that support (Knight, 2019). Finally, Philadelphia District Attorney Larry Krasner voiced approval for the planned OPS in his community (Krasner & Krinsky, 2020).

Thus far, none of those efforts have led to the successful opening of an OPS due to strong federal opposition. Under the Trump Administration, the US Department of Justice has opposed OPSs under far-reaching interpretation of the Controlled Substances Act (CSA). OPSs were not contemplated by Congress at the time the CSA was passed, and the intent of the so-called "crack house statute" was to reduce illicit drug use, not bar public health interventions (Beletsky, Davis, Anderson, & Burris, 2008). Nonetheless, DOJ has argued that the CSA prohibits OPSs and fear of federal prosecution has derailed efforts by states to embrace OPSs, including a bill in California in 2018 vetoed by then-Governor Jerry Brown (Associated Press, 2018). However, the current litigation over the planned OPS, Safehouse, in Philadelphia, represents a viable avenue for a federal court to deem OPSs legal under the CSA, and 85 criminal justice leaders joined in an amicus brief in support of the legality of Safehouse, arguing that OPSs provide a lifesaving service critical to public safety (Fair and Just Prosecution, 2020a).

The context for this support of OPSs is a broader movement among reform prosecutors in the USA away from carceral approaches toward public health harm reduction interventions. Many chief prosecutors have embraced some level of decriminalization; choosing either to use their prosecutorial discretion to decriminalize certain substances or offences or advocating for legislative reform. For example, in Seattle, Prosecuting Attorney Satterberg has stopped charging virtually all personal possession cases of small amounts of drugs (Jouvenal, 2019), Baltimore (Maryland) State's Attorney Marilyn Mosby decriminalized cannabis possession (Dewan, 2019), and SA Sarah George (in Burlington, Vermont) has stopped prosecuting possession of the opioid treatment buprenorphine (Aloe, 2018). Over 20 prosecutors spoke out in favor of the MORE Act, which would federally decriminalize cannabis (Fair and Just Prosecution, 2020b). And Los Angeles's DA-elect, Gascon, has expressed support for the Portuguese model, which combines decriminalization of all drugs with a robust harm reduction infrastructure (Jaeger, 2019). Likewise, a growing number of law enforcement leaders and prosecutors are embracing more public health-oriented diversion or deflection models, such as Law Enforcement Assisted Diversion (Fair and Just Prosecution, 2017).

A Growing Prosecutorial Voice Is Embracing New Thinking

While reform-minded prosecutors represent a small fraction of the 2500 elected prosecutors in the United States, they hail from many major cities, as well as smaller communities, and represent a significant portion of the US population. Therefore, the growing support for decriminalization and public health models among these reformers reflects meaningful trends in prosecutorial culture. First, the rise of evidence-based justice decision-making has driven many prosecutors toward new solutions: the data shows that the "war on drugs" has failed and demands new approaches (Fair and Just Prosecution, 2019). Second, racial equity is a core value of the reform prosecutor movement in the USA, and many of these prosecutors are eager to move away from the carceral drug policies that have driven racial disparities (Fair and Just Prosecution, 2018). Third, these prosecutors have reached toward public health interventions as they redefine prosecutorial success, measuring "wins" not just in number of convictions, but also in improvements in the health and wellbeing of their community (Fair and Just Prosecution. (2020c). Fourth, they are also redefining their role to include preventing harm, not simply prosecuting it. And finally, they are affirming the worth and dignity of the lives of people who use drugs.

At their core, OPSs are antithetical to traditional punitive approaches to drug use because they affirm the value of the lives of people who use drugs over the strict enforcement of prohibition. By raising their voices in support of OPSs, this new generation of prosecutors in the USA are saying they agree, and signaling their support for safer, healthier, more equitable communities where the lives of even the most marginalized people matter.

References

Africa Check. (2019). Fact Sheet: South Africa's crime statistics for 2018/19. https://africacheck. org/factsheets/factsheet-south-africas-crime-statistics-for-2018-19/

Aloe, J. (2018). *Chittenden County prosecutor Sarah George wants to help drug users -- not lock them up*. Burlington Free Press. https://www.burlingtonfreepress.com/story/news/politics/ elections/2018/10/18/sarah-george-chittenden-opiate-opioid-harm-reduction-safe-injection/ 1565883002/

American Hospital Association. (2020, July 16). *CDC: Drug overdose deaths up 4.6% in 2019*. https://www.aha.org/news/headline/2020-07-16-cdc-drug-overdose-deaths-46-2019.

American Medical Association. (2020). *Issue brief: Reports of increases in opioid- and other drug-related overdose and other concerns during COVID pandemic*. https://www.ama-assn.org/ system/files/2020-11/issue-brief-increases-in-opioid-related-overdose.pdf.

Asijiki Coalition. (2020). *Sex Work and Covid-19 Webinar – Unlawful Policing*. https:// genderjustice.org.za/publication/asijiki-coalition-sex-work-and-covid-19-webinar/.

Associated Press. (2018). Gov. Brown Vetoes Bill To Open Safe Injection Sites In San Francisco. CBS Sacramento. https://sacramento.cbslocal.com/2018/09/30/gov-brown-vetoes-bill-to-open-safe-injection-sites-in-san-francisco/.

Beletsky, L., Davis, S. D., Anderson, E., & Burris, S. (2008). The law (and politics) of safe injection facilities in the United States. *American Journal of Public Health, 98*(2), 231–237. https://doi. org/10.2105/AJPH.2006.103747

Bazelon, E., & Krinsky, M. (2018). *There's a wave of new prosecutors. And They Mean Justice*. The New York Times. https://www.nytimes.com/2018/12/11/opinion/how-local-prosecutors-can-reform-their-justice-systems.html

Bogan, J. (2020). *Spike in drug overdose deaths of African Americans in St. Louis and St. Louis County causes alarm*. St. Louis Post-Dispatch. https://www.stltoday.com/lifestyles/health-med-fit/health/spike-in-drug-overdose-deaths-of-african-americans-in-st-louis-and-st-louis-county/ article_3d0e644f-515a-52a9-8d15-afcd173d43dd.html

Centers for Disease Control and Prevention. (2019). *Morbidity and Mortality Weekly Report: Drug and Opioid-Involved Overdose Deaths – United States, 2013–2017*. https://www.cdc.gov/ mmwr/volumes/67/wr/mm675152e1.htm?s_cid=mm675152e1_w

Centers for Disease Control and Prevention. (2020). *Health Equity Considerations & Racial & Ethnic Minority Groups, Coronavirus Disease*. https://www.cdc.gov/coronavirus/2019-ncov/ community/health-equity/race-ethnicity.html

Dewan, S. (2019). *A growing chorus of big City prosecutors say no to marijuana convictions*. The New York Times. https://www.nytimes.com/2019/01/29/us/baltimore-marijuana-possession. html

Evans, D. & Walker, R. (2018). The policing of sex work in South Africa: A research report on the human rights challenges across two south African provinces. Sonke Gender Justice. https:// www.saferspaces.org.za/be-inspired/entry/positive-policing-partnership, https://genderjustice. org.za/publication/the-policing-of-sex-work-in-south-africa/

Evans, D. (2017). *Interim case study report on sex worker and policing challenges in South Africa*. Sonke Gender Justice. http://www.genderjustice.org.za/publication/sex-worker-policing-human-rights-challenges

Evans, D., Richter, M., & Katumba, M. (2019). Policing of sex work in South Africa: The positive policing partnership approach. *Journal of Community Safety & Well-Being, 4*(4), 80–85. https:// doi.org/10.35502/jcswb.107

Fair and Just Prosecution. (2017). Promising practices in prosecutor-led diversion. https:// fairandjustprosecution.org/wp-content/uploads/2017/09/FJPBrief.Diversion.9.26.pdf

Fair and Just Prosecution. (2018). 21 Principles for the 21st Century Prosecutor. https:// fairandjustprosecution.org/wp-content/uploads/2018/12/FJP_21Principles_Interactive-w-desti nations.pdf.

Fair and Just Prosecution. (2019). Harm reduction responses to drug use. https:// fairandjustprosecution.org/wp-content/uploads/2019/08/FJP_Brief_HarmReduction.pdf

Fair and Just Prosecution. (2020a). More than 80 criminal justice leaders call for access to life saving overdose prevention sites. https://fairandjustprosecution.org/wp-content/uploads/2020/ 07/FJP-Safehouse-Appeals-Court-Amicus-Release-FINAL.pdf

Fair and Just Prosecution. (2020b). Joint Statement in Support of the MORE Act, https:// fairandjustprosecution.org/wp-content/uploads/2020/08/LEAP-FJP-MORE-Act-Letter.pdf.

Fair and Just Prosecution. (2020c). Researchers launch new tool to measure success in prosecutors' offices, https://fairandjustprosecution.org/wp-content/uploads/2020/09/PPI-Launch-Media-Release_FINAL.pdf.

Fick, N. (2006a). Sex workers speak out – policing and the sex industry. *South African Crime Quarterly, 15*, 13–18. https://journals.assaf.org.za/sacq/article/viewFile/1003/776

Fick, N. (2006b). Enforcing fear – Police abuse of sex workers when making arrest. *SA Crime Quarterly, 16*, 27–33. https://doi.org/10.17159/2413-3108/2006/v0i16a994

Gould, C., & Fick, N. (2008). *Selling sex and human trafficking in a south African City.* Institute for Security Studies. https://issafrica.org/research/books/selling-sex-in-cape-town-sex-work-and-human-trafficking-in-a-south-african-city

Haley, D., & Saitz, R. (2020). The opioid epidemic during the COVID-19 pandemic. *JAMA, 324* (16), 1615–1617. https://doi.org/10.1001/jama.2020.18543

Harm Reduction International. (2018). The Global State of Harm Reduction. https://www.hri. global/files/2019/02/05/global-state-harm-reduction-2018.pdf.

Human Rights Watch & SWEAT. (2019). *Why Sex Work Should Be Decriminalised in South Africa.* https://www.hrw.org/report/2019/08/07/why-sex-work-should-be-decriminalised-south-africa

Jaeger, K. (2019). *Los Angeles prosecutor candidates back drug decriminalization at debate.* Marijuana Moment. https://www.marijuanamoment.net/los-angeles-prosecutor-candidates-back-drug-decriminalization-at-debate/

Jouvenal, J. (2019). *No charges for personal drug possession: Seattle's bold gamble to bring 'peace' after the war on drugs.* The Washington Post. https://www.washingtonpost.com/local/ public-safety/no-charges-for-personal-drug-possession-seattles-bold-gamble-to-bring-peace-after-the-war-on-drugs/2019/06/11/69a7bb46-7285-11e9-9f06-5fc2ee80027a_story.html

Katumba, M. (2018). Lessons learnt: The south African police service's dignity, Diversity and Policing Project: The Promotion And Protection Of Human Rights, Dignity And Safety For All. https://international.coc.nl/wp-content/uploads/2018/12/LL-48-October-2018_Original.pdf

Knight, H. (2019). *SF DA candidate knows pain of prison: His radical dad is locked up.* San Francisco Chronicle. https://www.sfchronicle.com/bayarea/heatherknight/article/SF-D-A-candi date-knows-pain-of-prison-His-14444513.php

Krasner, L., & Krinsky, M. (2020). *As pandemic continues, safe injection sites could save more lives.* The Philadelphia Inquirer. https://www.inquirer.com/opinion/commentary/safe-injection-site-philadelphia-safehouse-harm-reduction-20200708.html

Manoek, S. (2017). Stop harassing us! Tackle real crime! In *A report on the human rights violations by police against sex workers in South Africa.* Sex Worker Education & Advocacy Taskforce & Women's Legal Centre. http://wlce.co.za/wp-content/uploads/2017/02/210812-FINAL-WEB-version.pdf

Murray, E. (2017). *Top officials at odds over need for safe injection sites in Vermont.* Burlington Free Press. https://www.burlingtonfreepress.com/story/news/local/2017/11/29/safe-injection-sites-needed-vermont-saysstudy-group/902666001/

Pauw, I., & Brener, L. (2003). You are all just whores: You can't be raped. Barriers to safer sex practices among women street workers sex workers in Cape Town. *Culture, Health & Sexuality, 5*(5), 465–481. https://doi.org/10.1080/136910501185198

Scorgie, F., Vasey, K., Harper, E., Richter, M., Nare, P., Maseko, S., & Chersich, M. (2013). Human rights abuses and collective resilience amongst sex Workers in Four African Countries:

A qualitative study. *Globalization and Health, 9*(33), 165–178. https://doi.org/10.1186/1744-8603-9-33

Singer, J. (2018). *Harm reduction: Shifting from a war on drugs to a war on drug-related deaths.* Cato Institute. https://www.cato.org/sites/cato.org/files/pubs/pdf/pa-858.pdf

Sonke Gender Justice & the Positive Policing Partnership. (2019). *Positive Policing Practices and Sex Work. Proceedings of a Roundtable Discussion.* Cape Town, 22 May 2019. https://genderjustice.org.za/publication/positive-policing-practices-and-sex-work/.   Accessed 21 December 2020.

South African Police Service (2019). *Annual Crime Report 2018/19.* https://static.pmg.org.za/SAPS_Annual_Crime_Stats_201819.pdf and also https://www.saps.gov.za/services/crimestats.php ISBN NUMBER: 978–0–621-47567-8.

South African Sexual Offences Act 1957. (Act 23 of 1957). https://www.gov.za/documents/sexual-offences-act-previous-short-title-immorality-act-12-apr-1957-0000.

South African Women's Legal Centre (2016). *Police Abuse of Sex Workers: Data from cases reported to the Women's Legal Centre between 2011 and 2015.* http://wlce.co.za/wp-content/uploads/2017/02/Police-abuse-of-sex-workers.pdf

Stats S. A.. (2020). *PO341 Victims of Crime Statistical Release – Governance, Public Safety & Justice Survey.* http://www.statssa.gov.za/publications/P0341/P03412018.pdf

Stremple, C. (2019). *Court ruling could pave way for safe injection sites in San Francisco.* KALW. https://www.kalw.org/post/court-ruling-could-pave-way-safe-injection-sites-san-francisco#stream/0

SWEAT. (2019). #SayHerName report 2014-2017. http://www.sweat.org.za/wp-content/uploads/2019/08/Sweat-Say-Her-Name-Report_HI-RES.pdf.

Whelan, A. (2020). *Philadelphia's drug pandemic, like COVID-19, now puts the heaviest burden on black residents, data show.* Philadelphia Inquirer. https://www.inquirer.com/health/opioid-addiction/overdose-deaths-philadelphia-black-residents-20200826.html

Part III
Special Issues in Law Enforcement and Public Health

Chapter 12
Moving Beyond the War on Drugs? The Rhetoric and Reality of Harm Minimisation in Australia

Elida Meadows, Zoe Kizimchuk, Juani O'Reilly,
Isabelle Bartkowiak-Théron, and Shirleyann Varney

Introduction

For more than two decades, the unintended effects of the 'war on drugs'[1] have been extensively examined in scholarly and policy documentation worldwide. In 1985, Australia introduced 'harm minimisation' across all Australian state and federal government drug policy, with the launch of the National Campaign against Drug Abuse and the subsequent National Drug Strategy. This significant paradigm shift came as experts, state and non-state actors recognised that the 'war on drugs' policies were causing more harm than good to individuals and communities (Wisotsky, 1990; Groves, 2018). As of 2020, harm minimisation, which must in principle consider all the harmful (health, social and economic) consequences of alcohol and other drug use on both the individual and the community, remains the prominent drug policy guideline in Australia, in shaping alcohol and other drugs laws and responses across all areas of government. However, current evidence suggests that

---

[1] Although the expression has been used by MPs from different jurisdictions over time, there has never been an official policy named "War on Drugs" in Australia. It has been more about an approach which prioritises law enforcement. For a timeline of Australian Drug Policy see: NDARC The Australian (illicit) drug policy timeline: 1985–2019, https://ndarc.med.unsw.edu.au/sites/default/files/ndarc/resources/Australian%20Illicit%20Drug%20Policy%20Timeline%20-%201985-2019%20-%20FINAL.pdf.

E. Meadows · Z. Kizimchuk · S. Varney (✉)
Drug Education Network, Hobart, TAS, Australia
e-mail: shirleyannvarney@den.org.au

J. O'Reilly
Australian Federal Police, Canberra, ACT, Australia

I. Bartkowiak-Théron
University of Tasmania, Hobart, TAS, Australia

greater effort is required to scale up harm minimisation, increase access to treatment and other medical and health services, and remove the stigma of possession for drug use.

This chapter examines harm minimisation strategies implemented in the two specific case studies: personal cannabis use, and pill testing. In analysing such cases, we suggest that there is an inconsistent application of the principles of harm minimisation across the Australian States and Territories. Political hesitation world-wide and minimalist implementation frameworks are two of the many factors that contribute to slowing down the implementation of harm minimisation approaches for alcohol and other drug harms.

After providing an overview of the history and background to Australian drug policy, we consider the constraints that prevent Australia from implementing more comprehensive drug harm minimisation strategies, and the inconsistent application of current strategies across Australia. Our argument, of course, is not new. There is and has been vigorous discussion internationally, calling on all countries to explore alternative approaches. A consensus has emerged that public health and human rights should underpin every country's response to alcohol and other drugs. The aim is for this consensus to now, slowly but surely, make its way through govern-ment, non-government agencies, and communities.

Background

It has been 35 years since the term 'harm minimisation' was first used in the Australian drug and alcohol policy discourse. The National Campaign Against Drug Abuse, launched in 1985, and the National Drug Strategy which followed in 1993, were 'the starting point for a range of policies based on a harm minimisation approach, and intended to "have a significant impact on the everyday work of frontline workers, especially in the way they interact and intervene with young people"' (Australian Department of Health, 2004). This shift, with its strong empha-sis on prevention and treatment as opposed to prohibition, has been acknowledged worldwide as an enlightened approach, based on human rights and people's health and wellbeing (Groves, 2018). If the early strategy achieved only one thing, it is that it began to move the discourse away from the traditional ideology of substance users as underclass, sick, or deviant individuals which were essentially considered 'police property' (Groves, 2018; Reiner, 1998).

It was with the arrival of the AIDS epidemic in the 1980s that the idea of harm minimisation gained new momentum, with the particular set of drug-related strate-gies designed to prevent the spread of the HIV (Bastos & Filho, 2015). Needle and Syringe Programmes (NSPs) were put in place as a public health measure to reduce the spread of blood-borne viral infections such as HIV and hepatitis C among injecting drug users. However, despite the stated harm minimisation intent of Australian drug policy—including the NSPs, the court and police diversion programmes, safe injecting rooms and the agreement that drug use sits in the health arena and not in criminal justice—governments in Australia have for the most part been straddling the fence about decriminalising drugs for the past several years.

Notwithstanding a strong philosophical rhetoric of harm minimisation, in practice government policy remains conservative in its approach, prioritising law enforcement strategies and zero-tolerance policies. This is despite evidence of their limited effectiveness, as well as growing support from experts, academics and the community highlighting the need for an alternative approach. Conservative government policy and the political will has been clearly displayed by the Australian Federal Cabinet when, in August 1997, it rejected the proposed trial of prescription heroin in the Australian Capital Territory (ACT), even though the ACT Government had approved the trial (McKay, 1998). Several national surveys and empirical studies have shown that although drug use is illegal, there is a widespread support that harm minimisation and public health-focused strategies are, at least, equally worthwhile (Groves, 2018, p. 10).

The National Drug Strategy 2017–2026 approach is to reduce 'the harms of use through coordinated, multi-agency responses that address the three pillars of harm minimisation. These pillars are demand reduction, supply reduction and harm reduction' (Australian Department of Health, 2017). However, according to a position paper by Directions Health Services,[2] 'in practice, policy and funding has heavily focused on the 1st pillar and very little is expended on the 3rd pillar'. The Australian government allocates $1.7 billion in response to illicit drugs. Sixty-six per cent (66%) of this ($1.1billion) is spent on law enforcement. Thirty-two per cent (32%) is allocated to treatment ($361million), and two per cent (2%) to harm reduction ($36million). The result: Australia has the highest rate of policing drug use in the world (Directions Health Services, 2019).

In the last 12 months, 81 per cent of drug offences were for personal use, not supply. 'Aboriginal and Torres Strait Islander people and other disadvantaged populations are disproportionately represented' (Directions Health Services, 2019). Disproportionately targeting disadvantaged people is an unintended but real consequence of policies which lean towards illicit drugs and law enforcement.

Despite this lean towards illicit drugs and law enforcement, efforts continue to be made to reduce the harms of licit substances: Initiatives across the three pillars to prevent the harms from alcohol and tobacco have been successful to some extent, possibly because the focus here is less on law enforcement and more on health promotion, prevention and early intervention. The *National Drug Strategy Household Survey 2019* found that more Australians are giving up or reducing their alcohol intake, driven by health concerns even though there was little change in the proportion of people drinking at risky levels (Australian Institute of Health and Welfare (AIHW, 2020). The use of nicotine, another legal drug harmful to the user, has also

---

[2]Directions Health Services is a specialist drug treatment service that has provided treatment and support to people and concerned others impacted by alcohol, drugs, and other addictions for more than 40 years. It is funded primarily by ACT Health and the Australian Government Department of Health.

been in decline with 11% Australians smoking daily in 2019, down from 12.2% in 2016 and 24% in 1991. Many smokers reported that they were taking steps to reduce their tobacco consumption in 2019 (Australian Institute of Health and Welfare (AIHW, 2020, p. vii).

It has been established that some drugs, which are openly and legally available, may be more harmful than certain illicit substances (Bonomo et al., 2019), which leads us to wonder on what criteria normative legality is based if not harm minimisation. Melbourne University and Curtin University researchers assert that history, not harm, dictates why some drugs are legal and others aren't. They point out that 'at various times around the world, coffee has been illegal and cocaine has been widely available [and that] many drugs that currently carry criminal penalties began life as useful medicinal therapies, such as opiates, cocaine, MDMA and amphetamines. They were often available over the counter at pharmacies or through licensed sellers' (Friedman, 1998; Lee & Bartle, 2019). However, arguments around the relative harms of particular drugs do not negate the fact that all substances, regardless of legality, have the potential to cause harm.

Depenalisation and Diversion

In recent times, the system of criminalisation of personal drug use has been increasingly called into question. There are differences in how 'decriminalisation' is defined and implemented (Global Commission on Drug Policy, 2016). However, more than 25 countries have removed criminal penalties for the personal possession of some or all drugs, contributing to the growing global shift away from punitive drug policies. Portugal complemented its policy of decriminalisation by allocating greater resources across the drugs field, expanding and improving prevention, treatment, harm reduction and social reintegration programmes (Transform Drugs Drug Policy Foundation, 2018).[3]

In Australia, where legislation is state- and territory-based, differing penalties apply to different drugs in different jurisdictions. It is therefore unsurprising to note some inconsistency in the application of laws in relation to the decriminalisation (which removes criminal penalties) of drug use and possession across the Australian

---

[3] Decriminalisation may replace criminal penalties with civil penalties. These could include referral to an education or treatment program, or a fine. Civil cases do not have to go through the court system and may be dealt with by tribunals. While records may be kept by a tribunal, these are not criminal records and will not affect employment, housing or travel opportunities. The key difference to a criminal model is that in a decriminalised model, while penalties still apply for use and possession of drugs, they are no longer criminal charges. However, decriminalisation is not legalisation. If drug possession and personal use are decriminalised, it is still illegal to possess and use drugs. Selling and manufacturing drugs still carry criminal penalties. See: https://adf.org.au/talking-about-drugs/law/decriminalisation/overview-decriminalisation-legalisation/#:~:text=The%20key%20difference%20to%20a,to%20possess%20and%20use%20drugs.

states and territories, with a current mix of *de jure* (by law) and *de facto* (by practice) (Hughes et al., 2016; Lee & Ritter, 2016).

South Australia, the ACT and Northern Territory have decriminalised personal use of cannabis by applying civil penalties if a person meets certain eligibility criteria. All Australian states have depenalisation systems in place for cannabis, meaning that charges of possession can be subject to 'diversion' by police or the court, allowing offenders to avoid a criminal penalty. Non-attendance at education, assessment or treatment sessions as part of bail conditions can still lead to criminal charges.

Options for police to divert adult offenders away from the criminal justice system are limited in many parts of Australia. In a report of a project which sought to provide the first comprehensive analysis of Australian criminal justice responses relating to personal use and possession of illicit drugs and the reach of Australian drug diversion programmes, the National Drug and Alcohol Research Centre made the point that 'Experts showed unanimous support for drug diversion in Australia, recognising that it is more cost effective, pragmatic and consistent with a harm minimisation approach, as well as a means to reduce workloads and pressures on both police and courts. There was a universal view, including among jurisdictions with relatively low and relatively high levels of diversion, that there needs to be more diversion for possession for personal use in Australia, including to counter the recent national trend of reducing rates of drug diversion' (Hughes et al., 2016, p. 5). The view is 'echoed by Victoria Police in their recent parliamentary submissions, including to the Inquiry into the supply and use of methamphetamines', which stated that there is clearly scope to further increase use of the Victorian Illicit Drug Diversion Initiative (*IDDI*)[4] by police. This sentiment was also echoed in the Northern Territory (Victoria Police, 2017; Parliament of Victoria, 2018; Legislative Assembly of the Northern Territory, 2015) which confirmed that the need for additional and stronger diversion measures was triggered by a documented declining national trend and the observation of pronounced differences in access to diversion options and services nationally.

However, the streamlining of diversion requires the careful consideration of a number of issues, such as (see, for example, Hughes et al., 2016):

- a strong belief among some agencies that diversion is a 'soft option',
- how diversion can be (or be seen as) procedurally complicated,
- the availability of services across states and territories, and across rural, regional and urban areas,
- political leadership and willingness to encourage diversion as policy.[5]

---

[4]The Victorian Illicit Drug Diversion Initiative (IDDI) involves offering a caution to a person detained for use or possession of an illicit drug other than cannabis on the condition that they undertake a clinical drug assessment and enter any prescribed drug treatment.

[5]A good example of such a statement is the demise of the ACT Heroin Trial. The 1996 proposal came up at the tail end of a 'year feasibility study sponsored by drug treatment and policy experts' (Bammer & Douglas, 1996). The proposal was rejected in 1997 by the Federal Cabinet. That rejection was followed by much pressure from medical practitioners to see to such a trial.

At this stage of our argument, it is important to note that many of the people funnelled through the diversion systems are not necessarily those with dependency issues and are occasional cannabis users who may not require treatment for dependency or health related issues (Australia21 Ltd., 2016). This over-representation of 'low hanging fruit' can impede the system from helping those people with significant drug-related health issues, particularly those with dependency issues. It suggests a need for another layer of diversion to appropriately utilise available resources in an equitable and effective manner.

The Push for Decriminalisation

Cannabis possession and use is still currently illegal in Australia, although there has been increasing advocacy from experts and commentators for change. One argument has been that the enforcement of drug laws through policing, the courts and prisons use resources that could be more productively directed towards health and prevention programmes. In recent times, a number of prominent retired high-ranking police, magistrates and judges, and ex-politicians have publicly announced their support for decriminalising illicit drugs for personal use, and calling for the reframing of drugs use as a public health issue to increase support for vulnerable people (Beyer et al., 2002). These advocates for treating drug use as a health issue rather than a law enforcement one include Mick Palmer, who was the Commissioner of the Australian Federal Police from 1994 to 2001 (Caldwell, 2019), former state premiers Bob Carr and Jeff Kennett (Hunt, 2017), former ACT Supreme Court Justice Richard Refshauge (Giannai, 2019), former Police Sergeant Greg Denham (Gregoire, 2019) and many others. Greg Denham is an Australian representative for Law Enforcement Action Partnership (LEAP),[6] an international organisation comprised of both current and former police officers, advocating for an end to drug prohibition and the establishment of a legal and regulated market. In 2020, the Canadian Association of Chiefs of Police collectively backed the decriminalisation of drugs for personal use. 'At the news conference releasing the report, those presiding said repeatedly that police should, in general, not be the first responders regarding homelessness, mental health issues and drug dependence' (Bogart, 2020).

Two specific areas that have seen some movement towards a decriminalisation approach, mostly in other countries, is the harm minimisation and educational initiative for party drug use: pill testing and the decriminalisation of cannabis. Subtle changes within the politic arena with former politicians and some former senior police in Australia promoting the move from justice to health, have contributed to

---

[6]LEAP is a not-for-profit organisation of police, prosecutors, judges, corrections officials and other law enforcement officials advocating for criminal justice and drug policy reforms that will make communities safer and more just. LEAP believes that adult drug misuse is a public health problem and not a law enforcement matter while recognising that drugs can be dangerous and addictive.

these two specific drug initiatives being somewhat endorsed. Studies have shown that community attitudes are also in favour of such a shift (Australian Institute of Health and Welfare (AIHW, 2020), and that the community sector is also ready for a harm minimisation and drug education initiative such as pill testing and the decriminalisation of cannabis. The 2019 edition of the National Drug Strategy Household Survey (Australian Institute of Health and Welfare (AIHW, 2020, p. ix) noted a change in attitudes towards cannabis use and the testing of drugs:

> 'In 2019, for the first time, more people said they supported the legalisation of cannabis than opposed it (41% compared with 37%). It was also the first time the proportion of Australians who supported cannabis being used regularly by adults was greater than the proportion that supported regular tobacco smoking (19.6% compared with 15.4%). (. . .) Almost 3 in 5 Australians (57%) supported potential drug users being able to test their pills or other drugs at designated sites. There has also been a shift towards education, rather than law enforcement, as the preferred strategy to reduce the use of illicit drugs—when asked where money should be spent, people allocated more funds to education than to law enforcement for the first time in 2019'. (Australian Institute of Health and Welfare (AIHW, 2020, p. ix)

In the case of these two areas for potential decriminalisation, any movement by decision makers to take a more substantial decriminalisation route is not apparent. This lack of discernible action prompts us to reflect upon the rationalisation of specific approaches and attitudes towards decriminalisation.

One visible action in this space is the Queensland Productivity Report which recommends the decriminalisation of 'lower harm drugs' as a pathway to legalisation. In fact, the Report has sketched out a plan that travels a pathway from decriminalisation to legalisation (Queensland Productivity Commission, 2019, p. 23):

> The first stage should be to decriminalise the use and possession of lower harm illicit drugs, such as cannabis and MDMA. Consideration will need to be given to the regulatory framework around use, including, for example, the regulation of use in public places. At the same time, the government should expand the provision of health support and drug treatment services to reduce drug harms. The next stage should establish a regulatory framework for the supply of low harm drugs. As for other potentially harmful activities (such as liquor and gaming), the framework should establish the arrangements for supply, including licensing for production and retail, and regulation of licenced premises, with a regulator, to oversee this framework. The final stage of the reforms should be to legalise the use and regulated supply of cannabis and MDMA. The government should also move to adopt a regulatory approach to other illicit drugs. However, given the complexities in approaches to managing higher harm drug use, a reform pathway will need to be developed.

Pill Testing

As a drug education and harm-minimisation intervention, festival pill testing services have been operating in some form for more than 25 years in several European countries including the Netherlands, Switzerland, Austria, Belgium, Germany, Spain and France (Ritter, 2018). Often the pill testing debate gets mired in discussions focusing on the imperfections of the pill-testing regime. Dr. Andrew Groves, lecturer in Criminology at Deakin University, notes that 'Pill testing cannot eliminate the harms of drug use, but it is not intended to. It represents a model that best functions as one part of a much wider harm reduction strategy, to provide less punitive and more pragmatic responses to drug use for the protection of a generation of young club and music festival attendees, clearly establishing its worth in the Australian drug context' (Groves, 2018, p. 11).

Groves describes the process used in pill testing as part of harm minimisation programmes where organisations such as DanceSafe, operating in the USA, focus on harm minimisation through peer education. In Europe, pill testing and information services are 'typically undertaken in mobile facilities located near or inside venues to allow timely feedback to users (approx. 30 min). Results are then "posted" anonymously on information boards or event websites (often using red/yellow/green colour-coding), so users can review feedback clearly and discreetly. These practices are possible through partnerships between event promoters, healthcare services and local police, and a strong harm reduction philosophy' (Groves, 2018, p. 2). It is critical to emphasise that this is a process that partners with those who run the business of said events, healthcare services and police. This is one of several areas where policing has a clear role in reducing the health burden of alcohol and other drugs: Police are an essential partner in such initiatives, and take an active part in the education and support of young people attending these events.

Following a number of recent drug-related fatalities in Australia at music festivals, a pill testing trial was first introduced in the ACT in 2018 at the Groovin' the Moo Festival and again in 2019. The pill testing service involved experts working closely with festival organisers, ACT Policing, ACT Ambulance and ACT Health (Vumbaca et al., 2019). The pilot was independently evaluated by experts from the Australian National University. The independent evaluation report showed that pill testing provided relevant and good health information to patrons who planned to use illicit drugs, had led to harm reduction behaviours among patrons, disposing of highly dangerous drugs once identified, provided valuable new information on current drug markets and detected dangerous substances in circulation (Olsen et al., 2019). The ACT Government has subsequently announced further investigation of pill testing in Canberra city centre.

However, the early implementation of pill testing in specific settings, and lack of guidelines on the role of law enforcement in the process, left many police officers unsure of the various processes that had to unfold on their end. The management of the Amnesty Bins, in particular, left some police officers perplexed when it started in late 2019. While it was clear that Amnesty Bins are within a 'no questions asked and police will leave you alone' framework, there has been some hesitation around their limited use at festivals mainly due to this lack of clarity around management: the details of how these bins would be supervised and emptied, among other things, require clear guidelines.

Such lack of clarity can be found in other areas, such as safe injecting rooms, where the role of police was never clarified for operational purposes. The Law Enforcement and HIV Network (LEAHN) drafting of guidelines for police working in Drug Consumption Rooms (DCR) (such as needle exchange programmes or opiate substitution programmes) was deemed a necessary exercise in situations 'where legislation in a jurisdiction legally enables the establishment of a DCR but does not provide clarity on the police role' (Denham and LEAHN Consultation Participants, 2018, p. 1). While admittedly, these guidelines are '*generic* in nature and cannot address every legal, social, cultural and political context', they consist of an operational framework that is flexible enough for operationalisation in a number of varied and legislatively different contexts. Recommendations include, with the aim to acknowledge the remit and purpose of drug consumption rooms, that: police exercise discretion, making sure that no customer is deterred from accessing services when coming to the rooms, avoid the enforcement of drug law unless absolutely necessary, that police enable the creation of collaborative therapeutic environments for the purpose of harm reduction, and for the provision of primary health service access.

With draft guidelines, clearly identified needs for progress, locally evaluated pilot programmes and the experience of international counterparts, the scene is well set for the implementation of pill testing or other related harm-reduction measures: we need only to act.

Cannabis

In several states and territories in Australia (Notably South Australia, ACT and Northern Territory, although it may be that these jurisdictional approaches have greater visibility than others), a small amount for personal use is decriminalised under a variety of cannabis cautioning schemes, administered by police officers in the field. For example, the New South Wales Cannabis Cautioning Scheme has been in operation by the New South Wales Police Force since 2000. In the ACT, new rules around personal use of cannabis came into effect on 31 January 2020. Cannabis is still illegal, but its possession in small amounts is not a criminal offence.[7]

In Tasmania the health Promotion, Prevention and Early Intervention (PPEI) work led by the Drug Education Network demonstrates how attention can be drawn to positively affect health outcomes regarding substance use. Such efforts consist of putting in place appropriate efforts to educate the community about risks, advertising bans, and other regulatory interventions or programmes that help the most disadvantaged people build their resilience and self-worth. Police can and do contribute to promoting and building community members' resilience and self-worth in many ways, not least through Police and Community Youth Clubs (PCYC) programmes whose mission is to 'provide low cost, positive, sporting, recreational, social and cultural programmes in a safe environment primarily for "at risk" youth'.[8]

---

[7]With the initiative dubbed an "unusual legalisation scheme"; see https://adf.org.au/insights/cannabis-act/.

[8]http://www.pcyctas.org/.

The push to take advantage of the potential therapeutic effects of cannabis extracts has become muddied by the campaign to legalise recreational use. The promotion of medicinal cannabis has resulted in some confusion between medicinal cannabis and recreational cannabis, resulting in a general acceptance in the community of cannabis being a beneficial drug and people using the plant as 'herbal medicine' because they cannot secure a script for medicinal cannabis (Ieraci, 2017). This is an area that requires an increased focus on community education and information.

International studies (e.g. Hakkarainen et al., 2019; Hall & Lynskey, 2016, Blickman, 2018) have found that there is evidence of blurring of boundaries between medical and recreational cannabis, partly due to an overlap between medicinal and recreational cannabis use. This blurring of boundaries revealed by multi-faceted research is concerning and should be taken as a call to action for more in-depth health education and community awareness programmes on such matters. This is particularly urgent, in light of other research which warns that there remain some significant unknowns with regard to cannabis use and both its purported negative and positive effects. Two issues of particular concern are the connection of cannabis use with mental health conditions and the use of cannabis by pregnant women and its potential impact on their foetus (Di Forti et al., 2019).

The compelling evidence of 'a statistical association between cannabis use and the development of schizophrenia or other psychoses, with the highest risk among the most frequent users' (National Academies of Sciences, Engineering, and Medicine, 2017; Di Forti et al., 2019) should give further momentum to the call for more investment into education campaigns and studies on the exact effects of the substance. Research by the World Health Organization (2016) found that:

> the strongest independent predictors of whether any given individual would have a psychotic disorder or not were daily use of cannabis and use of high-potency cannabis. The odds of psychotic disorder among daily cannabis users were 3.2 times higher than for never users, whereas the odds among users of high-potency cannabis were 1.6 times higher than for never users. Starting to use cannabis by 15 years of age modestly increased the odds for psychotic disorder but not independently of frequency of use or of the potency of the cannabis used.

These negative effects of cannabis on pregnancy (Gibson & Ehiri, 2015) and mental health might seem to reinforce a case for penalisation; however, they remain, at their core, issues that sit neatly in the realm of health discipline. As such, they should primarily be dealt with from a health perspective: there is widespread, and growing, agreement, including from the law enforcement sector, that this should be the case.

Conclusion

The 2016 Global Commission on Drug Policy's *Advancing drug policy reform: a new approach to decriminalisation* report outlines the harms created through implementing punitive, prohibitive drug policies. In addition to providing a description of decriminalisation in their final report, authors suggest that although it has been poorly implemented and designed in the past, decriminalisation is a framework that can only improve public health and social outcomes. They offer several examples from countries which have decriminalised drugs in some way. Authors support the idea that low level supply in the drug trade need alternatives to punishment (particularly for those engaging in this behaviour to alleviate socioeconomic marginalisation). This has also been addressed by *Law Enforcement Action Partnership (LEAP)*.

A recent event organised by LEAP UK and LEAP US examined the question: 'Should Police be leading reform?' The focus of the discussion was diversion schemes, decriminalisation and drug consumption rooms. Panel members made up of former police officers addressed the event and spoke about the need for 'champions', change leaders within the police force and the imperative to improve relationships between police and communities. A former US Chief of Police made the point that: 'Police leaders are being forced to find creative ways to get the criminal justice system out of the way so that we can help people – not punish them. . . We are way past the point of knowing that our antiquated drug policies keep the war on drugs running strong. We also have far too much evidence that harm reduction methods save lives. . . Police are heading reform because they know reform is needed and they cannot wait for official reforms to take place. . . They are doing this despite the other political pressure to do otherwise' (UN Commission on Narcotic Drugs, 2020).

With these issues in mind: a 'war on drugs' with unintended consequences and a quiet harm minimisation framework ready for reinvigorating; inconsistent policy across the country and increasing calls for decriminalisation; potential measures such as pill testing and the decriminalisation of cannabis being primed for rollout; and the agreement of police and the alcohol and other drug sector of the new direction in which to head, the time is therefore ripe to renew efforts dedicated to informing discussions and policy reform around harm reduction and the necessary police/health therapeutic collaborations in approaching drug and alcohol issues.

References

Australia21 Ltd. (2016). *Can Australia respond to drugs more effectively and safely?: Roundtable report of law enforcement and other practitioners, researchers and advocates*. Australia21 Ltd. https://smartrecoveryaustralia.com.au/can-australia-respond-to-drugs-more-effectively-and-safely-report/

Australian Department of Health. (2004). Overview of current national drug policies and programs. In *Historical publications: Young people, society and AOD*. Australian Government. https://www1.health.gov.au/internet/publications/publishing.nsf/Content/drugtreat-pubs-front5-wk-toc~drugtreat-pubs-front5-wk-secb~drugtreat-pubs-front5-wk-secb-7~drugtreat-pubs-front5-wk-secb-7-1

Australian Department of Health. (2017). *National Drug Strategy 2017–2026: A national framework for building safe, healthy and resilient Australian communities through preventing and minimising alcohol, tobacco and other drug related health, social and economic harms among individuals, families and communities*, p. 6. https://www.health.gov.au/sites/default/files/national-drug-strategy-2017-2026_1.pdf

Australian Institute of Health and Welfare (AIHW). (2020). *National Drug Strategy Household Survey 2019. Drug statistics series no. 32, PHE 27* (p. vii). AIHW. https://www.aihw.gov.au/getmedia/3564474e-f7ad-461c-b918-7f8de03d1294/aihw-phe-270-NDSHS-2019.pdf.aspx?inline=true

Bammer, G., & Douglas, R. M. (1996). The ACT heroin trial proposal: An overview. *Medical Journal of Australia, 164*(11), 690–692.

Bastos, F. I., & Filho, C. L. V. (2015). Critical remarks on strategies aiming to reduce drug related harm: Substance misuse and HIV/AIDS in a world in turmoil. *Revista Brasileira de Epidemiologia, 18*(Suppl 1), 120–130. https://doi.org/10.1590/1809-4503201500050009

Beyer, L., Crofts, N., & Reid, G. (2002). Drug offending and criminal justice responses: Practitioners' perspectives. *International Journal of Drug Policy, 13*(3), 203–211. https://doi.org/10.1016/S0955-3959(02)00063-4

Blickman, T. (2018). The elephant in the room: Cannabis in the international drug control regime. In A. Klein & B. Stothard (Eds.), *Collapse of the global order on drugs: From UNGASS 2016 to review 2019* (pp. 101–131). LOC: Emerald Publishing Limited. https://doi.org/10.1108/978-1-78756-487-920181005

Bogart, B. (2020). Canadian police chiefs want drugs decriminalised – And there has been a reaction. *Policing Insight*. https://policinginsight.com/author/billbogart/

Bonomo, Y., Norman, A., Biondo, S., Bruno, R., Daglish, M., Dawe, S., Egerton-Warburton, D., Karro, J., Kim, C., Lenton, S., Lubman, D. I., Pastor, A., Rundle, J., Ryan, J., Gordon, P., Sharry, P., Nutt, D., & Castle, D. (2019). The Australian drug harms ranking study. *Journal of psychopharmacology (Oxford, England), 33*(7), 759–768. https://doi.org/10.1177/0269881119841569

Caldwell, F. (2019). *Retired AFP commissioner argues for decriminalization of drugs for personal use. Brisbane Times*. https://www.brisbanetimes.com.au/politics/queensland/retired-afp-commissioner-argues-for-decriminalisation-of-drugs-for-personal-use-20190425-p51h28.html

Denham, G., & LEAHN Consultation Participants. (2018). *Guidelines for police working with drug consumption rooms*. Law Enforcement & HIV Network (LEAHN). http://www.leahn.org/archives/5249

Di Forti, M., Quattrone, D., Freeman, T. P., Tripoli, G., Gayer-Anderson, C., Quigley, H., Rodriguez, V., Jongsma, H. E., Ferraro, L., La Cascia, C., La Barbera, D., Tarricone, I., Berardi, D., Szöke, A., Arango, C., Tortelli, A., Velthorst, E., Bernardo, M., Del-Ben, C. M., et al. (2019). The contribution of cannabis use to variation in the incidence of psychotic disorder across Europe (EU-GEI): a multicentre case-control study. *The Lancet Psychiatry, 6*(5), 427–436. https://doi.org/10.1016/S2215-0366(19)30048-3

Directions Health Services. (2019). *Position Paper Decriminalisation to reduce harm and positively impact on drug use*. https://www.directionshealth.com/wp-content/uploads/2019/12/Directions-Position-Paper-Decriminalisation-Nov-2019.pdf

Friedman, S. R. (1998). The political economy of drug-user scapegoating—And the philosophy and politics of resistance. *Drugs: Education, Prevention and Policy, 5*(1), 15–32. https://doi.org/10.3109/09687639809035768

Giannai, D. (2019). Drug decriminalisation needed to reduce harm says former ACT supreme court justice. *About regional*. https://aboutregional.com.au/drug-decriminalisation-needed-to-reduce-harm-says-former-act-supreme-court-justice/

Gibson, S. J., & Ehiri, J. E. (2015). The effects of prenatal cannabis exposure on fetal development and pregnancy outcomes: A protocol. *BMJ Open*. https://doi.org/10.1136/bmjopen-2014-007227

Global Commission on Drug Policy. (2016). *Advancing Drug Policy Reform: A New Approach to Decriminalization 2016 Report*. https://www.globalcommissionondrugs.org/wp-content/uploads/2016/11/GCDP-Report-2016-ENGLISH.pdf

Gregoire, P. (2019). Drug policing causes Most of the harms: An interview with former Police sergeant Greg Denham. *Sydney Criminal Lawyers*. https://www.sydneycriminallawyers.com.au/blog/drug-policing-causes-most-of-the-harms-an-interview-with-former-police-sergeant-greg-denham/?utm_source=Mondaq&utm_medium=syndication&utm_campaign=LinkedIn-integration

Groves, A. (2018). Worth the test? Pragmatism, pill testing and drug policy in Australia. *Harm Reduction Journal, 15*(12), 1–13. https://doi.org/10.1186/s12954-018-0216-z

Hakkarainen, P, Decorte, T., Sznitman, K., Karjalainen, K., Barratt, M., *Frank, V.A.,* Lenton, S., Potter, G., Werse, B., & Wilkins, C. (2019). Examining the blurred boundaries between medical and recreational cannabis – Results from an international study of small-scale cannabis cultivators. *Drugs: Education, Prevention and Policy.* 26(3), pp. 50-25. DOI: https://doi.org/10.1080/09687637.2017.1411888.

Hall, W., & Lynskey, M. (2016). Evaluating the public health impacts of legalizing recreational cannabis use in the United States. *Addiction (Abingdon, England), 111*(10), 1764–1773. https://doi.org/10.1111/add.13428

Hughes, C., Ritter, A., Chalmers, J., Lancaster, K., Barratt, M., & Moxham-Hall, V. (2016). *Decriminalisation of drug use and possession in Australia: A briefing note.* Drug Policy Modelling Program. NDARC, UNSW, Australia.

Hunt, E. (2017). Former premiers and Australian police chiefs call for drug decriminalisation. *The Guardian.* https://www.theguardian.com/australia-news/2017/mar/20/former-premiers-and-australian-police-chiefs-call-for-drug-decriminalisation#_=_

Ieraci, S. (2017). *Time to unmuddy the cannabis waters.* InsightPlus MJA. https://insightplus.mja.com.au/2017/26/time-to-unmuddy-the-cannabis-waters/

Lee, N. & Bartle, J. (2019). History, not harm, dictates why some drugs are legal and others aren't. *The Conversation.* https://theconversation.com/history-not-harm-dictates-why-some-drugs-are-legal-and-others-arent-110564

Lee, N., & Ritter, A. (2016). *Australia's recreational drug policies aren't working, so what are the options for reform? Resource document.* National Drug & Alcohol Research Centre, UNSW, Australia. https://ndarc.med.unsw.edu.au/blog/australias-recreational-drug-policies-arent-working-so-what-are-options-reform

McKay, P. (1998). Alternative treatments for heroin addiction. In *Current issues brief 3.* Social Policy Group, Parliament of Australia. https://www.aph.gov.au/About_Parliament/Parliamentary_Departments/Parliamentary_Library/Publications_Archive/CIB/cib9899/99CIB03

National Academies of Sciences, Engineering, and Medicine. (2017). *The health effects of cannabis and cannabinoids: The current state of evidence and recommendations for research.* The National Academies Press. https://doi.org/10.17226/24625

Olsen, A., Wong, G., & McDonald, D. (2019). *Act pill testing trial 2019.* Australian National University. https://www.health.act.gov.au/sites/default/files/2019-12/ACT%20Pill%20Testing%20Evaluation%20report%20FINAL.pdf

Parliament of Victoria. (2018). *Inquiry into drug law reform: Report.* Parliament of Victoria.

Queensland Productivity Commission. (2019). *Inquiry into imprisonment and recidivism imprisonment and recidivism: Final report. Resource document.* Queensland Productivity Commission. https://qpc.blob.core.windows.net/wordpress/2020/01/SUMMARY-REPORT-Imprisonment-.pdf

Reiner, R. (1998). *The politics of the Police* (3rd ed.). Oxford University Press.

Ritter, A. (2018). *Six reasons Australia should pilot 'pill testing' party drugs. Resource document.* National Drug & Alcohol Research Centre (NDARC). https://ndarc.med.unsw.edu.au/blog/six-reasons-Australia-should-pilot-pill-testing-party-drugs

Transform Drugs Drug Policy Foundation. (2018). Drug decriminalisation in Portugal: Setting the record straight. Resource document. https://transformdrugs.org/drug-decriminalisation-in-portugal-setting-the-record-straight/

UN Commission on Narcotic Drugs. (2020). Blog: Should Police be leading reform? Diversion schemes, decriminalisation and drug consumption rooms. March 3, 2020. http://cndblog.org/2020/03/should-police-be-leading-reform-diversion-schemes-decriminalisation-and-drug-consumption-rooms/ .

Victoria Police. (2017). *Submission to the Victorian Government inquiry into drug law reform committee*. Victoria Police.

Vumbaca, G., Tzanetis, S., McLeod, M., & Caldicott, D. (2019). Report on the 2nd ACT GTM pill testing pilot: A harm reduction service. Resource document. Pill Testing Australia. https://www.harmreductionaustralia.org.au/wp-content/uploads/2019/08/2nd-Pill-Testing-Pilot-August-2019.pdf

Wisotsky, S. (1990). *Beyond the war on drugs*. Prometheus Books.

World Health Organization. (2016). The health and social effects of nonmedical cannabis use. Resource document. https://www.who.int/substance_abuse/publications/msbcannabis.pdf?ua=1.

Chapter 13
Refugees: Sitting at the Nexus of Law Enforcement and Public Health

Penny Egan-Vine, Isabelle Bartkowiak-Théron, and Roberta Julian

Introduction

The Black Lives matter movement has brought about a much-needed resurgence of debate about race, law enforcement, and social justice. Concerns relating to race and ethnicity have been at the forefront of policing inquiries worldwide, starting (albeit modestly) with the UK Scarman report in 1981 and the 1999 Macpherson report and followed by prominent commissions into law enforcement (Bartkowiak-Théron & Asquith, 2015). These inquiries have had some impact on policing, how it is done and how it is scrutinised by the public and third parties. They have been landmarks in bringing to prominence, matters relating to ethnicity in policing, racial profiling, and over-policing among the broader public. Missing from these inquiries, however, are the nuances between numerous socio-cultural groups, with different languages, and different experiences of trauma. Among these few examples of groups struggling at the intersection of law enforcement and public health (LEPH), few reports are more striking than those of refugees. Despite a significant increase in global refugee numbers over recent decades, the heated debates focused around international rights to health and safety have failed to address the primary health, mental health, and social justice issues faced by refugees around the world. In this chapter, by carefully dissecting two recent, de-identified, Australian case studies, we consider and unpack the nature of the difficulties refugees face in accessing health services and justice, during and after their resettlement journey. We argue that the refugee experience amplifies the risk of negative outcomes at the interface of police, the individual and their families. There develops a distress that increases over time and impacts greatly

P. Egan-Vine (✉)
Murray Valley Sanctuary Refugee Group, Albury, NSW, Australia
e-mail: pcvine46@gmail.com

I. Bartkowiak-Théron · R. Julian
Tasmanian Inst. Law Enforcement Studies, University of Tasmania, Hobart, TAS, Australia

on future interactions, not only with law enforcement services, but with society in general. The importance of considering a stigma-free and respectful response is promoted in this chapter and the positive gains that come from such a response cannot be underestimated.

Background and Definitions

It has long been established that racial profiling and institutional racism are endemic in policing (Bartkowiak-Theron & Asquith, 2019). Racial profiling consists of the intended steering of policing activities or processes towards an individual on the basis of their racial or ethnic attributes (also, occasionally, nationality or religion), rather than specific circumstances, while institutional racism was defined by Macpherson (1999, 6.34) as:

> the collective failure of an organisation to provide an appropriate and professional service to people because of their colour, culture, or ethnic origin. It can be seen or detected in processes, attitudes and behaviours which amount to discrimination through unwitting prejudice, ignorance, thoughtlessness and racist stereotyping which disadvantages minority ethnic people.

Considerations of these phenomena have essentially focused on the broad category of visible, racial minorities in communities. More specifically, inquiries in the UK, the USA, Europe, and Australia have mostly considered indigenous, black or Asian minorities. However, the nuances around the identity of each individual, their lived experiences and attitudes towards government agencies, whether law enforcement[1] or public health, has to a certain extent been omitted in 'blanket' considerations of race and belonging in most inquiries into public services. However, the experiences of refugees can be vastly different from other vulnerable groups. The extended pain and trauma experienced by refugees justifies their positioning at the nexus of law enforcement and public health service delivery and warrants careful attention (Egan-Vine & Fraser, 2012).

According to the United Nations, a 'refugee' is defined as a person who:

> has been forced to flee his or her country because of persecution, war or violence. A refugee has a well-founded fear of persecution for reasons of race, religion, nationality, political opinion or membership in a particular social group. Most likely, they cannot return home or are afraid to do so. War and ethnic, tribal and religious violence are leading causes of refugees fleeing their countries (United Nations, 2020).

---

[1] Throughout this chapter, we distinguish between 'law enforcement' (the non-negotiable application of legislation and police powers) and 'policing', which comprises the above, as well as a variety of negotiated, consultative, and community-oriented initiatives.

In 2018, international relief agencies recorded 70.8 million refugees around the world, with many claiming asylum each year (United Nations, n.d.). In 2019, the United Nations recorded two million such claims (United Nations, 2020).[2]

Global movement and migration have been an enduring feature of humanity. Most outcomes of this geographical mobility are peaceful and acknowledged as a much welcome aspect of democratic societies, with the local infusion of skilled labour and socio-cultural diversity (Egan-Vine & Fraser, 2012). Discourses of 'cosmopolitanism' and multiculturalism highlight the ways in which a country is enriched through a variety of experiences, cultures, foods, music, and a critical engagement with these discourses is well documented in sociological literature (Julian, 2015). However, unlike 'cosmopolitan' migration, the displacement of communities and families due to war and conflict fundamentally changes the dynamics of displacement (Bhuyan & Senturia, 2005), with people being uprooted from their homes, and relocated, often after lengthy negotiations and waiting periods, to estranged countries and local communities. As we have indicated before (Egan-Vine & Fraser, 2012, 132), the entry of newly arrived refugees in local communities around the world does have an impact on the social fabric of that local community, with 'the law and management of difference [including] all aspects of the interface of new and existing communities and each arriving individual vulnerable to stereotyping, ignorance, and resistance to change'.

The challenge of arriving and settling in a different country, which requires critical assistance from international and local agencies, as well as from 'the locals', needs to be understood in the context of the experiences of refugees prior to their arrival (Julian, 2015, 2019). While most community members in the country of destination are aware of and (more or less) comfortable with navigating the complexity of public health and government service provision, refugees may not be able to identify community leaders or service providers and 'are denied the chance to develop conventional pathways to positions of influence and authority' (Egan-Vine & Fraser, 2012, 134). Experiences of war, violence, abuse (rape, beating, torture) at the hands of local or invading forces (often involving law enforcement, para-militarised militia), deprivation and ill-health, are compounded by experiences of living in a refugee camp, where additional risks of violence, abuse, theft, malnutrition, or ill-health present themselves. Such experiences of hardship and of 'getting by' in order to survive camp conditions mean that refugees often view government services with fear and resentment (Campbell & Julian, 2007). Refugee trauma cannot be understated if we want to comprehend the difficulties experienced by refugees in accessing public health and safety services in their country of resettlement.

---

[2] The Refugee Council of Australia provides links to a number of interactive maps where one can follow the paths of refugees around the world, as well as refugee numbers. See https://www. refugeecouncil.org.au/interactive/.

Case Study 1: 'Fidele'[3]

Fidele

'Fidele' became a refuge in 1992, when, at the age of 19, he fled for his life. He had responded to the president's promise of democratic elections by becoming actively involved in encouraging other young people to vote. A week before the election was due, opposition supporters were gathered at a hall. The building was surrounded by the Armed Forces, which then opened fire on those inside. Fidele managed to escape to a nearby house but soon the police arrived and he was stabbed and beaten unconscious. After 2 weeks recovering in hospital, he was discharged to his uncle's house. His uncle gave him a little money and advised him to leave the country as the police were searching for him. Fidele sought asylum in the neighbouring country. Elections were never held in his country but government agents continued to hunt for opposition supporters and many people were killed or 'disappeared'.

Arriving in Australia at the age of 35, with little English, with a wife and three children, Fidele found work as soon as he could, learning English on the job. Four years later, on New Year's Eve, he was working until 9 pm. A non-drinker, he was persuaded by his workmates to try a beer, 'because it was New Year's Eve'. He had a mouthful but did not like the taste, so he consumed only a little of the drink in order to be polite, then excused himself and headed home.

As a P-Plater (a newly licenced driver) out in the evening of New Year's Eve, he was pulled over for a routine breath test, by a police car manned by two recent police academy/college graduates who were on duty that night. Four attempts to obtain a breath test were unsuccessful, as he seemed unable to sustain enough breath to register. His breathing became increasingly tight and he appeared agitated and unable to understand what was being said to him. He was accused of refusing to submit to a breath test, told that this was a criminal offence, handcuffed, put in the back of the police car and taken to the station.

Seven additional attempts to obtain a breath test at the police station were again unsuccessful and he was noted to have a glazed expression, blood-shot eyes, sweating profusely, smelling of alcohol, and appeared confused and agitated. Difficulty locating an interpreter, on New Year's Eve, meant that a blood test was unable to be performed. He was charged with failure to submit to breath analysis and booked to attend court a few weeks later.

At court, his legal aid lawyer, whom he had met, without an interpreter, a few minutes earlier, advised him to plead guilty. He received a fine and loss of

(continued)

---

[3] Names and other personal identifiers in both case studies have been changed to protect privacy and confidentiality.

licence for a year. (In consequence, he also lost his job, for which a driver's licence was a prerequisite.)

After his arrest, and the subsequent court case, Fidele became increasingly withdrawn from his family, restless and irritable. He slept poorly, frequently waking, screaming, from nightmares. He refused overtures of comfort from family and friends and would spend hours alone walking. He had told no one of his arrest and so had not received any informed guidance in managing the charge.

At school his children began to perform poorly—the girls became withdrawn and were sitting back in class, no longer actively engaged in learning, and the son became disruptive and getting into fights. His wife felt unsafe because of his irritability and was seeking ways to leave the marriage. It was her actions that alerted friends to their situation and they encouraged Fidele to appeal his conviction.

It was not until after the appeal that he had access to counselling. There he spoke of an underlying fear that had persisted since he had left his country, that the police would eventually find him and kill him. With regard to his recent arrest, he could not understand why he could not produce a breath test, but knew that it was hard to breathe and he could not think. When he was told that he had committed a crime, handcuffed, and put in the police car, he believed that he was about to be killed. He said that his head was full of memories of his encounter with police in Africa and he felt extremely unsafe. As police had described his actions as criminal, he believed that he was regarded as a very bad person and would be severely punished. He did try to be cooperative in the hope of being allowed to live, but found that he could not understand what was being said, however hard he tried.

On his return home, and in the subsequent weeks after the arrest, he found he was preoccupied with the memories of the assault by police in Africa and was overwhelmed by flashbacks and nightmares. He complained of bad headaches and felt deeply ashamed, anxious, and fearful. Fortunately, a local refugee-assistance agency and some community members (some speaking Fidele's language) became involved, and a pro bono lawyer was found. Thus a clearer history of events was obtained and Fidele's past experience disclosed. The affidavit presented to the magistrate during the appeal included information on the attempts on his life by the police in his country of origin. Fidele was assisted by a bilingual community member. He was acquitted without charge, his licence was reinstated, but his disturbed moods continued. At this stage of our narrative, it needs to be noted that the court judge severely reprimanded attending police for their ignorance and lack of empathy. She also requested a full report on what cultural awareness training was being taught at their registered training organisation.

(continued)

Fortunately, Fidele responded well to post-traumatic stress disorder (PTSD) intervention, after he obtained access to counselling. His life had been settled before an assault in his youth and there had been no other significant traumas in his life. The relationship difficulties in his family settled and the children's school performances improved as he returned to being the gentle and caring man they had known him to be. He found a new job close to home and pursued a lifelong ambition to become a chef—a silver lining to come out of this event.

Individual Vulnerabilities

Such a positive outcome, in addition to the intervention of such a culturally aware and involved judge, is welcome but often unusual. Fidele was fortunate in encountering both a number of helpful community members and a lawyer who was fluent in his language. He was also in the extraordinary position of having no further experience of trauma in his life other than those mentioned in the above vignette. However, he had no understanding of the cause of his distressed behaviour (not being able to link it to past trauma created by civil war in his country of origin), and the disruption to his family felt beyond his control. To him, it was further proof of what a bad person he was. His wife and children had no information that could enable them to explain his behaviour. They turned in on themselves and were trapped in a feeling of helplessness.

The public health ripple effect from one individual under traumatic arrest circumstances onto the close family circle also needs considering. The situation directly impacted the school performance and behaviour of his children, as well as his relationship with his wife (those closest to the person are the ones most affected by the emergence of PTSD). Such consequences could have had significant long-term effects on mental as well as overall health, lives, and future careers. The previous high achievement of the children at school made behavioural pattern changes more noticeable, but any assistance offered by the school, in this case, would not have dealt with the core difficulty—their father's distressed behaviour.

The breakdown in the marriage and the loss of a skilled worker—Fidele had been in the workforce for 4 years and making tax contributions—would have been additional long-term consequences. He had emerged as a leader in the community, helping new arrivals and being consulted on matters of dispute. This would have been a loss to the whole community of new settlers. His wife could also have been kept out of the workforce as she struggled with her own circumstances with the young children and she may have been ostracised by her community because she had left her husband.

Trauma and Iatrogenic[4] Vulnerability

The deep-seated nature of Fidele's trauma and the timeline are worthy of attention. While it may not read as such in our narrative, which we have limited to relevant events for the purpose of this chapter, there had actually been a long time gap between the event that caused him to flee his country of origin and the New Year's Eve arrest. To many of the people involved in this case, including Fidele and his family, the displacement and experience of conflict and abuse at the hand of law enforcement in his country of origin had seemed left in the past, until the triggers of police officers standing close to him and appearing to be angry, the use of the word 'crime' and the absence of any support people brought long-forgotten trauma back to the surface.

Some elements of this incident are particularly relevant to the breakdown in Fidele's mental health. The police officers were recent graduates and appeared to have little experience of not only this vulnerable population, which is however a standing feature of the local community (and of local demographic statistics), but also lacked any capacity to assess individual and ontological vulnerability[5] as it presents in the field. Their actions and decision-making, isolated and devoid of any kind of joint, health-based responses to a person in distress, had a significant impact on case procedure and on the wellbeing of all involved. The event took place on a day when excessive drinking is common behaviour and access to interpreters is also reduced during public holidays and at such a late hour of the night. But the lack of contextualisation of the needs of a community member under duress, and in a state of escalating physical (inability to breathe properly) and mental health crisis, is glaring. Furthermore, the situational vulnerability[6] of Fidele was neither considered nor effectively assessed by arresting police officers; the fact that their very interaction was a tipping point in the escalation of the situation did not seem to compute either. In a 'law enforcement' (one with the main point of enforcing road rules and alcohol abuse at key times of the year) rather than a 'policing' mode, looking for alternate explanations to what could be common deviant behaviour did not seem important, and to police, it made sense that business-as-usual protocols applied. That there were overlaps in the signs and behaviour of excessive intake of alcohol with those of acute PTSD did not seem to spring to mind in such a context. The reddened eyes, a common finding among African peoples, is also a distractor. The absence of an interpreter and a support person, at the police station and during the court case, are indicators of failure to comply with due process but probably could be argued as

---

[4] Iatrogenic vulnerability refers to the harms (intentional or not) associated with treatment or interaction with a service. The policing process can exacerbate the harms experienced by a person. See Bartkowiak-Théron & Asquith, 2012; see also Chap. 4 in this collection.

[5] An ontological vulnerability refers, universally, to the fragile nature of a human being. See Bartkowiak-Théron & Asquith, 2012; see also Chap. 4 in this collection.

[6] A situational vulnerability refers to the circumstances in which harm can be done. See Bartkowiak-Théron, 2012; see also Chap. 4 in this collection.

likely to have had no additional impact, as the initial triggers would have been enough to set off the PTSD.

Case Study 2: 'Jason'

Jason

'Jason', a young African, came to Australia 2 years before the events we are about to describe, with his older brother, 'John', and sister, 'Sara' on a Humanitarian refugee visa. All of them were under twenty years of age when they arrived. Their parents and their other siblings had disappeared, without a trace, ten years earlier during the conflict that had driven them from their country.

They had settled well. Sara had recently married, John had work and Jason was doing well at school. A few weeks before the incident, another recently arrived member of their community, a young single refugee, 'Stephen', one of John's co-workers, had moved in to share accommodation with them, occupying Sara's room and helping with the rent. Their lives seemed to be so well-managed and well on track that their caseworker had significantly reduced the level of support being offered.

However, they were unfortunate in their neighbour, 'Mary'. Mary, then in her mid-thirties, had difficulties with substance abuse and paranoia. On several occasions, and with increasing frequency and boldness, Mary stood on the unfenced boundary to their land and screamed abuse, calling on them to come and fight, to stop being cowards and threatening to 'get them'. She accused them of being Sudanese thugs (they were not from Sudan). This behaviour generally happened when Jason was returning from school to an empty house.

However, on two occasions, after Mary began moving over the boundary onto their block, Stephen recorded her aggressive behaviour on a smartphone. On video, Stephen is heard stating that he was going to call the police. Mary seemed undaunted and walked further onto their land. She continued to yell abuse and appeared quite inebriated. She was carrying a weapon that she claimed was a machete.

After this significant incident, Jason became fearful and uncertain about what to do. He also became frightened of being alone at home. When Mary threatened him as he walked from the street into his home, he felt paralysed and unable to talk. The behaviour, along with the video of the behaviour, had been reported to the police, without any action taken that was apparent to Jason. He felt that he had little to protect him. One Friday night, John came back from work with Stephen and had taken Jason to do some shopping. Stephen stayed in town to meet with some friends. Back home, John went

(continued)

inside to sleep and Jason stayed in the car talking on the phone to a friend. After about 30 minutes, he was startled to find Mary and two other people banging on the car windows, waving a machete and sticks and screaming abuse. Jason was terrified and rang Stephen, as John was not answering his phone (John slept inside the house through the whole event and only heard about what happened later).

Stephen quickly arrived with some friends and came upon the attack on the car. They pulled Jason from the car and attempted to go inside the house. Mary rushed after them, waving a machete, and they struggled to stop her entering the house. At this point the police arrived and charged them all with affray (a charge of unlawful fighting with a disturbance of the peace), as there were accusations and counter-accusations. The court case took place 8 months later.

The boys were given the contact number for Victims of Crime and allowed to go free. Information about the incident was not shared with any settlement agency and their successful lives had led their caseworkers to relax and not be in frequent contact. They were alone, stunned, and could not understand why they had been charged when they were the victims, especially when they had already reported Mary's behaviour, with video evidence to the police. This charge seemed incomprehensible to them and to be mimicking the corrupt behaviour of the police 'back home' where criminals would bribe policemen to falsify the evidence. Also perhaps, as newcomers, they had criticised an Australian and felt that was another reason that they were in trouble.

Individual and Situational Vulnerabilities

In this case study, the resettlement situation seems to have stabilised, and access to public health services (health, education, employment, housing, etc.) seemed to be smooth. Like many refugees settling in their new country, the boys felt safe and relatively protected from violence in Australia. However, the verbal and physical violence they encountered from their neighbour, fuelled by prejudice, ignorance, and stereotype, had the effect of retriggering significant trauma. The presence of the machete as a weapon of choice, in particular, was disturbing. Stephen started having flashbacks, going back to his childhood when the rebels killed the person beside him with a machete as they ran to safety. Jason also discovered that he did have memories of his childhood, and he was plagued by a recurring image of his parents being butchered many years before.

The ripple effects translate across to their everyday lives, as when John and Stephen were at work, Jason was alone at home. He found it hard to concentrate on his schoolwork, and even when the others were at home, Jason was not sleeping well. They were waiting for the neighbour to attack again and this time were certain that the police would not help. Rather, they felt that they would be in trouble for criticising an Australian.

Stephen and Jason stated that they did not feel safe anywhere and wondered when the next attack would happen. Their friends—those involved in trying to protect their property as well as those who heard about the incident—felt that their view of Australia as a safe place had been shattered. They described themselves as being devout Christians and were appalled that they were being accused of violence, as non-violence had been a significant tenet of their faith (countering the alternative desire to take up arms against those who had driven them from the homeland).

Iatrogenic Inefficiencies

It is well-documented that in cases of crisis or uncertainty, refugees have a tendency to feel defeated in the face of hardship, and stoicism and prayer are often the sole resort. A sense of fatalism has been documented, even after resettlement (Asgary & Segar, 2011). Intrusive thoughts and fears are unquestioned, despite evidence of threats, and while it would seem logical to reach to authorities to help with problem-solving, as indicated before, the comprehension of 'public health and police organisations as helpful entities' is not automatic in the minds of refugees. In the psyche of these young boys, the phone number for Victims of Crime was meaningless; police were perceived as a force of corruption and abuse. The young people were not talking to anyone who would challenge that interpretation and who could provide them with information and reassurance. The fact that the boys were still working on their English and did not yet trust community members to reach out for help in such an unpredictable world were compounding factors.

Two weeks after the event a chance visit by a volunteer—seeking to find out how they were going in the suddenly cold autumn—brought the news to the attention of the caseworkers. Still, what could be done to help them was not clear. The Community Legal Centre could not help in a criminal case. A couple of potential lawyers had conflicts of interest in having been involved in representing Mary in the past. Things moved slowly and it took a few months before a person was found to assist them in their case and give them legal guidance.

Discussion

Refugees resettling in a new country are a welcome addition to socio-cultural diversity and to the workforce (Bartkowiak-Theron & Asquith, 2019; Birma, 2013; Parsons, 2013; Hugo, 2014). However, the conditions they are leaving behind (isolation in camp, lack of access to public health services) necessitate a joint approach to helping with a smooth transition that is likely to require government services being perceived in a different light. Australia currently delivers a 'package' to new arrivals, which consists of a social worker, housing assistance, Centrelink help, and an offer of 500 hours of English tuition. For the duration of their first

6 months in Australia, they are offered assistance to navigate new ways of life and service access (Egan-Vine & Fraser, 2012).

One issue, however, is that refugees often perceive government services with suspicion. Coming from situations of deplorable public health provisions in the camps, refugees often struggle to access the most basic of primary health services. It is even documented that due to 'biopolitical othering' (the institutionalisation of difference according to the intersecting fields of human biology and politics), refugees in Europe are excluded from the most basic of public health services in housing, education, and primary health (Dhesi et al., 2018). Refugees arriving in democratic countries from camps suffer from a range of health and trauma effects caused by social and political injustice—which cannot be understated and underestimated:

> Upon arrival at their destination, refugees – most of whom tend to be women and children – may suffer severe anxiety or depression, compounded by the loss of dignity associated with complete dependence on the generosity of others for their survival (Toole & Waldman, 1997, p. 302).

This has consequences for how refugees perceive, and engage with, public health providers and law enforcement agencies in the country of resettlement. The limited knowledge of the health care and policing systems among refugees may mean they fail to see the relevance of reporting a crime or being prescribed (or renewing) medication; resign themselves to sub-optimal health; distrust medical practitioners and police officers and fear deportation or loss of legal status (Asgary & Segar, 2011). Also, due to limited financial resources, an inability to pay for health services (and a lack of awareness of bulk-billing or Medicare mechanisms) may prevent refugees from seeking assistance in accessing primary healthcare services altogether. Shame, stigma, and cultural understandings of power may also counteract efforts by police to support vulnerable refugees (for example, females in the case of sexual abuse, or children in a situation of domestic violence; Bhuyan & Senturia, 2005; Campbell & Julian, 2007).

A lack of knowledge among refugees about the policing system in the country of resettlement has flow-on effects (Campbell & Julian, 2007). Governments in countries like Australia have organised for a number of agencies (often including law enforcement, military forces and social work) to be trained to collaborate in public health emergencies (Toole & Waldman, 1997). However, the deployment of democratic armed forces to facilitate emergency relief or the involvement of law enforcement in helping with resettlement through community policing activities or initiatives can be confusing for many refugees. The involvement of the military and the police in these types of community and public health activities lies in stark contrast with refugees' experiences of these agencies in their countries of origin. These two different ways of engaging with citizens lie at opposite ends of the scale in terms of power dynamics and use of coercive power. Therefore, while police in Australia are often seen as a first port-of-call in addressing many social and non-criminal matters (Bartkowiak-Théron & Asquith, 2012; Boulton et al., 2017), or viewed as jacks-of-all-trades (Bartkowiak-Théron & Julian, 2018), among refugees whose experiences of police have typically been negative, they are viewed as the last ones one should be relying on. The idea of police being brokers of social services or interventionists on a public health continuum aligns with a framework of service provision that cannot be any further from refugees' experiences and perceptions. As such, they are not trusted (Asquith & Bartkowiak-Théron, 2017; Campbell & Julian, 2010).

Health services can also be perceived as a threat in the new, unfamiliar environment. Lack of knowledge of democratic health care systems and fear of deportation can play a significant part in the difficulties faced by refugees (Asgary & Segar, 2011). At the same time, service providers may find that current settlement policies hinder rather than support their efforts to meet the various needs of refugees as they go through the settlement process (James & Julian, 2020). In the two case studies presented above, it is evident that these difficulties are not immediate and can unfold long after refugees have established a routine and their background refugee experience is longer perceived as relevant to them or to others.

The provision of refugee settlement services in Australia is both complex and fragmented (James & Julian, 2020). The current structure of programs established to help refugees with the broad range of difficulties they face upon arriving in their country of resettlement relies heavily on a siloed provision of social services and the idea that 'they will now be fine' (Bhuyan & Senturia, 2005). Furthermore, despite the specificity of their situation, and the (documented) depth of their trauma, they are not considered a specialisation within Australian policing liaison initiatives, as the 'refugee' social category is either 'covered' by ethnic liaison officers or subsumed within broader community liaison portfolios. Given the circumstances and experiences discussed in this paper, we argue that approaching the situation of refugees from a multidisciplinary, interagency, and collaborative angle (which incorporates the refugees themselves, their views and their voices) can frame their vulnerability more comprehensively and would help to improve public health and criminal justice responses.

Achieving such comprehensive and attentive responses requires much more than simply engaging with refugee communities, or prominent members of refugee communities through a one-way communication process (Campbell & Julian, 2010). It requires an attentive, comprehensive, and inclusive dialogue between public health service providers, police organisations, and various members of refugee communities in order to comprehend the nuances of their experiences. Such dialogue should also include, for example, officially recognised community leaders as well as young people, women, people with a disability, people who identify as LGBTIQ. This requires an LEPH approach to addressing the settlement needs of refugees; that is, one that adopts a holistic approach to settlement through interagency collaboration, relies on the establishment of long-term relationships with community members, and comes to recognise the diverse experiences within these communities. This community policing approach that involves working in partnership with public health agencies enhances the likelihood that trust—in people, service providers, and institutions—will slowly develop. A successful LEPH approach thus acknowledges the strengths and agency of refugees in the settlement process. It is predicated on public health and police agencies working *with* refugees rather than trying to solve problems for them through the top-down delivery of siloed services.

The point needs to be made that refugee status is transient and people with that title usually move on to become citizens and members of the general community. Their life experiences of being a refugee become the past and no longer seem as relevant to their identity and to their current lives. No more significant than being a new parent or graduate.

Conclusion

The United Nations, as well as the European Union Agency for Fundamental Rights, advocate that appropriate public health environments and access to justice should be a basic right for all migrants and refugees (United Nations, 2020, n.d.). Moreover, Dhesi et al. (2018, 150) also argue that any kind of denial of public health services, or the 'denial of publicly acceptable health conditions, is a tool of coercive governance, the aim no longer being to forcefully remove refugees and asylum seekers'. To a certain extent, the blind application of law enforcement with no consideration of context or individual circumstances is no way to achieve positive health and justice outcomes.

It is necessary to institutionalise a comprehensive knowledge of refugees' circumstances in order to facilitate the unfolding of services at the nexus of law enforcement (policing) and public health. This is a significant challenge requiring structural and cultural change (Julian et al., 2017). Services need to become more culturally competent and accessible. Within such a multidisciplinary paradigm, police need to reinvigorate their efforts as 'guardians' rather than 'warriors' (Wood & Watson, 2017). It is worth noting, however, that such a transition to any 'guardianship' role is unlikely, or will remain limited, when security and crime control policies, as opposed to protective and trauma-informed practices, continue to dominate police organisations. Health services also need to be perceived in terms of their major objective, namely as facilitators of health and wellbeing as opposed to threats to visas and government spies. Much educational effort needs to be placed along those lines in order to achieve positive health and justice outcomes for all citizens in a democratic country.

References

Asgary, R., & Segar, N. (2011). Project muse: Barriers to health care access among refugee asylum seekers. *Journal of Health Care for the Poor and Underserved, 22*(2), 506–522.

Asquith, N. L., & Bartkowiak-Théron, I. (2017). Police as public health interventionists. In N. L. Asquith, I. Bartkowiak-Théron, & K. Roberts (Eds.), *Policing encounters with vulnerability* (pp. 145–170). Palgrave.

Bartkowiak-Théron, I., & Asquith, N. L. (2012). *Policing vulnerability*. Federation Press.

Bartkowiak-Theron, I., & Asquith, N. L. (2019). Policing ethnic minorities: Disentangling a landscape of conceptual and practice tensions. In S. Ratuva (Ed.), *The Palgrave handbook of Ethnicity* (pp. 1–24). Palgrave Macmillan.

Bartkowiak-Théron, I. & Julian, R. (2018). Collaboration and Communication in Police Work: The 'Jack-Of-All-Trades' Phenomenon. https://connect42.org/collaboration-and-communication-in-police-work-the-jack-of-all-trades-phenomenon/

Birma, E. (2013). How refugees stimulate the economy. La Trobe University. https://www.latrobe.edu.au/news/articles/2013/opinion/how-refugees-stimulate-the-economy

Bhuyan, R., & Senturia, K. (2005). Understanding domestic violence resource utilisation and survivor solutions among immigrant and refugee women. *Journal of Interpersonal Violence, 20*(8), 895–901.

Boulton, L., McManus, M., Metcalfe, L., Brian, D., & Dawson, I. (2017). Calls for police service: Understanding the demand profile and the UK police response. *The Police Journal, 90*(1), 70–85.

Campbell, D., & Julian, R. (2007). Community policing and refugee settlement in regional Australia: A refugee voice. *The International Journal of Diversity in Organisations, Communities and Nations, 7*(5), 7–16.

Campbell, D., & Julian, R. (2010). *Community policing and newly arrived refugee communities in regional Australia. A Conversation on Trust. Final Report to the Australian Research Council.* Tasmanian Institute of Law Enforcement Studies, University of Tasmania.

Dhesi, R., Isakjee, A., & Davies, T. (2018). Public heath in the Calais refugee camps: Environment, health and exclusion. *Critical Public Health, 28*(2), 140–152.

Egan-Vine, P., & Fraser, K. (2012). Policing vulnerable offenders: Police early encounters with refugees. In I. Bartkowiak-Théron & N. L. Asquith (Eds.), *Policing Vulnerability*. Federation Press.

Hugo, G. (2014). The economic contribution of humanitarian settlers in Australia. *International Migration, 52*(2), 31–52. https://doi.org/10.1111/imig.12092

James, I., & Julian, R. (2020). Policy implementation and refugee settlement: The perceptions and experiences of street-level bureaucrats in Launceston, Tasmania. *Journal of Sociology*. https://doi.org/10.1177/1440783320931585

Julian, R. (2015). Ethnicity and immigration: Challenging the National Imaginary? In D. Holmes, K. Hughes, & R. Julian Australian (Eds.), *Sociology: A changing society* (4th ed., pp. 90–129). Pearson Australia.

Julian, R., Bartkowiak-Theron, I., Hallam, J., & Hughes, C. (2017). Exploring law enforcement and public health as a collective impact initiative. *Journal of Criminological Research and Practice, 3*(2). https://doi.org/10.1108/JCRPP-03-2017-0014

Julian, R. (2019). Ethnicity, health and multiculturalism. In J. Germov (Ed.), *Second opinion: An introduction to health sociology* (6th ed., pp. 180–204). Oxford University Press.

Macpherson, W. (1999). *The Stephen Lawrence inquiry*. Home Office.

Parsons, R. (2013). *Assessing the economic contribution of refugees in Australia. Reference document*. Analysis and Policy Observance. https://apo.org.au/node/35435

Slee, C. (2020, April 14). Victorian police crack down on refugee rights campaigners. *Green Left Weekly, 1261*, 1–3.

Toole, M. J., & Waldman, R. J. (1997). The public health aspects of complex emergencies and refugee situations. *Annual Review of Public Health, 18*, 283–312.

United Nations. (n.d.). https://www.un.org/en/sections/issues-depth/refugees/

United Nations. (2020). What is a refugee? https://www.unrefugees.org/refugee-facts/what-is-a-refugee/

Vaughan, C., Davis, E., Murdolo, A., Chen, J., Murrary, L., Block, K., Quiazon, R., & Warr, D. (2016). *Promoting community-led responses to violence against immigrant and refugee women in metropolitan and regional Australia: The ASPIRE project: Key findings and future directions* (p. 8). Research to Policy and Practice.

Wood, J. D., & Watson, A. C. (2017). Improving police interventions during mental health-related encounters: Past, present and future. *Policing and Society, 27*(3), 289–299.

Chapter 14
First Responder Stress and Resilience as a Matter of the Public Health: A Scientific Approach to Police Commander's Testimonial About Police Work Challenges Following Practical Implications

Grant Edwards, Katy Kamkar, and Konstantinos Papazoglou

Introduction: Presenting the Issue

Depression, anxiety disorders, trauma, and stressor-related disorders, in particular, posttraumatic stress disorder (PTSD), and substance use disorders are among the many psychological conditions that are being addressed as part of workplace mental health education, prevention, and interventions. Depression is the third highest cause of burden of disease and is predicted to be the leading cause of burden and disease in 2030 (World Health Organization, 2008). Prevention and early interventions are essential given negative outcomes resulting from common mental health conditions left untreated and for a prolonged period of time (World Health Organization, 2001).

One of the many pathways to build and optimize prevention involves interventions at both individual and organizational levels—creating a healthy positive organizational culture and improving workplace mental health promotion by

Parts of the chapter have been published previously in: *Moral Challenges: Vocational Wellbeing Among First Responders* (Tom Frame, Ed.); Chapter 9; Katy Kamkar & Konstantinos Papazoglou. Mitigating Risk Factors and Building Protective Factors as Prevention Strategies, Pages 126–152, Copyright © 2020. Reproduced with permission of Connor Court Publishing.

G. Edwards
Aspect Frontline, Sydney, NSW, Australia

K. Kamkar (✉)
Centre for Addiction and Mental Health (CAMH) University of Toronto, Toronto, ON, Canada
e-mail: katy.kamkar@camh.ca

K. Papazoglou
The POWER Institute, San Diego, CA, USA

ProWellness Inc., Toronto, ON, Canada

© The Author(s), under exclusive license to Springer Nature Switzerland AG 2022   201
I. Bartkowiak-Théron et al. (eds.), *Law Enforcement and Public Health*,
https://doi.org/10.1007/978-3-030-83913-0_14

reducing workplace risk factors and identifying and building individual as well as organizational strengths and protective factors.

Occupational stressors can increase the risk of mental health conditions, both at clinical and sub-clinical levels, including depression, anxiety disorders, burnout, and psychological distress (e.g., Memish et al., 2017; Harvey et al., 2017; Joyce et al., 2016) both at individual and organizational levels (e.g., Memish et al., 2017; Martin et al., 2014). Analogously, both potential traumatic events and occupational stressors (organizational stressors and operational stressors) have been found to be associated with mental health conditions and with occupational stressors being significant contributors after controlling for traumatic exposure (e.g., Carleton et al., 2020).

A Testimonial from a Veteran Police Officer

The first author of this manuscript is a veteran police officer who has responded to a myriad of critical incidents and in this part he shares his narrative of experiences and insights as a veteran police officer:

> Policing is one of the most rewarding careers one can have. There are so many positives being able to help your society and serve your community and country like; saving lives, taking the worst criminals like murderers and rapists off the streets; ensuring child sex offenders are bought to justice; taking huge quantities of drugs out of the community; helping developing societies or those post conflict nations to enable peace and security just to name a few.
>
> However, it is also one of the toughest and most dangerous career choices you could embark upon. After all, what other profession requires you to continually deal with the worst of humanity? What other job causes you to be in a constant state of hyper vigilance yet at the same time remain calm enough to be a counsellor, a social worker, a psychologist, a medic, a lawyer, a teacher or a prison warden. What other profession authorizes you at law to take a person's liberty, or at worse execute deadly force on another human being, but then mandates that you render assistances to the person who has just tried to harm or kill? What job causes you to wonder whether you will come home to your loved ones at the end of your shift each day?
>
> Most people don't call upon a police officer when everything is conventional; people call when the situation is beyond their control. What seems to be generally forgotten by society though is that Police are human beings. We are mums, dads, brothers, sisters, sons, and daughters. We feel pain, we cry, we bleed just like the rest of society does. But the main difference is we are Human Beings dealing with inhumane things. Having been a police officer for 34 years and involved in competitive sport for over 40 years I did not expect the two disparate elements would fundamentally entwine my identity.
>
> Competitive sport would help me through some difficult times during my life. I would be fortunate enough to represent my country in many sports, however, it was the sport of strongman that unintentionally would define me both as a person and a police officer through my life. On the exterior, I was the strong guy that could pull large trucks, buses, trams, planes and sailing ships and locomotive trains. I would secure a spot in the 1997 Guinness Book of Records for pulling a 201-tonne steam locomotive. Scratch the surface though and you would find a troubled, insecure and mentally fragile person.
>
> Joining the AFP was one of the most important days of my life. I couldn't wait to get out there amongst the crime and take criminals off our streets. I went to work each and every day

to make a difference, to do something positive and I loved my job. From the time I entered the academy as a fresh faced recruit I was taught all elements of the profession, bought to the peak of physical fitness, skilled and educated in how to maintain neutrality with my emotions and to remain composed and calm in situations where others weren't. I was shaped to distrust and question everything which would be so pervasive it would eventually permeate all facets of my work and personal life.

What I wasn't taught or exposed to, however, was how to deal with the stress and trauma I would experience throughout my career. Throughout a policing career it's not unreasonable to expect to be verbally abused, physically assaulted, spat at, bitten, have urine or some other bodily fluid thrown at you. You will suffer physical injuries, cuts, abrasions, sprains and broken bones. You may deal with horrendous things; homicides, rapes, assaults, fatal motor vehicle accidents; seeing another human being beheaded, or; the horrendous impact of chemical weapons used on young innocent children in a conflict zone.

You could experience the devastation and catastrophe of natural disasters. You will remove children from their home who are suffering welts and sores from a flea infested, maggot riddled household where the filth and stench permeates every element of your senses. You could be present in a surgical theatre alongside doctors trying to save the life of a drug courier who had swallowed pellets containing drugs, or dealing with the body of a drug overdose victim whose 'so-called friends' were so drugged that they used the cord of an iron in an attempt to electrically jump-start his heart. You may experience children who are sexually assaulted and violently molested, some as young as six months of age, abused and filmed for distribution over the internet, listening to their distraught screams, their sobs, their distressed pleas begging for the abuse to stop.

You may be deployed overseas to hostile environments where you are vigorously removed from a vehicle at gunpoint by the local military and threatened, or be attacked by Taliban insurgents in Afghanistan who detonate their bomb vests and indiscriminately shoot at anyone or anything that moves. The public will monitor and film your every move by mobile devices and selectively post elements that will be scrutinized, assessed and adjudicated on popular digital media sites without the full context being known.

When you get to court you will be questioned at length by defence lawyers and have your integrity, professionalism and credibility attacked. In some cases, you are ridiculed, patronised and mocked before your peers, the jury and the legal profession without the opportunity of rebuttal. Worst of all, criminals will physically and psychologically threaten and intimidate you and your family. You will work incessant hours, develop poor sleeping and nutritional habits, cease physical activities, form a reliance on alcohol and medications and withdraw from family and loved ones. You will miss many Christmases, birthdays, significant family events, your children's milestone events, be away from family and the home for extended periods, isolate yourself, become angry and intolerant, cry and sob and eventually suffer absolute exhaustion.

You will attend far too many unnecessary funerals of colleagues. This is not an exhausting list, but these examples are all personal experiences that have happened to me. Many others in the policing profession have suffered and been exposed to far worse. Law enforcement culture is very strong. As Police we see ourselves as the protectors or guardians of society and we are viewed by society as infallible which we strive to maintain. We value strength of character, self-reliance, controlled emotions, and competency in handling the worst of situations. These values discourage help-seeking behaviour, and there is a sense of having lost control by asking someone else to help fix the problem. Fearful of being perceived as weak and untrustworthy, suffer potential sanctions or loss of professional opportunities, officers are therefore unlikely to reach out and seek help, even privately.

Seemingly with little other options death by suicide would be the only option for some. I did my utmost to protect our broader community but without realising it, the stress and trauma of my job ate away at me until I was left psychologically vulnerable and exposed.

Whilst I used my smile as a mask, my relentless fight to preserve my job took every ounce of energy from me. Declaring a mental health issue to my superiors in my mind was a career killer.

I didn't trust anyone, my work colleagues, friends, not even my family. I wasn't sure where to go and didn't know who was there for me. I had become so physically and mentally exhausted and the brain fog so severe that I no longer had the will to fight the daemons inside my head. Early 2014 following my return from Afghanistan a sinister turn occurred to me. The voice inside my head would assure me the misery I was battling could be ended by committing suicide. I was internally tortured by the thoughts, but I would eventually commence meticulously planning my own suicide. I had progressed to executing it—but thankfully one thought kept pushing me not to. That thought was the feelings of pain, abandonment, anger and weight the suicide of my grandfather and the profound impact that had on me as a 10-year-old. I couldn't put my loved ones through the same. So, of course I'm here today thankfully and abandoned my plans.

Barriers to Mental Health Use Services and Pathways to Care

The officer's story as portrayed in the previous pages highlights a number of barriers that have prevented him from asking for help. It appears that the toxic impact of exposure to a plethora of potentially traumatic events in the line of duty was accumulating over the years of service. Nevertheless, it was some of the values of traditional police culture that expect its members to be invincibly strong. Let alone, such expectations are not merely met in police context but also the general public expects officers to be strong and "invincible" so that they resolve any threat or danger that appears to jeopardize social welfare. Undeniably, law enforcement officers are present and in moments when civilians escape to avoid danger law enforcement officers are the ones who despite the risks heading toward the threatening situation to protect the public. However, as officer's story mentioned previously, officers are still human beings and in moments of challenge or desperation they should have to seek help. However, in order for this movement to occur community and organizations in general need to be conducive toward this direction. Over the previous years many steps have been made toward changing the whole notion of encouraging officers to seek help if needed. To name a few, most agencies at this point have wellness units in which wellness coordinators make sure that wellness programs and services are officers to law enforcement officers. Let alone, most agencies have police clinical psychologists and other health professionals who are highly trained to address officers' challenges. As well, peer support programs in police agencies have proven to be quite effective in helping officers ventilate their concerns and challenges to blue brothers and sisters who dedicate their time to be present and help. However, another important part in these situations is also the role of prevention and the preventative interventions that need to be embedded in the police organizations and it will be discussed in the following sections in this chapter.

Mental health conditions are associated with the loss of productivity (Birnbaum et al., 2010). In fact, research findings suggest that workers experiencing depression are more productive when receiving treatment than workers with depression who are not receiving treatment (Dewa et al., 2011). Mojtabai et al. (2011) identified three types of mental health service use barriers, including not recognizing that help is needed, structural factors (e.g., financial concerns; whether services are available) and attitudinal factors (e.g., stigma; wanting to cope with the health condition independently; questioning the efficacy of treatment). In addition, they found that attitudinal barriers—in particular wanting to cope with the illness independently—is the most common and frequent type of barriers to seeking treatment than structural barriers (Mojtabai et al., 2011).

In a study by Dewa and Hoch (2015), researchers tried to look at the impacts on work productivity of three types of barriers to mental health service use, with the goal of targeting interventions to increase service use. They found that the largest reduction in productivity loss occurs when all three service use barriers are removed, including not recognizing when help is needed; structural factors; and attitudinal factors. Specifically, among a population-based survey of Canadian workers, they found that removing the service need recognition barrier is associated with a 33% decrease in work productivity losses; however, a 49% decrease in productivity loss when all three mental health service use barriers are removed.

The authors recommend a collaboration among government, healthcare system, and employers in order to help overcome barriers to care. Taken together, prevention and intervention efforts toward building awareness of mental health symptoms and stigma reduction are indicated. The findings also show that a comprehensive system strategy needs to include:

- Collaboration among all stakeholders;
- The need for education and for any learning to be translated into work and practiced;
- Prevention at primary, secondary, and tertiary levels of continuum of care;
- Interventions at both worker and organizational levels;
- Ensuring access to resources and treatment and case management and disability management for return to work, better prognosis and recovery, and work productivity.

Mental Health Risk Factors

Building pathways to resilience involve strategies and interventions aimed at reducing risk factors at both individual levels and organizational levels (e.g., Harvey et al., 2017; Memish et al., 2017). A comprehensive strategy to workplace mental health entails identifying and assessing multiple risk factors, including burnout, mental health disorders, as well as occupational stressors, including organizational and operational stressors, work demands, work resources, workplace culture and leadership. A comprehensive understanding of sources of stress help toward optimal education, prevention and interventions, optimal treatment interventions and return work, and strengthening resiliency pathways at both organizational and worker levels.

Burnout

Burnout has been found to have an adverse impact on health and work performance (e.g., Borritz et al., 2010; Fragoso et al., 2016). Burnout is characterized by exhaustion, depersonalization or cynicism, and lack of professional efficacy (Maslach et al., 1996). The experience of exhaustion is often emotional, psychological, and physical, often marked with elevated fatigue, low energy, and insomnia. There is growing cynicism toward the value of one's occupation and ability to complete job duties and elevated fatigue resulting from work demands (Maslach et al., 1996). The depersonalization or cynicism can lead to emotional numbness or feeling emotionally distant from one's work, reduced interest in activities, losing motivation or interest in what was once a passion and/or reduced care. Reduced professional efficacy is associated with low self-confidence, low self-efficacy where one is doubting their capability of performing their work to the best of their ability, negative views of self and negative self-evaluation. One can view burnout as a loss and grief given the emotional numbness related to the self, loss of identity and loss of self-confidence, loss of motivation, or one's added value to work. The exhaustion component of burnout has also been found to result from an imbalance between job demands and job resources (Bianchi et al., 2015). A systematic review and meta-analysis by Koutsimani et al. (2019) looking at the relationship between burnout, depression, and anxiety found no conclusive overlap between burnout and depression and between burnout and anxiety. The results indicated that they are all different constructs. Hence, the need for prevention and interventions efforts to include all the above constructs to ensure a comprehensive approach is taken.

In a 1-year longitudinal study, both job demands and job resources were found to predict burnout and symptoms of depression over time (Hatch et al., 2019) while also being associated with symptoms of depression independent from burnout. The authors found evidence that both burnout and symptoms of depression change in the same direction and that no construct has a stronger temporal relation over the other. They also found that employee's mental health needs to include assessment of burnout, depression symptoms, and job-related stressors.

In officer's case portrayed in this chapter it was described how police work demands and expectations may lead to the sense of low productivity, reduced performance, and physical and mental exhaustion that can make one more vulnerable to the mental and physical health issues. Considering that police work is quite challenging as also described eloquently in the officer's story it is also important the fact that officers many times may feel that the organization does not care other than having the job done. If this perspective occurs or if officers internalize this notion, then trust toward the agency is violated and any chance for seeking help is jeopardized.

Compassion Fatigue[1]

If you review officer's story in this chapter you may note that he listed numerous situations where he was in the line of duty supporting victims of crimes or human beings who suffered in some capacity. To this end, he even stated that police work often appears to be that of a psychologist, social worker, or even a medic meaning that officers are not always crime fighters but they also respond to support those who suffer due to critical incidents. Let alone, officers are often the ones who respond first to the crime scenes or the critical incident scene and until other professionals arrive (e.g., paramedics, social services) they are the ones who are present and support those who suffer. However, this ongoing exposure to human suffering and support for those who suffer may come with a cost especially if the officers are not trained mentally to cope with these issues to some capacity that would help them make meaning of the value of their services. In this section, we present the compassion fatigue and we discuss extensively its potential impact on officers' health and wellbeing.

The occupational demands of first responders' work often entail officers being exposed to individuals who have been hurt, abused, injured, or even killed. First responders' work is an occupation marked with dangerous and distressing incidents (Burke & Mikkelsen, 2007; Crank, 2004; Cross & Ashley, 2004; Karlsson & Christianson, 2003; Kelley, 2005; Violanti et al., 2006; Waters & Ussery, 2007). The foundation of first responders' work includes serving and protecting with calls ranging from monotonous to life-threatening (Cross & Ashley, 2004; Henry, 2004; Papazoglou et al., 2017; Slate et al., 2007; Violanti et al., 2006; Waters & Ussery, 2007; Weiss et al., 2010). First responders are regularly exposed to critical incidents (e.g., vehicular accidents and fatalities, cases of abuse and mistreatment of vulnerable populations, dealing with violent subjects, etc.) that have long-lasting effects on their overall mental health (Cross & Ashley, 2004; Karlsson & Christianson, 2003). It is not a normal condition for the human brain to be exposed to human misery at the heightened levels experienced by many first responders. In addition, sustained and continuous exposure to stress and critical incidents can contribute to declining mental function (Heim & Nemeroff, 2009). This is particularly worrying since mental functioning is a necessity in this type of work. First responders must enter a career with exceptional mental health and are expected to remain that way for the duration of their careers.

The cost of caring (Figley, 1995) in first responders work is seen in the form of compassion fatigue and can have adverse effects on the physical, emotional, and

---

[1] Parts of this section on "compassion fatigue" have been published previously in: *Power: Police Officer Wellness, Ethics, and Resilience* (Konstantinos Papazoglou & Daniel M. Blumberg, Eds.); Chap. 7; Chuck Russo, Prashant Aukhojee, Brooke McQuerrey Tuttle, Olivia Johnson, Mark Davies, Brian A. Chopko, and Konstantinos Papazoglou; Compassion fatigue & burnout, Pages 97–115, Copyright © Elsevier 2020. Reproduced with permission of Elsevier. https://doi.org/10. 1016/B978-0-12-817872-0.00007-0

mental health of first responders, which is directly and indirectly related to overall work performance (Andersen & Papazoglou, 2015). Seeing the worst parts of society, along with caring for victims, can negatively influence job performance. For example, first responders may misplace aggression and anger in the form of excessive use of force issues and citizen complaints, both of which can lead to liability issues. In addition to job performance concerns, officers may struggle on a personal level both physically and mentally when combatting compassion fatigue. First responders are skilled at concealing their emotions such that others may be unaware that something is going on in the officer's life until problematic behavior surfaces.

First responders are often reluctant to admit that they may be struggling, especially with mental health issues (Olson & Wasilewski, 2016). Issues that can affect one's mental and emotional health often carry a stigma, even more so within subcultures like law enforcement (Violanti et al., 2018; Workman-Stark, 2017). First responders' professional culture influences how incidents are framed and how they are perceived by officers (Waters & Ussery, 2007). First responders' feelings of reluctance toward mental health improvement programs exemplify the dark side of first responders' culture where seeking help is stigmatized as weakness (Hohner, 2017; Workman-Stark, 2017). Hohner (2017) adds that first responders are worried about peer support programs backfiring, as they fear that their expression of concerns and negative experiences might be conveyed to management. Additionally, availability and accessibility to mental health resources within agencies may prevent first responders from receiving the help they need (Violanti et al., 2012). Generally, first responders that expressed job dissatisfaction due to organizational and departmental factors were more likely to experience symptoms of depression, anxiety, and traumatic stress (Gershon et al., 2009).

First responders play a key role in critical incidents that constitute a vital protective factor critical in shifting the victims' lives away from a trajectory toward poor, long-term outcomes (Akers & Kaukinen, 2009; Garrett, 2004; Marans et al., 2012; Marans & Hahn, 2017). When properly equipped, police officers may simultaneously play a critical role in advancing victims' recovery from traumatic experiences while more broadly contributing to the strengthening of relationships between agencies and communities (Akers & Kaukinen, 2009; Manzella & Papazoglou, 2014; Marans & Hahn, 2017). In this context, "compassion satisfaction" (Stamm, 2002) refers to the satisfaction that caregiving professionals derive from helping those who suffer. However, research has also shown that a considerable number of police officers do not appear to value the importance of their services in the communities they serve (Papazoglou, 2017). Therefore, while these first responders still serve their communities, their inability to view their work as valuable increases the likelihood that they will approach their duties in a perfunctory manner ("*just the facts, ma'am*"). In other situations, first responders may suppress their emotions or be emotionally disengaged because their attention is solely focused on investigation-related aspects of the incident and they fail to appreciate the value of additional, trauma-informed approaches that may not only be critically helpful to victims and witnesses as well as strengthening their contributions to the investigative process itself.

Research has indicated that frontline professionals who experience compassion satisfaction feel a greater sense of success and increased motivation because they are able to appreciate the value their services add to the lives of the individuals and the communities they serve (Papazoglou, 2017). In addition, other studies have concluded that police officers with high levels of compassion satisfaction tend to show greater job performance, more commitment to their duties, and higher levels of self-perceived wellbeing.

Perhaps unsurprisingly, research has revealed that compassion satisfaction is negatively associated with compassion fatigue; that is, an increase in compassion fatigue appears to be associated with a decrease in compassion satisfaction, and vice versa. One possible explanation for this relationship is that compassion fatigue symptoms (e.g., feeling overwhelmed, hypervigilance, irritability) may preclude officers from experiencing compassion satisfaction. Although more research is required in order to substantiate this negative association, it seems clear that frontline professionals with high levels of compassion satisfaction are able to appreciate the importance of their services despite being exposed to overwhelming experiences as a result of caring for trauma victims in the line of duty. In addition, the negative association between compassion fatigue and compassion satisfaction indicates that using various techniques to strengthen compassion satisfaction can mitigate or entirely neutralize the virulent experience of compassion fatigue.

Individual first responders have varying reactions when exposed to traumatic or potentially traumatic incidents. Those who may have a negative reaction to an incident will often refuse to come forward, for fear of what their peers may think. This leaves many first responders suffering in silence. The repression of emotions among police officers has been associated with poor health holistically (Wastell, 2002), and those who suffer in silence may revert to maladaptive coping mechanisms, such as the use of drugs and/or alcohol abuse to try to deal with their stress and trauma (Cross & Ashley, 2004; Hackett & Violanti, 2003; Violanti & Samuels, 2007; Waters & Ussery, 2007). Asking for help in police work is difficult for many first responders, because many believe that doing so could cost them their career, livelihood, and the respect of fellow officers. An occupation that operates at societal extremes reiterates the necessity to reinforce such cultural beliefs (Crank, 2004; Karlsson & Christianson, 2003; Kelley, 2005).

The impact of compassion fatigue on first responders' health and wellbeing is one side of the spectrum. Alternatively, it should be considered that compassion fatigue is very likely to affect officers' performance at work. Trauma scholars mentioned that caregiving professionals may even experience dissociation during their work with traumatized individuals (Danieli, 1996). Mathieu (2007) mentions that while each individual may express certain unique symptoms of compassion fatigue; those entering in the danger zone of compassion fatigue may show warning signs of "intrusive imagery or dissociation." Healthcare professionals experiencing compassion fatigue have often felt that they were "frequently dissociated [and] walked around in an altered state..." (Babbel, 2012). Similarly, police officers support numerous victims of crimes, accidents, or natural catastrophes over the course of their career. Therefore, compassion fatigue may create ripple effect of poor health and mental malfunctioning. Research has shown that those who suffer from previous mental health challenges are more likely to develop PTSD in the experience of a life-threatening situation (McFarlane, 2000; Sayed et al., 2015).

First responders' personal and family lives are also impacted by compassion fatigue (Sprang et al., 2007). At the end of their shift, first responders return to their homes, where their families are waiting for them. There, they assume the role of a parent, spouse, son/daughter, and friend. Officers who suffer from police compassion fatigue may become cynical, apathetic, negative, and aloof which could negatively influence their interactions with family and friends (Cox et al., 2017; Fuller, 2003). As a result, a snowball phenomenon may occur and mundane or minor family or personal issues may remain unresolved and aggravate over time until they lead to family discord or potential divorce (Miller, 2007).

Moral Injury[2]

In the officer's story it was mentioned that law enforcement work entails dealing with violent offenders and human suffering. Human suffering especially when relates to vulnerable individuals such as children and elders often has impact on officers' moral values and creates inner moral conflicts that often transgress one's value system. In situations, as described in officer's story, when officers, for instance, respond to abused children or battered woman it would lead to officers' guilt or even sense of hopelessness believing that s/he would have prevented this suffering from happening. As already discussed, officers are often wired to believe that they are invincible strong superheroes that can impede virulent criminal offenses from occurring in their neighborhoods. However, this is not always the case and when violent crimes occur that also entail suffering of a human being this assumptive notion is violated. When officers realize that they cannot really prevent everything and anything in the community and suffering occurs due to criminal activity, trauma, or neglect those experiences may impact officers moral value system by creating moral conflicts that often are accompanied by guilt, shame, helplessness, and hopelessness. In the following paragraphs we extensively present and discuss different types of moral risks experienced in the law enforcement.

The idea of moral injury has been pervasive in human societies for thousands of years, and perhaps since the existence of humankind. In the Greco-Roman tradition,

---

[2]Parts of these three consecutive sections on "moral injury" and "moral distress" have been published previously in: *Power: Police Officer Wellness, Ethics, and Resilience* (Konstantinos Papazoglou & Daniel M. Blumberg, Eds.); Chap. 8; Katy Kamkar, Chuck Russo, Brian A. Chopko, Brooke McQuerrey Tuttle, Daniel M. Blumberg, and Konstantinos Papazoglou; Moral injury in law enforcement, Pages 117–128, Copyright © Elsevier 2020. Reproduced with permission of Elsevier. https://doi.org/10.1016/B978-0-12-817872-0.00008-2

warrior narratives reference the experience of moral conflicts on the battlefield (called miasma or "μίασμα"—moral pollution and purification), defining it as a situation wherein someone with legitimate and recognized authority betrays what is right in a critical situation (Shay, 2014). In the modern era, conceptualization of moral injury is derived from research and clinical work with US military personnel and veterans. It became apparent through both research and clinical practice that veterans who served in combat zones were exposed to traumas that altered their moral beliefs and values systems; that is, some veterans experienced a violation of their morals or beliefs during their service and became skeptical about whether or not the world is a just, benevolent, and safe place. Thereby, a formal definition refers to moral injury as exposure to unprecedented traumatic life events wherein one perpetrates, fails to prevent, or witnesses actions that "transgress deeply held moral beliefs and expectations" (Litz et al., 2009, p. 1). Similarly, the U.S. Marine Corps uses the term "inner conflict" when referring to experiences involving moral injury (Nash & Litz, 2013). Inner conflict may occur not only when a Marine experiences extraordinary violence (e.g., terrorists using children as "shields") but also in moments when they are ordered to leave a wounded comrade behind in order to save their own lives.

Events that may lead to moral injury include handling/uncovering human remains, the inability to render help to severely wounded victims, involvement in friendly fire incidents, being present when noncombatants are harmed or killed by accident, witnessing others injure or kill unnecessarily without intervening to stop their actions, or observing war-related destruction of property, and killing enemy soldiers (Drescher et al., 2011; Frankfurt & Frazier, 2016; Litz et al., 2009). These experiences violate individuals' moral belief systems and share core features of guilt and shame for having been involved in these events.

The Impact of Moral Injury in Police Officers' Health and Work

The experience of moral injury carries negative physical and psychological effects for officers. Moral injury, although not recognized as a mental health disorder within the *Diagnostic and Statistical Manual of Mental Disorders, Fifth Edition* (DSM-5) (American Psychiatric Association, 2013), can lead to lasting emotional and psychological impact. It is, therefore, a significant mental health issue that needs to be recognized during mental health assessment for a more comprehensive case conceptualization; while also being targeted throughout treatment interventions; and an essential part of evidence-based education around mental health prevention and promotion. Moral injury has been associated with intrusion, avoidance, and arousal symptoms of PTSD (Feinstein et al., 2018); depression, suicidal ideation, and anger (Bryan et al., 2014; Gaudet et al., 2016); and, as discussed earlier, with guilt and shame (Nazarov et al., 2015). Taking a broader perspective approach also helps to further understand the impact of moral injury and related diagnoses such as posttraumatic stress disorder (PTSD) or depression, which are all part of operational stress injuries (OSI).

Initially conceptualized within the Canadian Armed Forces (Standing Senate Committee on National Security and Defence, 2015), OSI include any persistent psychological difficulties resulting from operational or service-related duties. Common mental health problems at the core of OSI include PTSD, anxiety disorders, depression, substance use disorders, suicidal ideation, or any other conditions that may interfere with a person's level of functioning, personal, social, or occupational. Stressors related to employment, finances, family, relationships as well as pain and physical health issues and changes within role or identity can all be part of OSI which, in turn, cause further pain, suffering, and impaired functioning.

OSI, and in particular trauma, can shatter an individual's core belief system whereby one's views of self, others, the future, and the world can fundamentally change. How events, circumstances, or situations are perceived, interpreted, or viewed can drastically change following traumatic events and, as well, often reflect elements of moral injury. This can lead to potential difficulty regulating emotions, experiencing intense mixed and negative emotions, difficulty making healthy decisions and taking proactive strategies, difficulty resuming regular work duties, decreased work productivity, reduced self-efficacy at work, and feeling incompetent. As well, over time, any future events or situations tend to be filtered through the lens that has been altered, thus, further compounding suffering and impaired functioning.

Individual response varies between officers, depending on how each person processes events or circumstances. What may set in motion a fundamental change in one individual may have an entirely different effect on another individual or possibly even no impact. This makes understanding, recognizing, and treating OSI far more difficult compared to physical injuries experienced by officers.

While most attention has been given to emotions such as anxiety and fear resulting from traumatic incidents that police officers have often faced in line of duty, other emotions such as guilt and shame have received less attention despite their contributions to health and work outcomes (e.g., Wright & Gudjonsson, 2007; Cohen et al., 2011). Mixed emotions related to guilt and shame often result in internal conflict within the self where actions of self or others are not in harmony with one's moral values, standard, beliefs, or conscience. Guilt and shame are related to maintaining and exacerbating psychopathology, interpersonal conflict, self-isolation and avoidance, disruption in work activities, prolonged recovery, and present a significant barrier to personal, social, and occupational functioning. First responders often report difficulty with resuming their regular work activities or with the return to process after a period of absence as a result of feeling ashamed, or not wanting to go out to public places or attending social events out of fear of seeing people or colleagues due to guilt or shame. Those emotions can lead at times to more self-isolation and prominent avoidance than other emotions, such as fear or anxiety.

Other Types of Moral Distress

In addition to the risk for moral injury presented by operational stressors already discussed (e.g., shooting someone after believing the person had a gun and realizing afterwards the person did not possess a weapon; witnessing horrific crime scenes), organizational stressors can also present risk for moral distress. Common organizational stressors related to job stress and burnout (Cooper & Marshall, 1976; Finney et al., 2013) include stressors intrinsic to the job; role in organization and rewards; supervisory relationships and organizational structure and climate. Organization stressors can lead to first responders' feeling they have little or no control over their work. For example, just being "along for the ride" may be a common sentiment among those experiencing organizational stressors.

In the work of first responders, risk for moral injury related to organization stressors can occur and be compounded by excessive work demands that are difficult to manage; limited opportunities for training and limited resources; heavy workloads; lack of support; dissatisfaction around one's role in the organization (e.g., role ambiguity or the role not fitting one's interest, skills or training); unclear responsibilities; strained relationships with supervisors; unresolved interpersonal conflicts; harassment and bullying in the workplace; or lack of perceived organizational support following high-profile police incidents. When first responders are unable to pursue what they believe or perceive to be the right plan of action or decision, or fail to meet their own expectations due to, for instance, work related obstacles, interpersonal conflicts, and limited resources or circumstances beyond their control, they may subsequently feel guilty, demoralized, and/or helpless. Any of the stressors named above can lead to internal conflict or transgression of one's moral values and belief system and, in turn, set the stage for moral injury.

Moral distress is also related to a variety of other emotional, psychological, and physiological reactions such as sleep disturbance, bad dreams, appetite changes, feelings of worthlessness, reduced sense of self-confidence, and headaches (Fry et al., 2002). The emotional and psychological impact of moral distress can also over time increase the risk for burnout (Fumis et al., 2017). Traumatic incidents noted above, including operational and organizational stressors, can lead to not only trauma reactions that are fear-based or trauma reactions that are loss-based, but also to moral injury-based trauma reactions (Gray et al., 2012; Held et al., 2018; Litz et al., 2016).

Trauma reactions that are fear-based can include, for instance, fear for safety of self or others following increased violence, assaults, gang related incidents, or as a result of limited staffing in smaller communities. They can also include fear of impending doom; fear of something bad happening to self or others; and anxiety being in social situations or in public places and witnessing interpersonal conflicts or arguments. Trauma reactions that are loss-based can include, for instance, losing a colleague to suicide; death of a colleague following a shooting incident; or a death scene that resembled an officer's personal life (e.g., having a child of same age; a house looking the same as the officer's house). For moral injury-based trauma reactions, the symptoms can be similar to OSI symptoms and may include mixed emotions such as feelings of shame, guilt, remorse, or anger; irritability, negative beliefs about oneself; self-blame; avoidance and self-isolation; withdrawal from social situations; distressing intrusive memories of traumatic incidents and related nightmares; difficulties with sleep; and difficulties with concentration and making decisions. The symptoms related to moral injury can also contribute to maintenance and/or exacerbation of psychological disorders related to OSI.

Taken together, building awareness of the harmful impact of moral injury, providing education around moral injury, and recognizing the signs and symptoms of moral injury can inform prevention initiatives and contribute to resilience building among officers and help optimize treatment interventions to improve quality of life and wellbeing, and personal and occupational functioning. At the organizational level, creating healthy culture, providing a people-oriented culture and people focused leadership, building organizational capacities and resources, and implementing psychological health and safety strategies to alleviate organizational stressors could help reduce the risk of moral injury.

Morally injurious experiences are prevalent in first responders' work. Current scholarly literature shows that moral injury violates the moral belief system of the individual, leading to negative and distressing views of self, others, and the world. It also results in a host of negative emotional reactions with guilt and shame as predominant emotions experienced. Taken together, moral injury can have a virulent impact on first responders' health, wellbeing, and overall functioning. Nevertheless, emphasis should be placed on the fact that moral injury is not an inevitable condition. When addressed early, or through prevention, the negative impact of moral injury on officers can be reduced. It is possible that first responders may be inclined to employ unhealthy ways of coping (e.g., alcohol, isolation, cynicism) to battle moral injury symptoms as a desperate way to prevent the negative impact of moral injury in their lives. In many occasions, first responders may not be familiar with healthy ways of coping or preventative strategies to protect them against the incapacitating impact of moral injury.

Research on first responders' moral injury is still in its infancy. However, as discussed in the current chapter, first responders and scholars can translate military moral injury knowledge into first responders' work. That way, police officers will become cognizant of moral injury in their work. The successful application of moral injury research findings in first responders' work requires a synergistic effort emanated from police leaders, police clinicians, police families, and officers themselves. It is essential that the possibility of moral conflicts is addressed at the organizational level within police departments. When moral injury is openly addressed in an unapologetic and de-stigmatizing way, first responders will feel more comfortable to share about moral distress experienced on the job. Such dialogue should take place during department meetings because they are facilitated in a collective context in which officers have the opportunity to get feedback from their colleagues and supervisors. This would allow for early signs of moral injury or any inner conflict to be verbalized and processed within a supportive context.

Analogously, first responders' moral dilemmas and conflicts should be addressed during police training and, hence, incorporated into police training curricula. The authors of the present chapter suggest that first responders' training should encompass the different nuances of critical incidents (e.g., moral dilemmas, stress levels, decision making, use of force) and such incidents should not solely be approached from an operational perspective. Moral injury can potentially affect first responders' capacity for decision making during critical moments (e.g., to shoot or not to shoot) and affect their clarity of judgment in the line of duty. First responders' trainers should encourage first responders to share any moral dilemmas they experience during training so that they are best prepared for real life situations of police work where moral dilemmas and conflicts are omnipresent.

The role of clinicians in preventing and treating moral injury is vital. Clinicians may collaborate with officers who are part of peer support units and help them identify peers who struggle with moral injury, moral conflicts, and moral dilemmas. In addition, clinical treatment, especially in regard to stress and trauma, should explore any morally injurious symptoms experienced by first responders who participate in treatment. Assessing for moral injury allows treatment to address the holistic needs of first responders. Often, issues experienced by first responders in the past have remained unaddressed or ignored because the severity of such issues was undervalued or understudied. In addition, clinicians may guide and encourage first responders to practice strategies that can help them prevent the impact of moral injury in their lives. For instance, prior research with veterans has shown that volunteerism, journaling, mindfulness, and gratitude letters are some ways that can help first responders express their moral conflicts while engaging in activities where they can realize that the world has potential for kindness and fairness and not just violence and unfairness.

Psychological health and safety in the workplace should include education around moral injury in first responders' work as well as increased efforts to reduce likelihood of moral injury or moral distress resulting from operational or organizational stressors. Further research, education, and training are needed to better identify all aspects of moral injury in the first responders' population and to inform prevention and intervention around moral injury in first responders' field.

The Integral Role of Prevention in the Organizational Level

In an international review of guidelines on workplace mental health by Memish et al. (2017), key themes included: (1) taking an integrated approach to workplace mental health; (2) interventions are preventative when risk factors related to work are modified or minimized; protective factors are promoted and illnesses are managed; and (3) prevention approaches, primary, secondary and tertiary, must occur at both worker and organization-level factors (LaMontagne et al., 2007, 2014). Any education and mental health promotion and interventions at primary prevention would lead to the most effective outcome when carried out along with secondary and tertiary prevention with interventions at both worker and organizations levels (e.g., Memish et al., 2017; Giga et al., 2003; LaMontagne et al. 2007).

Prevention involves any kind of intervention aimed at preventing the onset, recurrence, severity, and impact of health conditions. Primary prevention is aimed toward reducing the onset or likelihood of an illness. It generally involves building resiliency through a two-step process: reducing risk factors and building protective factors. Any proactive education and mental health promotion can fall within the primary prevention care (e.g., online resiliency training). Secondary prevention involves any interventions aimed at identifying and addressing health problems at an early stage (e.g., screening tests). Tertiary prevention care involves evidence-based treatment and interventions, and disability management (e.g., evidence-based cognitive behavioral treatment with work interventions) aimed at reducing disability and improving overall functioning and return to work. Any interventions that are provided at secondary and/or tertiary prevention care can also be included within primary prevention care including, for instance, peer support, ways of accessing resources to care, the need for any work modification or accommodation, learning problem-solving skills, and proactive and healthy coping strategies to cope with life or work stressors.

Mental Health Promotion and Education

Shann et al. (2019) studied an online workplace mental health intervention for leaders to help reduce stigma related to depression. Results showed depression related stigma were much lower among leaders who completed the online program than the control group. The authors concluded that strong knowledge or positive attitudes are not sufficient to transfer learning or knowledge into workplace and that other key elements such as the work atmosphere and attitudes, organizational readiness and capability, and the political context impact the transfer of learning into workplace.

With stigma identified as largest barrier to help seeking (Lasalvia et al., 2013), continuous effort and creative strategies need to be delivered for stigma reduction. A meta-analysis (Corrigan et al., 2012) on stigma reduction found that both education and contact (having personal contact with someone with a mental health condition) were effective at reducing stigma with contact being more effective.

Building pathway to care and treatment include:

- Identifying signs and symptoms of psychological distress that are increasing over time and causing functional impairment;
- Recognizing that help is needed;
- Workers feeling safe sharing their experiences and not being afraid of stigma and in particular workplace stigma where they might feel judged, not being considered for promotion or any other opportunities, or not feeling supporting during disability leave or after leave of absence;

- Deciding to receive treatment and knowledge of effectiveness of treatment;
- Access to treatment that is evidence-based and resources with expertise;
- Engagement in treatment and benefit from treatment;
- Receiving treatment that includes return to work interventions;
- A system that ensures collaborative care model that helps to increase therapy outcome, positive prognosis, increase overall functioning, in particular occupational functioning and the likelihood of return to work and work productivity and recovery.

Protective Factors

Healthy and proactive coping is known to be a protective factor against negative health outcomes following traumatic events and further contributor to resiliency and wellbeing (e.g., Galatzer-Levy et al., 2012; Feder et al., 2013). As discussed earlier, workplace mental health needs to involve increase in protective factor as part of resiliency. To this end, coping flexibility is the ability to utilize flexibility different coping strategies in a particular situation (Bonanno et al., 2011) and has been found to be associated with lower levels of posttraumatic stress and depressive symptoms after controlling for comorbid symptoms, age and time since the traumatic event (Park et al., 2015). The authors of those studies found that lower coping flexibility was associated with higher PTSD symptoms as the number of traumatic events increased, with conclusion that coping flexibility is a protective factor for PTSD and depression and the risk for mental health conditions following series of trauma is higher with lower coping flexibility.

Similarly, Dahm et al. (2015) have researched modifiable factors that are related to PTSD and functional impairment to optimize interventions and to that effect studied mindfulness and self-compassion. They looked at the relation of both mindfulness and self-compassion with PTSD symptom severity and disability in veterans, both mindfulness and self-compassion have each been found to be negatively associated with PTSD symptom severity and functional disability, even after controlling for PTSD symptom severity. The findings indicated that prevention and interventions aimed at building mindfulness and self-compassion can help toward reducing the functional disability related to PTSD. Mindfulness involves regulating emotion and attention in the moment and present time by identifying thoughts and emotions and looking at them from an objective standpoint to help reframing thoughts and put them into perspective (e.g., Teasdale et al., 2002). Self-compassion involves being mindful of one's suffering and thoughts and emotions and putting them into perspective, self-kindness and providing self with support and a sense of humanity by acknowledging that everyone is human, no one is perfect and any human can make mistake and suffering is part of humanity (e.g., Neff, 2003, 2012).

In an article published by American Psychological Association, Sprang et al. (2019) stated that the expert panel defined Secondary Traumatic Stress (STS) as a construct directly related to or very closely parallels the components of PTSD as defined in DSM-5 (re-experiencing symptoms of trauma; avoidance related symptoms; alternations in mood and cognitions; and arousal symptoms) with an additional domain to reflect the likely changes in personal and professionals systems of meaning and beliefs that might result from other stress reactions such as moral distress, reduced empathy, or professional self-efficacy. Compassion satisfaction that refers to the satisfaction and gratification that one feels after helping others (Stamm, 2010) has also been found to be a protective factor. To this end, compassion satisfaction has been found to be negatively related to secondary traumatic stress and burnout and a likely protective factor against those health risk factors (Simon et al., 2006). And more recently, Cummings et al. (2018) found that burnout is a strong predictor of vicarious trauma and secondary traumatic stress, however, compassion satisfaction might be a protective factor against experiencing both. The authors concluded in the importance of prevention and interventions to reduce burnout and increase compassion satisfaction.

Conclusion

The main focus of this chapter was to highlight the many pathways that exist to build workplace mental health and resiliency at both individual and organizational level factors. Workplace Risk factors as well workplace strengths and protective factors were discussed. Taken together, there is a need to optimize mental health education, prevention, and interventions at both individual and organizational levels to further positive organizational culture and workplace mental health.

References

Akers, C., & Kaukinen, C. (2009). The police reporting behavior of intimate partner violence victims. *Journal of Family Violence, 24*(3), 159–171.

American Psychiatric Association. (2013). *Diagnostic and statistical manual of mental disorders* (5th ed.). American Psychiatric Publishing.

Andersen, J. P., & Papazoglou, K. (2015). Compassion fatigue and compassion satisfaction among police officers: An understudied topic. *International Journal of Emergency Mental Health and Human Resilience, 17*(3), 661–663. https://doi.org/10.4172/1522-4821.1000259

Babbel, S. (2012, July 4). Compassion fatigue: Bodily symptoms of empathy. *Psychology Today.* https://www.psychologytoday.com/ca/blog/somatic-psychology/201207/compassion-fatigue

Bianchi, R., Schonfeld, I. S., & Laurent, E. (2015). Burnout-depression overlap: A review. *Clinical Psychology Review, 36*, 28–41. https://doi.org/10.1016/j.cpr.2015.01.004

Birnbaum, H. G., Kessler, R. C., Kelley, D., Ben-Hamadi, R., Joish, V. N., & Greenberg, P. E. (2010). Employer burden of mild, moderate, and severe major depressive disorder: Mental health services utilization and costs, and work performance. *Depression and Anxiety, 27*, 78–89.

Bonanno, G. A., Pat-Horenczyk, R., & Noll, J. (2011). Coping flexibility and trauma: The perceived ability to cope with trauma (PACT) scale. *Psychological Trauma: Theory, Research, Practice, and Policy, 3*, 117–129.

Borritz, M., Christensen, K. B., Bültmann, U., Rugulies, R., Lund, T., Andersen, I., Villadsen, E., Diderichsen, F., & Kristensen, T. S. (2010). Impact of burnout and psychosocial work charac-teristics on future long-term sickness absence. Prospective results of the Danish PUMA study among human service workers. *Journal of Occupational and Environmental Medicine, 52*(10), 964–970. https://doi.org/10.1097/JOM.0b013e3181f12f95

Bryan, A. O., Bryan, C. J., Morrow, C. E., Etienne, N., & Ray-Sannerud, B. (2014). Moral injury, suicidal ideation, and suicide attempts in a military sample. *Traumatology, 20*(3), 154–160. https://doi.org/10.1037/h0099852

Burke, R. J., & Mikkelsen, A. (2007). Suicidal ideation among police officers in Norway. *Policing: An International Journal of Police Strategies & Management, 30*(2), 228–236. https://doi.org/10.1108/13639510710753234

Carleton, R. N., Afifi, T. O., Taillieu, T., Turner, S., Mason, J. E., Ricciardelli, R., McCreary, D. R., Vaughan, A. D., Anderson, G. S., Krakauer, R. L., Donnelly, E. A., Camp, R. D., Groll, D., Cramm, H. A., MacPhee, R. A., & Griffiths, C. T. (2020). Assessing the relative impact of diverse stressors among public safety personnel. *International Journal of Environmental Research & Public Health, 17*(4), 1234. https://doi.org/10.3390/ijerph17041234

Cohen, T. R., Wolf, S. T., Panter, A. T., & Insko, C. A. (2011). Introducing the GASP scale: A new measure of guilt and shame proneness. *Journal of Personality and Social Psychology, 100*(5), 947–966. https://doi.org/10.1037/a0022641

Cooper, C. L., & Marshall, J. (1976). Occupational sources of stress: A review of the literature relating to coronary heart disease and mental ill health. *Journal of Occupational Psychology, 49* (1), 11–28. https://doi.org/10.1111/j.2044-8325.1976.tb00325.x

Corrigan, P. W., Morris, S. B., Michaels, P. J., Rafacz, J. D., & Rüsch, N. (2012). Challenging the public stigma of mental illness: A meta-analysis of outcome studies. *Psychiatric Services, 63*, 963–973. https://doi.org/10.1176/appi.ps.201100529

Cox, S. M., Marchionna, S., & Fitch, B. D. (2017). The police culture and work stress. In *Introduction to policing* (3rd ed., p. 177).

Crank, J. P. (2004). *Understanding police culture* (2nd ed.). Anderson Publishing.

Cross, C. L., & Ashley, L. (2004). Police trauma and addiction: Coping with the dangers of the job. *FBI Law Enforcement Bulletin, 73*(10), 24–32.

Cummings, C., Singer, J., Hisaka, R., & Benuto, L. T. (2018). Compassion satisfaction to combat work-related burnout, vicarious trauma, and secondary traumatic stress. *Journal of Interpersonal Violence*, 1–16. https://doi.org/10.1177/0886260518799502

Dahm, K., Meyer, E. C., Neff, K., Kimbrel, N. A., Gulliver, S. B., & Morissette, S. B. (2015). Mindfulness, self-compassion, posttraumatic stress disorder symptoms, and functional disability in U.S. Iraq and Afghanistan war veterans. *Journal of Traumatic Stress, 28*(5), 460–464.

Danieli, Y. (1996). Who takes care of the caregiver? In R. J. Apfel & B. Simon (Eds.), *Minefields in their hearts: The mental health of children in war and communal violence* (pp. 189–205). Yale University Press.

Dewa, C. S., & Hoch, J. S. (2015). Barriers to mental health service use among workers with depression and work productivity. *Journal of Occupational & Environmental Medicine, 57*(7), 726–731.

Dewa, C. S., Thompson, A. H., & Jacobs, P. (2011). The association of treatment of depressive episodes and work productivity. *Canadian Journal Psychiatry, 56*(12), 743–750.

Drescher, K. D., Foy, D. W., Kelly, C., Leshner, A., Schutz, K., & Litz, B. (2011). An exploration of the viability and usefulness of the construct of moral injury in war veterans. *Traumatology, 17* (1), 8–13. https://doi.org/10.1177/1534765610395615

Feder, A., Ahmad, S., Lee, E. J., Morgan, J. E., Singh, R., Smith, B. W., Southwick, S. M., & Charney, D. S. (2013). Coping and PTSD symptoms in Pakistani earthquake survivors: Purpose in life, religious coping and social support. *Journal of Affective Disorders, 147*(1–3), 156–163. https://doi.org/10.1016/j.jad.2012.10.027

Feinstein, A., Pavisian, B., & Storm, H. (2018). Journalists covering the refugee and migration crisis are affected by moral injury not PTSD. *JRSM Open, 9*(3), 1–7. https://doi.org/10.1177/2054270418759010

Figley, C. R. (1995). *Compassion fatigue: Coping with secondary traumatic stress disorder in those who treat the traumatized. BrunnerMazel psychosocial stress series*. Bruner/Mazel.

Finney, C., Stergiopoulos, E., Hensel, J., Bonato, S., & Dewa, C. S. (2013). Organizational stressors associated with job stress and burnout in correctional officers: A systematic review. *BMC Public Health, 13*(1), 82. https://doi.org/10.1186/1471-2458-13-82

Fragoso, Z. L., Holcombe, K. J., McCluney, C. L., Fisher, G. G., McGonagle, A. K., & Friebe, S. J. (2016). Burnout and engagement: Relative importance of predictors and outcomes in two health care worker samples. *Workplace Health & Safety, 64*(10), 479–487. https://doi.org/10.1177/2165079916653414

Frankfurt, S., & Frazier, P. (2016). A review of research on moral injury in combat veterans. *Military Psychology, 28*(5), 318–330. https://doi.org/10.1037/mil0000132

Fry, S., Harvey, R., Hurley, A., & Foley, B. (2002). Development of a model of moral distress in military nursing. *Nursing Ethics, 9*(4), 373–387. https://doi.org/10.1191/0969733002ne522oa

Fuller, M. E. (2003). *Living with a cop: A handbook for police officers and their families. Resource document*. https://opus.uleth.ca/bitstream/handle/10133/1150/Fuller_Merle_E.pdf

Fumis, R. R. L., Amarante, G. A. J., Nascimento, A. F., & Junior, J. M. V. (2017). Moral distress and its contribution to the development of burnout syndrome among critical care providers. *Annals of Intensive Care, 71*(7), 1–8. https://doi.org/10.1186/s13613-017-0293-2

Galatzer-Levy, I. R., Burton, C. L., & Bonanno, G. A. (2012). Coping flexibility, potentially traumatic life events, and resilience: A prospective study of college student adjustment. *Journal of Social and Clinical Psychology, 31*(6), 542–567. https://doi.org/10.1521/jscp.2012.31.6.542

Garrett, P. M. (2004). Talking child protection: The police and social workers "working together". *Journal of Social Work, 4*(1), 77–97. https://doi.org/10.1177/1468017304042422

Gaudet, C. M., Sowers, K. M., Nugent, W. R., & Boriskin, J. A. (2016). A review of PTSD and shame in military veterans. *Journal of Human Behavior in the Social Environment, 26*(1), 56–68. https://doi.org/10.1080/10911359.2015.1059168

Gershon, R. R. M., Barocas, B., Canton, A. N., Xianbin Li, L., & Vlahov, D. (2009). Mental, physical, and behavioral outcomes associated with perceived work stress in police officers. *Criminal Justice and Behavior, 36*(3), 275–289. https://doi.org/10.1177/0093854808330015

Giga, S. I., Noblet, A. J., Faragher, B., & Cooper, C. L. (2003). The UK perspective: A review of research on organisational stress management interventions. *Australian Psychologist, 38*(2), 158–164. https://doi.org/10.1080/00050060310001707167

Gray, M. J., Schorr, Y., Nash, W., Lebowitz, L., Amidon, A., Lansing, A., Maglione, A., Lang, A. J., & Litz, B. T. (2012). Adaptive disclosure: An open trial of a novel exposure-based intervention for service members with combat-related psychological stress injuries. *Behavior Therapy, 43*(2), 407–415. https://doi.org/10.1016/j.beth.2011.09.001

Hackett, D. P., & Violanti, J. M. (2003). *Police suicide: Tactics for prevention*. Charles C. Thomas.

Harvey, S. B., Modini, M., Joyce, S., Milligan-Saville, J. S., Tan, L., Mykletun, A., Bryant, R. A., Christensen, H., & Mitchell, P. B. (2017). Can work make you mentally ill? A systematic meta-review of work-related risk factors for common mental health problems. *Occupational & Environmental Medicine, 74*(4), 301–310. https://doi.org/10.1136/oemed-2016-104015

Hatch, D. J., Potter, G. G., Martus, P., Rose, U., & Freude, G. (2019). Lagged versus concurrent changes between burnout and depression symptoms and unique contributions from job demands and job resources. *Journal of Occupational Health Psychology, 24*(6), 617–628. https://doi.org/10.1037/ocp0000170

Heim, C., & Nemeroff, C. B. (2009). Neurobiology of posttraumatic stress disorder. *CNS Spectrums, 14*(1 Suppl 1), 13–24.

Held, P., Klassen, B. J., Brennan, M. B., & Zalta, A. K. (2018). Using prolonged exposure and cognitive processing therapy to treat veterans with moral injury-based PTSD: Two case examples. *Cognitive and Behavioral Practice, 25*(3), 377–390. https://doi.org/10.1016/j.cbpra.2017.09.003

Henry, V. E. (2004). *Death work: Police, trauma, and the psychology of survival.* Oxford University Press.

Hohner, C. (2017). *'The environment says it's okay': The tension between peer support and police culture. Resource document.* Western Libraries. https://ir.lib.uwo.ca/etd

Joyce, S., Modini, M., Christensen, H., Mykletun, A., Bryant, R., Mitchell, P. B., & Harvey, S. B. (2016). Workplace interventions for common mental disorders: A systematic meta-review. *Psychological Medicine, 46*(4), 683–697. https://doi.org/10.1017/S0033291715002408

Karlsson, I., & Christianson, S. (2003). The phenomenology of traumatic experiences in police work. *Policing: An International Journal of Police Strategies & Management, 26*(3), 419–438. https://doi.org/10.1108/13639510310489476

Kelley, T. M. (2005). Mental health and prospective police professionals. *Policing: An International Journal, 28*(1), 6–29. https://doi.org/10.1108/13639510510510580959

Koutsimani, P., Montgomery, A., & Georganta, K. (2019). The relationship between burnout, depression, and anxiety: A systematic review and meta-analysis. *Frontiers in Psychology, 10* (284), 1–19. https://doi.org/10.3389/fpsyg.2019.00284

LaMontagne, A. D., Keegel, T., & Vallance, D. (2007). Protecting and promoting mental health in the workplace: Developing a systems approach to job stress. *Health Promotion Journal of Australia, 18*(3), 221–228. https://doi.org/10.1071/HE07221

LaMontagne, A. D., Martin, A., Page, K. M., Reavley, N. J., Noblet, A. J., Milner, A. J., Keegel, T., & Smith, P. M. (2014). Workplace mental health: Developing an integrated intervention approach. *BMC Psychiatry, 14*(131). https://doi.org/10.1186/1471-244X-14-131

Lasalvia, A., Zoppei, S., Van Bortel, T., Bonetto, C., Cristofalo, D., Wahlbeck, K., Bacle, S. V., Audenhove, C. V., Weeghel, J., Reneses, B., Germanavicius, A., Economou, M., Lanfredi, M., Ando, S., Sartorius, N., Lopez-Ibor, J. J., & Thornicroft, G. (2013). Global pattern of experienced and anticipated discrimination reported by people with major depressive disorder: A cross-sectional survey. *The Lancet, 381*(9860), 55–62. https://doi.org/10.1016/S0140-6736(12)61379-8

Litz, B. T., Lebowitz, L., Gray, M. J., & Nash, W. P. (2016). *Adaptive disclosure: A new treatment for military trauma, loss, and moral injury.* The Guilford Press.

Litz, B. T., Stein, N., Delaney, E., Lebowitz, L., Nash, W. P., Silva, C., & Maguen, S. (2009). Moral injury and moral repair in war veterans: A preliminary model and intervention strategy. *Clinical Psychology Review, 29*(8), 695–706. https://doi.org/10.1016/j.cpr.2009.07.003

Manzella, C., & Papazoglou, K. (2014). Training police trainees about ways to manage trauma and loss. *International Journal of Mental Health Promotion, 16*(2), 103–116. https://doi.org/10.1080/14623730.2014.903609

Marans, S. & Hahn, H. (2017). *Enhancing police responses to children exposed to violence: A toolkit for law enforcement.* Office of Juvenile Justice and Delinquency Prevention, Office of Justice Programs, US Department of Justice.

Marans, S., Smolover, D., & Hahn, H. (2012). Responding to child trauma: Theory, programs, and policy. In E. L. Girgorenko (Ed.), *Handbook of juvenile forensic psychology and psychiatry* (pp. 453–466). Springer.

Martin, A., Karanika-Murray, M., Biron, C., & Sanderson, K. (2014). The psychosocial work environment, employee mental health and organizational interventions: Improving research and practice by taking a multilevel approach. *Stress & Health, 32*(3), 201–215. https://doi.org/10.1002/smi.2593

Maslach, C., Jackson, S. E., & Leiter, M. P. (1996). *MBI: Maslach burnout inventory.* CPP, Incorporated.

Mathieu, F. (2007). Running on empty: Compassion fatigue in health professionals. *Rehabilitation & Community Care Medicine, 4*, 1–7.

McFarlane, A. C. (2000). Posttraumatic stress disorder: A model of the longitudinal course and the role of risk factors. *Journal of Clinical Psychiatry, 61*(5), 15–23.

Memish, K., Martin, A., Bartlett, L., Dawkins, S., & Sanderson, K. (2017). Workplace mental health: An international review of guidelines. *Preventive Medicine, 101*, 213–222. https://doi.org/10.1016/j.ypmed.2017.03.017

Miller, L. (2007). Police families: Stresses, syndromes, and solutions. *The American Journal of Family Therapy, 35*(1), 21–40. https://doi.org/10.1080/01926180600698541

Mojtabai, R., Olfson, M., Sampson, N. A., Jin, R., Druss, B., Wang, P. S., Wells, K. B., Pincus, H. A., & Kessler, R. C. (2011). Barriers to mental health treatment: Results from the National Comorbidity Survey Replication. *Psychological Medicine, 41*(8), 1751–1761. https://doi.org/10.1017/S0033291710002291

Nash, W. P., & Litz, B. T. (2013). Moral injury: A mechanism for war-related psychological trauma in military family members. *Clinical Child & Family Psychology Review, 16*(4), 365–375. https://doi.org/10.1007/s10567-013-0146-y

Nazarov, A., Jetly, R., McNeely, H., Kiang, M., Lanius, R., & McKinnon, M. C. (2015). Role of morality in the experience of guilt and shame within the armed forces. *Acta Psychiatrica Scandinavica, 132*(1), 4–19. https://doi.org/10.1111/acps.12406

Neff, K. D. (2003). Development and validation of a scale to measure self-compassion. *Self and Identity, 2*, 223–250. https://doi.org/10.1080/15298860309027

Neff, K. D. (2012). The science of self-compassion. In C. Germer & R. Siegel (Eds.), *Compassion and wisdom in psychotherapy* (pp. 79–92). Guilford Press.

Olson, A., & Wasilewski, M. (2016). Suffering in silence: Mental health and stigma in policing. *Police One*. https://www.policeone.com/police-products/human-resources/articles/218917006-Suffering-in-silence-Mental-health-and-stigma-in-policing/

Papazoglou, K. (2017). The examination of different pathways leading towards police traumatization: Exploring the role of moral injury and personality in police compassion fatigue. *Dissertation Abstracts International: Section B: The Sciences and Engineering, 79*(3-B).

Papazoglou, K., Koskelainen, M., McQuerrey Tuttle, B., & Pitel, M. (2017). Examining the role of police compassion fatigue and negative personality traits in impeding the promotion of police compassion satisfaction: A brief report. *Journal of Law Enforcement, 6*(3), 1–14.

Park, M., Chang, E. R., & You, S. (2015). Protective role of coping flexibility in PTSD and depressive symptoms following trauma. *Personality and Individual Differences, 82*, 102–106. https://doi.org/10.1016/j.paid.2015.03.007

Sayed, S., Iacoviello, B. M., & Charney, D. S. (2015). Risk factors for the development of psychopathology following trauma. *Current Psychiatry Reports, 17*(8), 612. https://doi.org/10.1007/s11920-015-0612-y

Shann, C., Martin, A., Chester, A., & Ruddock, S. (2019). Effectiveness and application of an online leadership intervention to promote mental health and reduce depression-related stigma in organizations. *Journal of Occupational Health Psychology, 24*(1), 20–35. https://doi.org/10.1037/ocp0000110

Shay, J. (2014). Moral injury. *Psychoanalytic Psychology, 31*(2), 182–191. https://doi.org/10.1037/a0036090

Simon, C. E., Pryce, J. G., Roff, L. L., & Klemmack, D. (2006). Secondary traumatic stress and oncology social work: Protecting compassion from fatigue and compromising the worker's worldview. *Journal of Psychosocial Oncology, 23*(4), 1–14. https://doi.org/10.1300/j077v23n04_01

Slate, R. N., Johnson, W. W., & Colbert, S. S. (2007). Police stress: A structural model. *Journal of Police and Criminal Psychology, 22*(2), 102–112. https://doi.org/10.1007/s11896-007-9012-5

Sprang, G., Clark, J. J., & Whitt-Woosley, A. (2007). Compassion fatigue, compassion satisfaction, and burnout: Factors impacting a professional's quality of life. *Journal of Loss and Trauma, 12*(3), 259–280. https://doi.org/10.1080/15325020701238093

Sprang, G., Ford, J., Kerig, P., & Bride, B. (2019). Defining secondary traumatic stress and developing targeted assessments and interventions: Lessons learned from research and leading experts. *Traumatology, 25*(2), 72–81. https://doi.org/10.1037/trm0000180

Stamm, B. H. (2002). Measuring compassion satisfaction as well as fatigue: Developmental history of the compassion satisfaction and fatigue test. In C. Figley (Ed.), *Treating compassion fatigue* (pp. 107–119). Routledge.

Stamm, B. (2010). *The concise ProQOL manual: The concise manual for the professional quality of life scale* (2nd ed.).

Standing Senate Committee on National Security and Defence. (2015). *2015 Interim report on the operational stress injuries of Canada's veterans*. https://sencanada.ca/content/sen/Committee/412/secd/rep/rep17jun15-e.pdf

Teasdale, J. D., Moore, R. G., Hayhurst, H., Pope, M., Williams, S., & Segal, Z. V. (2002). Metacognitive awareness and prevention of relapse in depression: Empirical evidence. *Journal of Consulting and Clinical Psychology, 70*(2), 275–287. https://doi.org/10.1037/0022-006X.70.2.2775

Violanti, J. M., Castellano, C., O'Rourke, J., & Paton, D. (2006). Proximity to the 9/11 terrorist attack and suicide ideation in police officers. *Traumatology, 12*(3), 248–254. https://doi.org/10.1177/1534765606296533

Violanti, J. M., Mnatsakanova, A., Burchfiel, C. M., Hartley, T. A., & Andrew, M. E. (2012). Police suicide in small departments: A comparative analysis. *International Journal of Emergency Mental Health, 14*(3), 157–162.

Violanti, J. M., Owens, S. L., McCanlies, E., Fekedulegn, D., & Andrew, M. E. (2018). Law enforcement suicide: A review. *Policing: An International Journal, 42*(2), 141–164. https://doi.org/10.1108/PIJPSM-05-2017-0061

Violanti, J. M., & Samuels, S. (2007). Trauma and police suicide ideation. In J. M. Violanti & S. Samuels (Eds.), *Under the blue shadow: Clinical and behavioral perspectives on police suicide* (pp. 89–118). Charles C Thomas Pub Ltd.

Wastell, C. A. (2002). Exposure to trauma: The long-term effects of suppressing emotional reactions. *The Journal of Nervous and Mental Disease, 190*(12), 839–845. https://doi.org/10.1097/01.NMD.0000042454.90472.4F

Waters, J. A., & Ussery, W. (2007). Police stress: History, contributing factors, symptoms, and interventions. *Policing: An International Journal of Police Strategies & Management, 30*(2), 169–188. https://doi.org/10.1108/13639510710753199

Weiss, D. S., Brunet, A., Best, S. R., Metzler, T. J., Liberman, A., Pole, N., Fagan, J. A., & Marmar, C. R. (2010). Frequency and severity approaches to indexing exposure to trauma: The Critical Incident History Questionnaire for police officers. *Journal of Traumatic Stress, 23*(6), 734–743. https://doi.org/10.1002/jts.20576

Workman-Stark, A. L. (2017). Understanding police culture. In A. L. Workman-Stark (Ed.), *Inclusive policing from the inside out* (pp. 19–35). Springer.

World Health Organization. (2001). *World health report 2001. Mental health: New understanding, new hope*. World Health Organization.

World Health Organization. (2008). *The global burden of disease: 2004 update*. World Health Organization.

Wright, K., & Gudjonsson, G. H. (2007). The development of a scale for measuring offence-related feelings of shame and guilt. *Journal of Forensic Psychiatry & Psychology, 18*(3), 307–316. https://doi.org/10.1080/14789940701292810

Chapter 15
Law Enforcement and Public Health: A Framework for Analysis of LEPH in Lower- and Middle-Income Countries (LMICs)

Melissa Jardine and Auke van Dijk

Introduction

Approaches for protecting public safety and enhancing community wellbeing at the intersection of law enforcement and public health (LEPH) are increasingly being examined with a view to developing a theoretical framework for analysing their multiple intersections (van Dijk et al., 2019). Yet, explorations of LEPH issues are concentrated in the Global North (Punch & James, 2017). This is despite more than half of the world's population being located in the Global South and in much more diverse contexts, including lower- and middle-income countries (LMICs). In this chapter, we begin by outlining examples of variations in the way some health and social issues manifest or are problematised under different conditions—as they relate to policing. Following this, we identify a number of broad variables which shape the nature of a problem or concern, possible solutions or strategies for mitigating harm. We outline a framework that can account for diversity in the analysis and development of LEPH initiatives across both Global North and South. We argue that these variables interact in myriad ways that are not necessarily unidirectional or linear, and subsequently have important implications for understanding the role of police and health agencies in the protection of public health and safety across all forms of political institutions and resources (or lack of)—both tangible and intangible. While the focus here is on examples in the Global South, the framework has global utility.

M. Jardine (✉)
Centre for Law Enforcement and Public Health, Sydney, NSW, Australia
e-mail: melissa.jardine@gmail.com

A. van Dijk
Agora Police & Security, Dutch Police Service, Amsterdam, the Netherlands

Defining LMICs and the Global South

This chapter refers to lower- and middle-income countries (LMICs), as well as the Global South. While there is significant overlap, these descriptors are not neatly interchangeable or clearly delineated.

The World Bank refers to LMICs, as a way to group countries or regions for economic assessment, and classified mainly by geographic region, by income group and by operational lending categories (World Bank, 2020). Countries (or economies) are measured using gross national income (GNI) per capita, in US dollars and grouped according to: low, lower-middle, upper-middle and high income. The data is useful for guiding lending practices to countries that have limited financial ability to borrow, as well as determining the allocation of financial support, such as foreign aid.

In defining the 'Global South', we do not simply refer to the geography of the southern hemisphere, but rather a sociological perspective of power dynamics. Connell (2007) explicates these dynamics as they relate to the production of knowledge in the social sciences using Southern theory, pointing out that the result of Western empires, colonisation and exploitation of much of the Global South has contributed to privileging knowledge (and practice) from the Global North. Similarly, these dynamics have shaped dominant perceptions of criminal justice and policing practices (Carrington et al., 2016).

While defining LMICs and the Global South lend themselves to a macro conceptualisation, the intersection of low per capita income and a lack of access to power (e.g. political, cultural, social or symbolic) also exist at a localised level and on micro scales within larger geographic areas. For example, there may be sub-cultures within police agencies with varying levels of corruption and varying levels of skills, infrastructure or commitment to respond to community concerns. Similarly, the extent that civil society can hold police to account can also influence community safety outcomes.

The Sustainable Development Agenda 2030 and LEPH

The United Nations Sustainable Development Agenda (UN General Assembly, 2015) was adopted by all Member States in 2015 to reduce poverty and other deprivations and advance strategies for development. Two of the 17 Sustainable Development Goals (SDGs) within the Agenda (UN General Assembly, 2015) that are directly relevant to health and policing are:

SDG Goal 3 on 'Good health and wellbeing' includes targets relating to reducing maternal mortality (3.1), achieving universal health coverage (3.7) and supporting research and development of vaccines and medicines (3b), as examples.

A number of targets have direct or indirect implications for policing and law enforcement. Target 3.3 includes inter alia ending the AIDS epidemic and water-borne and other communicable diseases. Policing practices have a direct influence on whether people who inject drugs access health services which contribute to preventing human immunodeficiency virus (HIV). Additionally, target 3.6 aims to reduce deaths and injuries from road traffic collisions, an area where policing has a significant role.

SDG Goal 16 on 'Peace, justice and strong institutions' includes targets relating to reducing violence, abuse, exploitation and trafficking (especially of children), which have implications for good health and wellbeing. Other targets include combating transnational crimes, promoting the rule of law, enhancing access to justice and inclusivity and participation in institutional decision-making.[1]

The Sustainable Development Agenda is a framework in which examples of LEPH collaborations are striking. While SDG 16 focuses on (some) institutions, and participation in those institutions, the police contribute to the achievement of other SDGs through not only enforcing laws, but also through problem-solving, mediation, making referrals to other services and search and rescue operations. As examples, police have a role in: eliminating, dumping and minimising release of hazardous chemicals and materials (SDG 6: Clean water and sanitation); reducing deaths and mitigating negative impacts of disasters, and protecting the poor and vulnerable (SDG 11: Sustainable cities and communities); and eliminating all forms of violence and harmful practices against women and girls, such as trafficking, forced marriage and female genital mutilation, among others (SDG 5: Gender equality).

Fundamentally, the Sustainable Development Agenda aims to improve global governance to address inequality. In advanced economies, government structures, urbanisation and infrastructure development, access to education and access to technologies mean that particular approaches to preventing or responding to LEPH issues/vulnerability can draw on these resources. In contrast, LMICs may have limited access to these resources or they may be constituted differently compared to high-income countries. However, a lack of some resource types may mean reliance on or inclusion of different stakeholders than police or formal institutions or interventions, with more varied perspectives and contributions to solving complex social problems. Subsequently, the relationships between some institutions or actors and others can vary considerably.

What Is LEPH in LMICs and the Global South?

Crucially, police globally are always in transition. Therefore, processes of considering and exploring new practices is normal as a means to find new ways of working in a changing structural environment. In LMICs, due to lack of economic resources, police are more likely to find themselves at the frontline of poverty and deprivation.

Moreover, what is a policing concern in one country or context, may not be a concern in another. For example, homosexuality is criminalised in 72 countries mostly in Africa (Human Dignity Trust, 2020). The death penalty is a possible

---

[1] For more analysis and critique on the 'Rule of Law' as part of the SDGs, see Watson et al. (2021).

punishment in 11 countries.[2] Although the enforcement of legislation prohibiting same-sex sex is uneven, there are implications for the ways agencies or individuals undertake policing of these crimes. The criminalisation of homosexuality is also the result of North-to-South power dynamics, given legislation prohibiting homosexuality was enacted on the African continent under colonisation from countries or empires from the North. Notably, some of the colonising countries or empires have now removed prohibition of homosexuality from their statutes and expunged historical homosexual convictions. Importantly, LEPH approaches are viable across all contexts and is a call to action to identify the nature of a solution's configuration.

What constitutes a LEPH issue in a LMIC may share similarities with high-income countries, yet their instigation and response may vary. As examples relating to individual behaviours, police diverting people with drug use issues to treatment may not be possible because there is no treatment available. Similarly, a person with ill mental health or a psychiatric disorder who comes to the attention of police, cannot be referred to experts who do not exist. Lessons from high-income countries may be of no use in this context, but this does not reduce the need.

On a different scale of LEPH issues, weak enforcement, if any, of anti-pollution protections may mean entire communities have no access to safe, clean drinking water or police may be responsible for ensuring local dog populations are given rabies vaccinations. Therefore, problems that can be addressed through LEPH solutions may leverage resources in different ways.

Below are three case studies which draw attention to ways police contribute to public health in LMICs.

Case Study 1: HIV Prevention in Africa

This case study relates to the role of police in HIV prevention in two countries, Kenya and Ghana. Both examples draw attention to small- and large-scale efforts of police to improve public health outcomes in environments where criminalisation of homosexuality and sex work remain significant barriers.

Kenya has the joint third-largest epidemic in the world, alongside Mozambique and Uganda (AVERT, 2020). HIV prevalence among men who have sex with men (MSM) is almost three times that among the general population. Sex between men is illegal in Kenya and highly stigmatised among the community resulting in many men feeling reluctant to seek medical treatment for fear that they may be bribed, arrested and/or prosecuted (with a maximum penalty of up to 14 years' imprisonment). A Kenyan government official described homosexuality as being 'as serious as terrorism'.

In 2014, a Police Inspector was invited by the Kenya National AIDS Control Programme to take part in the 5-day workshop in Nyanza province

(continued)

---

[2] Afghanistan, Brunei, Iran, Mauritania, Northern Nigeria, Pakistan, Qatar, Saudi Arabia, Somalia, United Arab Emirates and Yemen.

to highlight the importance of the health sector working with police to address issues among the MSM community (LEAHN, 2014). Specifically, the Inspector addressed the practice where some clinical officers would call on police to arrest MSM who were seeking health treatment. He explained that even though homosexuality was criminalised in Kenya, MSM were reluctant to seek or access health services due to fear of being reported to police. The clinical officers were encouraged to treat the health concerns of the MSM community with sensitivity and discretion so as not to deter them from pursuing health treatment. The Inspector said some doctors and clinical officers were reporting the activities of MSM to police when it was not necessary and that it made addressing the HIV epidemic in the country more challenging. He explained the role of the Law Enforcement and HIV Network to the participants and explained that whilst a collaborative approach between police and health was necessary, the role of police was not one of strict law enforcement but that police had a role in protecting the public health which meant balancing the overall needs of the community.

In **Ghana** in 2010, the United Nations Population Fund (UNFPA) partnered with the Ghana Police Service to conduct research investigating human rights concerns and public health implications of police treatment and abuse of female sex workers (see OSF, 2014). Some male officers were confiscating condoms and bribing women to exchange sex to not pursue an arrest. The researchers from UNFPA and the Ghana Police Service reported the findings to the Police inspector general. As a result, a series of rights-based changes were made in relation to the policing of sex workers. This included training to sensitise police to their human rights obligations, awareness of gender-responsive harm reduction interventions and the inclusion of peer workers from the sex work community to speak about the impacts of police behaviours.

Notably, 180 police focal points were encouraged to work with sex workers to create and implement joint action plans to improve the environments where sex workers were working. Police also worked towards stopping the use of raids as a tactic against sex workers and, if sex workers were arrested for other crimes, to ensure they had access to legal representation through civil society organisations. Not only did police stop confiscating condoms from sex workers, but a specific pouch was also designed to attach to police officers' equipment belts so they could carry and distribute free condoms to sex workers when on duty.

As a nation known for taking an innovative approach to the HIV epidemic, new HIV infections have decreased in Ghana by 33% since 2010 (UNAIDS, 2020).

Case Study 2: COVID-19 in Asia
Despite COVID-19 originating in China, regional neighbours—including LMICs—have fared better than some upper-income countries further afield. This has laid bare that a country's economic resources do not necessarily predict a more effective response to the pandemic. Across Asia, police involvement in responses to the pandemic have drawn on the strengths and resources of their particular countries. For example, Singapore's economy is significantly larger and more advanced than Vietnam's, yet Vietnam is currently a world leader in limiting the spread of COVID-19 despite sharing a border with China, particularly through the deployment of the police and security sector.

The two countries engaged police early in the response, but in different ways. In Singapore, police were called in to assist with hi-tech contact tracing efforts with the Ministry of Health and a lockdown was not introduced until April. Vietnam's response focused on low-tech alternatives and deployed police to go house-to-house to share information about the virus with residents, assess transmission risks at the community level, especially in relation to recently returned travellers from abroad, and enforce strict lockdown measures of entire villages, in some cases (Luong et al., 2020).

Even though COVID-19 case numbers among the general public in Singapore remained low, there was an explosion of cases among migrant workers' dormitories. The Ministry of Manpower, responsible for monitoring the conditions of the dorms, may have had limited capacity to assess public health risks resulting in a blind spot for authorities and major outbreak (Woo, 2020). Consequently, technologies and efficiencies may be of little consequence if they do not enable feedback loops with people outside these structures.

Case Study 3: The Role of Police in Improving Abortion Access
In some contexts, women and girls do not have access to legal, safe abortions which places them at risk of being arrested and incarcerated if they seek an abortion outside restrictive legal parameters.

A significant number of unsafe abortions are carried out in LMICs. Unsafe abortions contribute to maternal deaths or disability. Barriers to accessing safe abortion include (WHO, 2020):

- Restrictive laws
- Poor availability of services
- High cost
- Stigma
- Conscientious objection of healthcare providers

(continued)

- Unnecessary requirements, such as mandatory waiting periods, mandatory counselling, provision of misleading information, third-party authorisation, and medically unnecessary tests that delay care

While changes to legislation to ensure women and girls have access to legal, safe abortion are needed, some contexts have significant challenges to reach this point.

Ipas, a non-profit organisation, works to increase women's ability to exercise their sexual and reproductive rights, especially the right to safe abortion. Ipas identified policing as a key determinant of whether women can access safe abortion, especially in countries where abortion is criminalised. In these contexts, police can use the law to scare, shame or imprison women seeking abortion or those who help her end her pregnancy. Police may be the only law officials involved in a particular case, as incidences involving abortion and the police often do not reach lawyers or courts. In some cases, this is due to police bribery of vulnerable women. As authority figures, police can also perpetuate misconceptions about the law and may not understand the legal differences between post-abortion and safe abortion services.

Ipas has conducted trainings for police in some countries in Africa about the importance of safe access to abortion, and law enforcement authorities are key partners in Ipas's work to increase access to safe abortion care and promote women's human rights because police can (Skuster et al., 2016, p. 7):

- Refer women to safe providers or trained health professionals who can provide care for complications of unsafe abortion.
- Improve their understanding of women's perspectives and response to reported cases of abortion, even where it is legally restricted.
- Educate communities about the law and the dangers of abortion from unsafe providers.
- Speak to the danger of criminalising abortion and the need for legal or policy reform as authorities on law, order and safety.

The police training aims to minimise potential harm within the current criminalised environment while working towards law reform as an overall goal.

These case studies show that, in LMICs, police have an important role in public health, indeed sometimes especially so where circumstances are less than optimal such that police can have a role in mediating positive outcomes particularly in circumstances where certain behaviours are and are likely to remain criminalised, or where some reproductive rights are denied. In contrast to leveraging the police role as mediators, police in Vietnam were formal partners with the Ministry of

Health and included both strict and coercive powers to enforce lockdown rules, alongside direct and systematic involvement in the public health education campaign to prevent transmission of COVID-19.

Dimensions Shaping the LEPH Intersection

As indicated in our introduction, the ambition of this chapter is to develop a framework which practitioners can use to identify, assess and explore LEPH solutions to problems of public health and safety in LMICs, or analyse why a particular approach was effective (or not) in a particular situation. We therefore provide a preliminary framework for analysis in which the following questions are addressed:

1. What are the dimensions shaping problems with a LEPH intersection?
2. What are some examples of this in action?
3. What are the steps to applying the LEPH framework?

State responses to public health and safety issues are mediated by interpretations of the problem and its causes, as well as resources available to address them. In this context, resources may include access to knowledge or expertise, the ability to mobilise institutions or communities and may be formal or informal. These processes are inherently political because they are concerned with power dynamics in society that relate to access to wealth and wellbeing. There are similarities between the concept of a risk or enabling environment and political economy, in that they both identify constraints or opportunities to improve health or social conditions for a population or community (Rhodes et al., 2012).

Importantly, if resources that are tangible (e.g. health and social services or community groups) or intangible (e.g. local customs or influences) are located outside of the criminal justice system, these should be harnessed, built upon and elevated where they can be more effective. Community consultation and collaboration are central to the development of LEPH solutions, particularly at the micro and local levels.

In examining a LEPH problem, there are a myriad of dimensions to consider. For our purposes, we draw on van Dijk and Hoogewoning (2016) to identify seven dimensions which frame the analysis from a policing perspective (Fig. 15.1):

Analysis of each of the dimension may include, but is not limited to:

- Policing paradigm

    - The role of police in society, legacies of colonialism, the relationship between police and community, and community expectations of police, relationship to military, distribution of funding, formal and informal policing institutions and practices.

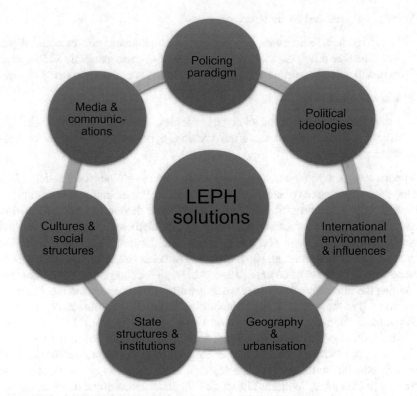

Fig. 15.1   LEPH analysis framework for policing

- Political ideologies
  - Nature of political structures and power dynamics, e.g. form of democratic governance, one-party state, monarchy, level of centralisation/decentralisation, political stability.
- International environment and influences
  - Nature of engagement with regional and global actors, e.g. on trade and security matters, foreign aid and development.
- Geography and urbanisation
  - Geo-strategic position, natural resources, built environment, population density, infrastructure.
- State structures and institutions (e.g. laws, policies, ministries and agencies for law enforcement, policing and health)
  - Availability of resources such as people, knowledge and technology, transparency and accountability, relationships between criminal justice system and other institutions, including private institutions, formal and informal economies.

- Societal cultures and social structures

  - Local cultures, ethnicities, and structures which shape norms, cultural practices, gender relations, intersectional identities, socioeconomic status, access to health and education, strength of civil society, social determinants of health.

- Media and communications.

  - Press freedom, communication technologies, freedom of speech, ability to access, understand and share information, cyber-enabled policing or health service delivery.

Importantly, these dimensions are relevant in both the global North and South and can have varying degrees of stability and complexity. For example, assumptions that the world order is heading towards an inevitably more democratic place following a linear trajectory are now clearly challenged. The elements which make up each dimension can be assessed according to whether they constrain and/or facilitate improving LEPH outcomes, and how these assessments can inform the development of an appropriate intervention or response. Although the state is used as a framework in defining the dimensions, this does not imply that uniform outcomes are implied. In many ways it is the opposite and all about the differences in outcomes, especially with regard to 'vulnerable populations' and how they are 'defined' by, for example, political ideologies and state structures. Emblematic is the position of so-called Indigenous populations, globally. For example, Australia is geographically in the Global South, but with many of the features and privileges of the Global North according to Connell's Southern Theory (2007). Indigenous populations continue to survive colonisation yet gain uneven benefit from the health and education systems and approaches to democratic participation as does the settler population. Notably, Indigenous people experience significantly higher levels of incarceration, as well as deaths in the custody of prison or police officers, than non-Indigenous people. Additionally, responses to people with ill mental health are often framed by states and cultures and dealt with (or ignored) by institutions and approaches. In sum, using the state to develop a framework also necessitates consideration of intersectional identities and micro-level contexts.

Table 15.1 outlines further detail with respect to the dimensions in relation to the example used in Case Study 2 regarding COVID-19 in Vietnam. This exercise can also be done comparatively to elucidate similarities and differences between different countries or regions. These details can then be further analysed according to specific vulnerabilities as well as any risks and constraints, and benefits and opportunities regarding a LEPH issue within the specific context.

This case study highlights how the dimensions can inform an understanding of the nature of Vietnam's response to COVID-19. In practice, a more thorough analysis of each dimension is necessary. Nonetheless, the following is a brief example analysis of the vulnerabilities, risks, constraints, benefits or opportunities on a macro scale, although analyses can also target the micro, local or individual levels:

Table 15.1 COVID-19 in Vietnam

LEPH analysis: COVID-19 in Vietnam	
Policing paradigm	Modern policing in Vietnam emerged through its fight against French and American colonisation in 1945; therefore, national and territorial security forms a core part of the police role which continues today, particularly in relation to the East Sea (South China Sea)
	The historical Confucian influence on wider national culture places high importance on education, including in policing. Commissioned officers and non-commissioned officers are required to undertake 4-year and 2-year training programmes (considerably longer than police in some jurisdictions)
	Police training emphasises their role in educating the community about laws, policies and morality
	Deploying police to educate the community about COVID-19 is consistent with policing practices prior to the pandemic
Political ideologies	Vietnam is a one-party state ruled by the Vietnamese Communist Party. Governance can function in a relatively decentralised manner with significant autonomy at the provincial level; however, there are increasing efforts by the party to increase centralisation
	As a one-party state, the government needs to establish legitimacy through its performance, for example, through a strong economy and successful management of national security issues
International environment & influences	In the 1980s, Vietnam was one of the poorest countries in the world. It now has a growing economy, increasing international trade, and is now regarded as a middle-income country, though at the lower end
	A large Vietnamese diaspora exists due to the outflux of refugees following the American war. Moreover, some citizens travel abroad (legally and illegally) to seek improved economic circumstances
Geography & urbanisation	Vietnam has both land and maritime borders. It shares a land border to its north with China, other porous land borders to the west with Lao PDR and Cambodia. Its proximity to Wuhan where the COVID-19 outbreak originated was a significant risk meaning rapid border closures were essential
	Vietnam's population is spread across 63 provinces. Some include remote areas with ethnic minority populations that are difficult to reach as well as for delivery of public services
State structures, institutions & practices	Vietnam has one of the largest security sectors in the world with estimates of a ratio that one in six people are affiliated with the public security sector. Subsequently, capability for physical surveillance and mobilisation is extensive
	Even though Vietnam has undergone significant health systems strengthening over recent decades, its capacity has limitations, especially for the poor who cannot afford to pay for private care
	Police are responsible for administering the *ho khau* (household registration) which holds detailed information about every individual in Vietnam and can determine access to education and social security
	The government established multi-sector pandemic response plans

(continued)

Table 15.1 (continued)

LEPH analysis: COVID-19 in Vietnam	
	in the aftermath of the 2003 severe acute respiratory syndrome (SARS) epidemic
Societal cultures & social structures	In Vietnam, it is common for multiple generations of a family to live together
	Government policies supporting gender equality means women generally have good access to education and employment, though are under-represented in government decision-making roles
	Mass organisations, such as the ho chi minh youth union and Women's union, provide established mechanisms for community mobilisation. Nonetheless, these unions function under the Communist Party structure and non-government affiliated civil society activities are limited
	There is population-level knowledge and experience of the 2003 SARS epidemic and the public health response
Media & communications	Vietnam's media institutions are state-owned and press freedom is restricted. The government regularly prosecutes people for violating legislation regarding dissenting views against the state or spreading false information
	Approximately 70% of the population are internet users

Vulnerabilities

Vietnam's proximity to China is a clear vulnerability, given the potential for the spread of COVID-19 across the border. Its status as a middle-income country means it has limited economic resources to invest or deploy. Internet usage among the population is moderate, thus, access to timely health information may be limited. Multi-generational family living conditions may lead to rapid spread to elderly populations if the virus gains a hold in the community. And, returning diaspora may bring COVID-19 into the country.

Risks and Constraints

Some elements which may be considered as risks or constraints include access to information about government activities due to restrictions on transparency. Civil society involvement may be limited and drawing attention to events or information perceived as against the interest of the one-party state can be punishable by imprisonment. This means potential feedback loops to improve procedures and processes may be overlooked or information may be excluded from the public domain. A large security sector with limited accountability mechanisms may create an environment of human rights abuses and over-policing, resulting in decreased trust and legitimacy. While the aforementioned elements may be considered risks or constraints on one hand, they may be mitigated, transformed or leveraged in different ways so they are neutralised or become benefits or opportunities.

Benefits and Opportunities

Vietnam's experience of the SARS epidemic in 2003 resulted in government investment for increased pandemic preparedness. In these pandemic plans, the government assigned the large security sector as partners with health with specific tasks and responsibilities. Activities including distributing personal protective equipment to the community and sharing information about how to reduce risk of COVID-19 transmission, such as social distancing and hand hygiene, contributed to building trust between the police and community. The police role in educating the community is consistent with police cultural identity and practice prior to the pandemic (Jardine, 2020). Moreover, the large security sector enabled the enforcement of strict border security measures, including using existing police barracks as quarantine centres. While sharing false information—or information deemed false by the state—can be prosecuted in Vietnam, it may contribute to ensuring restricting distribution of conspiracy theories or fake health information which is an advantage in terms of consistency and accuracy of health messages to the public. The existence of mass organisations provides mechanisms for information dissemination and mobilising the community to respond to official instructions with respect to COVID-safe behaviours.

Summary

Considering the selected vulnerabilities, risks and constraints detailed above, Vietnam may have been considered at high risk at the outset of COVID-19, especially due to its proximity to China. Yet, at the time of writing, Vietnam had recorded—in total—1500 COVID-19 cases and 35 deaths among a population of 96 million. In comparison, the United Kingdom recorded 2.7 million COVID-19 cases and 75,000 deaths among a population of 66 million. And, while Vietnam presents a good example of a successful law enforcement and public health partnership, the aim is not to suggest other countries increase the size of their police agencies so they may be deployed in similar ways. Rather, the aim is to identify the elements which determine what a strategy or intervention should be in a particular context, how it can be achieved and its political feasibility. In Vietnam, both historical and current national security concerns have resulted in a large security sector with significant power to shape and control government responses to a wide range of issues. In this context, the security forces are a viable partner in public health. In contrast, South Korea had a less prominent role for police in the management of COVID-19, and civil society emerged as important interlocutors with government in demanding improvements to some inequities in the response, especially in regard to distribution of and access to face masks (Kim, 2020). Therefore, the particular power dynamics among different institutions and actors need consideration.

What Does This Framework Contribute to Solving Future LEPH Problems?

The LEPH analysis framework for policing enables a systematic approach to better understand the dynamics of the processes that enable or hinder change and helps identify key entry points that are technically sound and politically feasible. Broad questions in these analyses include:

- What is the context?
- How do things get done?
- Who is or who should be involved?

These questions can be considered for each dimension of the framework separately, though it is paramount to understand how they function in relation to each other. Crucially, focus should be given to who has power and how it is used, motivations, incentives, actions, practices and informal institutions as well as formal institutions and structures. This analysis also enables a greater understanding of which approaches currently exist in a particular place and why, what could be built and what could deteriorate if not for intervention.

As an example, consider Case Study 3 on the role of police in improving abortion access. Alongside stigma, a major part of the problem is the criminalisation of abortion. In the current environment, Ipas saw police as important intermediaries to reduce harm associated with criminalisation; and thus, was an entry point for advocacy. Even though Ipas's intervention trains police to use discretion to facilitate improved access to abortion, their overall aim is to change or amend the legislation which prohibits it. Therefore, they need to build community and political support for legislative change. Moreover, any changes in attitudes towards supporting legislative change must be sustained, as it is possible for anti-abortion interest groups or prominent individuals to campaign in a way that contributes to a deterioration of gains made with respect to public sentiment towards improving access to legal abortion.

The LEPH analysis framework emphasises the importance of understanding context so that solutions can be foregrounded that are feasible and sustainable. However, this does not mean inspiration for problem-solving cannot be found elsewhere. Indeed, researching ways that others have addressed similar issues under very different conditions can inspire creativity and imagination and help to elucidate dynamics and processes that may otherwise be rendered invisible through familiarity or taken-for-granted cultural knowledge.

In addition to exploring the current evidence base, LEPH practitioners should consider which features or actors can be changed or influenced? What can be done differently and how? This may include:

- Training, education and awareness raising
- Developing standard operating procedures, establishing Memorandum's of Understanding

- Building networks, advocacy coalitions and communities of practice
- Undertaking research using new lenses of inquiry
- Conducting stakeholder analyses
- Leveraging under-used or under-recognised skillsets such as flexibility and facilitation and coaching skills
- Questioning and revising what success looks like and how it is measured
- and more

A critique of some LEPH interventions may be that they focus too much on pragmatic, short- to medium-term impacts, instead of focusing on large-scale reform. Yet, pathways to large-scale reform often include successfully demonstrating the efficacy of alternative approaches developed and implemented as a pilot, innovation or local-level concept. These smaller interventions contribute to testing hypotheses and theories of change, building an evidence base in specific contexts and exploring adaptations necessary for improvement. Small-scale or pilot interventions provide opportunities to reframe the nature of a problem or concern so that alternative solutions, responses and responders can be explored. On the latter point, responders may not necessarily be located within an institutional structure or sector, but from a coalition of problem-solvers within a community. Moreover, the benefits of initiating small- to medium-scale change is that they help refine advocacy strategies and craft key messages for different audiences who have the ability to constrain or promote change which take into account the context of systems in which policing functions.

Pragmatic approaches to change are also cognisant of the relational dynamic between the different dimensions identified above which means contexts and issues relevant to LEPH are not static and can change over time. For example, a change in one dimension (e.g. social norms about homosexuality) can initiate a change in another (e.g. changes in legislation and policing)—positively or negatively. Therefore, the impacts and consequences of any change or intervention should be measured over the short, medium or long term with iterative evaluation regarding changes in the environment as well as to ensure the objectives are being met and any unintended consequences can be assessed, addressed and mitigated. Even though police are an important stakeholder in community safety, searches for alternative approaches outside the criminal justice system contribute to building the capability of other sectors and civil society in developing solutions to complex social problems.

Returning to the United Nations Sustainable Development Goals on good health and wellbeing (SDG 3) and peace, justice and strong institutions (SDG 16), LEPH approaches can be an alternative model to the sectoral model, especially because success in one field is often dependent on success in another. As mentioned earlier, SDG 3 includes preventing HIV and reducing road traffic injuries and fatalities, areas where policing has direct impacts. Clearly, policing cannot be isolated from other institutions and their goals and vice versa and better understanding their intersections can contribute to advancing the SDGs in a fundamentally new way.

Conclusion

We have outlined a framework that can account for diversity in the analysis and development of LEPH initiatives across both Global North and Global South. Perspectives on LEPH from the Global South are important: they demonstrate there are often wider alternatives to understanding who the police are and what they should do than is described in dominant, typically Northern, literature. In the past, transfer of policies and approaches typically travelled from Global North to Global South—the result of imperialism, unequal power dynamics and the exploitation of people and environmental resources.

Policing approaches in the Global South are increasingly being documented in policing scholarship. Some approaches may be considered 'emerging' if they are recent responses to particular and shifting dynamics, while others may have existed for a long time, but they can be regarded as such because theory and practice from the Global South is often regarded as the being on the periphery, whereas the Global North is the norm or default. With regard to developing new practices in LEPH in a variety of contexts, there is no rationale to give prevalence to Northern solutions.

References

AVERT. (2020). *HIV and AIDS in Kenya*. www.avert.org/professionals/hiv-around-world/sub-saharan-africa/kenya

Carrington, K., Hogg, R., & Sozzo, M. (2016). Southern criminology. *British Journal of Criminology, 56*, 1–20.

Connell, R. (2007). *Southern theory: The global dynamics of knowledge in social science*. Allen & Unwin.

Human Dignity Trust. (2020). www.humandignitytrust.org/lgbt-the-law/map-of-criminalisation/

Jardine, M. (2020). A southern policing perspective and appreciative inquiry: An ethnography of policing in Vietnam. *Policing and Society, 30*(2), 186–205. https://doi.org/10.1080/10439463. 2019.1680673

Kim, J.-H. (2020). Mask dynamics between the Korean government and civil society in the COVID-19 era. International Institute for Asian Studies. *The Newsletter 87 Autumn 2020*. www.iias.asia/the-newsletter/article/mask-dynamics-between-korean-government-and-civil-society-covid-19-era

LEAHN. (2014). *Health seeking behaviour a risky business in Kenya for men: LEAHN CFP Inspector Edung*. www.leahn.org/archives/3199

Luong, H. T., Jardine, M., & Thomson, N. (2020). Mobilizing the police from the top down as public health partners in combatting COVID-19: A perspective from Vietnam. *Journal of Community Safety and Well-Being, 5*(2), 57–59.

OSF. (2014). To protect and serve: How police, sex workers, and people who use drugs are joining forces to improve health and human rights. Open Society Foundations.

Punch, M., & James, S. (2017). Researching law enforcement and public health. *Policing and Society, 27*(3), 251–260. https://doi.org/10.1080/10439463.2016.1205066

Rhodes, T., Wagner, K., Strathdee, S. A., Shannon, K., Davidson, P., & Bougois, P. (2012). Structural violence and structural vulnerability within the risk environment: Theoretical and methodological perspectives for a social epidemiology of HIV risk among injection drug users and sex workers. In P. O'Campo & J. R. Dunn (Eds.), *Rethinking social epidemiology: Towards a science of change*. Springer. https://doi.org/10.1007/978-94-007-2138-8_10

Skuster, P., DiTucci, T., Riley, D., & Randall-David, B. (2016). *A practical guide for partnering with police to improve abortion access*. Ipas.

UN General Assembly. (2015*). Transforming our world: The 2030 agenda for sustainable development, 21 October 2015, A/RES/70/1*. https://sdgs.un.org/2030agenda

UNAIDS. (2020). *UNAIDS data 2020*.

van Dijk, A. & Hoogewoning, F. (2016) *Policing, public health and vulnerable populations—A framework and issues from a police perspective*. Paper written for the International Consultation on Policing, Public Health and Vulnerable Populations (Amsterdam, 1 October 2016).

van Dijk, A. J., et al. (2019). Law enforcement and public health: Recognition and enhancement of joined-up solutions. *The Lancet, 393*(10168), 287–294.

Watson, D., Yap, A., Pino, N., & Blaustein, J. (2021). Problematising the rule of law agenda in the SDG context. In J. Blaustein, K. Fitz-Gibbon, N. Pino, & R. White (Eds.), *The Emerald handbook of crime, development and sustainable development*. Emerald Publishing Limited.

WHO. (2020). *Preventing unsafe abortion*. World Health Organization. www.who.int/news-room/fact-sheets/detail/preventing-unsafe-abortion

Woo, J. J. (2020). Policy capacity and Singapore's response to the COVID-19 pandemic. *Policy and Society, 39*(3), 345–362. https://doi.org/10.1080/14494035.2020.1783789

World Bank. (2020). *How does the World Bank classify countries?* The World Bank Group. https://datahelpdesk.worldbank.org/knowledgebase/articles/378834-how-does-the-world-bank-classify-countries

Chapter 16
Policing Pandemics: Developing Effective Policing Responses During Health Emergencies

Karl A. Roberts

Introduction

This chapter explores the role of police[1] during disease pandemics. Its purpose is to explore what police can contribute to public health outcomes, the challenges that they face and ways to mitigate them. An important aim of this chapter is to identify effective strategies for policing future pandemics.

At the time of writing, the world is in the grip of a major disease pandemic caused by a novel coronavirus referred to as 'Coronavirus,' or 'COVID-19',[2] and to which humans have little or no natural immunity. Like other pandemic-prone viruses, it is highly transmissible and is associated with a wide range of serious and sometimes fatal illnesses. Throughout the COVID-19 pandemic there has been a lot of attention paid to the role of the police. Much of this has been a critique about how they have enforced pandemic-related legislation and rather less attention has been paid to how police might learn from the COVID-19 experience and develop more effective pandemic policing strategies. COVID-19 provides us with many examples of the challenges faced by police, and whilst this chapter is not about policing during the COVID-19 pandemic per se, there are many lessons that can be learned, which will inform some of our discussion.

---

[1] For the purposes of this chapter 'police' is used to refer to agencies and other organisations who are generally understood to be responsible for ensuring compliance with laws designed by national governments. It is acknowledged that the use of police in this manner is contested and some prefer the term Law Enforcement to describe such agencies.

[2] The official name given to the virus that causes what has become known as COVID-19 is Severe Acute Respiratory Syndrome Coronavirus 2 (SARS CoV2). We will use the term COVID-19 as this is generally understood as a label to refer to the current pandemic.

K. A. Roberts (✉)
Western Sydney University, Sydney, NSW, Australia
e-mail: karl.roberts@westernsydney.edu.au

To help structure our discussion, we have identified five interrelated themes relevant to policing during pandemics. These are the policy and legislative context in which police operate during a pandemic, multiagency working and relationships between police and other stakeholders, police and community engagement during a pandemic, police organisational challenges during pandemics, and police wellbeing. In what follows, we will describe how each theme is relevant, some of the challenges for police and how the challenges may be mitigated. We will end the chapter with a consideration of planning strategies for future pandemics.

National Pandemic Plans, Policy, and the Legislative Context

In order to respond effectively to a health emergency such as a pandemic, prior planning is essential. Planning allows the specification of strategies to mitigate the effects of a health emergency. It is, however, important that plans clearly specify the resources that are required and the roles and responsibilities of various actors and agencies (Acheson, 1988; Steigenberger, 2016). Without adequate planning responses to emergencies are likely to be limited in their effectiveness (Steigenberger, 2016).

As part of their core duties, police are required to enforce the law ensuring compliance with relevant rules and regulations (Newburn, 2003). This means that in most jurisdictions during a pandemic, the police will have responsibility for ensuring compliance with all public health-related legislation. However, pandemic legislation is frequently developed without due consideration of the capability and capacity of the police to ensure compliance with it. Indeed, police have frequently been forgotten in the pandemic planning process and this has led to a lack of consideration of their needs and the challenges that they face. We will consider how this has arisen and possible ways this may be mitigated in the future.

National Pandemic Plans and the Police

Facing the threat of disease pandemics, the World Health Organization has led on the development of a set of international health regulations. The International Health Regulations (World Health Organization, 2008) aim to set minimum international standards for public health services and to aid nations and the international community in responding effectively to pandemic-prone diseases. The regulations first appeared in 1969 and have been variously updated with the most recent version appearing in 2005. The regulations place legally binding obligations upon nation states regarding minimum standards for the capacity and capability of their public health systems. Nations are required to contribute to worldwide disease surveillance processes and to notify the World Health Organization (WHO) of any new disease outbreaks. Importantly for our discussion, nation states are expected to develop individual pandemic plans setting out how they will respond to an outbreak of disease. In practice most pandemic plans focus upon the risk of pandemic influenza as this has to date been considered to be the most likely pandemic threat that the world faces (Levin et al., 2007) although these plans are theoretically applicable to any pandemic.

Pandemic plans have, quite properly, been strongly influenced by medical and public health considerations. They stipulate how hospitals will be used in the event of a pandemic, what medical contingencies are in place should hospitals be overwhelmed by cases of disease, the development and storage of stockpiles of vaccines (where one exists), personal protective equipment (PPE) and other medical supplies, and the various responsibilities of different actors relevant to the public health response. However, content analyses of national pandemic plans (Luna et al., 2007) have revealed that the police are rarely mentioned within them and even when they are the roles of police are described in vague generalities, such as suggesting that during a pandemic police will conduct their '*usual duties*' and '*any other duties*' as appropriate (Luna et al., 2007). This is perhaps surprising as in most policing jurisdictions, one of the central, or 'usual duties' of the police is the enforcement of legislation (Newburn, 2003). This means that the police are likely to be at the forefront of any public health response and it is they who would take responsibility for ensuring compliance with health rules and regulations. The activities of the police are therefore likely to be central to the success or otherwise of many pandemic-related responses.

It is unclear why the role of police during pandemics has been neglected. One reason may be that it reflects a lack of understanding among planners about what (or even if) police can contribute to public health outcomes, in general, and health emergencies, in particular, beyond simply enforcing the law. Certainly, a number of writers have commented upon a lack of recognition among many public health and other officials of the positive contributions police can and do make to public health (Van Dijk et al., 2019). Compounding this is the fact that police agencies generally have a wide remit, so it is often difficult to define explicitly what police can or even should do. Police are frequently seen as the public service of last resort with a remit to respond to all manner of situations (Bayley & Shearing, 1996; Lum & Nagin, 2017). Also, many police agencies have not recognised their own relevance to public health outcomes and have themselves not engaged well with public health stakeholders (van Dijk & Crofts, 2017). Despite the observation that many police activities have a direct impact upon a wide range of social and public health issues (see other chapters in this book; van Dijk et al., 2019).

As national pandemic plans greatly influence the way in which resources and responsibilities are allocated and managed during a pandemic, the lack of mention of the police in many plans means that their needs are likely to be forgotten. This can have a number of unintended consequences. Chief among these is that many governments, especially during the COVID-19 pandemic, have developed related legislation insensitive to the needs of police. In the next section we will discuss this in more detail and highlight the challenges that this has presented for the police.

Legislation, Police, and Pandemics

Throughout history, in response to pandemic disease, nations have developed a wide range of rules, regulations, and associated legislation designed to control infection (Huremović, 2019). This has included national and local lockdowns, quarantine, bans on social gatherings, closing of shops, public houses, and restaurants etc. However, as noted, it appears that, whilst expecting the police to enforce it, legislation has rarely been developed with any consideration as to the effect it might have upon the police. Frequently during the COVID-19 pandemic legislation has been enacted that has failed to consider how the police would be able to enforce it, what resources were required to enforce it or whether or not it could be enforced. For example, police agencies in the UK have reported receiving from government vague and unclear legislation, often with little or no notice prior to it coming into effect (Dood & Pidd, 2020; Merrick, 2020). The effects of this have been that police have often been unsure about the meaning and intentions of some legislation, what if any powers they have to enforce it, and they have frequently had little time to plan policing strategies in response.

Vague and unclear legislation has also resulted in confusion among police officers and members of the public, and has led to considerable variations in policing and enforcement practices. For example, in the UK vague COVID-19-related rules have led to inconsistencies in the administration of fines by police officers. Some officers have imposed fines on members of the public for breaches of regulations when for similar breaches other officers have not imposed fines (Dood & Pidd, 2020). More worryingly, in some jurisdictions where legislation has been unclear about the limits of police responses or where it has specifically mandated use of force, draconian and violent (including fatally violent) enforcement methods have been used (Faull, 2020). For example, in South Africa, Uganda, and Kenya many people have been injured and some killed by police using extreme force to ensure people did not leave their homes during various lockdowns (BBC, 2020; France 24, 2020; Namu & Reily, 2020). The impact of inconsistent or even violent policing has been to damage the relationship between the police and the public, increasing fear of the police and often eroding public trust in the police (where it existed at all) (Namu & Reily, 2020).

Moving forward, the challenges experienced by police in responding to various health regulations and associated legislation strongly indicate the need for their role to be considered more fully as part of pandemic planning processes, especially in the design of relevant legislation. Police have been integral to the public health response during COVID-19 and failure to clarify their role in future seems likely to result in operational uncertainty that may compromise even the most comprehensive health regulations. It is perhaps incumbent upon police leaders also to proactively engage with governments, planners, and policy-makers to clearly represent their needs more fully. Certainly, the experience of COVID-19 should convince police leaders and governments alike of the important role that police play during pandemics.

Multiagency Working: Police Engagement and Cooperation with Government, Public Health, and Other Stakeholders

Pandemics and other health emergencies are complex events involving a range of different groups who often share similar goals of protecting the public. As well as police agencies this includes both formal groups such as governments, public health, medicine and nursing, the military, civil society, and other emergency services, and informal groups such as community groups. Each of these has a wide range of skills and expertise that can complement the work of others. Similarly, each of these groups is likely to be privy to knowledge and information that is both important for their own work and also can aid in the work of others. The extant literature on emergency responding demonstrates the importance of multiagency working in achieving successful outcomes such as compliance with regulations, efficient use of resources, and optimum use of information (Shaluf & Said, 2003).

Where multiagency working is non-existent, cooperation and coordination between different agencies can be compromised and this can be highly detrimental to successful outcomes. This can include duplication of effort, failure to share relevant information, wasted resources, 'turf wars' concerning who has lead responsibility, and behaviour by one agency inconsistent with the aims or needs of another (Luna et al., 2007; Steigenberger, 2016). The COVID-19 pandemic has highlighted some of these challenges. For example, some police agencies have used tactics that are insensitive to the work and needs of other agencies. Use of draconian enforcement methods has engendered fear and some police agencies have used information about the health status of individuals to criminalise them. Pejorative terms such as 'COVID suspects' have also been used to negatively label individuals thought to be infectious and so a 'danger' to police and others (Faull, 2020). Most frequently the groups who have experienced this treatment have been the most vulnerable such as asylum seekers, illegal immigrants, and other disadvantaged groups (Chirambwi, 2016). When faced with police responses like these, individuals are likely not to access health advice or testing and may keep their infection status secret creating work-around strategies to avoid contact with the police (Richards, 2006). Indeed, direct evidence for these effects was observed during the recent Ebola epidemic in the Democratic Republic of the Congo as a result of a militarised policing response (Chirambwi, 2016). Clearly this has a negative effect on the ability of other agencies such as public health to do work such as contact tracing or encouraging sick individual to attend for treatment with a likely negative impact upon infection rates (Faull, 2020).

Police Relationships with Informal Groups

It is also important for agencies like police not to neglect relationships with informal actors such as community groups and other influential members of communities.

These relationships may be of a hybrid nature including both formal and informal links between actors. These relationships are important because informal groups may have substantial influence within a community. Compared with police officers, some of these may enjoy greater visibility and trust and may therefore be better placed to carry health and other relevant messages into communities that can aid in achieving compliance (Kapucu et al., 2010).

Identifying and working with informal groups and actors is especially important for police when attempting to engage with hard to reach communities who may have a distrust of police, for example, asylum seekers and illegal immigrant groups. These groups can be badly affected by pandemic illness but may be reluctant to come forward if ill, fearing deportation, or police retribution. There are many examples of successful engagement by official agencies with informal groups to facilitate health outcomes. In the Democratic Republic of the Congo during the recent Ebola epidemic, public health officials developed relationships with local mother's groups who, because of the social status of women as custodians of family health, were able to successfully spread health messages into their communities. Similarly, during the Ebola outbreak in Sierra Leone state actors engaged closely with informal groups, community groups, and non-governmental organisations (NGOs) including local witch doctors to explain the effects of the illness and strategies to avoid infection (House et al., 2014).

Strategies to Encourage Effective Multiagency Working

Whilst desirable, cooperative working between agencies is, however, often difficult and replete with various challenges (Atkinson et al., 2005). Important among these is that members of one group often have limited knowledge and understanding of the principles and practices of another. This is most often because many groups whose responsibilities might overlap during a pandemic rarely work with each other (Steigenberger, 2016). Another challenge is that because many groups have different operating procedures, strategic or political interests, this often leads to a lack of trust between them severely limiting opportunities for cooperation, especially the sharing of personnel and information. For example, police have often felt uncomfortable sharing information with Public Health agencies due to uncertainties about their security arrangements (Steigenberger, 2016; Olejarski & Garnett, 2010).

Effective multiagency working is built upon effective relationships between different groups. However, these are difficult to create from scratch during times of an emergency as these relationships take some time to develop (Luna et al., 2007). Different actors and agencies need time to develop familiarity with each other's practices, how their respective practices interact, and to identify any barriers to cooperation. Moving forward then it is important for all agencies who may have involvement in pandemics to start to develop or build upon existing relationships. This can be done effectively through joint planning, training, and emergency simulation exercises and this should be an ongoing feature of the working relationships between different agencies (Davis, 2013). Joint training and working also serves to develop informal relationships between members of different agencies that can be highly influential during a health emergency (Waugh Jr & Streib, 2006). Individuals may have someone to contact directly. Informal relationships between members of different agencies are also important and where individuals can identify relevant others in another agency. Another important requirement is to establish adequate structures for communication between agencies and the coordination of activities and resources, a process that is greatly aided by the development of personal relationships between individuals (Davis, 2013; Steigenberger, 2016).

Police and Community Engagement During a Pandemic

Police work involves substantial engagement with members of the public in order to get them to cooperate with instructions and follow rules. This is especially important during a pandemic because, as we have noted, the police are generally expected to ensure compliance with public health rules and regulations. However, the manner in which this is done is highly significant to public perceptions of the police and the likelihood that the public will comply with police requests and requirements (Hough et al., 2010).

There are many different approaches that can be taken to ensuring compliance with health regulations. These range from approaches where police officers offer encouragement and persuasion through to the threat of and actual use of force. However, the evidence suggests that the threat or use of force or other draconian methods produce a significant number of negative effects including fear of police, a reduction in trust for the police, and ultimately result in greater non-compliance with the rules and regulations that are being enforced (Ehrenfeld & Harris, 2020; Chirambwi, 2016). In contrast, what has been found during the COVID-19 pandemic is that the so-called engage and explain approaches where police seek to engage productively with members of the public, reassure them, explain rules and regulations clearly and where enforcement action has been the last resort have generally been more successful in achieving public support for the police, maintaining trust in the police, and enhancing compliance (Murphy et al., 2020).

It is important to explore why these engage and explain strategies have been more successful. There is substantial evidence that trust in police and cooperation with them is related to the style of communication and the manner in which individuals are treated by police (Palmer, 2020; Tyler & Lind, 2002). Police strategies for encounters with the public that have been shown to enhance perceptions of trustworthiness have been labelled as procedurally just (Tyler & Lind, 2002). Here police officers treat individuals with respect, listen to their concerns (the individuals should have a 'voice' in the interaction), provide explanations and reasons for police actions, and behave in a manner that is consistent and non-arbitrary towards different individuals. Police need to be clear about their actions, why they are doing them and be prepared to explain the limitations and uncertainties (Palmer, 2020). These are characteristic of the engage and explain strategies deployed by some police agencies during the COVID-19 pandemic.

Moving forward for police, procedurally just engagement and communication strategies should be integral to pandemic policing strategies as these have the greatest chance of achieving and maintaining maximum compliance. Whilst it is acknowledged that strict enforcement strategies, including use of force, may at times be necessary, such tactics should be used as a last resort not as a first response. This is because use of such tactics undermines trust in the police.

Police Organisational Challenges During Pandemics

As has been noted, pandemic plans, if they mention police at all, suggest that they will continue their usual duties. The experience of a pandemic does however present a number of key challenges to their successful completion. These challenges include protecting police staff from infection, the impact of loss of staff and police absenteeism, changes in crime patterns during a pandemic, the impact of changes within the broader criminal justice system upon policing, and the health effects upon police officers during a pandemic.

Protecting Police Staff from Infection

Police work at times involves close contact with other individuals who may be infected with a pathogen. This means that as part of officer safety considerations, and especially during a pandemic, it is important for police to familiarise themselves with the modes of transmission of pathogens that they may come into contact with. They also need to develop mitigation strategies to avoid infection. In the case of COVID-19, for example, the virus appears to be spread via exposure to respiratory droplets or through other contact routes such as touching surfaces containing the virus. This means that anyone whose activities involve regular close engagement with other individuals and/or their property, such as police officers, is at increased risk of exposure to the virus and therefore of becoming infected with it (Centre for Disease Control, 2020; Baker et al., 2020).

A number of strategies can be used to mitigate the risk of exposure to a pathogen. These include activities such as the use of social distancing, hand washing, Personal Protective Equipment (PPE), and regular cleaning of items that may come into contact with a pathogen. However, despite the evident sense in adopting these strategies, operational requirements and the type of encounters police sometimes have with members of the public may make it difficult for them to adopt some of these.

Restricting Access to Police Premises

Restricting access to police stations has been done as an infection mitigation strategy in most jurisdictions during the COVID-19 pandemic (Bates, 2020). In higher-income jurisdictions, police have made use of technologies such as video conferencing, electronic and social media to facilitate crime reporting, interviewing of victims and witnesses (and some suspects). However, these facilities may not be available in some jurisdictions, especially those within low-income nations. It may also not be possible to completely stop members of the public from attending police premises as some have to attend. This can include some individuals suspected of (serious) crimes, those without access to new technologies or for whom these technologies are unacceptable, and some crime victims and complainants who may for various reasons have to attend a police station for a forensic examination (for example, victims of sexual assault) or to give a statement to police where another location is not possible (for example, some victims of domestic abuse where it is unsafe to speak with them at their home). The need for some individuals to attend police premises obviously increases the risk of infection and police need to take steps to mitigate this risk. This has included checks such as measuring temperature as well as social distancing and Personal Protective Equipment use within premises.

How effectively police manage restriction of access to police premises is crucial. Where the expectations of members of the public are breached, such as when they are prevented from attending police premises or when subjected to long wait times prior to contact by police, this may damage their trust and confidence in police (Myhill & Quinton, 2011). It is crucial therefore, as mentioned earlier, for police to be willing to use procedurally just approaches towards members of the public. In particular, being willing to explain their reasons for particular procedures and actions and listening to the concerns of members of the public where their expectations have been thwarted during a pandemic (Hough et al., 2010).

Personal Protective Equipment

Personal Protective Equipment (PPE) can include items such as goggles, gloves, face masks, and body coverings and these items have been deployed by police during the COVID-19 pandemic. There are, however, challenges concerning the availability and use of PPE during this COVID-19 pandemic. Some agencies have noted, for example, shortages of PPE for their staff raising infection risks (Khan, 2020).

Where PPE is available, it is vital that police receive appropriate guidance and training concerning its use. Inappropriate, misleading, or incorrect advice can raise the risk of infection. The COVID-19 pandemic has raised a number of challenges. For example, police in the UK were given conflicting advice about what type of PPE and when to deploy it with reports suggesting that the advice had changed four times (Khan, 2020).

The suitability of PPE for the work of police is in itself a challenge. Some PPE is designed and is most suitable for medical staff treating sick and often immobile patients. However, materials such as masks, gloves, goggles, and body coverings may be an encumbrance to some police activities. PPE is uncomfortable to wear for long periods of time, may be inconvenient to deploy in an emergency, or may be damaged during a violent encounter. PPE is most effective for single use followed by careful disposal. During the COVID-19 pandemic there have been examples of police officers not using PPE due to issues of practicality and where there have been shortages of PPE examples of multiple use of the same items (The Independent, 2020, May 4)

Social Distancing

Whilst an effective method of infection control, social distancing may not be possible on all occasions. Police often have reason to encounter individuals who are resistant to police attention or may come into contact with others who wish them harm. Here physical contact involving restraint or self-defence strategies may be required. In these circumstances it is difficult to see how social distancing could be maintained. Whilst personal protective equipment may help reduce infection risks from close contact with others, as noted PPE may not always itself be suitable during certain encounters. How police manage social distancing given the nature of some of their activities is not clear. Where possible it is important to utilise it as a method of infection control, but police work is not always conducive to it.

Cleaning Premises and Equipment

Whilst it is possible to introduce regular cleaning of items including vehicles and police offices to limit infection risks, the practicality of this in the light of operational responsiveness has to be considered. In some jurisdictions where resources are scarce, it may not be possible to completely close offices or stop using vehicles in order to clean them. For example, reports from Southern Africa suggest that during the COVID-19 pandemic, police agencies had significant operational difficulty due to loss of police vehicles and some buildings whilst these were cleaned following suspected infection (Interpol, 2020). During COVID-19, some police agencies responded to some of these challenges by utilising outdoor spaces for some of their work, some have opened additional premises for some of their activities or have used strict prioritising rules for when certain facilities or equipment can be used and by whom (Scottish Government, 2020).

These challenges surrounding infection control are important and need to be addressed as part of pandemic planning. To be effective in infection control it is vital that protocols are identified for the availability of sufficient PPE, that it is suitable for the range of police working environments and officers are adequately trained in its use and deployment.

Police Absenteeism

As noted, police are at heightened risk of exposure to pandemic viruses. Within policing, as with other organisations, those exposed to a virus or who are symptomatic with disease are generally advised to remain at home. This, however, presents policing with the challenge of increased absenteeism during a pandemic which can significantly affect their capacity to effectively conduct their duties.

Prior to the COVID-19 pandemic, some police forces forecast the absentee rate during an influenza pandemic as between 10 and 80% of staff (Police Forum, 2007). It is, however, not clear how well these figures apply to the COVID-19 pandemic. This is mainly because police absentee rates due to COVID-19 generally have not been made available. It is possible to estimate the effect of COVID-19 upon police absenteeism using some data that was released by the United Kingdom Metropolitan Police in response to a freedom of information request (FIR).

In response to the FIR, the Metropolitan police reported that between February and June 2020 (the peak of the first wave of COVID-19 in the UK) there were 74 confirmed cases of COVID-19 amongst police officers and 2089 suspected cases (Metropolitan Police, 2020). This represented a total of 2163 officers or 6.3% of the total police officer staff who were at some point absent during this period. Assuming that the 2163 officers with COVID-19-related absences stayed away from work for just 14 days each as suggested by self-isolation guidelines (and many may have been off work for longer) that would amount to 30,282 days lost. This absentee rate is in addition to the usual rates of absenteeism that would occur irrespective of a pandemic. Data from the Metropolitan police for 2018 suggests that under normal circumstances 3.6% of the available workdays (143,175 days of a total of 3,966,709 possible) are lost per year due to police officers being ill (Metropolitan Police, 2018). The estimated number of days lost to COVID-19 equates to an additional 21% more days lost in the 5-month period between February and June 2020 than usual. In addition, further exploration of the COVID-19 absentee figures reveals that the vast majority were concentrated within front-line policing roles. On the basis of these (rough) estimates it seems that absenteeism due to COVID-19 has represented a significant loss of the police workforce above what may normally be planned for, and, importantly, it has been focussed upon certain front-line roles. This is likely to have put significant strain upon resources and the capability and capacity of police to deliver services (Laufs & Waseem, 2020).

Absenteeism may mean that some officers may be redeployed to roles for which they have limited experience or for which they are untrained. Officers may also be required to work for longer hours (Laufs & Waseem, 2020). In the context of increased staff absenteeism, some officers may feel a degree of pressure from some supervisors (or even themselves) to return early from self-isolation or not to isolate at all. Another major challenge for police is that some asymptomatic but infected individuals may attend for work, unknowingly infecting others. All of these challenges have been seen during the COVID-19 pandemic.

The challenge of redeploying police officers who are untrained or inexperienced in certain areas is significant and requires careful planning. Obviously, where possible they should be supervised by an experienced officer, a strategy that has been common during COVID-19 (Bates, 2020). Strategies to deal with staff returning to work early or not wishing to self-isolate requires police leaders and supervisors to develop a culture that stresses absenteeism during a pandemic is not only acceptable but is also a vital tool to protect all staff and the functioning of the organisation. More broadly, it is also vital for police to have access to testing facilities that provide rapid results so that those who may have been exposed to a pathogen can rapidly know if they have been infected by it and return to work if they test negative. At the time of writing during the COVID-19 pandemic there are many debates ranging as to whether police should be given priority in accessing scarce testing facilities.

Changes in Crime Patterns

Throughout history, disease pandemics have influenced changes in crime patterns as a function of changing opportunities and responses to the pandemic (Stickle & Felson, 2020). During the Spanish flu pandemic during the early twentieth century there was a significant reduction in overall crime levels (Persico, 1976). This has been repeated internationally, during the COVID-19 pandemic (ONS, 2020). It seems that quarantine and curfews have reduced overall crime levels because opportunities to engage in certain types of criminality such as burglary, road traffic offences, and street crimes were limited. However, opportunities for new types of crime have been created and rates of others have increased. For example, during the COVID-19 pandemic, increased public concern related to health has created opportunities for the sale of counterfeit medicines and vaccines, and government stimulus packages have created opportunities for financial fraud such as false claims for financial aid (Stickle & Felson, 2020; Hodgkinson & Andresen 2020; Ashby, 2020). One particularly pernicious effect of lockdowns during COVID-19 has also been an increase in incidents of domestic violence and abuse (ONS, 2020).

A reduction in overall crime levels is perhaps to be welcomed as this reduces some of the pressures on policing at a time when police absenteeism is a concern. During COVID-19 some police agencies were in fact able to redeploy officers during lockdown from activities such as roads policing to other activities due to a significant reduction in road traffic (Bates, 2020). However, because absenteeism among police has been uneven in its impact staffing gaps have arisen in particular areas of specialism associated with front-line officers. In addition, crime types that have increased during COVID-19 such as domestic violence and fraud require some staff with specialist training or expertise to investigate them, which may be compromised due to absenteeism or present significant challenges for redeployed staff due to limited experience or expertise in the crime type.

As well as changes to the distribution of crimes, during any pandemic police have to respond to new offences created as part of public health regulations. For example, during the COVID-19 pandemic, in many jurisdictions, legislation has included the power for police to issue on the spot fines for breaches of lockdown, quarantine, or non-wearing of face coverings. Police have also been given responsibilities outside their usual core activities such as policing social gatherings to ensure group sizes were within legislative guidelines, ensuring compliance with lockdowns, policing curfews, and even protecting hospitals, medical staff and supplies. In some jurisdictions, in particular within low-income countries, police have also been recruited to aid in contact tracing, transporting sick individuals to hospital, and transporting medical supplies and equipment. This has left some already stretched police agencies with the challenge of developing policing strategies to accommodate these additional demands. In addition, it has required training officers to respond to new offences and manage new powers.

Another significant challenge for police during pandemics and evidenced during COVID-19 has been the requirement, in many jurisdictions, for police to investigate all sudden deaths. During the peak of the pandemic, as hospital facilities became overburdened, there was an increase in sudden deaths especially where individuals have died alone at home (Onder et al., 2020). This placed an increased burden upon the officers with expertise in this type of investigation over what they would normally respond to, as well as other front-line officers who may have to respond to related reports of death. For example, one report found that one police officer had attended fifteen sudden deaths in one 24-h period (Dearden, 2020). Many of these officers were also exposed to particularly harrowing death scenes where deaths had not been discovered for some weeks for some weeks, with a significant risk of trauma for the officers (Dearden, 2020; Stogner et al., 2020).

Overall changes in crime patterns, the creation of new offences and new responsibilities creates significant challenges for the management of already stretched police resources. Clearly strategies are required to respond that are cognisant of the available staff levels and expertise, and that are able to respond to the changes in crime patterns with reduced levels of operational staff levels.

Pandemics, Policing, and the Criminal Justice System

During a pandemic absenteeism and infection controls significantly impact the capacity and capability not just of police agencies but also for the whole of the criminal justice system. For example, during the peak of the COVID-19 pandemic in the UK there was a general closure of magistrate and crown courts to limit infection risk. In addition, in a further attempt to reduce pressure on the court system, the Crown Prosecution Service (CPS) issued guidance suggesting that prosecutors should use alternative options or even consider dropping charges where an individual might otherwise need to attend court (CPS, 2020). The impact of this has been a substantial backlog in the number of cases awaiting trial. As of September 2020, this amounted to 500,000 cases (Grierson, 2020). This has also impacted the prison system with more individuals than usual on remand awaiting a trail. This has had an impact upon the capacity of prisons to take new inmates which, in turn, has impacted disposal options for courts (Shepherd & Spivak, 2020).

Whilst this has undoubtedly reduced pressure on the courts, there has been a downstream impact upon police. In particular, it has negatively impacted the time scales and even the likelihood of some criminal cases getting to trial and has affected the range of disposal options. Where prosecutions and other court cases are slowed or stopped this can have a significant impact upon the police and the public perceptions, especially confidence in the police and criminal justice system. Victims of crime generally wish to see timely justice and where this does not happen this challenges confidence and trust in the police and the criminal justice system (Hough et al., 2010). When cases do not progress despite the best efforts of police officers, this can also severely damage police morale, with already overstretched officers expressing frustration at delays and an inability to see progress in some cases (Roberts & Herrington, 2013).

Given these challenges to the capacity of the criminal justice system police have had to make increased use of discretionary powers and other sanctions such as cautions, on the spot fines, and other disposal methods. We have already stressed the importance of fairness and consistency of police procedures and the negative impact when police are perceived to have breached this (Myhill & Quinton, 2011). Certainly, it is important that, in this context, police do not let frustration with the system get the better of them as this will increase the risk of inconsistency in responses and may encourage summary justice or draconian responses.

Police Wellbeing

We have discussed the impact of staff absenteeism and the impact of new legislation and changes to crime patterns on the capacity of police organisations to fulfil their responsibilities. However, it is important to recognise that this also has an impact upon the individuals discharging these responsibilities (Laufs & Waseem, 2020). During COVID-19, for example, absenteeism has resulted in increased workloads resulting in increasing levels of tiredness and exhaustion among staff. In addition, some officers have been deployed to carry out tasks for which they have limited experience, training, or expertise (Bates, 2020). New pandemic legislation has placed some police officers under greater pressure as they struggle to enforce, sometimes vague, rules in the face of non-complaint members of the public. This has occurred all in a context of a heightened risk to the individual officer of contracting the virus, and associated fear concerning their own health, and that of friends, colleagues and their families. For example, during the COVID-19 pandemic there have been many reports of members of the public intentionally coughing or spitting at police officers and claiming to be infected with the virus (Farooqi, 2020; Byford, 2020; Bates, 2020). There have also been reports of officers being unsure whether vehicles and other resources had been appropriately cleaned (Bates, 2020).

In addition, reduced court capacity and attendant challenges in getting cases to court has been a source of frustration for some officers. There is also a significant risk of officers experiencing psychological trauma resulting from seeing deaths on a larger scale than is usual, and of officers at times being required to deal with grief, anxiety, and anger from members of the public. In some jurisdictions the pandemic has also seen public protests and significant criticism of police from the Black Lives Matter movement and calls to defund the police for perceived racism and brutality (Dave et al., 2020). Many of these challenges for officers can be further compounded by poor management styles of police leaders. This is especially the case where managers, who themselves may be under significant pressures resulting from similar personal stresses and depleted organisational resources, default to excessively bureaucratic or autocratic leadership styles. Such approaches are associated with increases in workplace stress, multiplying the effects of trauma upon burnout and absenteeism among subordinates (Roberts & Herrington, 2013). These issues are a significant challenge to police officer wellbeing. Indeed, the COVID-19 pandemic has seen a rise in occupational stress among police officers (Frenkel et al., 2020; Stogner et al., 2020).

In developing responses to pandemics, it is therefore important for police to develop strategies to mitigate workplace stress and enhance employee wellbeing. Occupational health systems need to be in place that allow officers to share their worries and concerns in an open and non-evaluative manner and to easily avail themselves of support that does not result in negative stigma. Whilst many of these are important under normal circumstance as policing is a generally stressful occupation, they perhaps take on greater significance due to the range of extra challenges faced by police during pandemics. Opportunities for breaks and leave are important as this can mitigate the effects of exhaustion, even though this is significantly challenging with reduced staffing levels.

Planning for Future Pandemics

It is clear that pandemics present significant and sustained challenges for police. Pandemics are dynamic and complex events. They evolve over time with different infection and death rates related to the characteristics of the pathogen, its transmissibility and lethality, the efficacy of the public health responses, and the levels of cooperation of the public with health rules and regulations. As we have seen, the expectations of and roles for police can change substantially and rapidly, both as a result of the changing needs of governments and society, and the needs of the police themselves in response to the context of a pandemic. Together this creates substantial uncertainty for policy-makers and for police in planning their response strategies. How then should the police respond? What can be learned from the recent and past pandemics to inform future pandemic policing strategies?

Complexity associated with pandemics presents police with a range of wicked problems, where strategies aimed at dealing with one issue can lead to a series of unintended consequences that themselves present new challenges. For example, during the COVID-19 pandemic, imposing lockdowns has been relatively successful in slowing the risk of infection. However, as time has moved on some members of the public have become disillusioned with the curtailment of their freedom, leading to increased lawlessness from some in terms of illegal gatherings or breaches to lockdowns. Because of this, police have come under some political pressure from governments to rigidly enforce regulations. However, rigid enforcement strategies in some jurisdictions has had a negative effect. It has led to the criminalisation of some members of the public, often those of lower socioeconomic status or members of ethnic minorities (Dewey, 2020). It has also resulted in protests and a general reduction in cooperation with police and compliance with regulations (Dave et al., 2020).

Whilst tried and tested or best-practice methods may be useful at times during pandemics, the complexity of pandemics means that policing strategies based solely upon such methods may be of limited utility (Adams & Stewart, 2015). This is because, within complexity, any responses that appear to be successful one day can, as a result of changing circumstances, rapidly become ineffectual, or even damaging. Indeed, one of the problems with a focus upon the so-called best-practice solutions is that they run the risk of repeating past mistakes and limit the chance of novel strategies being developed (Jones-Rooy & Page, 2012). It is therefore vital that any pandemic policing strategies are flexible, subject to regular review, and capable of modification at short notice. Police planners need to be willing to explore the evolving circumstances in as much detail as possible through the collection and analysis of a wide range of relevant evidence and data. They must be prepared to use this to test the utility of strategies and modify or reject them accordingly.

Within complex environments diversity of thinking among planners is also a vital tool (Page, 2010). This increases the likelihood of novel strategies being developed, minimises the risk of repeating failed strategies, and mitigates against the risk of group think among planners. Planning teams should therefore involve as wide a range of experience and expertise as possible, including multidisciplinary perspectives from a range of stakeholders. The need for diversity in thinking further highlights the importance of police developing good working relationships with different stakeholders so that knowledge and expertise can be effectively shared. Relevant here is the argument made at the outset of this chapter that police need to be part of the pandemic planning system working alongside government and public health so that the voice of police is heard when legislation is created. It is important to note here that we are not advocating that police should write the legislation; instead, we argue that police concerns need to be considered by those developing legislation so that police are not in the future faced with vague and unenforceable regulations.

The uncertainty caused by pandemics perhaps also invites police to consider their broader role in society. In many jurisdictions, as well as investigating crime and enforcing laws, a core element of policing is for the police to protect and reassure the public (Newburn, 2003). This role may be especially important both during and after a pandemic. This is because at times of greatest uncertainty individuals look for signs of safety and stability as this helps to show them that their world is, at least in part, predictable with at least some consistency (Pyszczynski, 2004). Here individuals often turn to those in positions of authority, such as the police, for help and support. Perhaps then, during a pandemic, some of the less tangible aspects of modern policing such as high police visibility, and direct engagement with the public providing advice and support, may take on far greater significance. As we have stressed throughout this chapter, the way in which police engage with the public is vital, and when done in a procedurally just manner maximises the sense of reassurance, trust, and legitimacy of police (Hough et al., 2010). Moving forward then the nature of police engagement with the public, its fairness and the perceived fairness and consistency of police responses is a crucial element in police achieving both the trust of the public, their compliance with rules and providing a sense of reassurance.

Summary and Conclusion

This chapter has explored many of the challenges that pandemics create for the police. It has illustrated a broad lack of clarity at both a policy and legislative level in what is expected of police, save that they will conduct their usual duties and enforce whatever legislation is created by governments. As well as these, police also face a wide range of operational challenges including protecting staff from infection, staff absenteeism, changes in crime patterns, the health and wellbeing impact upon police officers, whilst trying to carry out their usual duties.

We have noted that police need to avoid, as their default position, excessive and overly draconian enforcement approaches to health regulations as these are likely to be counter-productive, compromising trust in police and potentially leading to greater non-compliance. Instead, experience from COVID-19 and other pandemics shows us that effective police responses involve open engagement with a wide variety of stakeholders (in particular, those from public health and government) with a willingness to work together and to share information and expertise. In order to achieve greatest compliance with regulations, police need to be willing to engage in a procedurally just manner with the public. This includes being willing to explain health regulations, why they are responding as they are, have a willingness to listen to the concerns and challenges presented by members of the public, and to enforce regulations fairly and consistently. Indeed, to achieve public compliance any enforcement action should be the last and not the first response. It is also vital that police leaders take steps to enhance and maintain police staff wellbeing; they need to be supportive of staff and avoid draconian, overly bureaucratic or authoritarian approaches to management.

Pandemics create considerable uncertainty and complexity. As such, whilst some tried and tested policing strategies may be useful, we caution against an over-reliance on these. Some police strategies during a pandemic may be novel or even experimental, but there is an attendant need to review these regularly and be willing to change them rapidly if necessary. Ultimately, pandemics present police with a range of significant challenges and whatever strategies are developed, open engagement with stakeholders and flexibility on the part of the police are crucial.

References

Acheson, D. (1988). *Public health in England. The report of the committee of inquiry into the future development of the public health function.* HMSO.

Adams, T. M., & Stewart, L. D. (2015). Chaos theory and organizational crisis: A theoretical analysis of the challenges faced by the New Orleans police department during hurricane Katrina. *Public Organization Review, 15*(3), 415–431.

Ashby, M. P. (2020). Initial evidence on the relationship between the coronavirus pandemic and crime in the United States. *Crime Science, 9*, 1–16.

Atkinson, M., Doherty, P., & Kinder, K. (2005). Multi-agency working: Models, challenges and key factors for success. *Journal of Early Childhood Research, 3*(1), 7–17.

Baker, M. G., Peckham, T. K., & Seixas, N. S. (2020). Estimating the burden of United States workers exposed to infection or disease: A key factor in containing risk of COVID-19 infection. *PLoS One, 15*(4), e0232452.

Bates, J. (2020, April). How coronavirus is affecting police departments. *Time Magazine.*

Bayley, D., & Shearing, C. D. (1996). The future of policing. *Law and Society Review, 30*(3), 585–606.

BBC. (2020, July 23). Uganda—Where security forces may be more deadly than coronavirus. *BBC.* https://www.bbc.com/news/world-africa-53450850

Byford, C. (2020, April 7). Newport man jailed after coughing at police and threatening to infect them with Covid-19. *Southern Daily Echo.* https://www.dailyecho.co.uk/news/18364564.newport-man-jailed-coughing-police-threatening-infect-covid-19/

Centre for Disease Control. (2020). *Law Enforcement Officer exposure to Covid19.* https://www.theiacp.org/resources/document/law-enforcement-officer-exposure-to-covid-1

Chirambwi, K. (2016). Militarizing police in complex public emergencies. *Peace Review, 28*(2), 171.

Crown Prosecution Service. (2020). *Prosecution Statisti s 2020.* Retrieved July 2021 from https://www.cps.gov.uk/publication/cpsdata-summary-quarter-4-2020-2021

Dave, D. M., Friedson, A. I., Matsuzawa, K., Sabia, J. J., & Safford, S. (2020). *Black lives matter protests, social distancing, and COVID-19* (No. w27408). National Bureau of Economic Research.

Davis, J. M. (2013). Supporting creativity, inclusion and collaborative multi-professional learning. *Improving Schools, 16*(1), 5–20

Dearden, L. (2020, April 11). Coronavirus: Police trauma warning after one officer called to 15 Covid-related deaths in 24 hours. *The Independent.* https://www.independent.co.uk/news/uk/home-news/coronavirus-police-deaths-uk-lockdown-homes-mental-illness-a9459711.html

Dewey, J. (2020). *The solution is the problem: What a pandemic can reveal about policing.* In COVID-19 (pp. 61–71). Routledge.

Dood, V., & Pidd, H. (2020, March 27). Police acknowledge confusion over UK lockdown rules. *The Guardian.* https://www.theguardian.com/uk-news/2020/mar/27/police-acknowledge-confusion-over-uk-lockdown-rules

Ehrenfeld, J. M., & Harris, P. A. (2020, in press). *Police brutality must stop.* American Medical Association.

Farooqi, J. (2020, April 16). Man jailed for coronavirus threats to spit and cough on police officers. *Gazette & Herald.* https://www.gazetteherald.co.uk/news/18384920.man-jailed-coronavirus-threats-spit-cough-police-officers/

Faull A. (2020). *State abuses could match the threat of COVID-19 itself.* https://issafrica.org/iss-today/state-abuses-could-match-the-threat-of-covid-19-itself

France 24. (2020, April 1). Security forces use violent tactics to enforce Africa's coronavirus shutdowns. *France 24.* https://www.france24.com/en/20200401-security-forces-use-violent-tactics-to-enforce-africa-s-coronavirus-shutdowns

Frenkel, M. O., Giessing, L., Egger-Lampl, S., Hutter, V., Oudejans, R., Kleygrewe, L., & Plessner, H. (2020, in press). The impact of the COVID-19 pandemic on European police officers: Stress, demands and coping resources. *Journal of Criminal Justice.* https://reader.elsevier.com/reader/sd/pii/S0047235220302506?token=B8E28F7B032A78E9E86A8A34977A42AFD45F6EF2D8516AB29DFEB509E90DED0E8881A59DF9691E60C08C5BA66C2703A6

Grierson, J. (2020, August 19). Early-release scheme for prisoners in England and Wales to end. *The Guardian.* https://www.theguardian.com/society/2020/aug/19/prisons-inspector-england-wales-warns-of-mental-health-problems-from-severe-coronavirus-restrictions

Hodgkinson, T., & Andresen, M. A. (2020, in press). Show me a man or a woman alone and I'll show you a saint: Changes in the frequency of criminal incidents during the COVID-19 pandemic. *Journal of Criminal Justice, 69.*

Hough, M., Jackson, J., Bradford, B., Myhill, A., & Quinton, P. (2010). Procedural justice, trust, and institutional legitimacy. *Policing: A Journal of Policy and Practice, 4*(3), 203–210.

House, N., Power, L., & Alison, A. (2014). A systematic review of the potential hurdles of interoperability to the emergency services in major incidents: recommendations for solutions and alternatives. *Cognition, Technology & Work, 16*(3), 319–335.

Huremović, D. (2019). Brief history of pandemics (pandemics throughout history). In D. Huremović (Ed.), *Psychiatry of pandemics*. Springer.

Interpol. (2020, May). *Workshop on the impact of coronavirus on policing.*

Jones-Rooy, A., & Page, S. E. (2012). The complexity of system effects. *Critical Review, 24*(3), 313–342.

Kapucu, N., Arslan, T., & Demiroz, F. (2010). Collaborative emergency management and national emergency management network. *Disaster Prevention and Management, 19*(4), 452–468. https://doi.org/10.1108/09653561011070376

Khan, R. (2020). Police officers are working in dangerous situations without protection from coronavirus—And now they're getting ill. *The Independent.* https://www.independent.co.uk/voices/coronavirus-uk-ppe-shortages-police-policing-covid-19-postcode-lottery-a9519816.html

Laufs, J., & Waseem, Z. (2020). Policing in pandemics: A systematic review and best practices for police response to COVID-19. *International Journal of Disaster Risk Reduction, 51*, 101812. https://doi.org/10.1016/j.ijdrr.2020.101812

Levin, P. J., Gebbie, E. N., & Qureshi, K. (2007). Can the health-care system meet the challenge of pandemic flu? Planning, ethical, and workforce considerations. *Public Health Reports, 122*(5), 573–578.

Lum, C., & Nagin, D. S. (2017). Reinventing American policing. *Crime and Justice, 46*(1), 339–393.

Luna, A. M., Brito, C. S., & Sanberg, E. A. (2007). *Police planning for an influenza pandemic: Case studies and recommendations from the field.* Resource document. Police Executive Research Forum. https://icma.org/sites/default/files/5700_.pdf

Merrick, R. (2020, October 21). Police 'struggling' to enforce 'confusing' three-tier lockdown rules. *The Independent.* https://www.independent.co.uk/news/uk/politics/lockdown-tier-rules-police-fines-nspcc-coronavirus-covid-b1202034.html

Metropolitan Police. (2018). *Freedom of Information Request, Overall sickness absence data for the year 2016-17.* https://www.met.police.uk/SysSiteAssets/foi-media/metropolitan-police/disclosure_2017/december_2017/information-right-unit%2D%2D-overall-sickness-absence-data-broken-down-by-staff-groups-for-2017september-2017

Metropolitan Police. (2020). *Freedom of Information Request Reference No: 01.FOI.20.014553.* https://www.met.police.uk/cy-GB/SysSiteAssets/foi-media/metropolitan-police/disclosure_2020/august_2020/information-rights-unit%2D%2D-staff-absences-due-to-covid-19

Murphy, K., Williamson, H., Sargeant, E., & McCarthy, M. (2020, in press). Why people comply with COVID-19 social distancing restrictions: Self-interest or duty? *Australian & New Zealand Journal of Criminology.*

Myhill, A., & Quinton, P. (2011). *It's a fair cop? Police legitimacy, public co-operation, and crime reduction: An interpretative evidence commentary.* National Policing Improvement Agency.

Namu, J., & Reily, T. (2020). Nine weeks of bloodshed: How brutal policing of Kenya's Covid curfew left 15 dead. *The Guardian.* https://www.theguardian.com/global-development/2020/oct/23/brutal-policing-kenyas-covid-curfew-left-15-dead

Newburn, T. (2003). Policing since 1945. In T. Newburn (Ed.), *Handbook of policing.* Routledge.

Office of National Statistics. (2020). *Crime in England and Wales: year ending June 2020.* Retrieved January 2021 from file:///Users/karlroberts/Downloads/Crime%20in%20England%20and%20Wales%20year%20ending%20June%202020.pdf

Olejarski, A. M., & Garnett, J. L. (2010). Coping with Katrina: Assessing crisis management behaviours in the big one. *Journal of Contingencies and Crisis Management, 18*(1), 26–38.

Onder, G., Rezza, G., & Brusaferro, S. (2020, in press). Case-fatality rate and characteristics of patients dying in relation to COVID-19 in Italy. *JAMA, 323*(18), 1775–1776.

Page, S. E. (2010). *Diversity and complexity* (Vol. 2). Princeton University Press.

Palmer, D. (2020, in press). Pandemic policing needs to be done with the public's trust, not confusion. *Australasian Policing, 12*(3), 47.

Persico, J. E. (1976). *The great swine flu epidemic of 1918.* American Heritage Publishing Company, Incorporated.

Police Forum. (2007). *Police planning for an influenza pandemic.* https://www.policeforum.org/assets/docs/Free_Online_Documents/Public_Health/police%20planning%20for%20an%20influenza%20pandemic%20-%20case%20studies%20and%20recommendations%20from%20the%20field%202007.pdf

Pyszczynski, T. (2004). What are we so afraid of?: A terror management theory perspective on the politics of fear. *Social Research: An International Quarterly, 71*(4), 827–848.

Richards, E. P. (2006). *The role of law enforcement in public health emergencies: Special considerations for an all-hazards approach.* US Department of Justice, Office of Justice Programs, Bureau of Justice Assistance.

Roberts, K., & Herrington, V. (2013). Organisational and procedural justice: A review of the literature and its implications for policing. *Journal of Policing, Intelligence and Counter Terrorism, 8*(2), 115–130.

Scottish Government. (2020). *Coronavirus (COVID-19): International policing responses—Part 1—during lockdown. Resource document.* https://www.gov.scot/publications/part-1-international-policing-responses-covid-19-during-lockdown/

Shaluf, I. M., & Said, A. M. (2003). A review of disaster and crisis. *Disaster Prevention and Management, 12*(1), 24–32.

Shepherd, S., & Spivak, B. L. (2020, in press). Re-considering the immediate release of prisoners during COVID-19 community restrictions. *The Medical Journal of Australia.*

Steigenberger, N. (2016). Organizing for the big one: A review of case studies and a research agenda for multi-agency disaster response. *Journal of Contingencies and Crisis Management, 24*(2), 60–72.

Stickle, B., & Felson, M. (2020, in press). Crime rates in a pandemic: The largest criminological experiment in history. *American Journal of Criminal Justice*, *45*(4), 525–536.

Stogner, J., Miller, B. L., & McLean, K. (2020). Police stress, mental health, and resiliency during the COVID-19 pandemic. *American Journal of Criminal Justice, 45*(4), 718–730.

The Independent. (2020, May 4). Police officers warned against going for operations without protective equipment. *The Independent.* https://www.independent.co.ug/police-officers-warned-against-going-for-operations-without-protective-equipment/

Tyler, T. R., & Lind, E. A. (2002). Procedural justice. In J. Sanders & V. Hamilton (Eds.), *Handbook of justice research in law* (pp. 65–92). Springer.

van Dijk, A., & Crofts, N. (2017). Law enforcement and public health as an emerging field. *Policing and Society, 27*(3), 261–275.

van Dijk, A. J., Herrington, V., Crofts, N., Breunig, R., Burris, S., Sullivan, H., Middleton, J., Sherman, S., & Thomson, N. (2019). Law enforcement and public health: Recognition and enhancement of joined-up solutions. *The Lancet, 393*(10168), 287–294.

Waugh, W. L., Jr., & Streib, G. (2006). Collaboration and leadership for effective emergency management. *Public Administration Review, 66*, 131–140.

World Health Organization. (2008). *International health regulations (2005).* World Health Organization.

Chapter 17
Special Issues in Law Enforcement and Public Health: Community Voices

Isabelle Bartkowiak-Théron, Murray Billett, Franck David, Emily Diamond, Daniel J. Jones, and Lesslie Young

Introduction

Isabelle Bartkowiak-Théron

In showcasing the voices of practitioners, we wanted to highlight the extraordinary complexities of navigating vulnerability in a professional capacity. As indicated by James Clover in an earlier chapter of this collection, "when we have an opportunity to learn from practitioners outside our personal or professional sphere, we become enriched with a fuller understanding of what our clients and communities need". One of our specific concerns as editors was also to engage our readers in an expanded

I. Bartkowiak-Théron (✉)
Tasmanian Inst. Law Enforcement Studies, University of Tasmania, Hobart, TAS, Australia
e-mail: isabelle.bartkowiaktheron@utas.edu.au

M. Billett
Edmonton, AB, Canada

F. David (✉)
People First Scotland, Edinburgh, Scotland, UK
e-mail: admin@peoplefirstscotland.org

E. Diamond (✉)
Wright Institute, Berkeley, CA, USA
e-mail: ediamond@wi.edu

D. J. Jones (✉)
The University of Huddersfield, Edmonton, AB, Canada
e-mail: daniel.jones@hud.ac.uk

L. Young (✉)
Epilepsy Scotland, Glasgow, Scotland, UK
e-mail: lyoung@epilepsyscotland.org.uk

dialogue about a broad range of vulnerabilities, of diverse nature and forms, often obscured from the policing debate or from LEPH collaborations. These community voices bring an added dimension to our conversations about the various topics that bring, or should bring, professionals together. We are adamant that while it looks like these are new topics in policing, they are not new at all. Instead, their specific documentation and analysis in scholarly literature, while perhaps nascent, is broadening our understanding of the scope and diversity of vulnerabilities that should be under deeper scrutiny. As editors, we think it is crucial for the LEPH field to expand knowledge and literature further.

The compelling narrative by Daniel Jones demonstrates two critical components that underpin many of the critical messages in this book: vulnerability and strength. It demonstrates that we can all experience various forms of vulnerabilities, some of them unexpected, and Jones shows that when someone has faced extreme trauma and vulnerability they can be strong and offer this strength to others, sometimes without even knowing so. The division between strength and vulnerability are not always visible nor are they as far apart as we may perceive.

Murray Billett provides a thoughtful analysis of the social and normative barriers faced by minorities, not only in accessing services, but also in their everyday lives. This contribution strikes a tone in terms of the sheer enormity of navigating the heavily stigmatized structures that have shaped identities, or lead some individuals to hide those identities. Murray finishes on a hopeful note that every step made to accept difference is a step forward, and a good one; that every little thing counts, and that we all have our part to play in bringing forward a world shaped by diversity.

Stereotypes surrounding the issue of disability are rife. Here, Franck David provides us with a picture of the price one pays when disability is ignored or when support services are not provided to a person. The example of X and of the vicissitudes of a life of exploitation is heartbreaking, and is a perfect illustration of the chasms that can exist between law enforcement and public health services when the first does not understand the other.

As a police recruit educator, I have been pondering for a long time why we do not teach police more about all the many various forms of diversity and vulnerability, and I always strive to throw as wide a net as I can when I talk to my police recruits (according to a universal precautions model, which I have been unashamedly borrowing from public health for 15 years and counting). I often ponder, though, how many vulnerabilities are under the police radar, and how such unawareness or lack of knowledge can make professionals misread a situation altogether. I often find that my mentioning what can be seen as an "obscure" form of vulnerability in policing comes as a bit of a light bulb moment in class for students (a bit like a "But of course, why didn't I think of it before?" moment). This is always the case when I mention autism as a form of vulnerability. Barely any policing curriculum is dedicated to the topic, and yet it is a topic of crucial importance to frontline police, at least for the profound cognitive or behavioural complexities that autism can bring to a person's encounter with police, and I am always grateful, and indebted, for the work of my psychology colleagues, who inspire my teaching work in that area. Emily Diamond's piece is a wonderful, much needed, and timely addition to the topic of neurodiversity in the field of policing. Needless to say, I am immediately prescribing this contribution to my students.

Along the same line, some of the editors, as medical practitioners, have learnt about epilepsy and treated people with epilepsy and handled critical situations involving seizures—but always in situations where the diagnosis had been made or was apparent. The thought of untrained personnel, licensed to use force, being confronted with and having to handle potentially dangerous clinical situations— situations that are confronting and can be inherently frightening—is not one that was thought of until one becomes aware of Lesslie Young's work. The prepared police mind, the aware prosecutor, the existing and trusting partnership with health author- ities—all will go a long way to preventing and ameliorating the sort of situations described here.

I am thoroughly grateful for the following pieces, which go a long way to expand the knowledge of specific forms of vulnerability and their relevance to the policing process, and to law enforcement and public health collaborations. Our teaching and research in those areas can only be enriched by them.

Being Vulnerable with the Vulnerable

Daniel J. Jones

I started my career in law enforcement 26 years ago as a correctional officer; for the past 23 years, I have been a police officer in a major Canadian city. I have had amazing opportunities as a police officer working in areas such as Neighbourhood Foot Patrol, Gang Unit and Undercover Operations. I have been fortunate to be promoted to the rank of Inspector and have really enjoyed my career. When people ask me what the best part of policing is I always say the people. This is often interpreted as enjoying working with colleagues, or the police family; however, that is not what I mean. I mean the people that I have interacted with in my role as a police officer: community members, people involved in criminal behaviour, people who are experiencing homelessness, basically the people that make up community.

There is often a delineation made in society between good and bad, as if this is an easy concept to grasp. What I have learned over 26 years of policing and engaging in research on the prison population as a graduate student is that there are far more shades of grey than we are ever taught about as police officers. Long before I ever engaged in research, I learned this lesson and it was taught to me by people who I interacted with on a daily basis. It is amazing what we can learn from people when we allow ourselves to be vulnerable and open with them, regardless of their background.

One of the many people who taught me lessons in life was Gilroy.[1] I first met Gilroy when I arrested him for gang-related crimes including drugs and violence. He

---

[1] Gilroy is a false name to protect the identity of the individual.

was a tall, lean indigenous man with sullen eyes and a reputation on the street as a ruthless killer.

Our first interactions were professional and not very memorable. What happened next was an interesting lesson for me. Gilroy reached out to me for help in exiting the gang and dealing with his substance use issues. I asked him why he reached out to me and he said, "You have never hit me, called me a name or treated me like a piece of shit". I met with Gilroy to discuss possible options and opportunities for him to change his life. Gilroy worked very hard to be the man he wanted to be. Eventually Gilroy moved away from gang involvement and involvement in crime. We would talk often, and one day he accompanied me to present to a class at the local University to tell them his story. Gilroy went into far more detail about his life than I had ever heard: abuse, selling drugs at 7 years old for his mom, neglect and systems involvement with child welfare, then the criminal justice system.

After Gilroy presented at the University he and I debriefed what he had said and he expected that I would think less of him based on his own personal victimization. I told him it was the exact opposite and that I appreciated his honesty and that his strength in telling his story was admirable. He and I became friends but his demons kept coming for him, and his struggle with substance use kept a strong hold on him. When Gilroy would slip from sobriety and start using again we would talk and the shame of slipping could be heard in his voice. I would try to talk Gilroy into going to see someone to discuss his past and get some help. However, he was too proud to go for help. Eventually Gilroy died of an accidental drug poisoning. He was never able to be released from the demons from his past.

Gilroy's passing hit me hard. He tried to be the person he wanted to be and escape the person everyone thought he was but was unable to do this. Then I started to realize that Gilroy taught me a lesson; that was, to make sure that you do not try to deal with your demons alone. When I talk about demons I mean the things that impact us the most, things that may be out of our control. In 26 years of policing I have demons, flashbacks of murdered children, horrendous crime scenes that will never leave my memory, holding the hand of a teenager as they died from an overdose, to name a few. I saw Gilroy open up about his demons but never really get help. I also talked about my demons with Gilroy but knew that wasn't sufficient as a means of addressing these memories and the impact that they had on my life.

During one of the worst times I had in dealing with my demons my wife suggested that I seek professional help to address my mental health issues and I flat-out refused. As my life was spiralling downhill and the risk of losing my family became real I started thinking about the advice I gave Gilroy to go and get some help and that there was no shame in it. I listened to my wife, and let Gilroy's far-too-early exit be my motivation to get help. I did and I am in a much better place.

It wasn't colleagues or family that taught me that vulnerability is strength; it was Gilroy. I have spent the better part of my career after getting help trying to provide a platform for people involved in the justice system to have a voice, and justice systems actors to listen to that voice. We live in a complicated world where black and white bleed to be shades of grey and good and bad are often intersected. Gilroy is not the only person with whom I have worked with who has taught me lessons. I find the people who have had the greatest impact on my life are not who I expected they would be. If I did not let myself be vulnerable, there are lessons that I never would have learned.

Working with Diversity: The Case of GLBTQ2 Communities

Murray Billett

The essence of any minority interacting with police and public health can be complex, challenging and, for some, intimidating. Both professions are a powerful and compelling necessity in everyone's lives. I respectfully submit that those complexities are exacerbated by those that are within our diverse GLBTQ2S communities, to a lesser extent, their families and friends that share the burden of secrets, shame and stigma. There are those living in the shadows as an invisible minority, others a minority within a minority(s) navigating closeted lives while being elastic with the truth.

Today some fail to understand that all of the above are imbedded in every spectrum of age, race, gender, colour, religion and ethnicity. We need to be more informed and less opinionated on these topics. Many healthcare facilities are still faith-based; consequently, religion continues to be a challenge of significance. Some still offer conversion therapy/pray the gay away. Some choose to persecute, discriminate and alienate those that are GLBTQ2S or perceived to be. The magnitude and consequences can be draconian. The rejection of family, alienation and abandonment continues. This leads to homelessness, crime, survival sex/prostitution, drug use and omnipresent suicide. Similarly, closets are complex, many people are forced or choose to navigate a life of deceit, denial, risk, restraint and obligation. We marry, have children like I did, or date the opposite sex to hide our true selves. All the while taking health and mental health risks faced daily with deceit management in their personal and professional relationships.

A recent viral tweet by Alexander Leon captured the mental gymnastics of sexual and gender minorities:

> "Queer people don't grow up as ourselves, we grow up playing a version of ourselves that sacrifices authenticity to minimize humiliation & prejudice. The massive task of our adult lives is to unpick which parts of ourselves are truly us & which parts we've created to protect us".

While much has improved and changed in policing and public health in recent years, despite those advances, for many GLBTQ2S people the challenges and trepidation have not. The assumptions based on age, race, gender, colour, religion and ethnicity continue to occur too frequently. Why are you single? Why don't you have kids? What gender is that person? The assumption list goes on; a simple "what did you do over the weekend" can trigger a series of lies and delicate details that ensure no hint of homosexuality or gender fluidity is exposed.

As a very out activist for the last few decades, I've lived intimately with the above realities, witnessing the harm to our families and our communities with erosion of trust and misunderstandings. Police and public health leaders have the right, responsibility and obligation to do their part ensuring equality rights by leading by example. We cannot offer one segment of our population a gold card to equality yet others are left with the basic blue card based on unworthy assumptions, beliefs and past practice. They assume if you have children, you are heterosexual. They assume, gender and/or orientation, based on whom you may date or live with, the assumptions list goes on.

Professionally, I have served as a Labour Relations Officer and Educator for United Nurses of Alberta as well as serving on the Edmonton Police Commission. I can say with certainty that civilian oversight of law enforcement agencies is an integral path to change. I encourage readers to apply for boards, agencies and commissions. All can bring change. Change happens by building credibility and respect by being tough on the problem and easy on the people. In these professions we all understand that trust, truth and reliability is crucial.

In recent years, I have seen improvements of the significant variety by listening and learning from each other. Sadly, in policing and in health care, there are those, at every level, that knowingly or unknowingly don't follow their employer's mission, vision and values by imposing their own beliefs, priorities and bullying.

In the last few years, public scrutiny and expectations are at an all-time high. Social networks are loaded with examples of this. This is a wake-up call for all involved. More than ever, employer policy, training and supervisory responsibilities are increasingly relevant in working with the diverse communities of today. Leaders are change agents and must keep current and find the courage to ensure compliant professional conduct takes place at all times, all the way to the top.

The processes to make this effective have to be integrated daily. Each and every aspect of the social determinants of health impact our community from a young age: from Gay-Straight Alliances (GSAs), access to gender-appropriate change rooms/washrooms, to education and literacy.

What are they learning about two-Mom or two-Dad families? Do your organizations properly acknowledge today's diverse familial realities? These social determinants unfold daily in much of the public health and policing interactions. These need to be viewed from an equality rights mural rather than simply a snapshot. As a society we have slowly moved forward on understanding GLBTQ2S families and related issues. Every step forward has been a battle, every step forward is hindered by discrimination. I have learned that coming out hinders that discrimination. With our allies, our families and friends there is more to accomplish. That cannot happen without courageous leadership and activism. As has been historically stated, you are either part of the problem or part of the solution.

Working with Diversity: The Case of Disability

Franck David

X is a member of the Supporting Offenders with Learning Disabilities (SOLD) group set up by People First (Scotland). People First is the national disabled people's organization of adults with a learning disability in Scotland run by our members for our members. SOLD is a national network committed to improving support for people who have difficulty with communication and understanding, and are at risk of, accused, or convicted of committing a crime. This includes people with learning disabilities, autism, foetal alcohol spectrum disorder, acquired brain injury, or other cognitive or neurological impairment.

Delivered in partnership between ARC Scotland and People First Scotland, the work of SOLD is funded by the Scottish Government Community Justice Division.

X was involved in petty crime from a young age. Because of pressure, he committed a more serious crime resulting in a prison sentence. X moved to Edinburgh for a "new start" with the help from a Criminal Justice Social worker. X stayed in a hostel with no additional support, he was exploited and also caught back into crime. The process repeated itself for a number of years with orders and short-term prison sentences.

What changed?—support in the community!

X is a 53-year-old man with a learning disability. X was involved in petty crime from a young age after his mum died. Before X moved to a new area and a new flat in 2018, he "got in trouble a lot for years [...] people were calling me names and I was shouting back at them. They said things to me that made me very angry"[...] "it happened every time I was going out. It was violent and I felt angry". "In my younger years I was involved in gangs and I was fighting a lot". "I got a lot of abuse for many years [...] people always shouted at me when I was out and threw things at my windows; one day I called the police and they were with me in the house when someone kicked my door and broke in. The people got arrested". "People would knock on my door to ask me money, taking advantage of my learning disability. I gave them a lot of money". "In the street people would throw things at me and I would throw them back at them". "Life was violent, I ended up in jail". X received a 2-year probationary order. He received help from a Criminal Justice Social worker who helped him turn his life around and helped him move to Edinburgh.

X also saw a psychologist and he then found support through the Social Work Action Group for people with learning disabilities, which was another turning point. The Action Group supported X with shopping, cleaning and tidying up of the house. They helped him find a new house in a better area. In X's own words, "I'm happy now".

After X started receiving support, he said that "everyone saw new change in him". Importantly, now that he is settled X is very keen to say: "I will tell anybody that crime does not work. I'm happy now and I will never go back to crime, it's not worth it, it's not worth it...".

X is in still in contact almost every day with the Action Group. The Group has been very supportive and helps X with his invoices and managing money which was an area that X struggled with in the past. The Group also supports X with practical advice and correspondence such as letters.

X has been regularly attending the monthly SOLD meetings for a few years together with other members who have all been involved in the criminal justice system. X says that going to the group "is really good, [he] feels useful and has a lot to contribute and say to change the system and make things better for people who have a learning disability".

X has had a personal trainer for 2 years every morning during weekdays which helps him with his physical and mental health. He started going to the gym, developed an interest in computers, has regular online meetings with SOLD and is involved in various other meetings (supported by People First workers) to "help other people". X has been using his own experience to train professionals, e.g. Justice of the Peace. He is working on various projects (improving police custody suites, improving Appropriate Adults process).

X says that without the support he received he "would have gone back in jail probably on a long sentence".

A Word About Autism

Emily Diamond

There are a few consistencies about autism that I know: around the world it's always more boys than girls, and as environmental factors have a role in the increasing prevalence, the prevalence varies from place to place. In our Centers for Disease Control and Prevention studies, it's 1 in 32 in New Jersey, to 1 in 76 in Colorado. Most important of all is that neurodiversity means not only that people may be different than you would expect, they are uniquely different from each other.

Each of us is the combined genetics of our mother and father, and we know that there are environmental factors in autism which increase the prevalence. When we consider all of our genes, and all the other factors, one can understand how no two cases of autism or neuroatypicality may look the same, and the great majority have more than one diagnosis.

Here I look at data from my own research work for things which may most account for the victimization and tragedy that we often learn about. There are a triad of things that bring neuroatypical people into contact with law enforcement, and simultaneously make that interaction difficult. These are a difficulty in knowing when things are dangerous and caution is needed, face-blindness, and difficulty with using spoken language. None of these things are visible, which adds to the risks that this triad holds.

In an international study of autistic adults and their family members, I asked a range of questions of 783 participants. One was whether there was difficulty knowing when something is dangerous, or caution is needed. For 469 people, they reported it was an ongoing issue, or it was at some point in their life, or they weren't quite sure. I asked this because bolting into traffic, wandering away from home, placing trust where it isn't warranted, high rates of being victimized–these experiences are all too common. There are two kinds of interactions that can arise from this misapprehension of danger and risk.

When law enforcement is in the role of leading a search for a person who has wandered or eloped, finding them before they meet harm is the objective, and there are strategies for leading searches which work well. There's another kind of interaction which is complex in motive and variety, but also leads to police interaction. I have changed small elements to protect the writer's identity: "I was only diagnosed at 35 after I threw a heavy object at my boss when I was frustrated". Another wrote: "Mental health has been my biggest challenge, post meltdown and during meltdown—feelings of suicidal rage". That's a very dangerous thing in a police context, particularly with armed police. Here's someone who was sexually made use of: "Because of my ASD and not fully [understanding] about [how] to recognize danger I have been used by older men for their 'own pleasure'."

When autistic people make contact with law enforcement, there are two other invisible difficulties that shape the interactions profoundly. The first of these is face-blindness, sometimes called prosopagnosia. Some people have the remarkable ability to never forget a face. It's these people, known as super-recognizers, who sometimes help police in their work. On the other end of the spectrum are people like the neurologist Oliver Sacks, who couldn't recognize himself in a mirror, and taught himself to recognize himself by remembering what his beard and ears look like. This revelation of his face-blindness came later in life, as it does for many.

When I asked those in my study if they had trouble recognizing others by face, 518 of the 783 report some difficulty with this. This may be part of why a great many people who are autistic have difficulty looking people in the eyes. While a potential sign of dishonesty to some, perhaps when one is face-blind, the eyes don't hold the same significance to the billions of neurons that generally help us look, interpret, react and remember the faces in our lives. This is one of the main things that are asked of victims, *what did the perpetrator look like?* Not only might the person not know, they may not meet your eyes to tell you that.

To complete the triad is that many autistic people have difficulty using spoken language. Of the participants, 458 had some difficulty with using spoken language. One person wrote: "I did not know what anxiety was. I would describe a feeling as 'sharp white static' and it was not until I was 21 years old that someone pointed out that what I was feeling was anxiety".

"Speech inflection takes effort; often when tired I lose the skill. I have been mocked for failing to get it right".

"I often end up thinking one thing but saying another".

"I had been told that if anyone ever touched me inappropriately to tell an adult/my parents, but I didn't know what that meant. When I was raped by a group of boys years later, I didn't know what to call it or know what to do. I wish I had a more specific education of what a dangerous situation is and what to do after".

"During meltdowns, I can get a stutter, have echolalia, or even go completely nonverbal".

Echolalia is to repeat a person's phrase back to them, like an echo. Imagine there's a person in your custody and you ask if there are health problems you should know about, and they don't meet your eyes and say nothing, or they say, "Do you have any health problems I should know about?"

There are other dangerous things, like intellectual challenge and suicidality. What is important to remember is that the invisible disadvantage that put people in harm's way, is also the disadvantage that make safe and effective work more challenging.

Hidden in Plain Sight: Epilepsy and the Law

Lesslie Young

Epilepsy is the world's most common neurological condition with an estimated 50 million people living with epilepsy worldwide. Epilepsy is the tendency of an individual to have repeated seizures which originate in the brain. Seizures present in a myriad of ways. There can be impaired consciousness and cognition, automatism and inappropriate behaviour. The postictal[2] recovery phase may be associated with communication difficulties, confusion, impaired cognition, amnesia, emotional instability and postictal psychosis. Directed violence in either phase is rare. However, if the person interprets your voice, commands or any physical intervention as aggressive, they may well respond aggressively.

During seizure activity, people are unable to and do not appear to interact with the environment as you would expect them to if they were not having a seizure. They may not respond to verbal questioning and display inadvertently incongruous behaviour such as repeated aimless movements, lip smacking, urinating in public, taking their clothing off or exposing themselves. They may be seen as drunk or on drugs.

Case Study

JB, a young woman with the diagnosis of epilepsy, finds herself in handcuffs, leg restraints and in hospital but has no idea why. With great difficulty despite her family's support, JB has previously managed to extricate herself from an abusive relationship. The stress and physical abuse I thought to be the cause of

(continued)

---

[2]"ictal" means "during crisis" or "during a seizure". Postictal means "after or between seizures".

her epilepsy. She is a single mother. She has epilepsy and experiences generalized, tonic-clonic seizures without warning.

In her new house with her 6-year-old daughter and new boyfriend, who is aware of her epilepsy, JB begins to seizure. Her first is prolonged and aggressive. She does not fully recover before another starts. Concerned for her wellbeing and that of the 6-year-old daughter, her boyfriend calls for an ambulance. He also prepares her emergency medication which is a benzodiazepine.

When the paramedics arrived JB was not fully recovered and was in a state of postictal confusion. She was not co-operative and resisted all attempts made by the paramedics to get her into the ambulance. Because they perceived her behaviour to be aggressive, they called for backup from the police.

Still not fully recovered and additionally feeling the effects of the benzodiazepine, JB remained confused and resisted the police and the paramedics. She spat at the police. Forced to the ground, she was handcuffed, and leg restraints were also applied. Both caused significant injury. She was also referred to as a junkie even though her boyfriend told them about the epilepsy and the medication given. JB was physically lifted into the ambulance and taken to the hospital with a police escort.

The receiving Accident and Emergency Consultant commented on the unnecessary use of excessive force, the injuries sustained and the unacceptable treatment of a vulnerable young woman especially in front of her 6-year-old daughter. JB was kept in hospital until she was fully recovered from her seizures, her injuries were treated and dressed, and outpatient appointments were made.

JB was charged with three counts of assault. The standard prosecution report was submitted to the Crown Prosecution and Procurator Fiscal Service (COPFS). Epilepsy Scotland was informed of the incident by JB's father. He had already complained to the local Police Office and provided a detailed medical history, reminding them his daughter had no control over her actions, **and had no memory of them as they were the result of generalized seizure activity**.

Epilepsy Scotland has been working with Police Scotland and COPFS for many years. Guidance was sought by Epilepsy Scotland from the highest level as to how to progress. The local sergeant contacted JB's father apologizing for the use of force, informing him epilepsy training was being requested at a local level. The two dedicated Epilepsy Ambassadors at COPFS gathered all essential information and submitted it to the independent case marker. JB's father instructed a solicitor and sought further medical evidence.

It took many months for JB's physical injuries to heal and she has been left with irreparable nerve damage to her hands.

All charges were dropped. No police training has been provided.

Where there has been any suggestion that seizure activity or behaviour during the postictal recovery phase has been interpreted as a criminal act, it is vital to involve the general practitioner and/or medical services at the earliest stage, preferably before charges are brought. Having epilepsy and the effects of that is bad enough without having to deal with the threat of criminal action or charges being brought because of behaviour the person has no control over and no memory of.

If the police reported an epilepsy-related incident to the prosecutor, they must provide as much information as possible to help them make the correct decision. The prosecutor will look for some medical history in the antecedents section of the standard prosecution report as well as a detailed description from the reporting officer about what they saw. The prosecutors need answers to the following questions:

1. Is there evidence of seizure activity?
2. Did the person acknowledge the arrival of the police officers?
3. Does the person have a history of seizure-related behaviour? If so, is the incident within their usual/previously witnessed behaviour?
4. Is the incident within the boundaries of general seizure/postictal behaviour?
5. Is the behaviour out of character for that person?
6. Is there a motive for the alleged offence?

The thought of potentially having a criminal record because of seizure-related behaviour over which the person has no control and no memory has a significant and detrimental impact. It creates stress and anxiety which may trigger further seizure activity. There is a worsening of job prospects because of a pending court case. It has been noted to create family conflict, depression and suicidal ideation. Persons with focal epilepsy have up to 25 times greater risk of suicide than age-matched controls (Christensen et al., 2007).

The approach outlined is not intended to make police officers and all other first responders experts in epilepsy. The intention is to provide enough information to better inform decision-making.

This is a public health issue and one with potentially fatal consequences.

Reference

Christensen, J., Vestergaard, M., Mortensen, P. B., Sidenius, P., & Agerbo, E. (2007). Epilepsy and risk of suicide: A population-based case-control study. *The Lancet. Neurology, 6*(8), 693–698. https://doi.org/10.1016/S1474-4422(07)70175-8

Index

Printed in the United States
by Baker & Taylor Publisher Services